Shojo Beat

kimi ni todoke
From Me to You

Vol. 12
Story & Art by
Karuho Shiina

Volume 12

Contents

Episode 47: Just a Little Bit ------------------------- 3

Episode 48: Do I Look Normal? -------------------- 51

Episode 49: There's No Way
I Would Hate You --------------------- 91

Episode 50: You're Too Loud ---------------------- 133

Story Thus Far

Sawako Kuronuma has always been a loner. Though not by choice, this optimistic 16-year-old girl can't seem to make any friends. Stuck with the unfortunate nickname "Sadako" after the haunting movie character, rumors about her summoning spirits have been greatly exaggerated. With her shy personality and scary looks, most of her classmates will barely talk to her, much less look into her eyes for more than three seconds lest they be cursed. Thanks to Kazehaya, who always treats her nicely, Sawako makes her first friends at school, Ayane and Chizu.

After some misunderstandings and awkwardness, Sawako and Kazehaya are finally dating. While being considerate of the feelings of Kurumi and the other girls who like Kazehaya, Sawako is determined to be a good girlfriend. On their first date, Sawako is nervous. She prepares a box lunch and they celebrate Kazehaya's past birthday. Sawako finally gives Kazehaya the presents that she couldn't give him before. Both of them are happy now that they're sure of each other's feelings...

♥Episode 47: Just a Little Bit

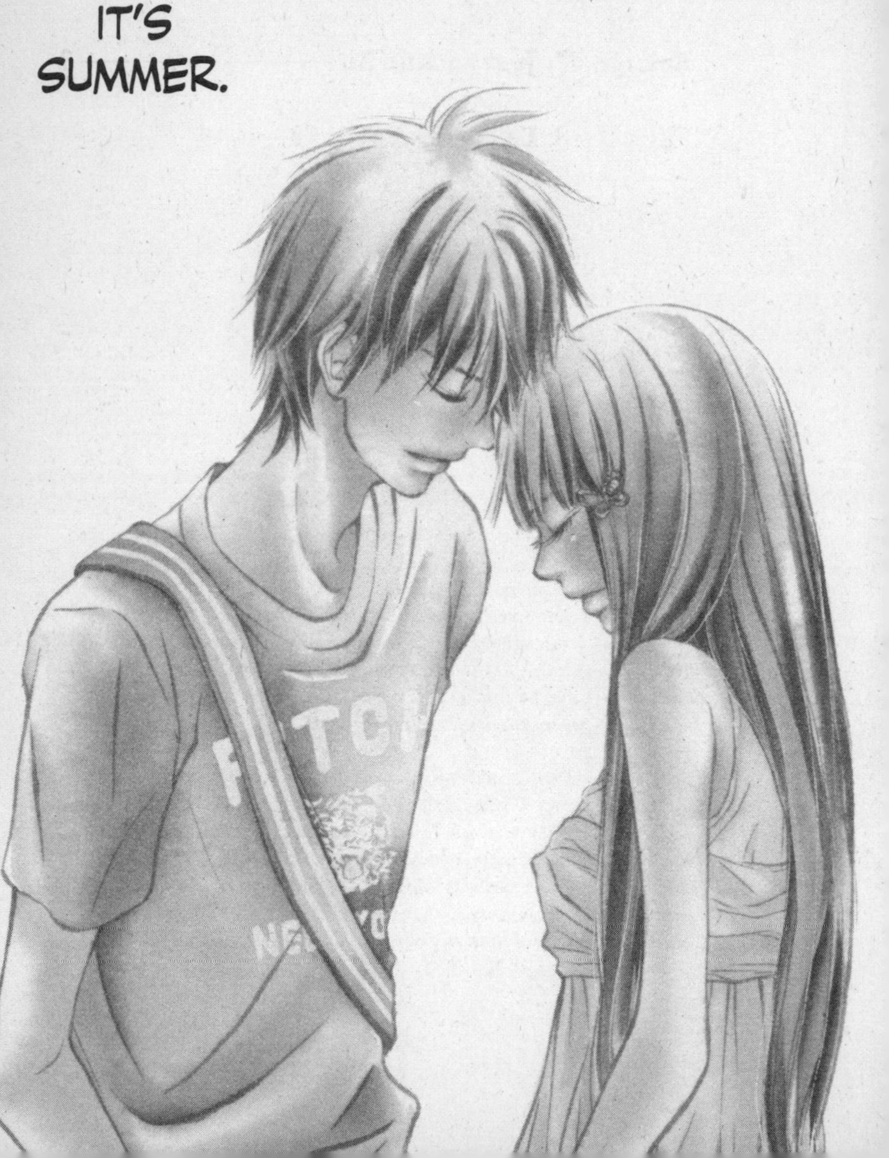
IT'S SUMMER.

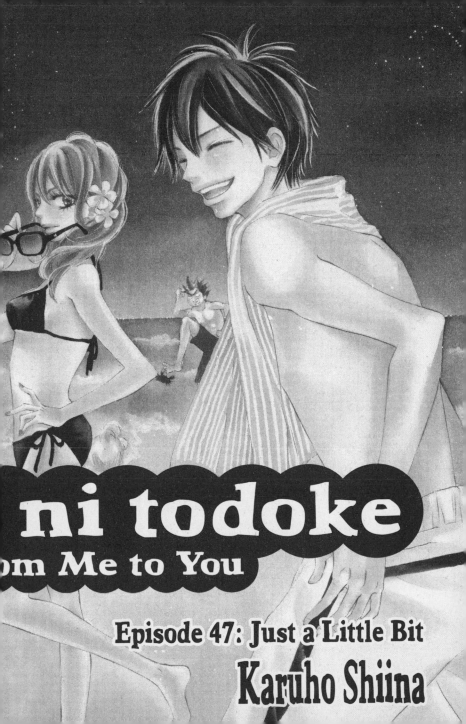

ni todoke

om Me to You

Episode 47: Just a Little Bit

Karuho Shiina

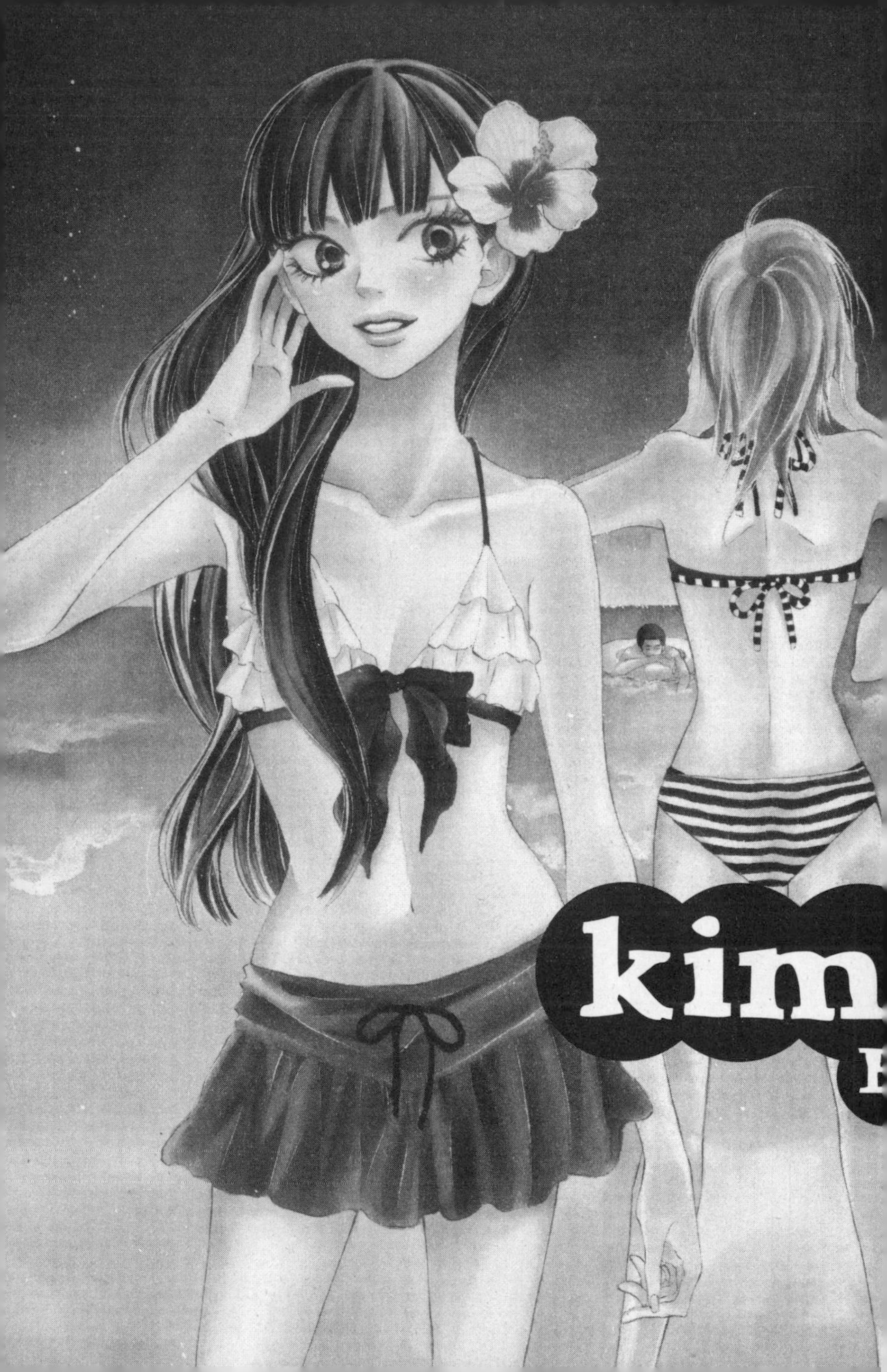
kim

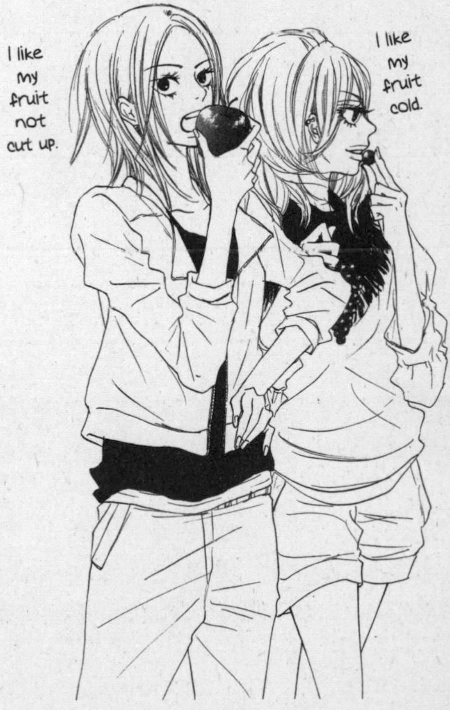
I like my fruit cold.
I like my fruit not cut up.

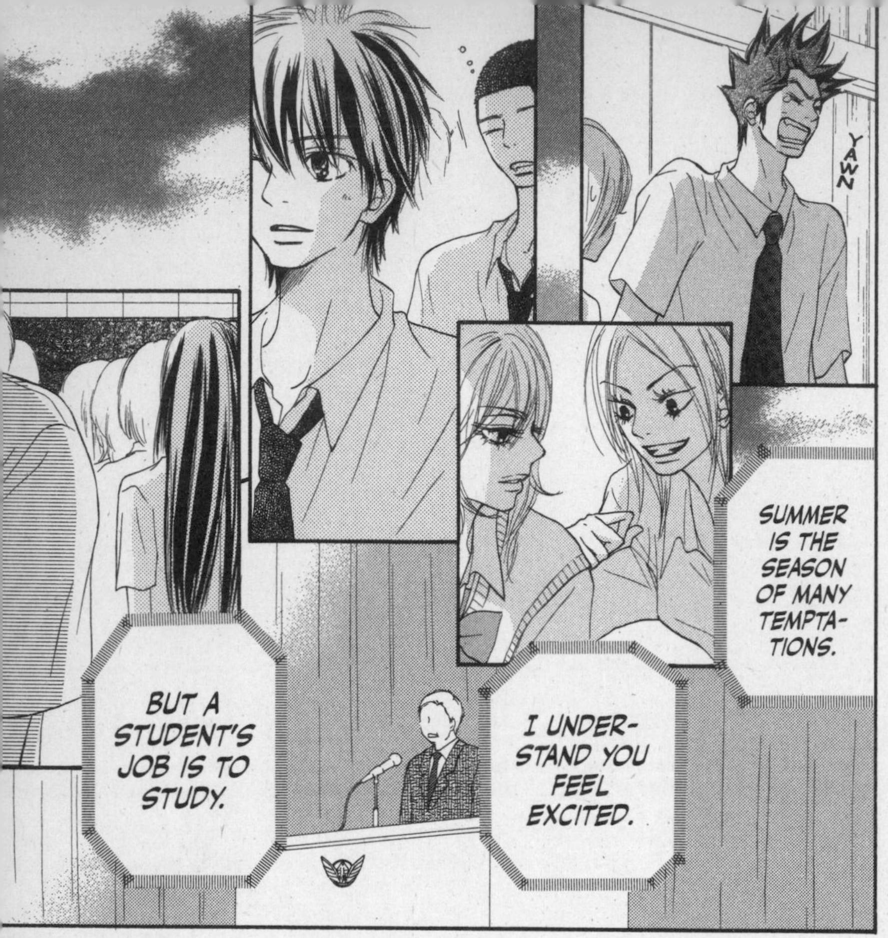
YAWN
SUMMER IS THE SEASON OF MANY TEMPTA-TIONS.
I UNDER-STAND YOU FEEL EXCITED.
BUT A STUDENT'S JOB IS TO STUDY.

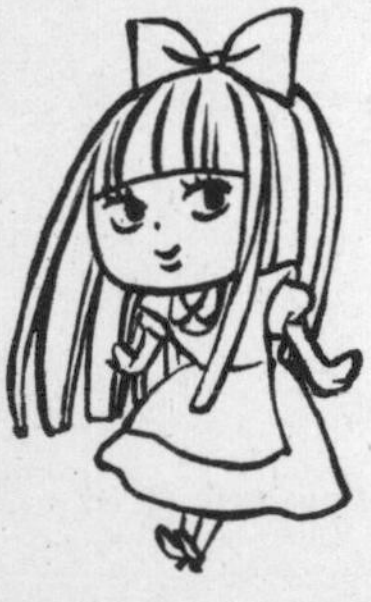

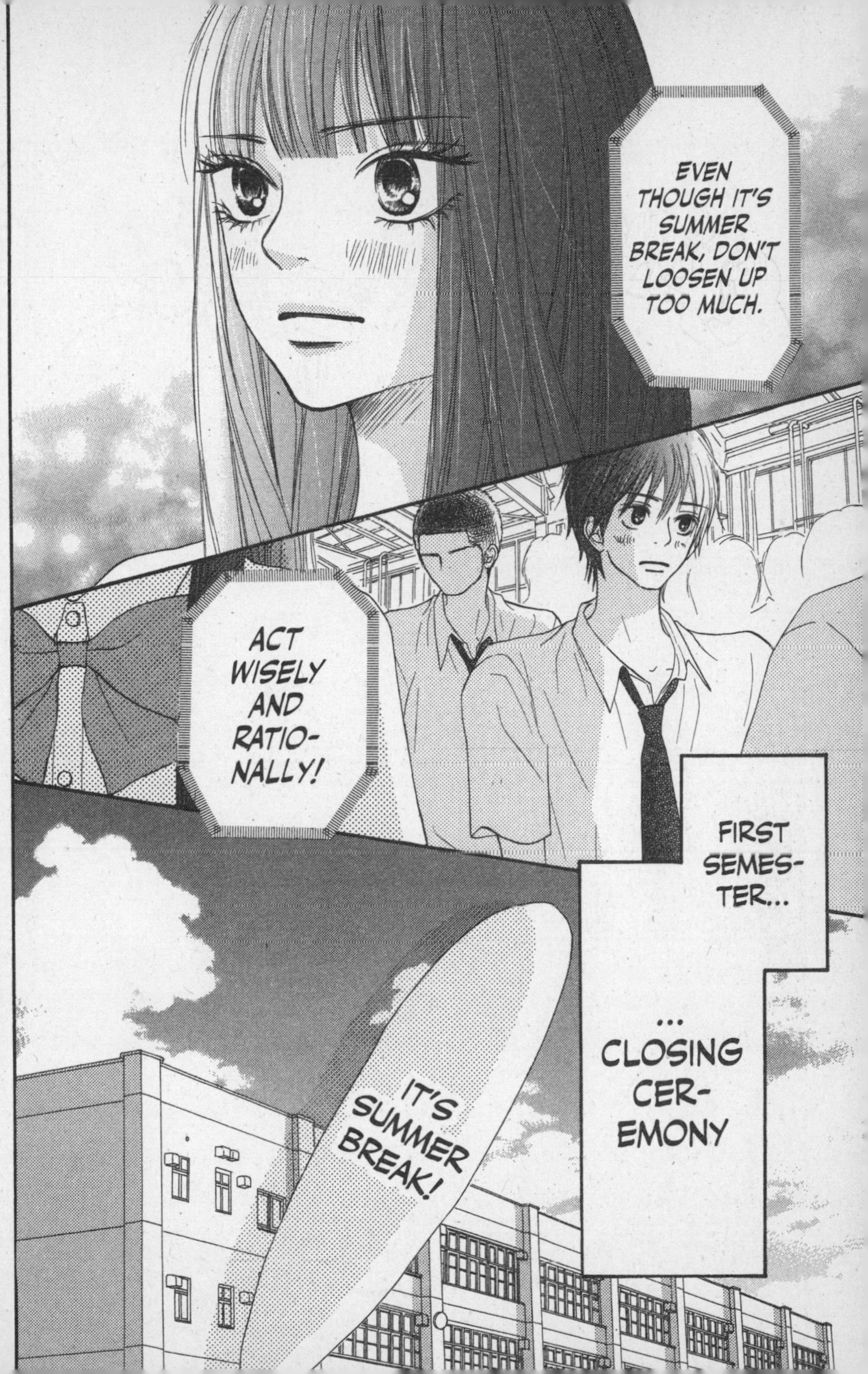
EVEN THOUGH IT'S SUMMER BREAK, DON'T LOOSEN UP TOO MUCH.
ACT WISELY AND RATIO-NALLY!
FIRST SEMES-TER...
...CLOSING CER-EMONY
IT'S SUMMER BREAK!

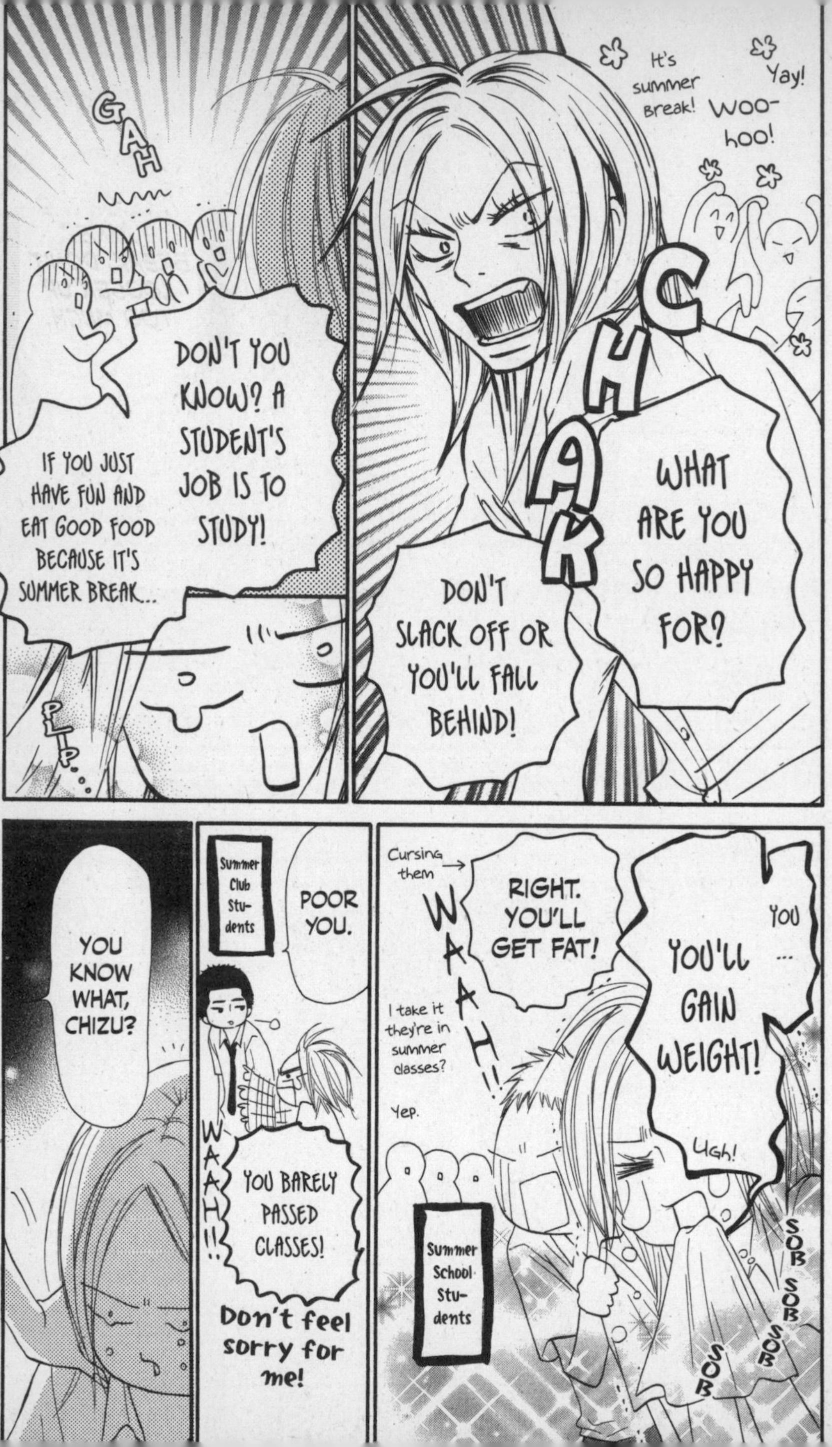
It's summer break!
Yay! Woo-hoo!
CHAAK
WHAT ARE YOU SO HAPPY FOR?
DON'T SLACK OFF OR YOU'LL FALL BEHIND!
GAH
DON'T YOU KNOW? A STUDENT'S JOB IS TO STUDY!
IF YOU JUST HAVE FUN AND EAT GOOD FOOD BECAUSE IT'S SUMMER BREAK...
PLIP...
YOU...
YOU'LL GAIN WEIGHT!
Ugh!
Cursing them
RIGHT. YOU'LL GET FAT!
WAAH!!
I take it they're in summer classes?
Yep.
Summer School Students
SOB SOB SOB SOB
Summer Club Students
POOR YOU.
WAAH!!
YOU BARELY PASSED CLASSES!
Don't feel sorry for me!
YOU KNOW WHAT, CHIZU?

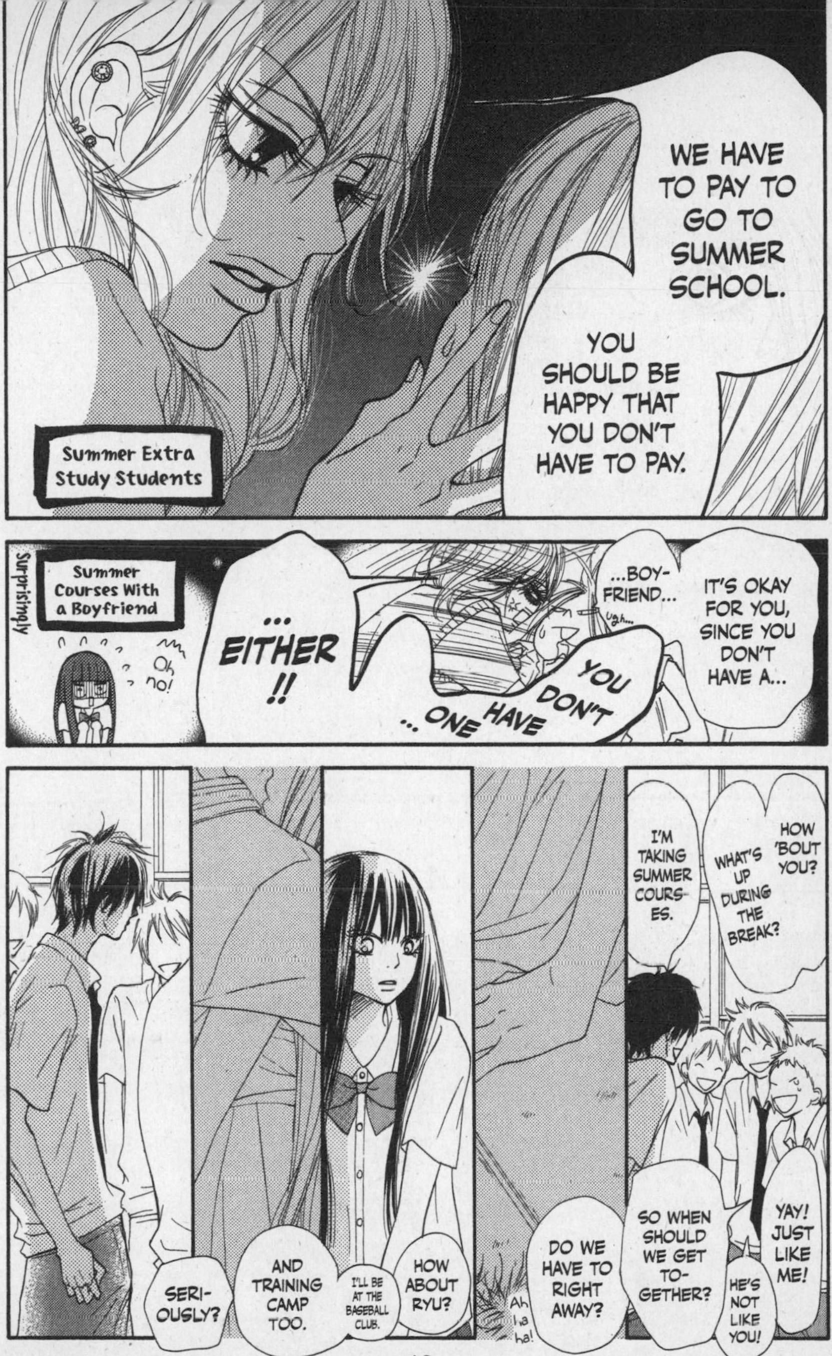
Summer Extra Study Students
WE HAVE TO PAY TO GO TO SUMMER SCHOOL.
YOU SHOULD BE HAPPY THAT YOU DON'T HAVE TO PAY.
Summer Courses With a Boyfriend
Surprisingly
IT'S OKAY FOR YOU, SINCE YOU DON'T HAVE A...
...BOY-FRIEND...
ugh...
YOU DON'T HAVE ONE...
...EITHER!!
Oh no!
HOW 'BOUT YOU?
WHAT'S UP DURING THE BREAK?
I'M TAKING SUMMER COURS-ES.
YAY! JUST LIKE ME!
HE'S NOT LIKE YOU!
SO WHEN SHOULD WE GET TO-GETHER?
DO WE HAVE TO RIGHT AWAY?
Ah ha ha!
HOW ABOUT RYU?
I'LL BE AT THE BASEBALL CLUB.
AND TRAINING CAMP TOO.
SERI-OUSLY?

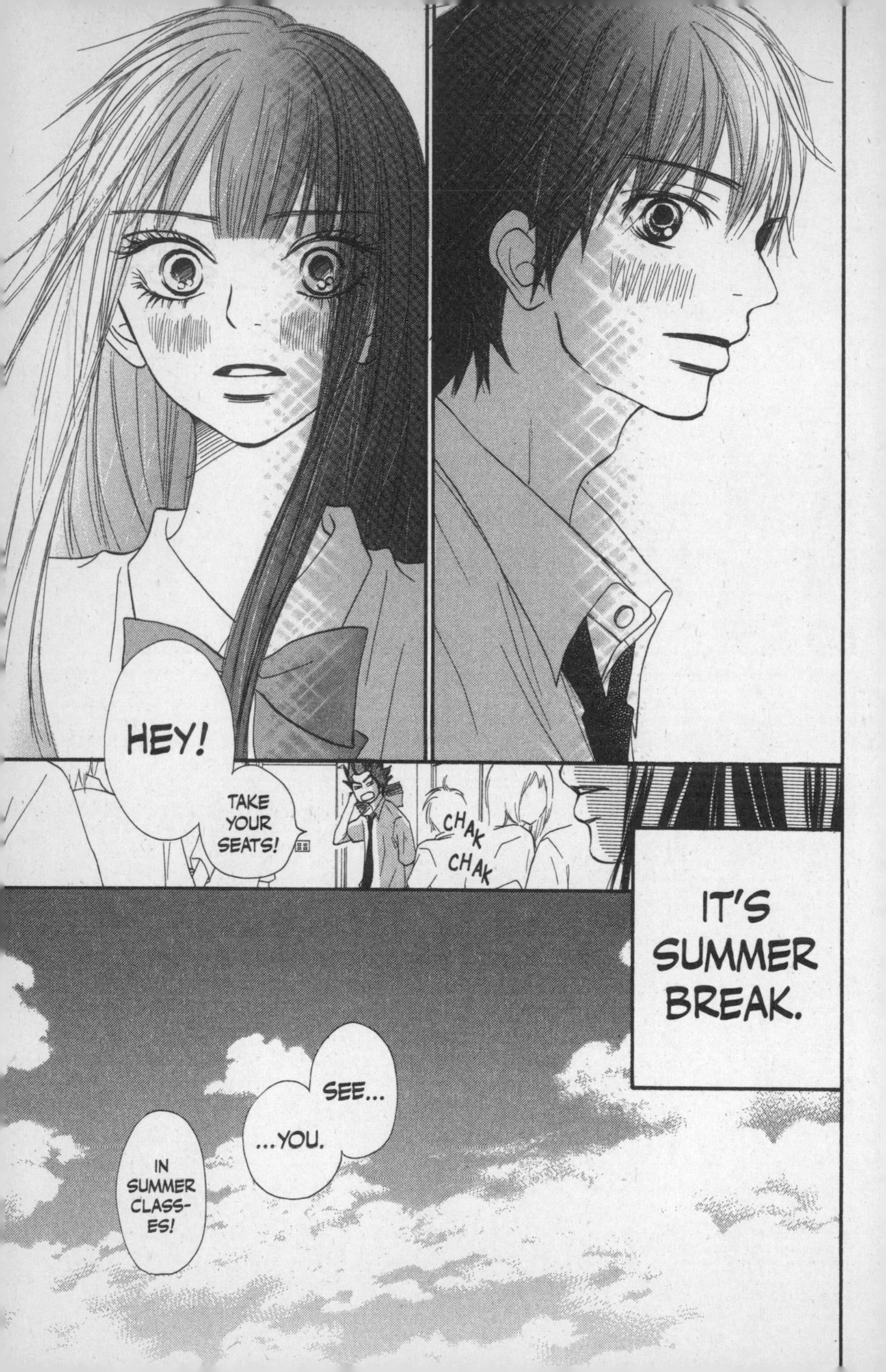
HEY!
CHAK CHAK
TAKE YOUR SEATS!
IT'S SUMMER BREAK.
SEE...
...YOU.
IN SUMMER CLASSES!

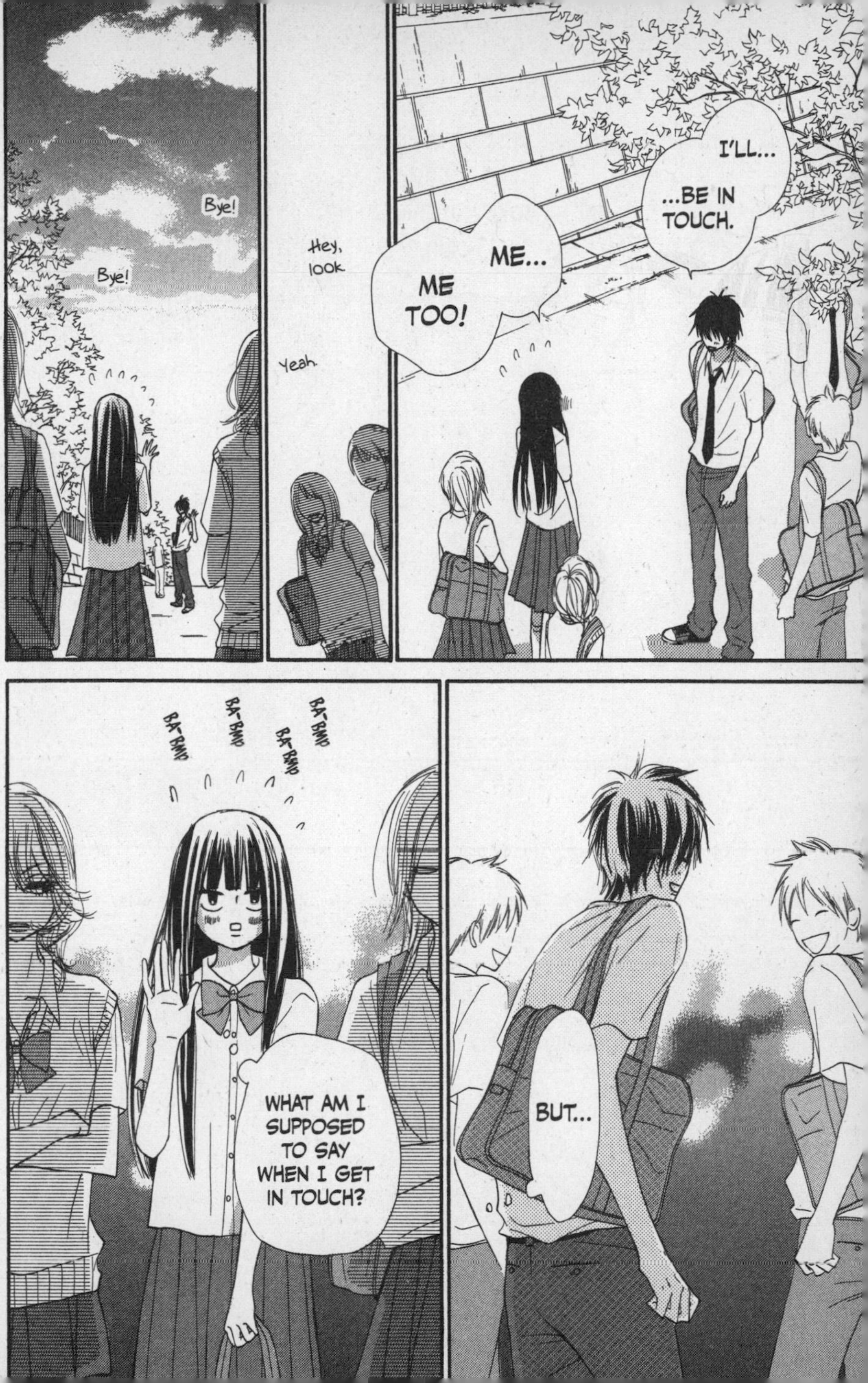
I'LL...
...BE IN TOUCH.
ME...
ME TOO!
Hey, look
Yeah.
Bye!
Bye!
BUT...
BA-BMP
BA-BMP
BA-BMP
BA-BMP
WHAT AM I SUPPOSED TO SAY WHEN I GET IN TOUCH?

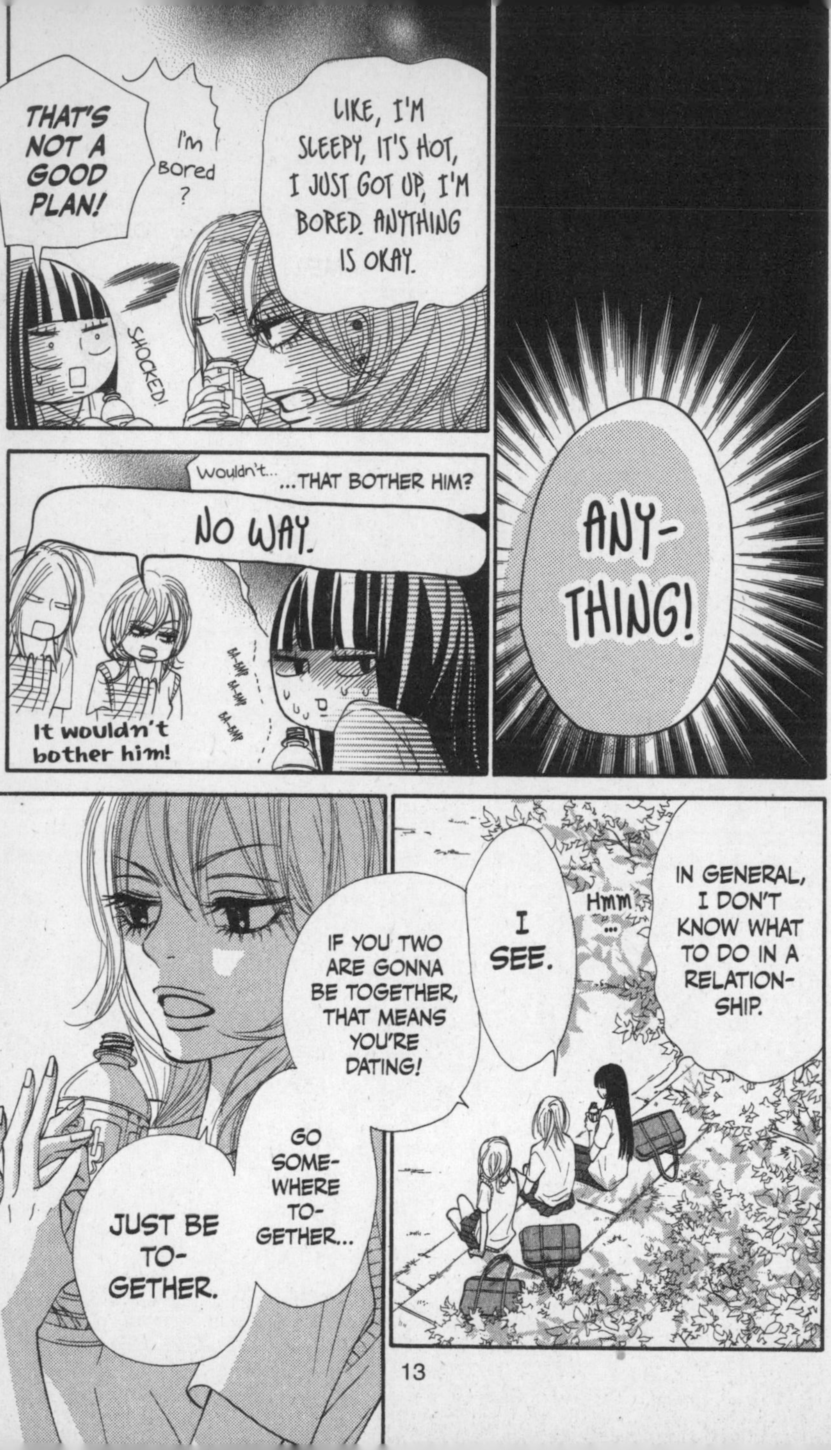
ANY-THING!
LIKE, I'M SLEEPY, IT'S HOT, I JUST GOT UP, I'M BORED. ANYTHING IS OKAY.
I'm Bored ?
THAT'S NOT A GOOD PLAN!
SHOCKED!
Wouldn't... ...THAT BOTHER HIM?
NO WAY.
BA-BUMP BA-BUMP BA-BUMP
It wouldn't bother him!
IN GENERAL, I DON'T KNOW WHAT TO DO IN A RELATION-SHIP.
Hmm...
I SEE.
IF YOU TWO ARE GONNA BE TOGETHER, THAT MEANS YOU'RE DATING!
GO SOME-WHERE TO-GETHER...
JUST BE TO-GETHER.

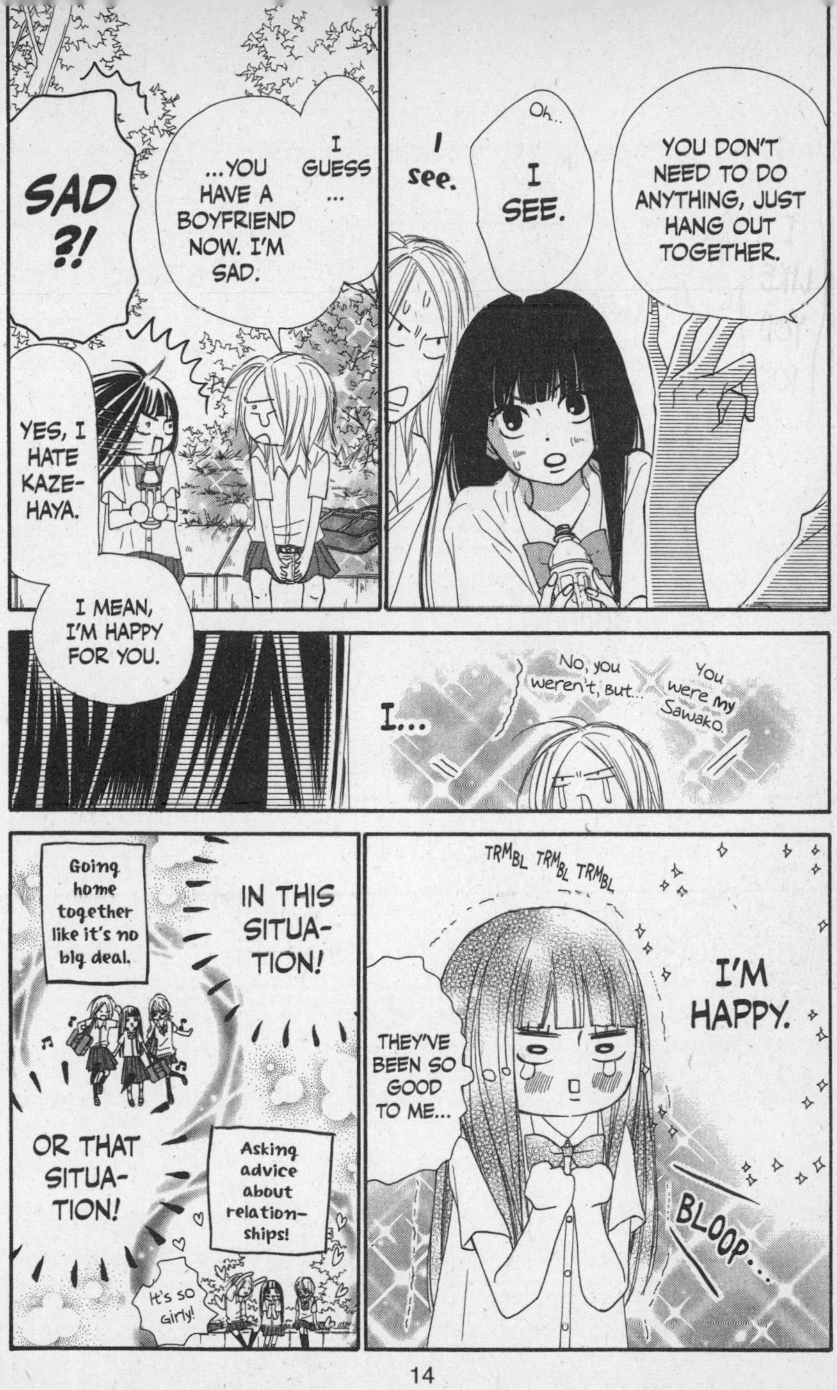
YOU DON'T NEED TO DO ANYTHING, JUST HANG OUT TOGETHER.
Oh... I SEE.
I see.
I GUESS... ...YOU HAVE A BOYFRIEND NOW. I'M SAD.
SAD?!
YES, I HATE KAZE-HAYA.
I MEAN, I'M HAPPY FOR YOU.
You were my Sawako.
No, you weren't, but...
I...
TRMBL TRMBL TRMBL
I'M HAPPY.
THEY'VE BEEN SO GOOD TO ME...
BLOOP...
IN THIS SITUA-TION!
Going home together like it's no big deal.
OR THAT SITUA-TION!
Asking advice about relation-ships!
It's so girly!

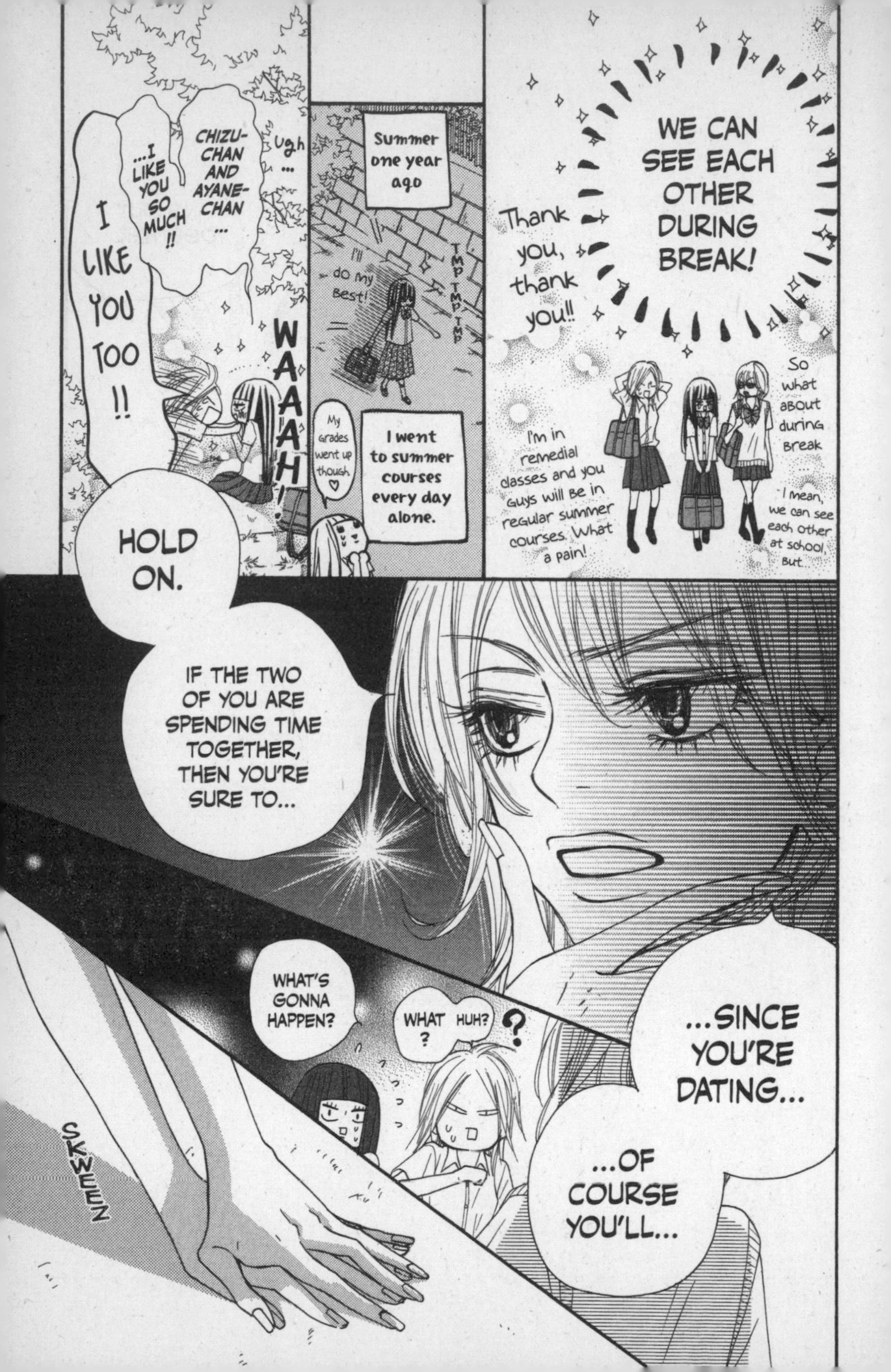
WE CAN SEE EACH OTHER DURING BREAK!
Thank you, thank you!!
So what about during break... I mean, we can see each other at school, but...
I'm in remedial classes and you guys will be in regular summer courses. What a pain!
Summer one year ago
TMP TMP TMP
I'll do my Best!
I went to summer courses every day alone.
My Grades went up though ♡
Ugh...
CHIZU-CHAN AND AYANE-CHAN...
...I LIKE YOU SO MUCH!!
I LIKE YOU TOO!!
WAAAAH!
HOLD ON.
IF THE TWO OF YOU ARE SPENDING TIME TOGETHER, THEN YOU'RE SURE TO...
...SINCE YOU'RE DATING...
...OF COURSE YOU'LL...
HUH?
WHAT?
WHAT'S GONNA HAPPEN?
SKWEEZ

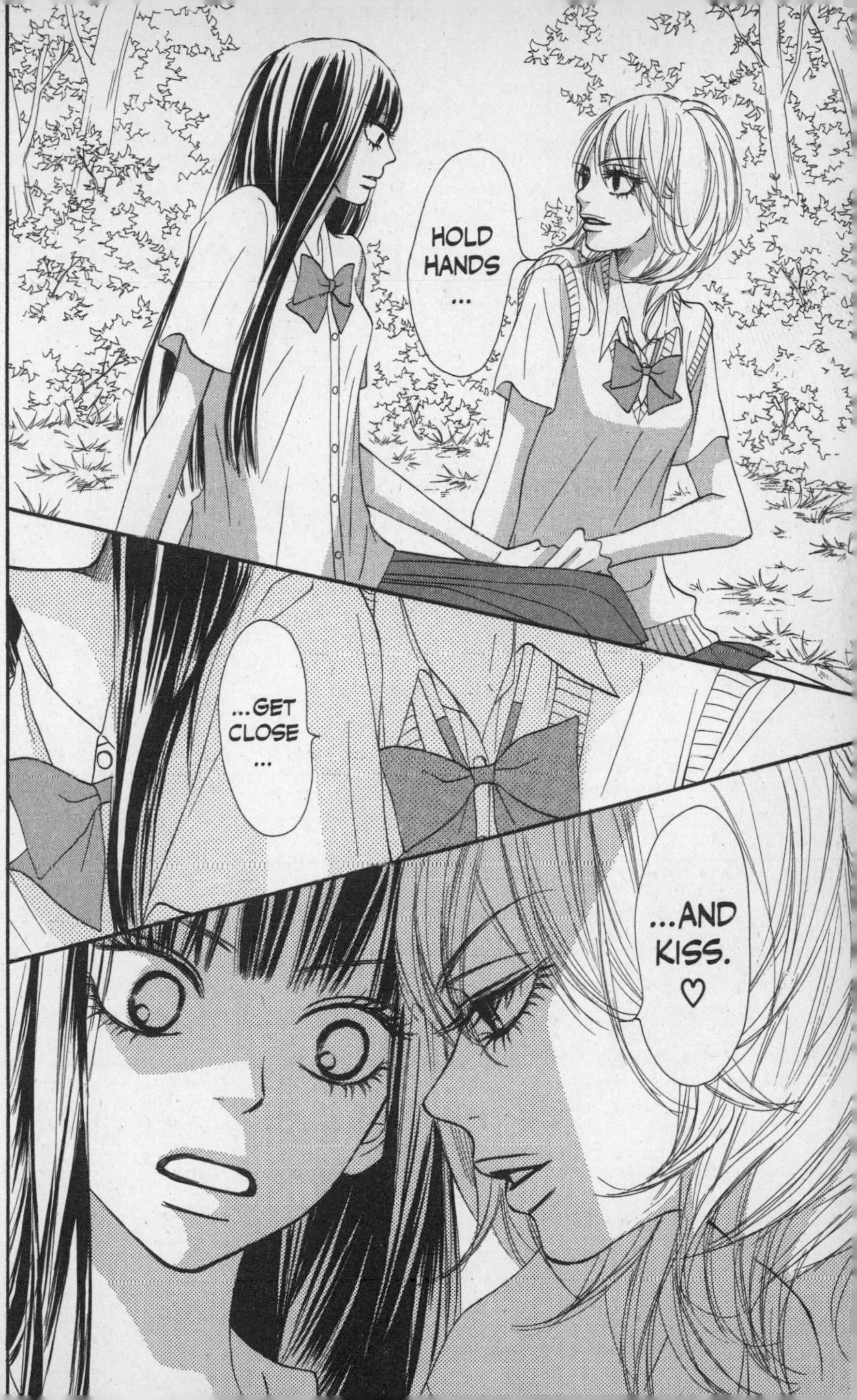
HOLD HANDS ...
...GET CLOSE ...
...AND KISS. ♡

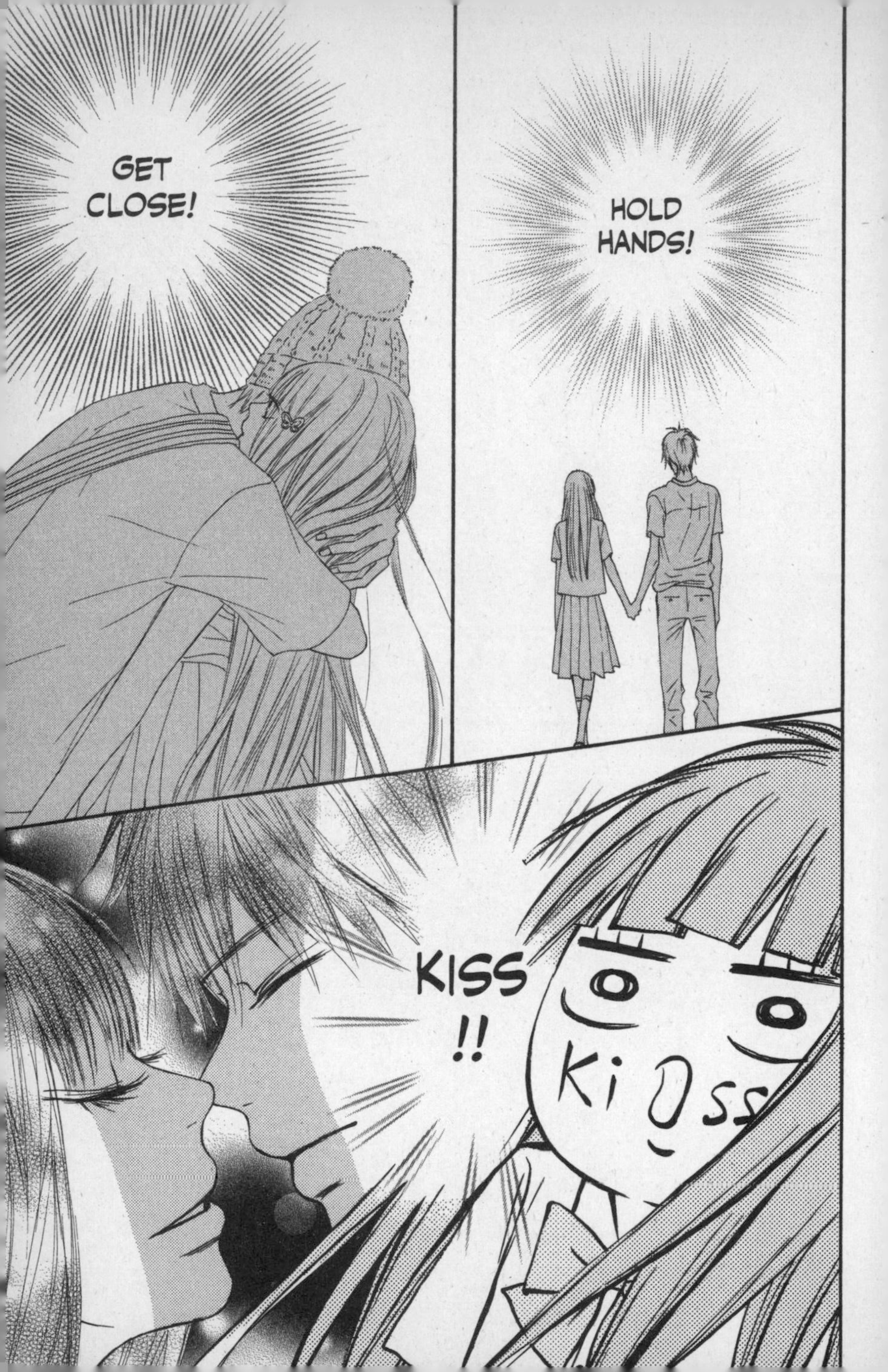
HOLD HANDS!
GET CLOSE!
KISS !!
Ki Oss

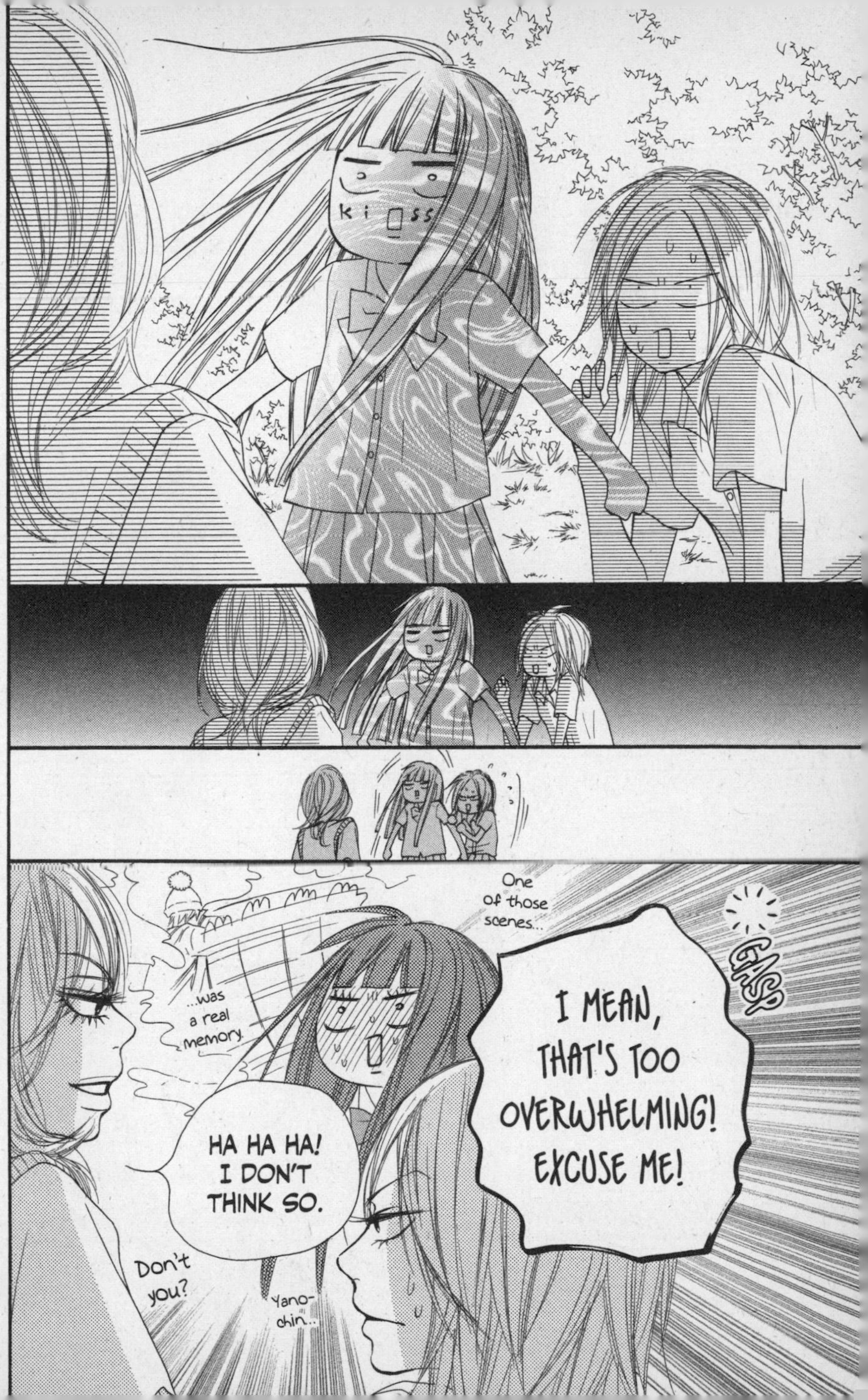
GASP
One of those scenes...
I MEAN, THAT'S TOO OVERWHELMING! EXCUSE ME!
...was a real memory.
HA HA HA! I DON'T THINK SO.
Yano-chin...
Don't you?

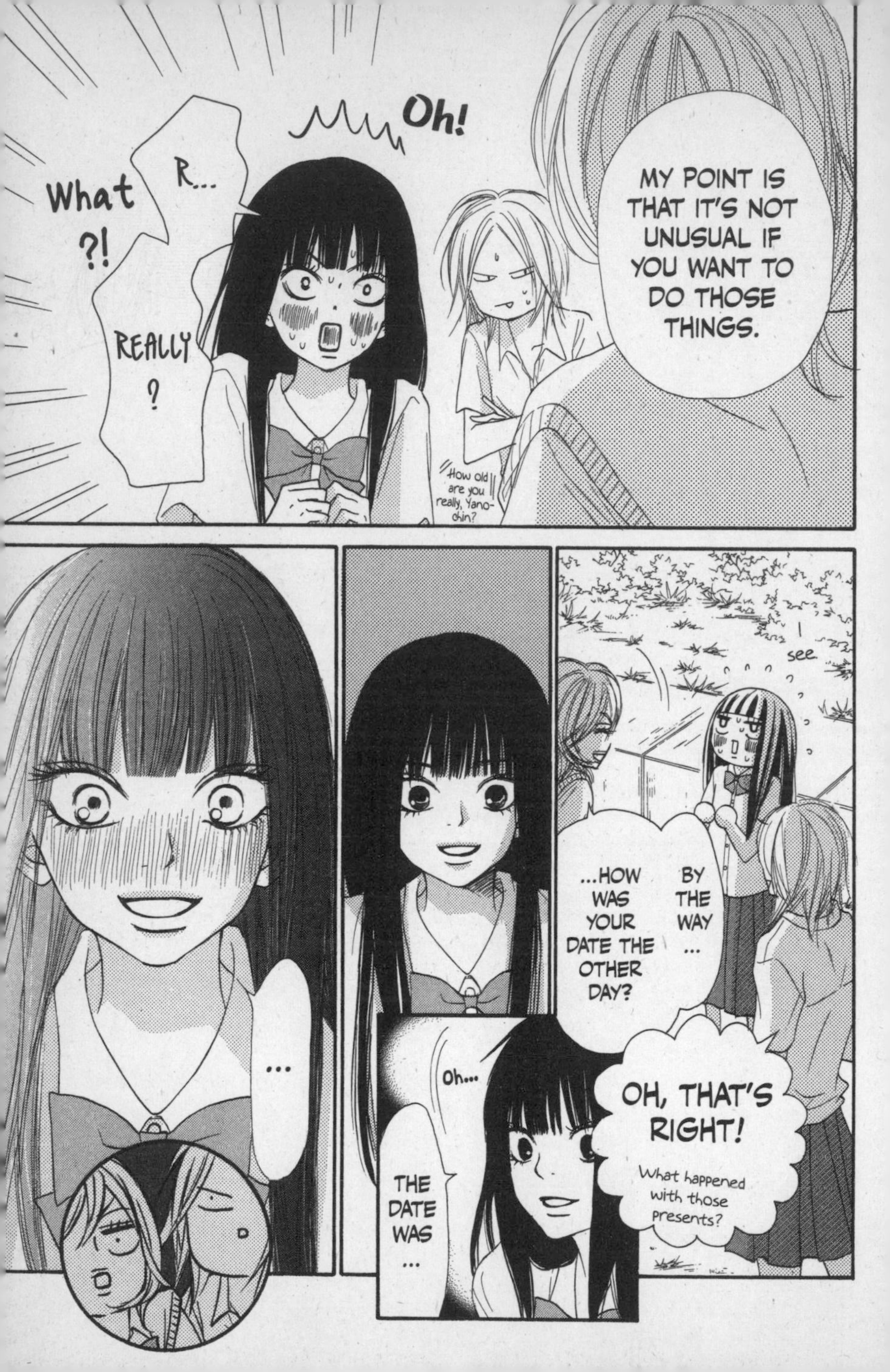
MY POINT IS THAT IT'S NOT UNUSUAL IF YOU WANT TO DO THOSE THINGS.
Oh!
R... REALLY?
What?!
How old are you really, Yano-chin?
I see
BY THE WAY...
...HOW WAS YOUR DATE THE OTHER DAY?
OH, THAT'S RIGHT!
What happened with those presents?
Oh...
THE DATE WAS...
...

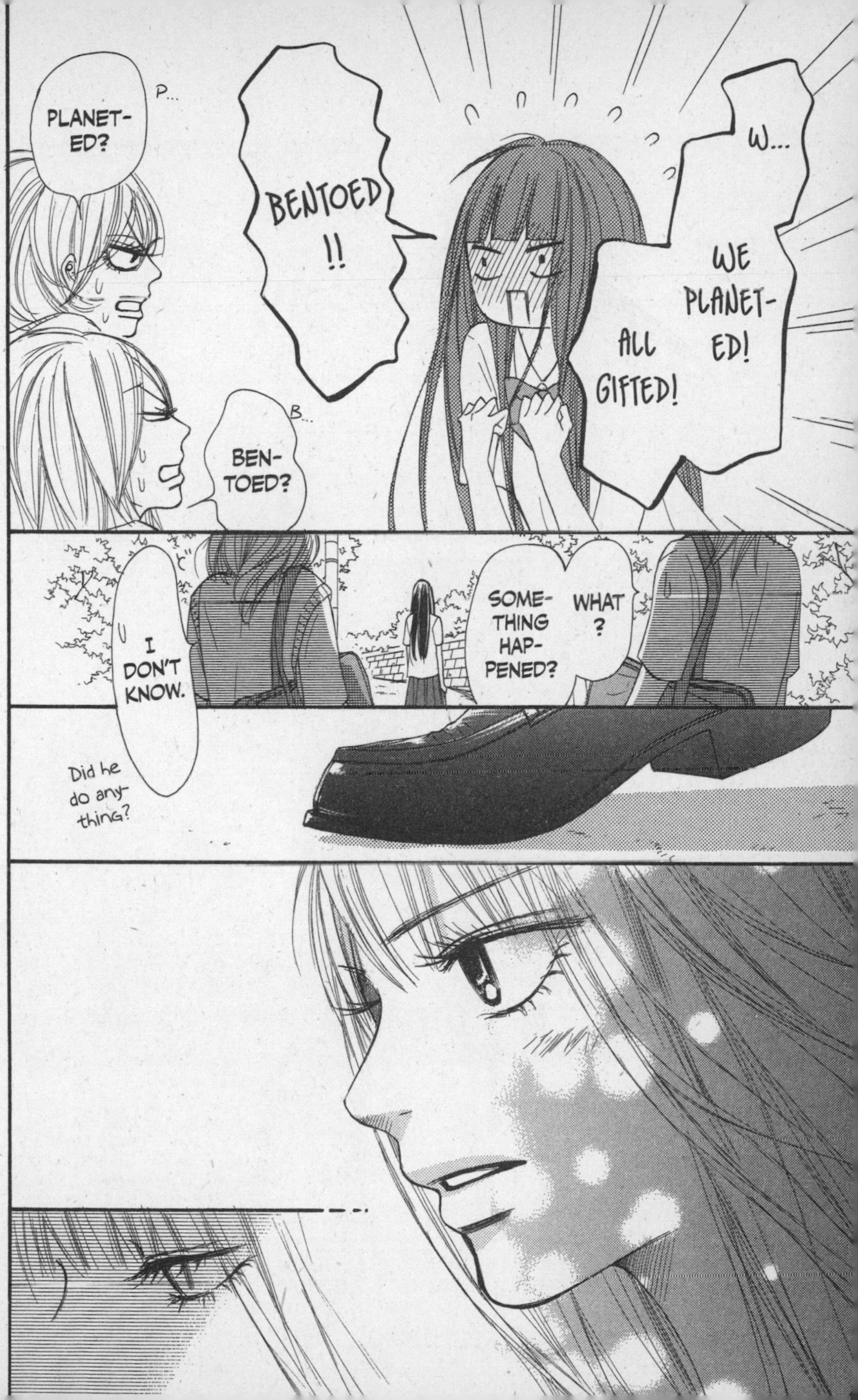
W...
WE PLANET-ED! ALL GIFTED!
BENTOED !!
P...
PLANET-ED?
B...
BEN-TOED?
WHAT ?
SOME-THING HAP-PENED?
I DON'T KNOW.
Did he do any-thing?

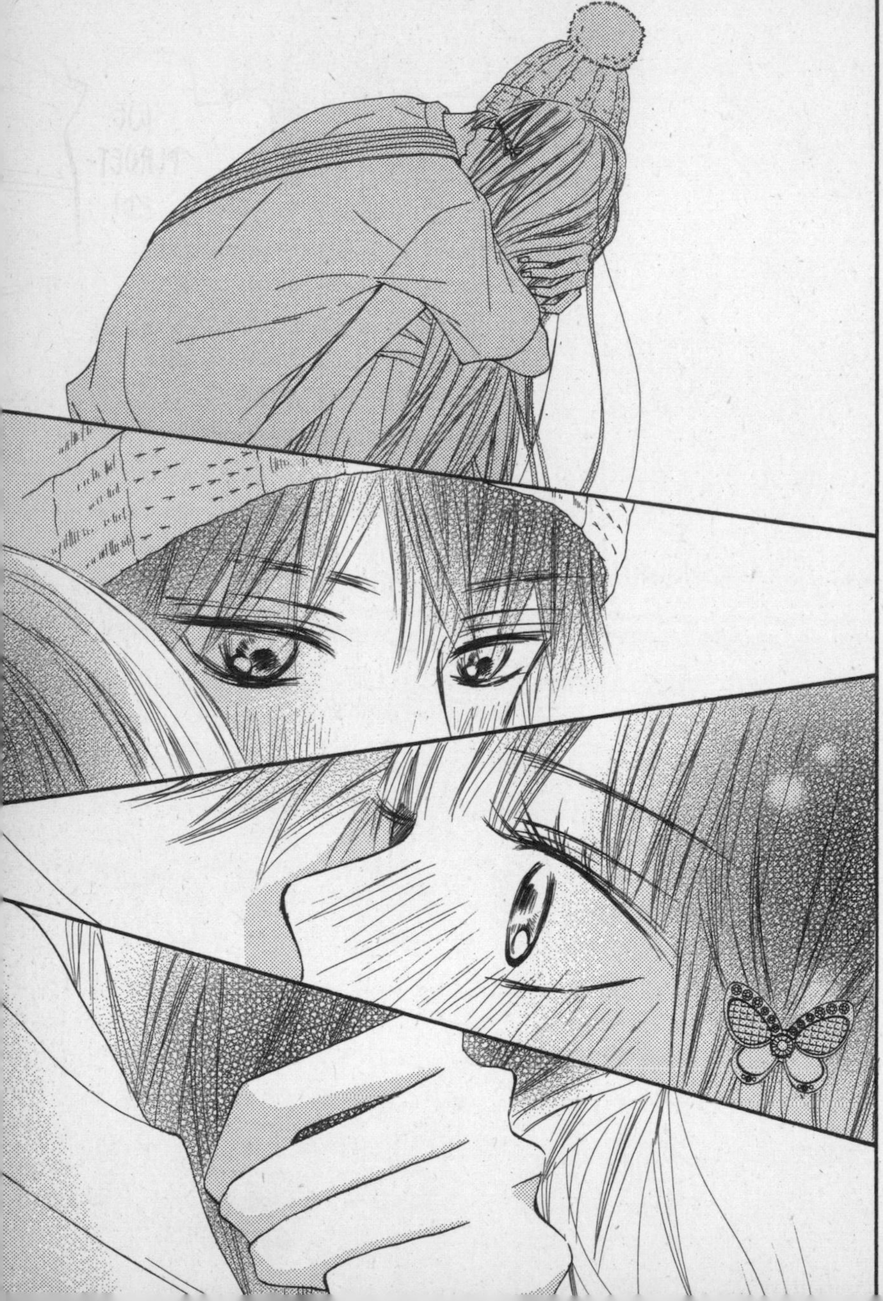

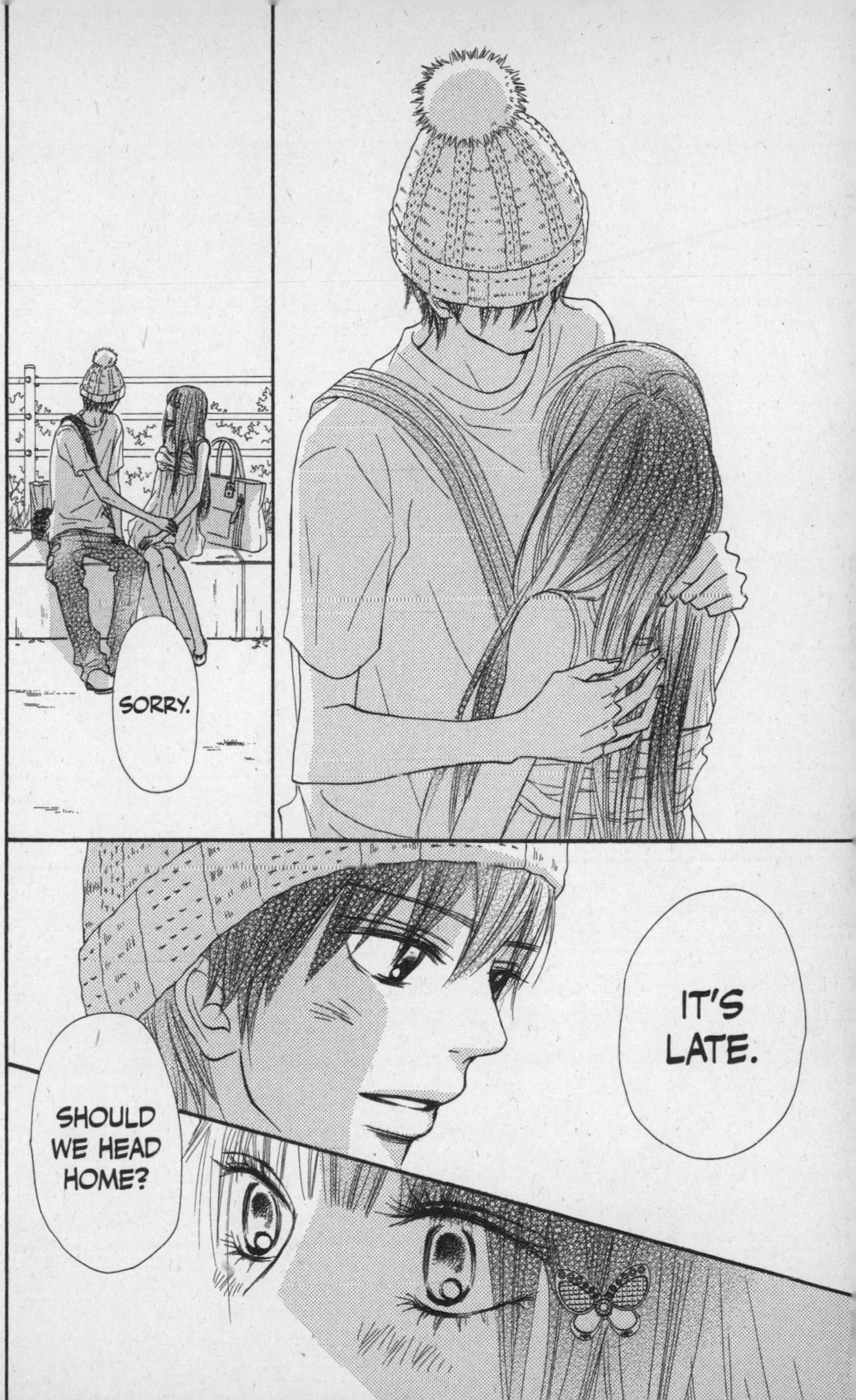
SORRY.
IT'S LATE.
SHOULD WE HEAD HOME?

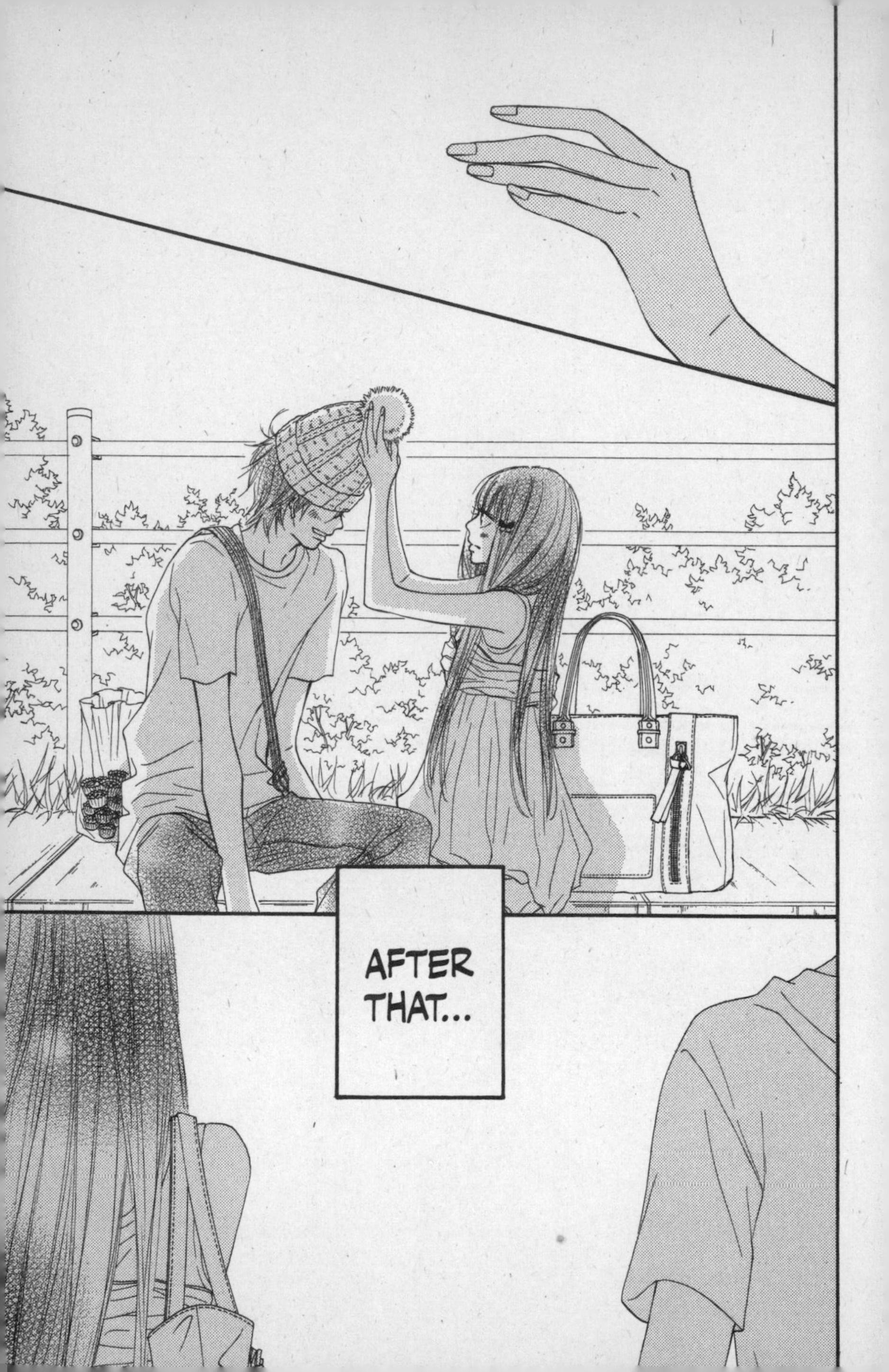
AFTER THAT...

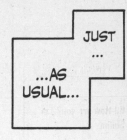

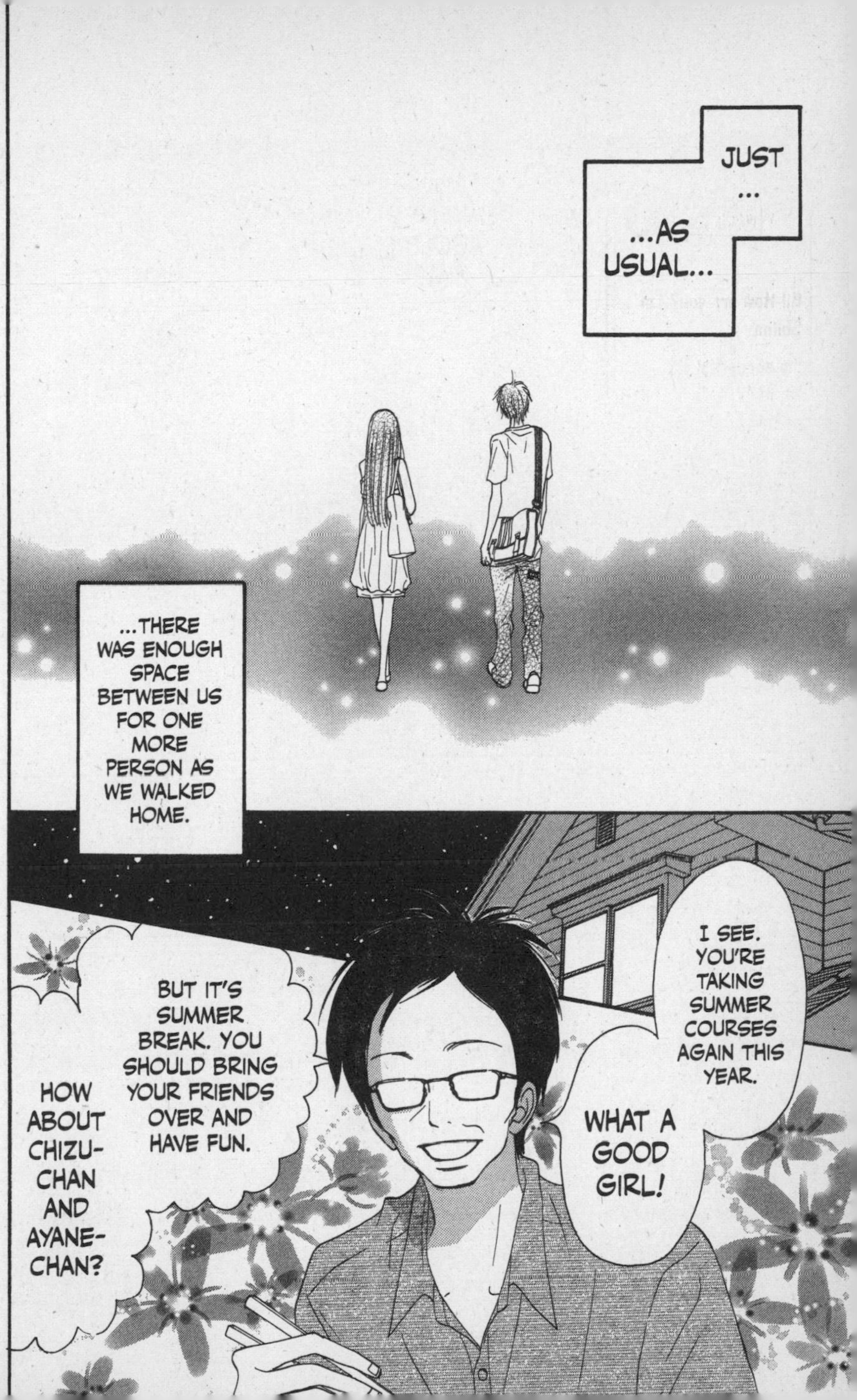

JUST
...

...AS
USUAL...

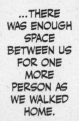

...THERE WAS ENOUGH SPACE BETWEEN US FOR ONE MORE PERSON AS WE WALKED HOME.

I SEE. YOU'RE TAKING SUMMER COURSES AGAIN THIS YEAR.

WHAT A GOOD GIRL!

BUT IT'S SUMMER BREAK. YOU SHOULD BRING YOUR FRIENDS OVER AND HAVE FUN.

HOW ABOUT CHIZU-CHAN AND AYANE-CHAN?

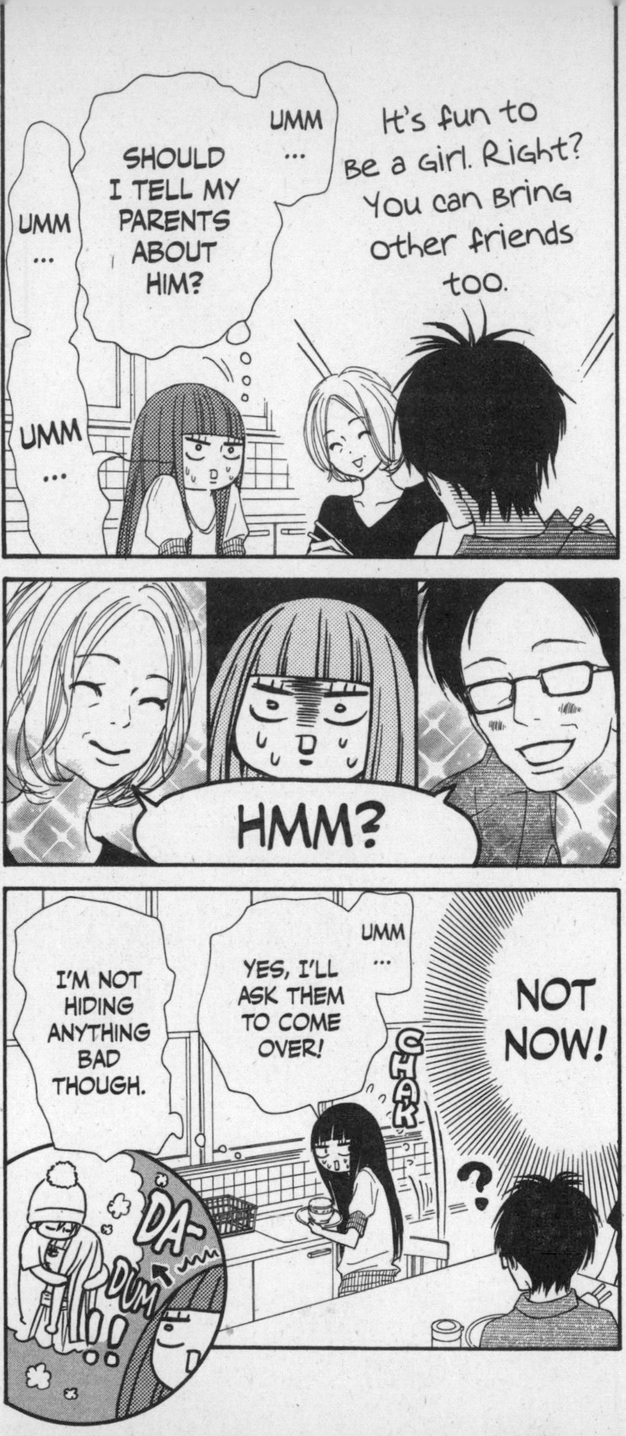
It's fun to be a girl. Right? You can bring other friends too.
UMM ...
SHOULD I TELL MY PARENTS ABOUT HIM?
UMM ...
UMM ...
HMM?
NOT NOW!
UMM ...
YES, I'LL ASK THEM TO COME OVER!
CHAK
?
I'M NOT HIDING ANYTHING BAD THOUGH.
DA-
DUM

KARUPIN on JAPAN 1

Hi! How are you? I'm Shiina.

I'm sorry that my handwriting looks like earthworms!

I think this volume comes out right before the opening of the movie. *Sigh!* Finally it's going to open. I'm so happy and excited, but sad (since it'll be over then!). I mean, I grew up in Hokkaido, so I always think about winter. I always think that winter will come after the summer solstice! (But that's when summer starts!) After July, I think winter will come! (But that's the middle of summer!) When August starts, I think summer is over! After the *bon* holiday, I expect TV commercials for heaters and snow tires to air. That's why I may have more fear of things ending than other people do! I'm scared!

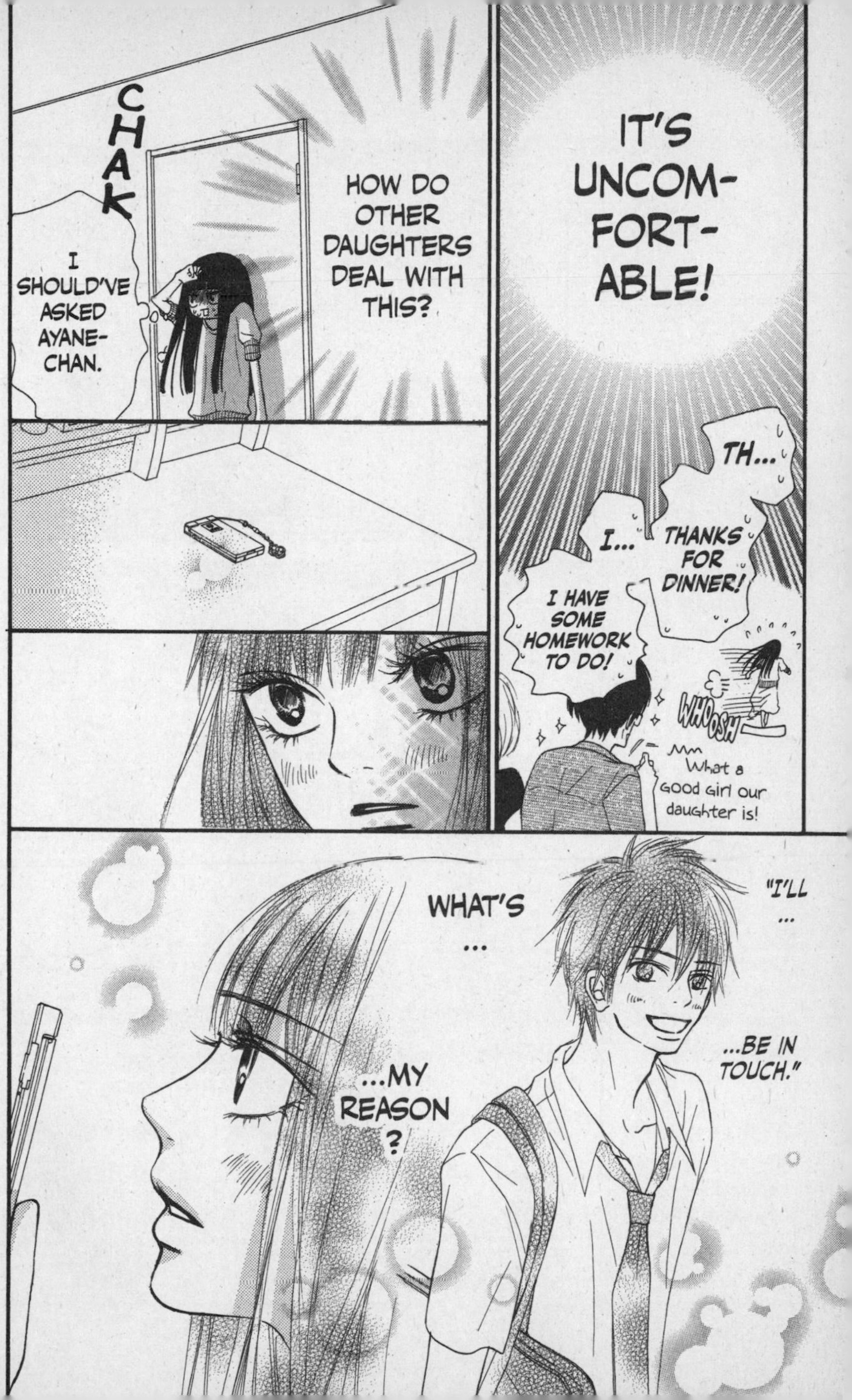
IT'S UNCOM-FORT-ABLE!
TH...
THANKS FOR DINNER!
I...
I HAVE SOME HOMEWORK TO DO!
WHOOSH
Mm
What a good girl our daughter is!
HOW DO OTHER DAUGHTERS DEAL WITH THIS?
CHAK
I SHOULD'VE ASKED AYANE-CHAN.
"I'LL ...
...BE IN TOUCH."
WHAT'S ...
...MY REASON?

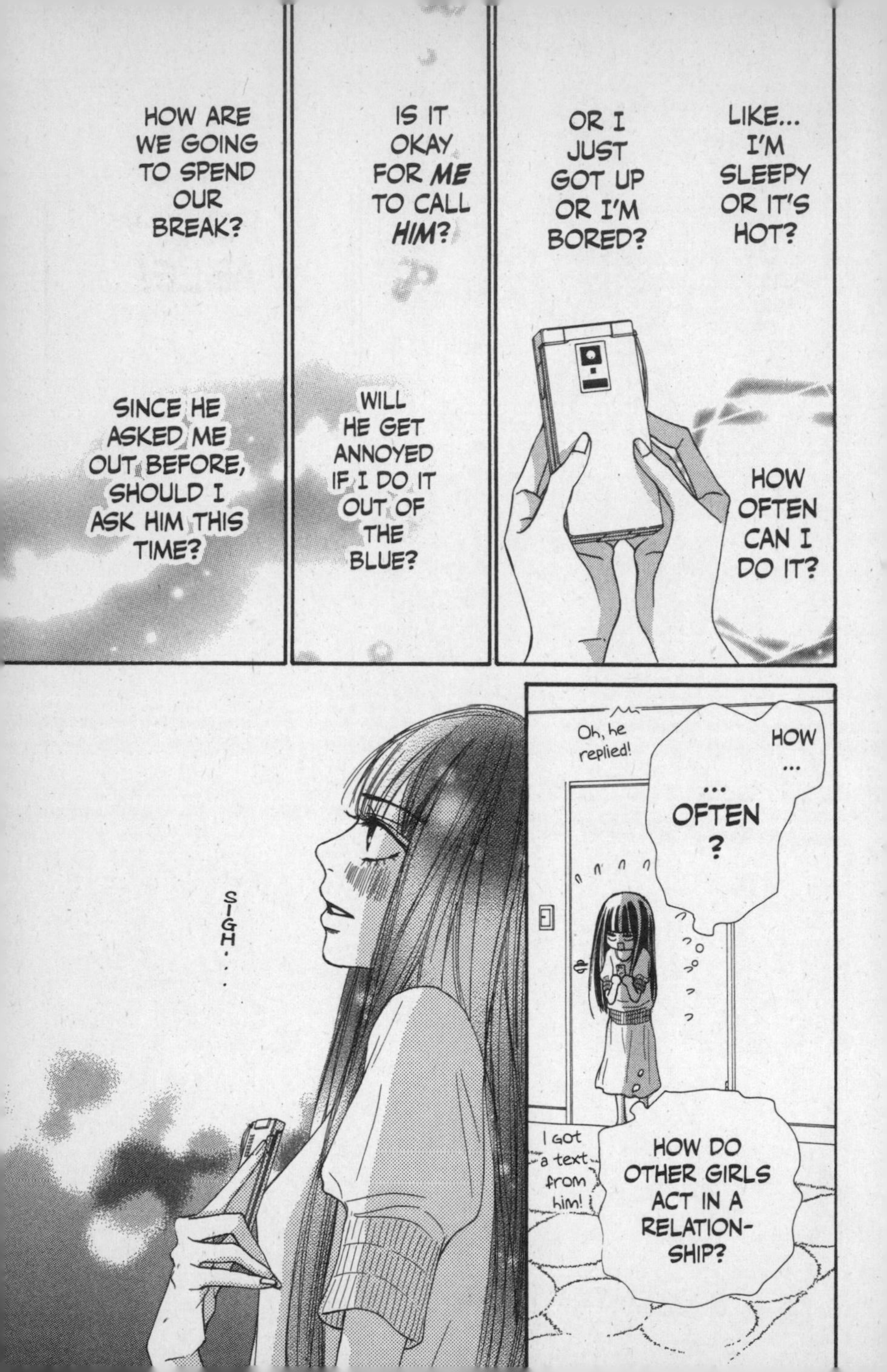
LIKE... I'M SLEEPY OR IT'S HOT?
OR I JUST GOT UP OR I'M BORED?
HOW OFTEN CAN I DO IT?
IS IT OKAY FOR *ME* TO CALL *HIM*?
WILL HE GET ANNOYED IF I DO IT OUT OF THE BLUE?
HOW ARE WE GOING TO SPEND OUR BREAK?
SINCE HE ASKED ME OUT BEFORE, SHOULD I ASK HIM THIS TIME?
Oh, he replied!
HOW... ...OFTEN?
I got a text from him!
HOW DO OTHER GIRLS ACT IN A RELATIONSHIP?
SIGH..

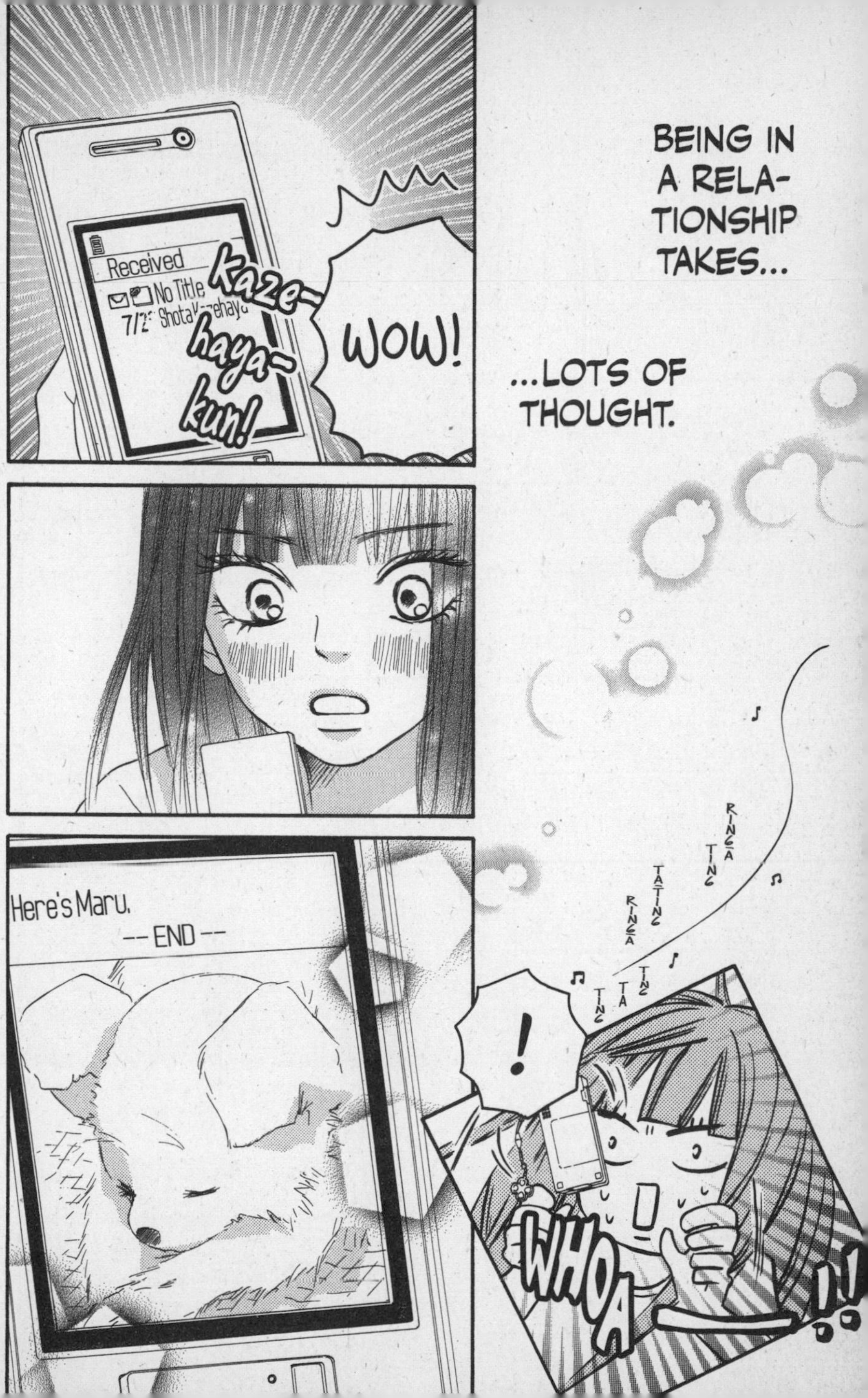
BEING IN A RELA- TIONSHIP TAKES...
...LOTS OF THOUGHT.
RINGA
TING
TATING
RINGA
TING
TA
TING
!
WHOA—!!
Received
No Title
Kaze-haya-kun!
WOW!
Here's Maru.
-- END --

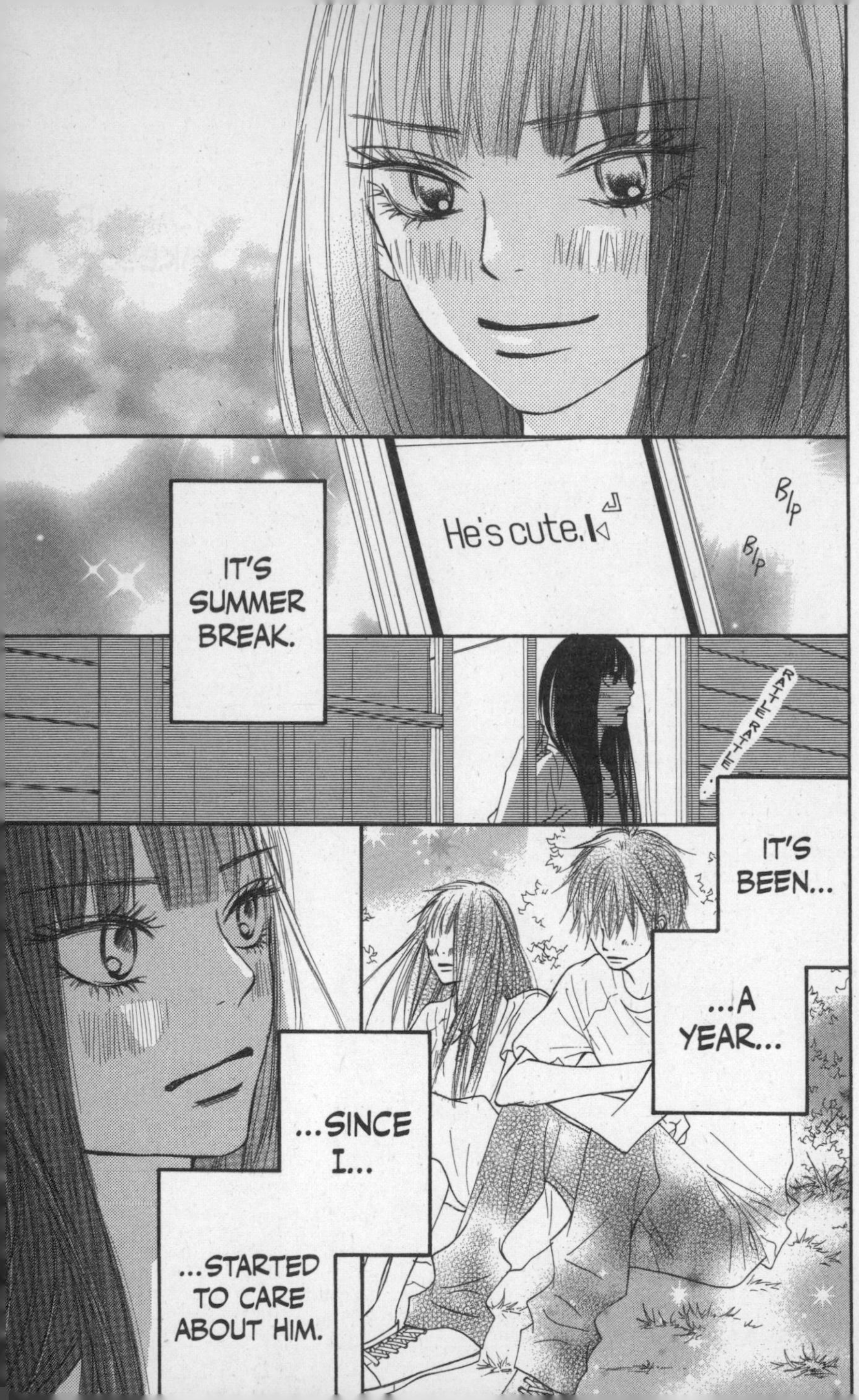
Blip
Blip
He's cute.
IT'S SUMMER BREAK.
RATTLE RATTLE
IT'S BEEN...
...A YEAR...
...SINCE I...
...STARTED TO CARE ABOUT HIM.

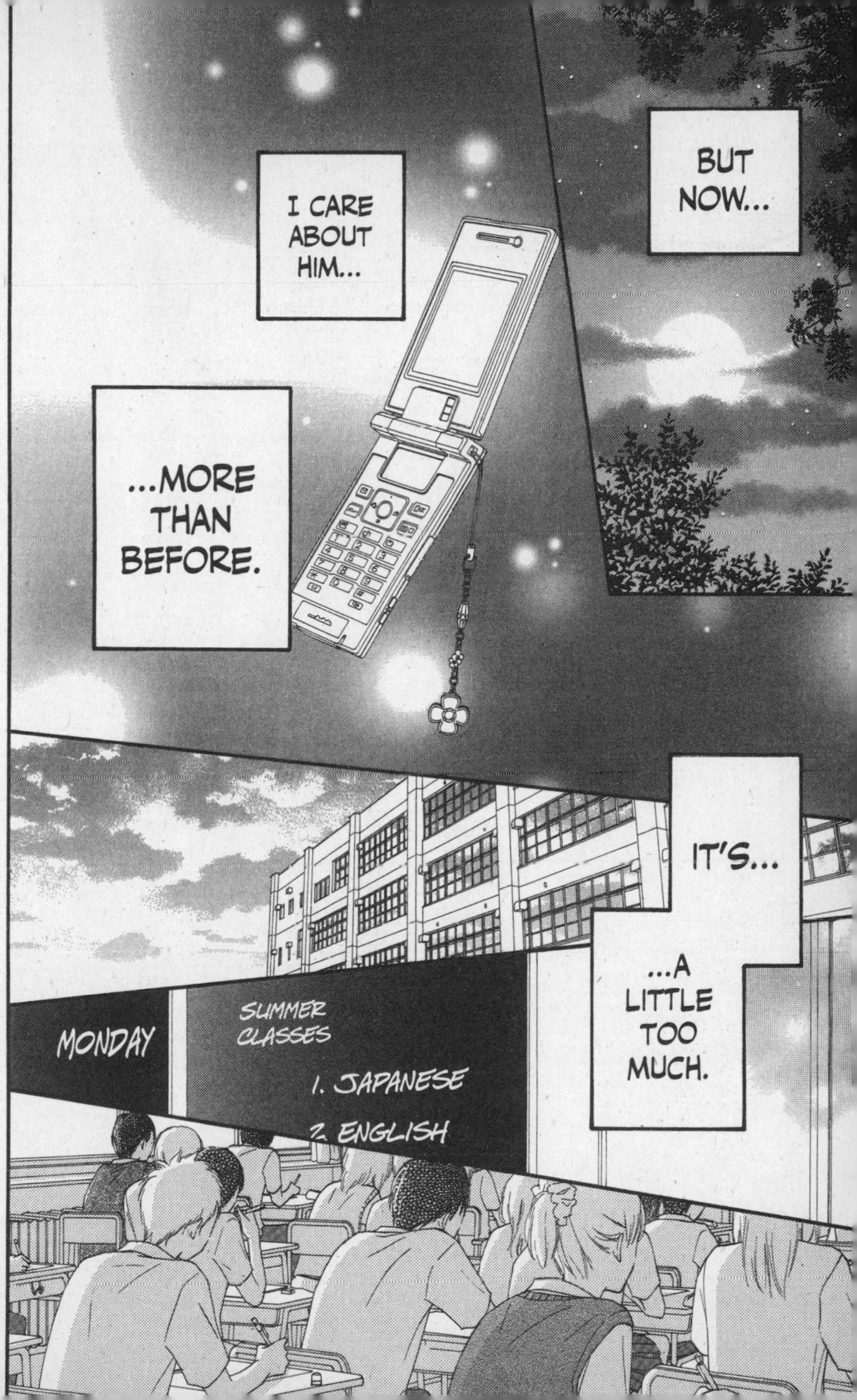
BUT NOW...
I CARE ABOUT HIM...
...MORE THAN BEFORE.
IT'S...
...A LITTLE TOO MUCH.
SUMMER CLASSES
1. JAPANESE
2. ENGLISH
MONDAY

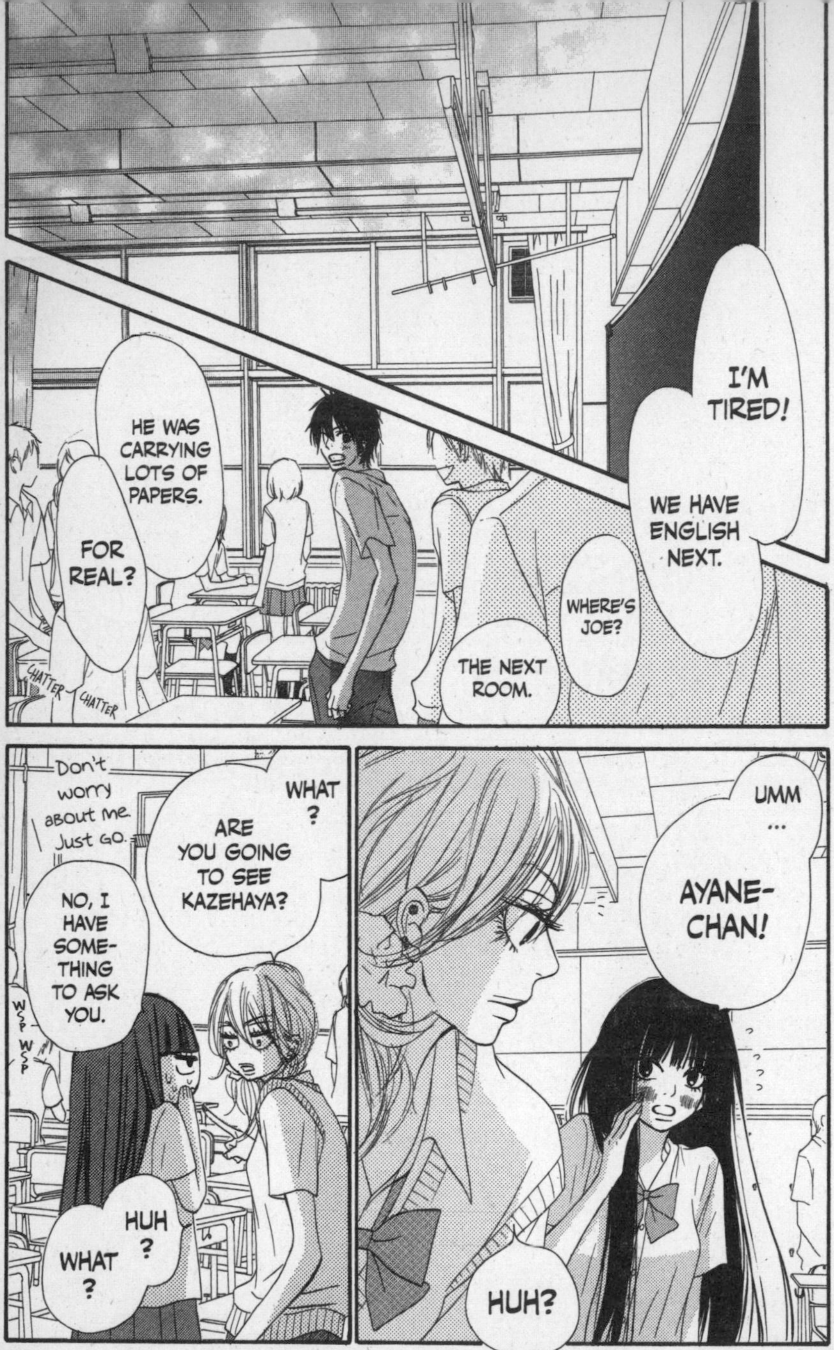
I'M TIRED!
WE HAVE ENGLISH NEXT.
WHERE'S JOE?
THE NEXT ROOM.
HE WAS CARRYING LOTS OF PAPERS.
FOR REAL?
CHATTER CHATTER
UMM ... AYANE-CHAN!
HUH?
WHAT?
ARE YOU GOING TO SEE KAZEHAYA?
NO, I HAVE SOMETHING TO ASK YOU.
Don't worry about me. Just go.
WSP WSP
HUH?
WHAT?

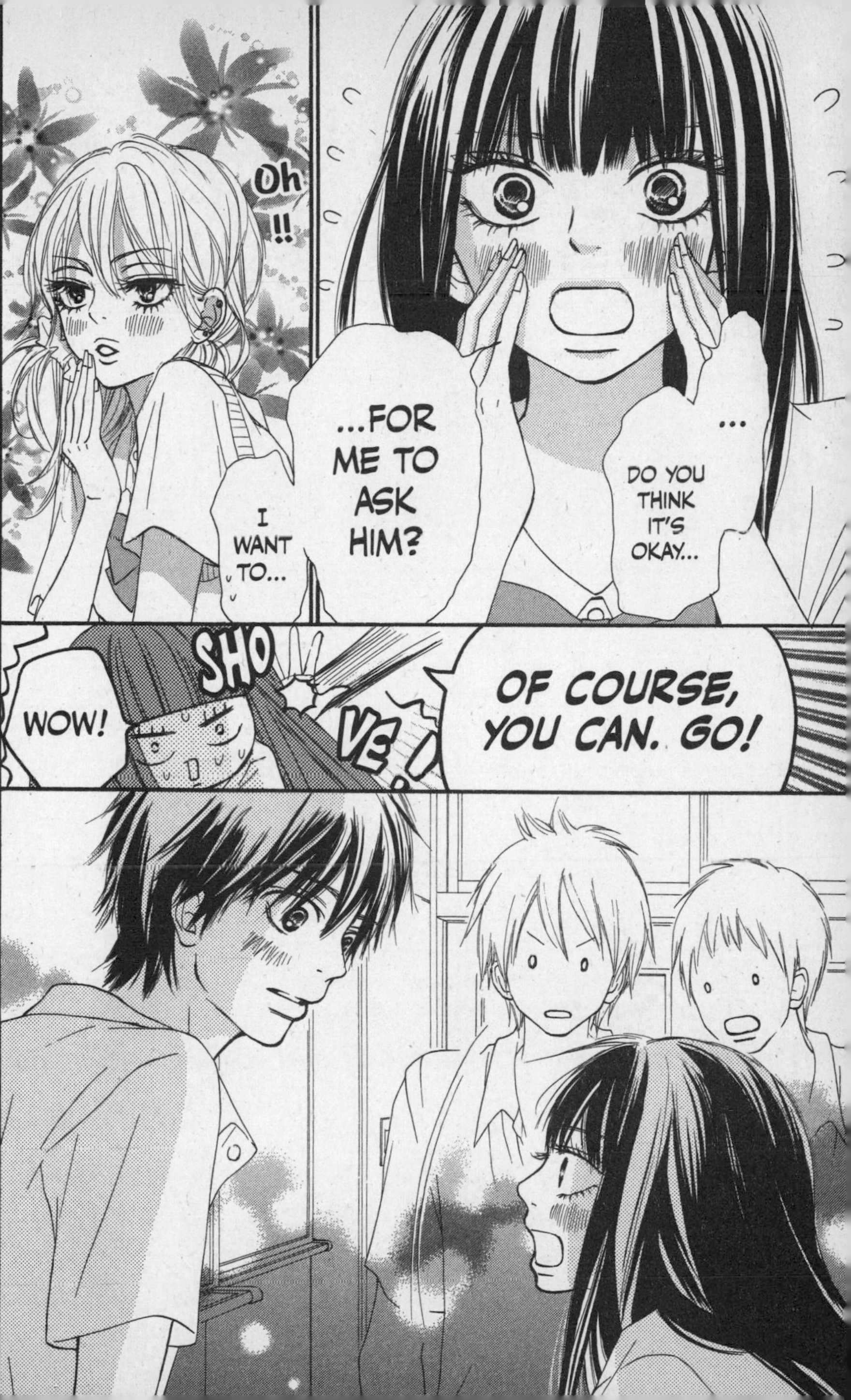
...
DO YOU THINK IT'S OKAY...
...FOR ME TO ASK HIM?
I WANT TO...
Oh !!
OF COURSE, YOU CAN. GO!
SHOVE
WOW!

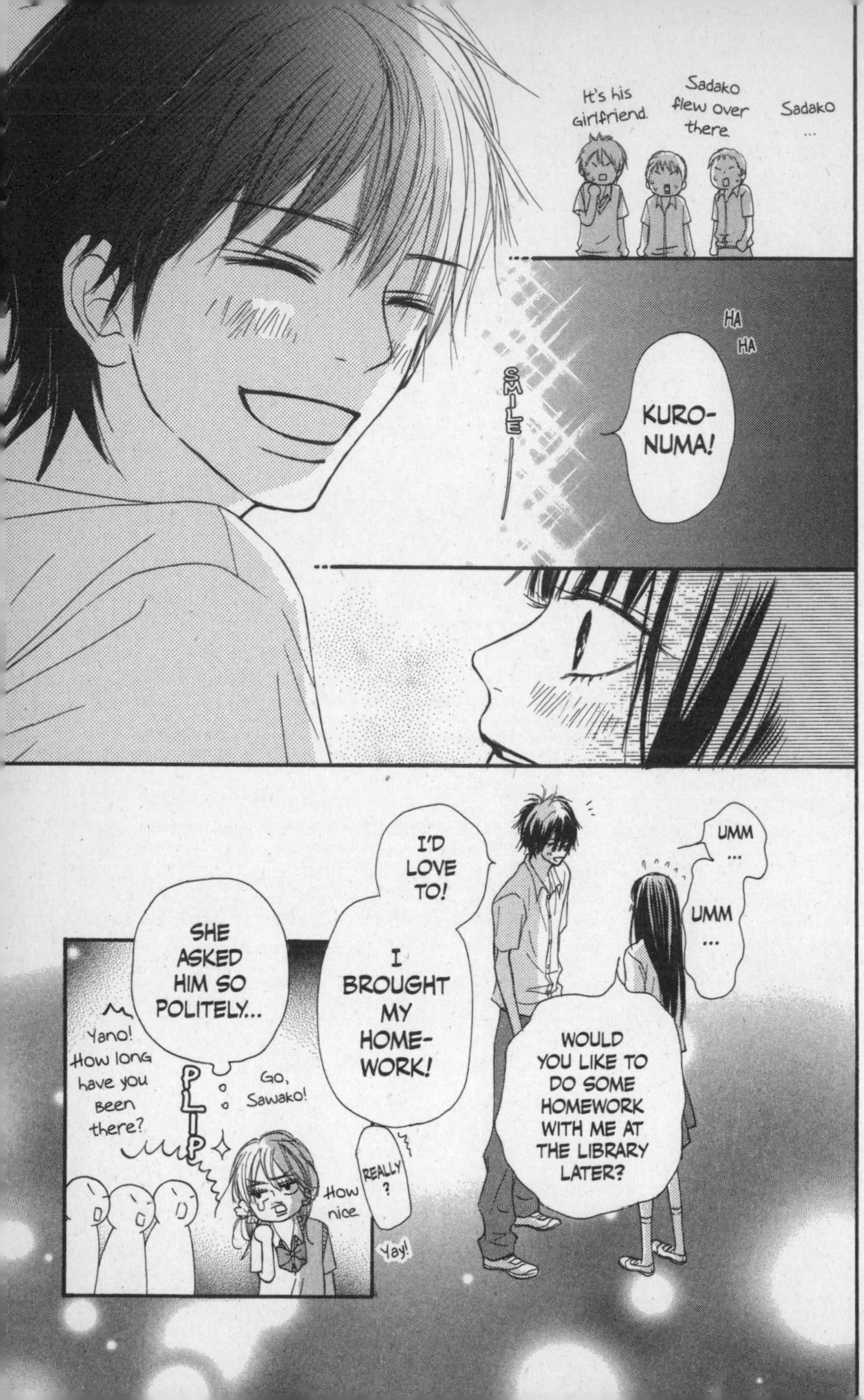
Sadako ...
Sadako flew over there.
It's his girlfriend.
HA HA
KURO-NUMA!
SMILE
UMM ...
UMM ...
WOULD YOU LIKE TO DO SOME HOMEWORK WITH ME AT THE LIBRARY LATER?
I'D LOVE TO!
I BROUGHT MY HOMEWORK!
REALLY?
Yay!
SHE ASKED HIM SO POLITELY...
Go, Sawako!
How nice.
PLIP
Yano! How long have you been there?

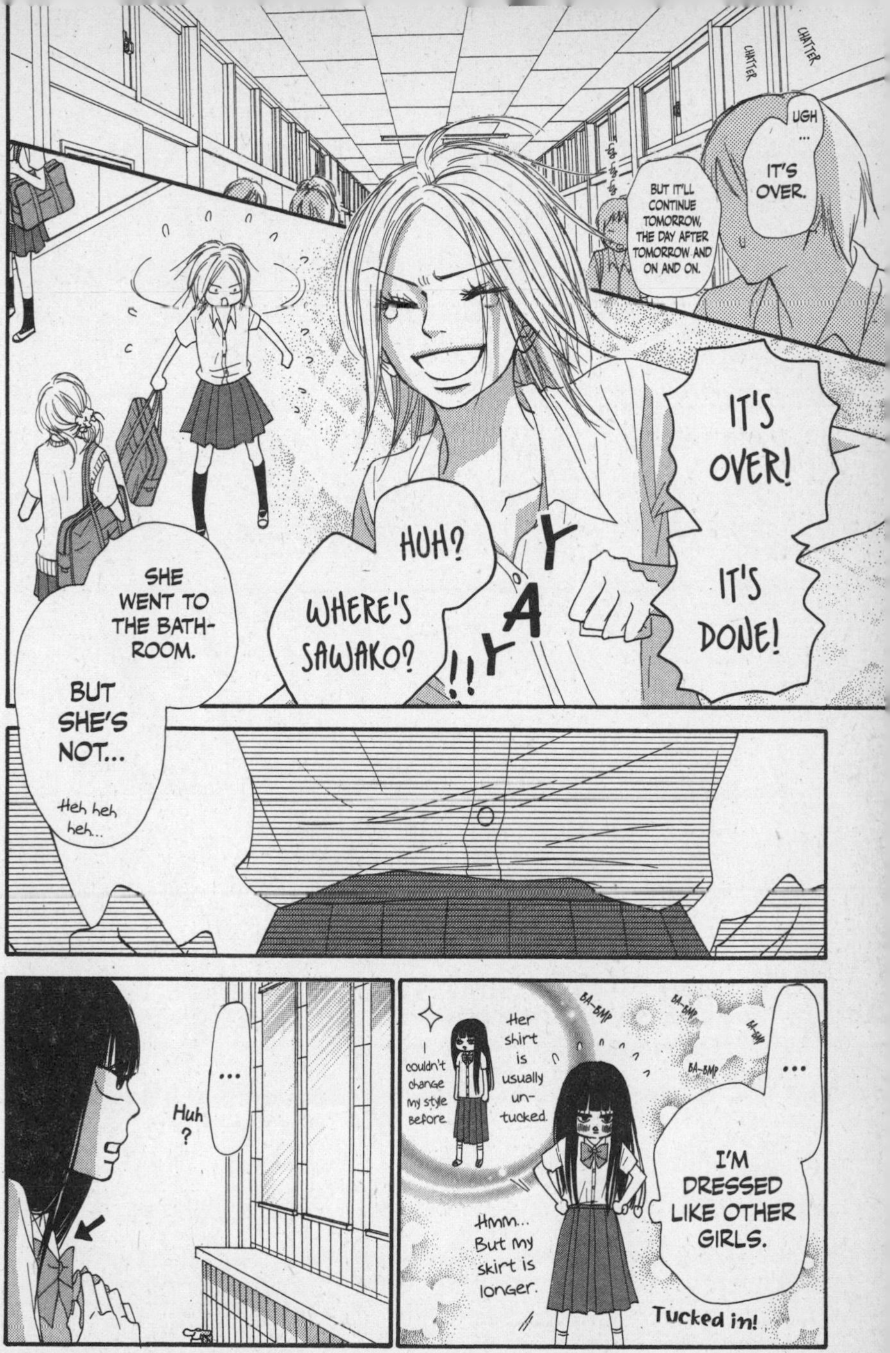
CHATTER
CHATTER
UGH ...
IT'S OVER.
BUT IT'LL CONTINUE TOMORROW, THE DAY AFTER TOMORROW AND ON AND ON.
IT'S OVER!
IT'S DONE!
YAY!!
HUH?
WHERE'S SAWAKO?
SHE WENT TO THE BATH-ROOM.
BUT SHE'S NOT...
Heh heh heh...
...
I'M DRESSED LIKE OTHER GIRLS.
BA-BMP
BA-BMP
BA-BMP
BA-BMP
Her shirt is usually un-tucked.
I couldn't change my style before
Hmm... But my skirt is longer.
Tucked in!
...
Huh?

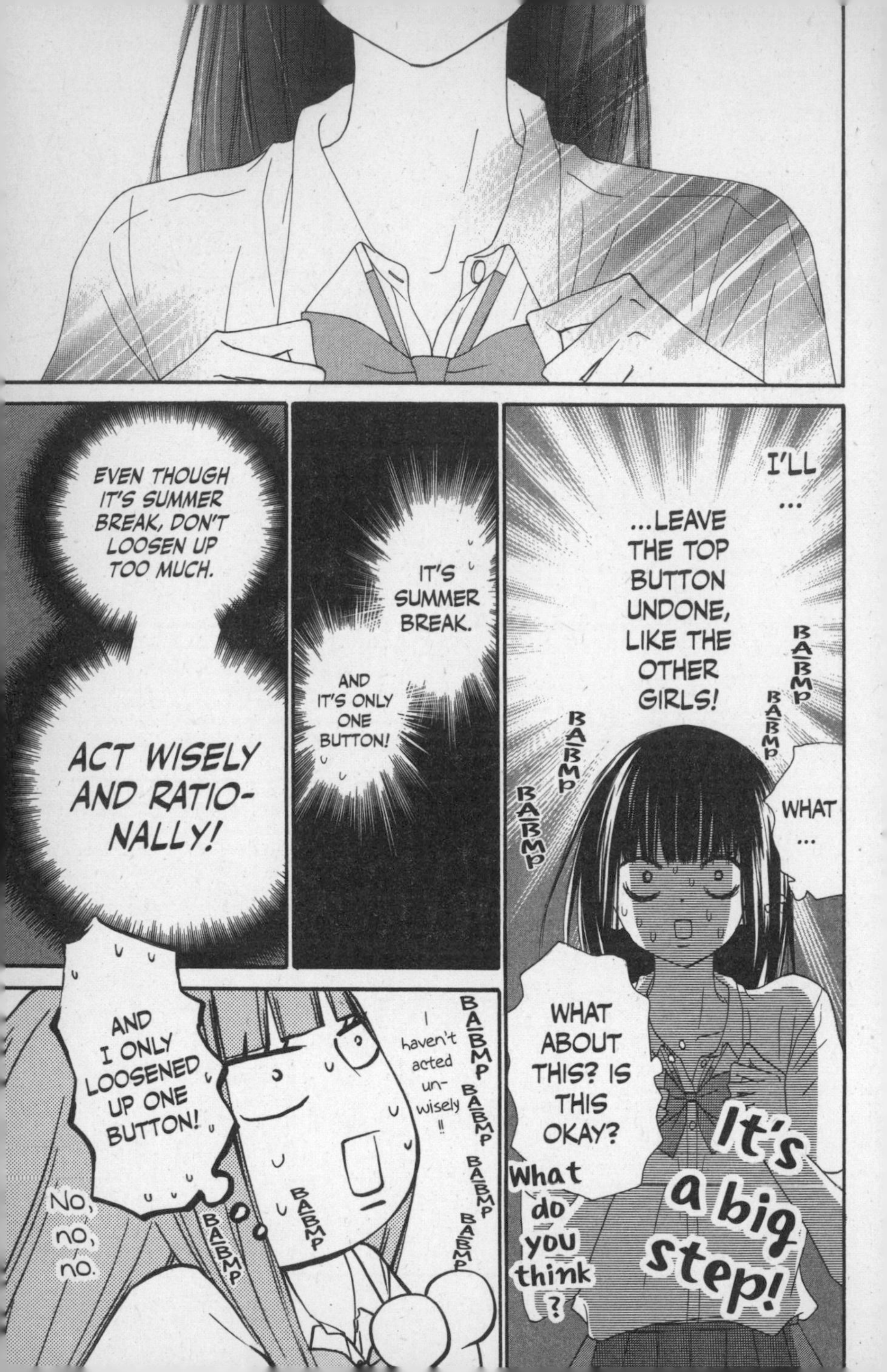
I'LL ...
...LEAVE THE TOP BUTTON UNDONE, LIKE THE OTHER GIRLS!
BABMP BABMP
BABMP BABMP
WHAT ...
WHAT ABOUT THIS? IS THIS OKAY?
It's a big step!
What do you think?
IT'S SUMMER BREAK.
AND IT'S ONLY ONE BUTTON!
EVEN THOUGH IT'S SUMMER BREAK, DON'T LOOSEN UP TOO MUCH.
ACT WISELY AND RATIO-NALLY!
BABMP BABMP BABMP BABMP
I haven't acted un-wisely!!
AND I ONLY LOOSENED UP ONE BUTTON!
BABMP
BABMP
No, no, no.

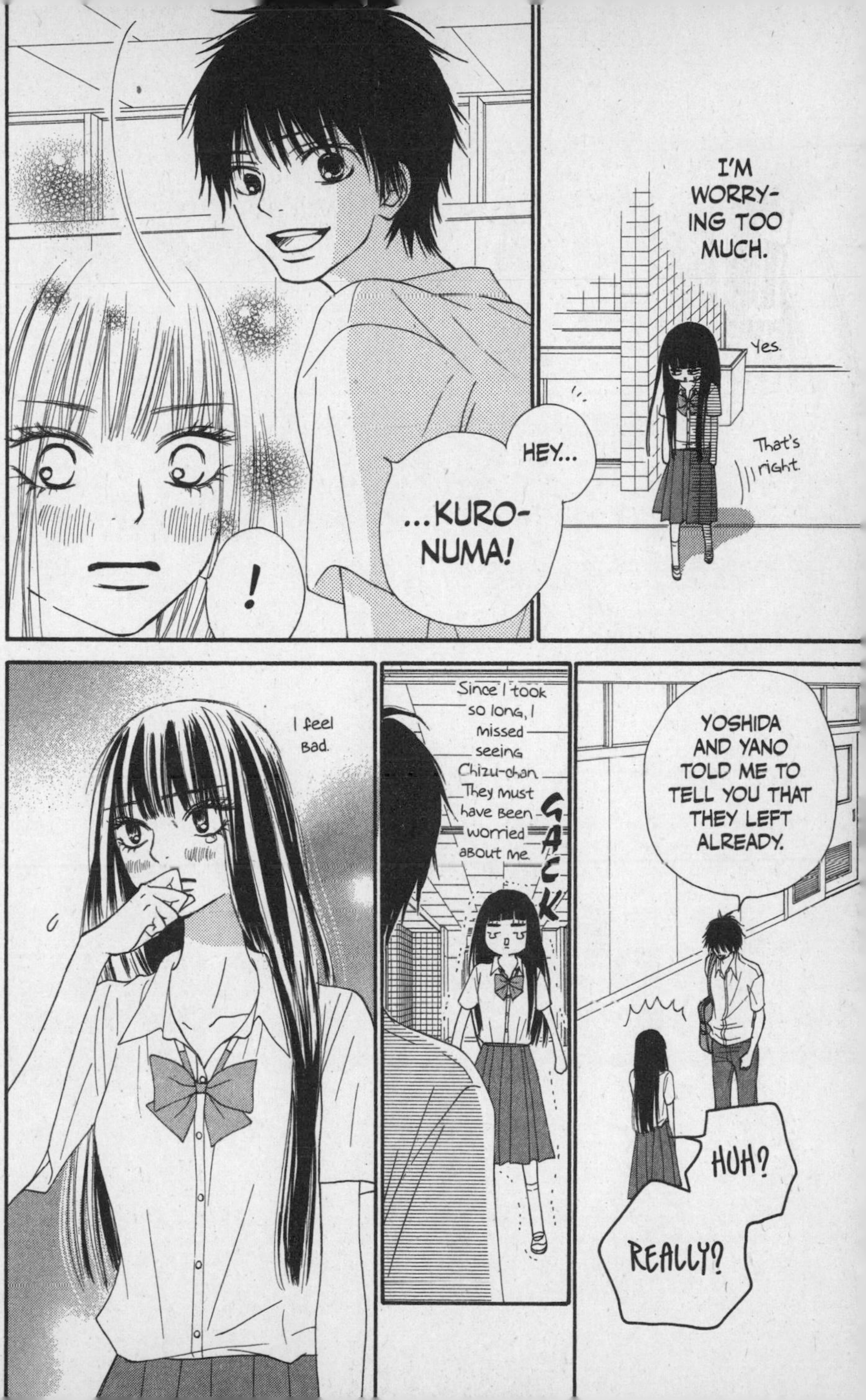
I'M WORRYING TOO MUCH.
Yes.
That's right.
HEY...
...KURONUMA!
!
YOSHIDA AND YANO TOLD ME TO TELL YOU THAT THEY LEFT ALREADY.
HUH?
REALLY?
Since I took so long, I missed seeing Chizu-chan. They must have been worried about me.
GACK
I feel bad.

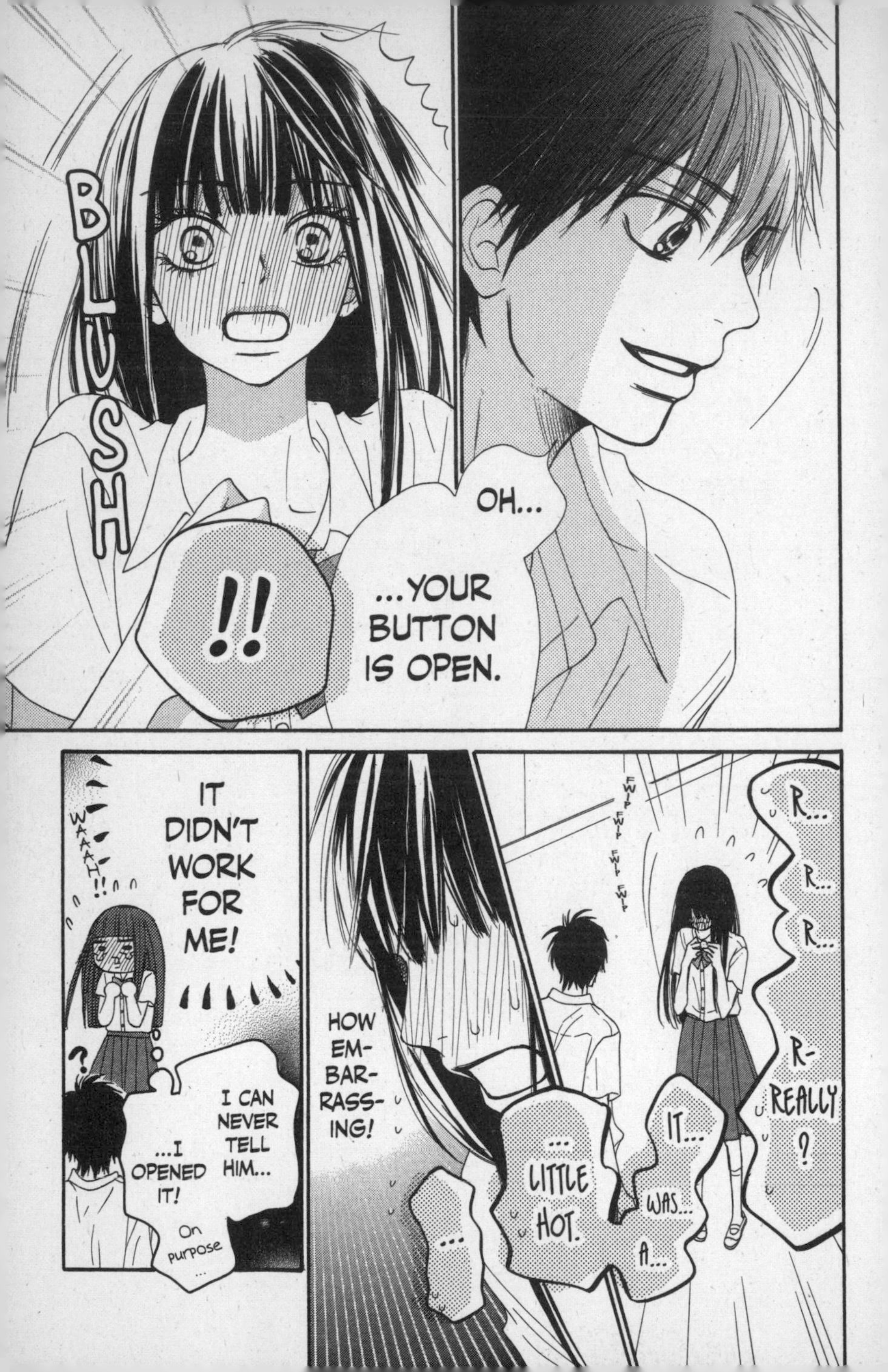
OH...
...YOUR BUTTON IS OPEN.
BLUSH
!!
R... R... R... R-REALLY?
FWIP FWIP FWIP FWIP
IT... WAS... A... LITTLE HOT.
...
HOW EMBARRASSING!
IT DIDN'T WORK FOR ME!
WAAAH!!
I CAN NEVER TELL HIM...
...I OPENED IT!
On purpose...

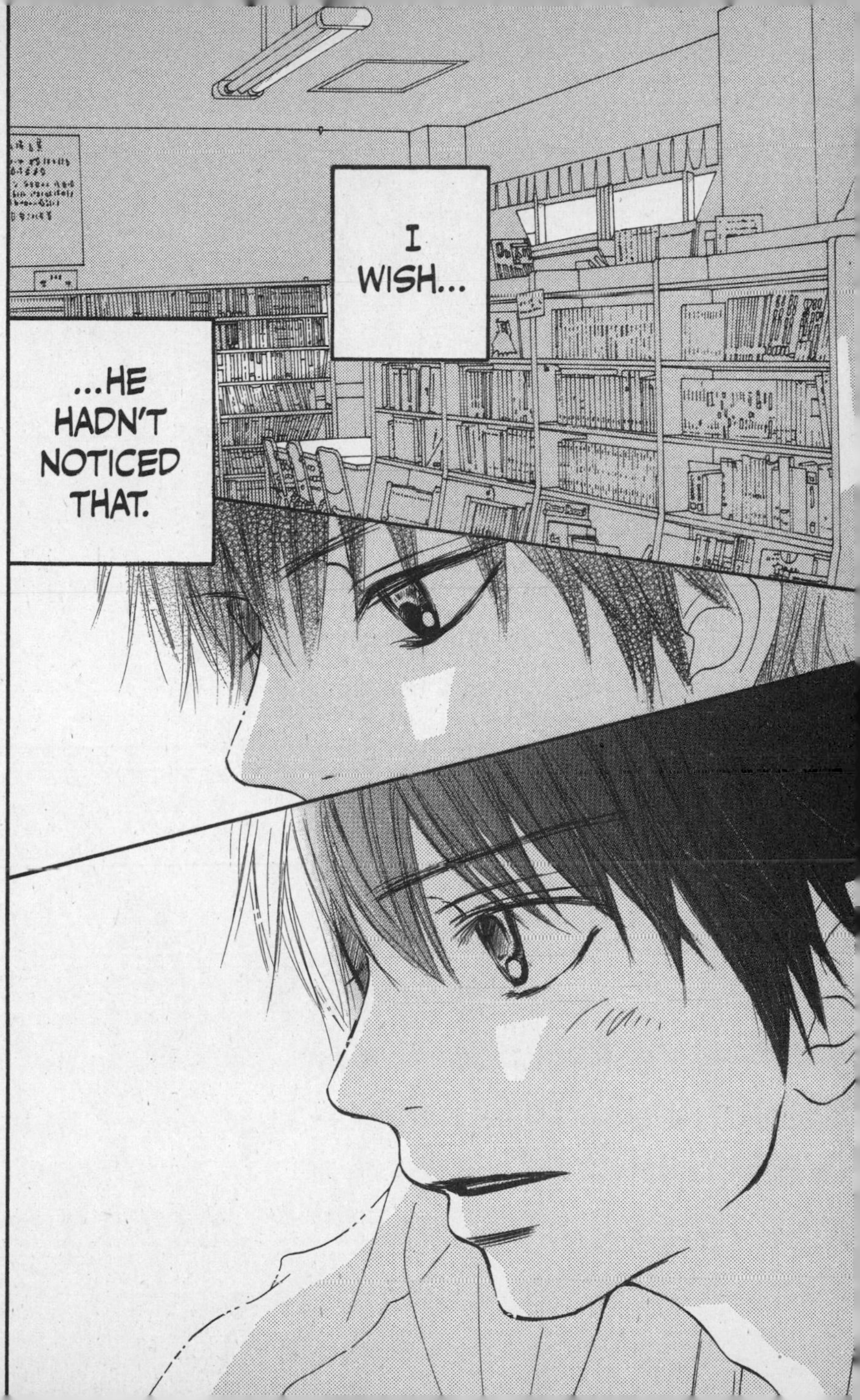
I WISH...
...HE HADN'T NOTICED THAT.

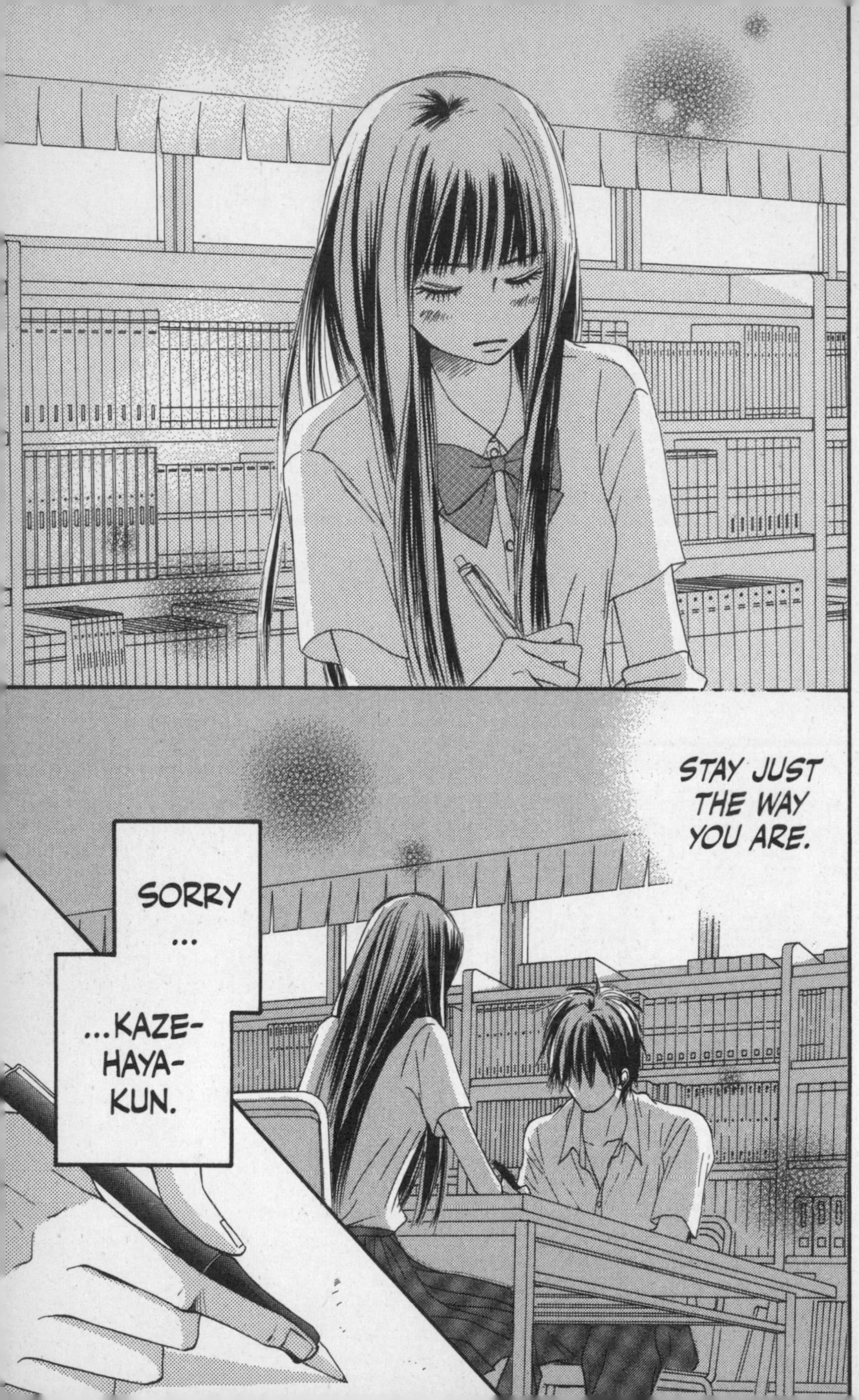
STAY JUST THE WAY YOU ARE.
SORRY ...
...KAZE-HAYA-KUN.

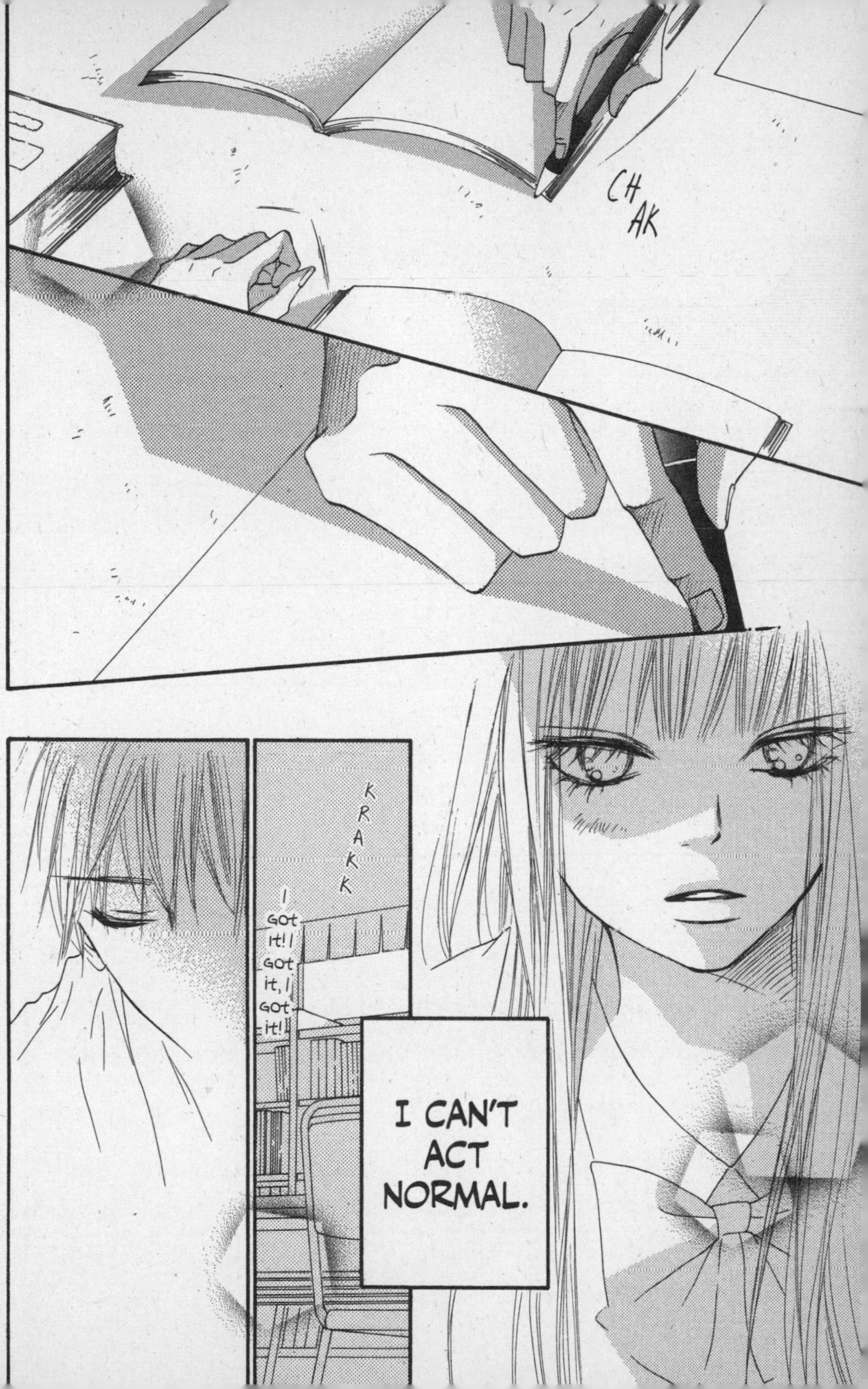
CHAK
I CAN'T ACT NORMAL.
KRAKK
I got it! I got it, I got it!

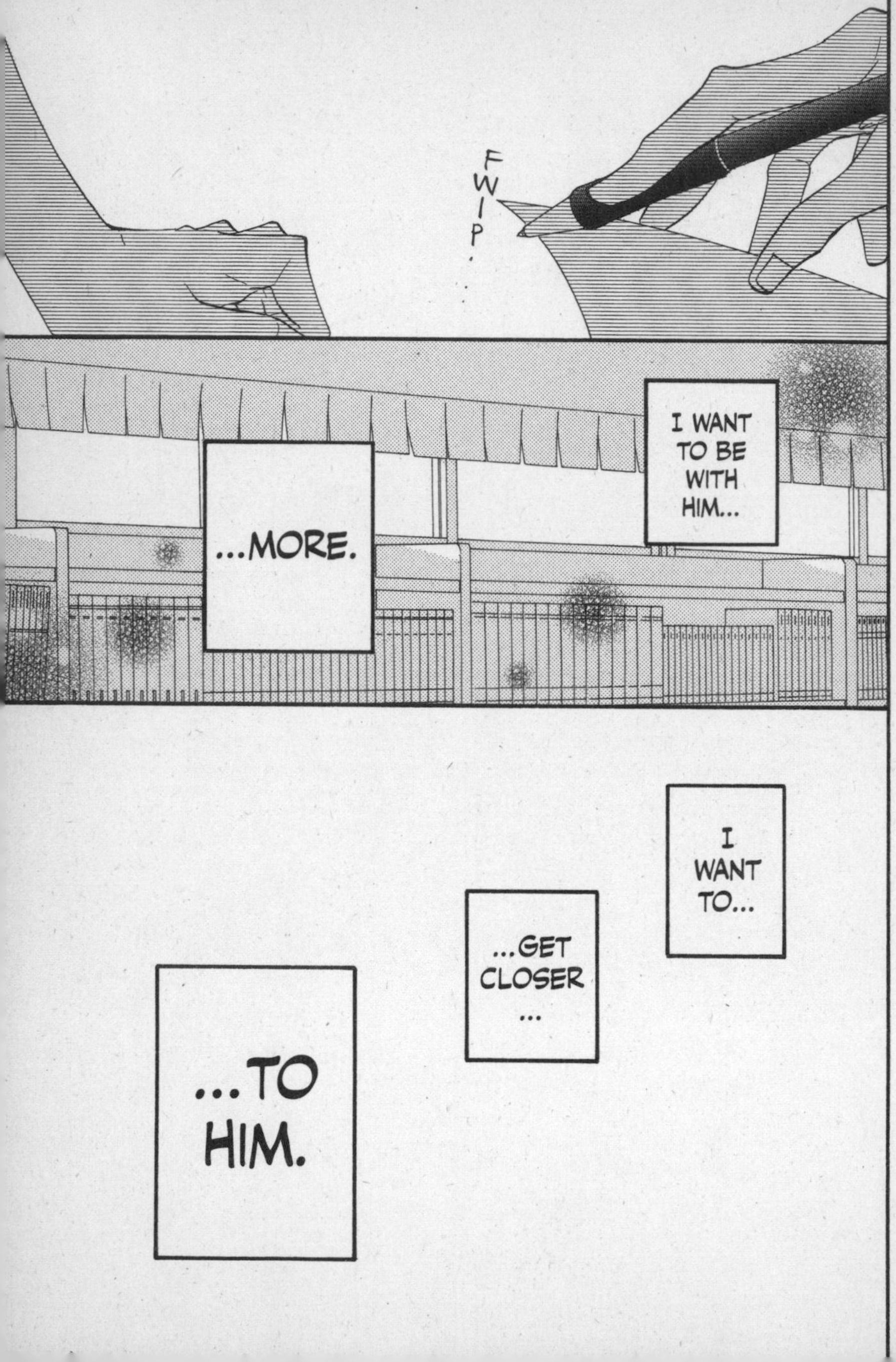
FWIP
I WANT TO BE WITH HIM...
...MORE.
I WANT TO...
...GET CLOSER ...
...TO HIM.

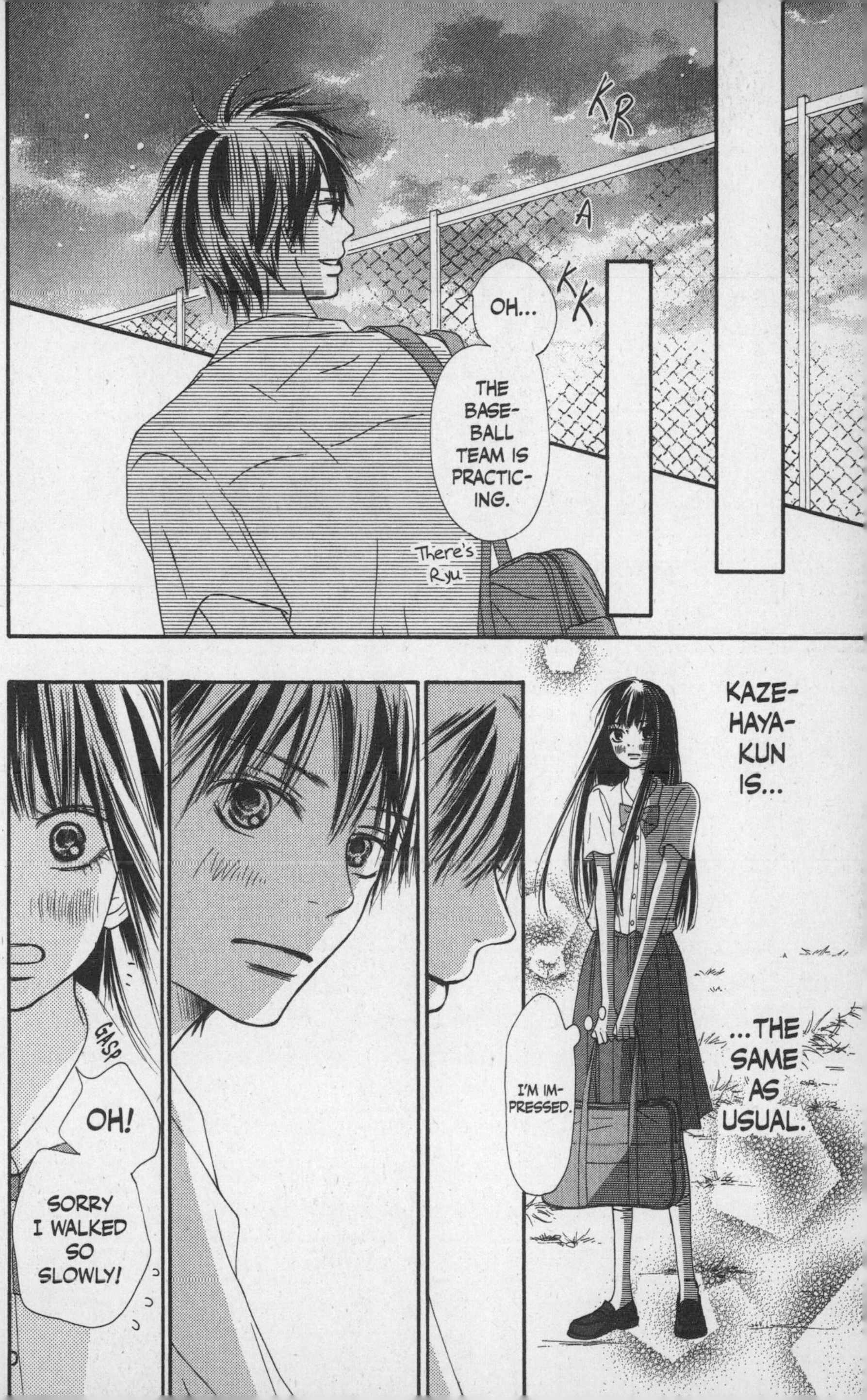
KRAKK
OH...
THE BASEBALL TEAM IS PRACTICING.
There's Ryu
KAZEHAYA-KUN IS...
...THE SAME AS USUAL.
I'M IMPRESSED.
GASP
OH!
SORRY I WALKED SO SLOWLY!

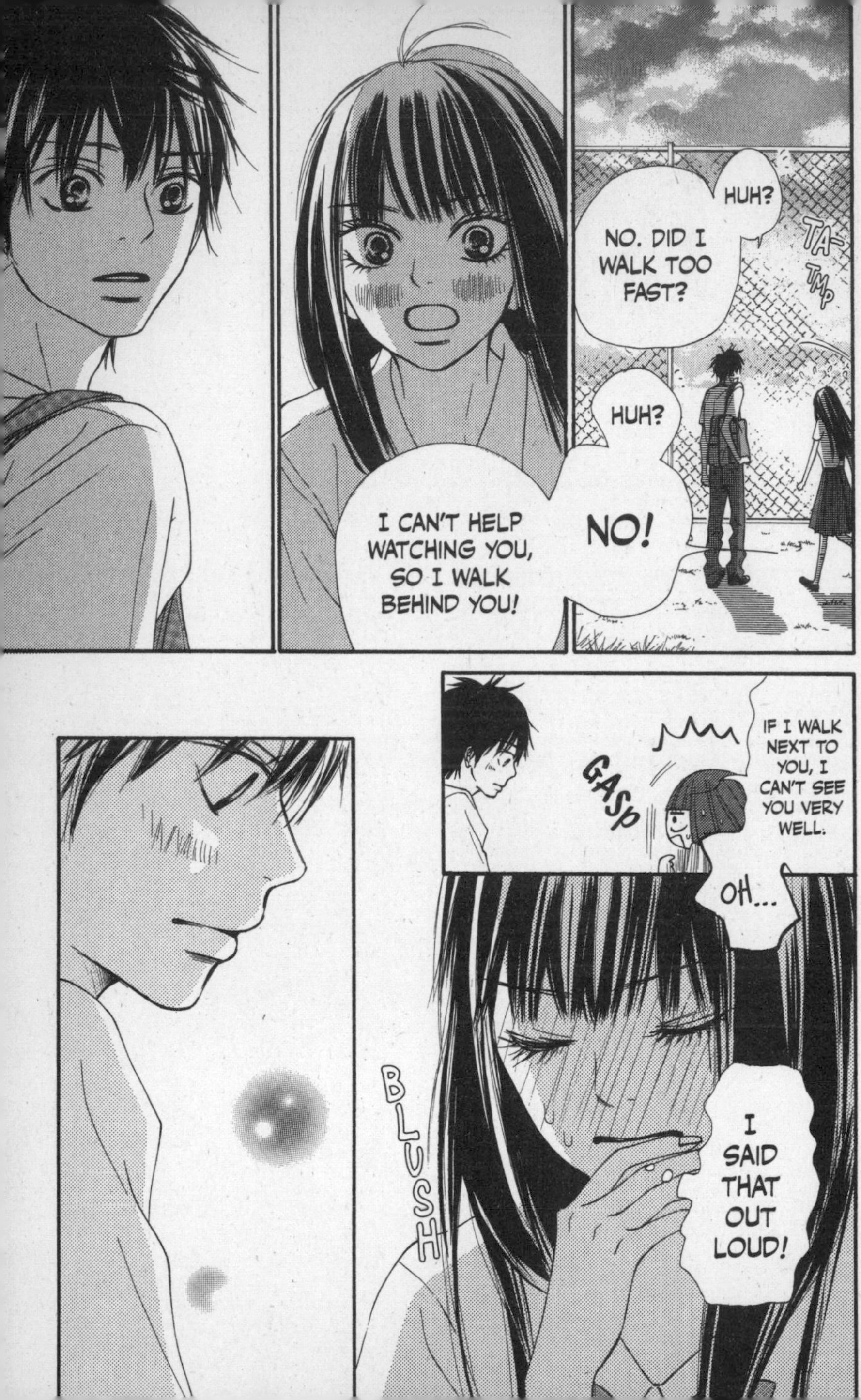
HUH?
NO. DID I WALK TOO FAST?
TA-TMP
HUH?
NO!
I CAN'T HELP WATCHING YOU, SO I WALK BEHIND YOU!
IF I WALK NEXT TO YOU, I CAN'T SEE YOU VERY WELL.
GASP
OH...
I SAID THAT OUT LOUD!
BLUSH

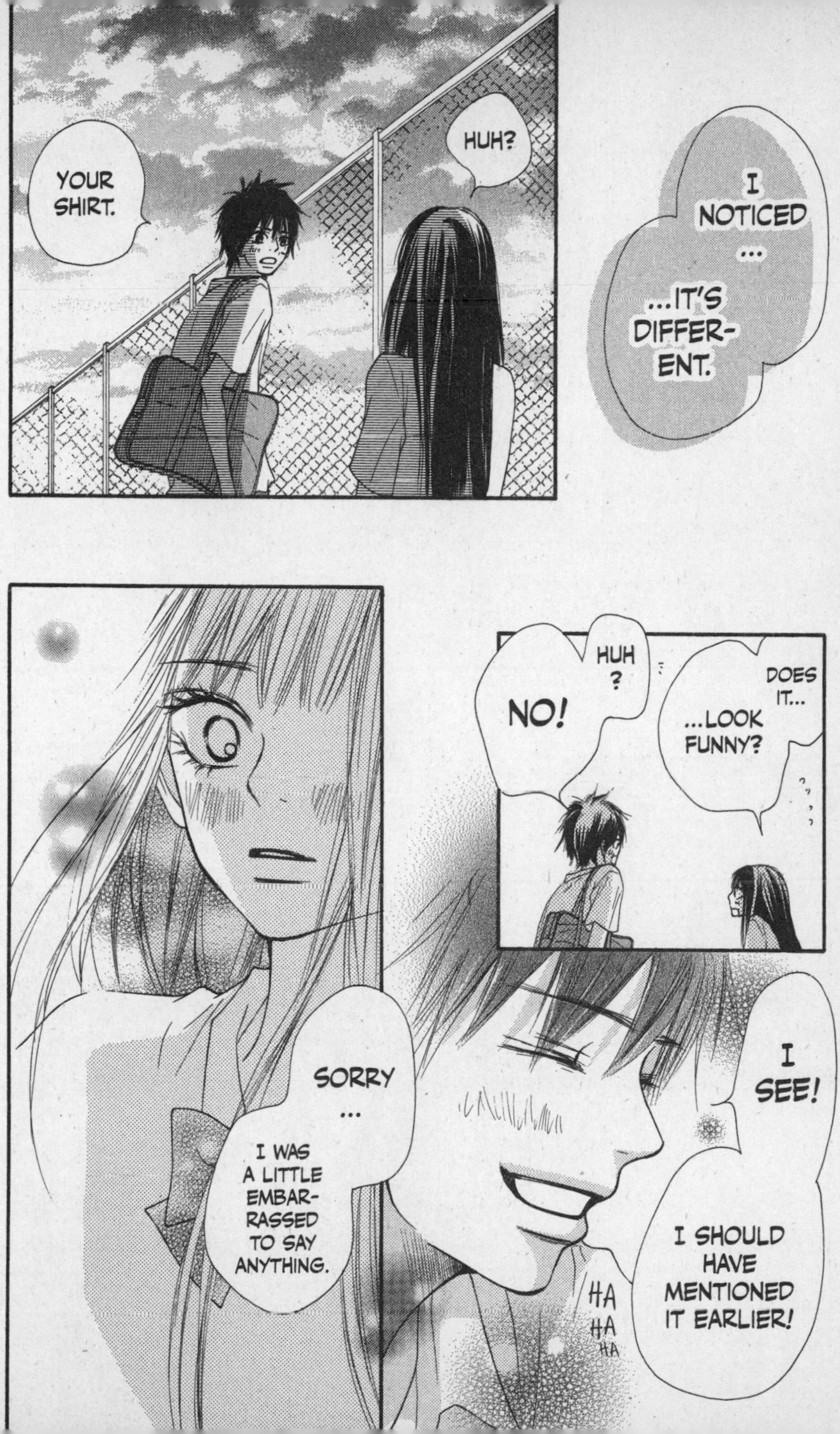
I NOTICED ...
...IT'S DIFFERENT.
HUH?
YOUR SHIRT.
DOES IT...
...LOOK FUNNY?
HUH?
NO!
I SEE!
I SHOULD HAVE MENTIONED IT EARLIER!
HA HA HA
SORRY ...
I WAS A LITTLE EMBARRASSED TO SAY ANYTHING.

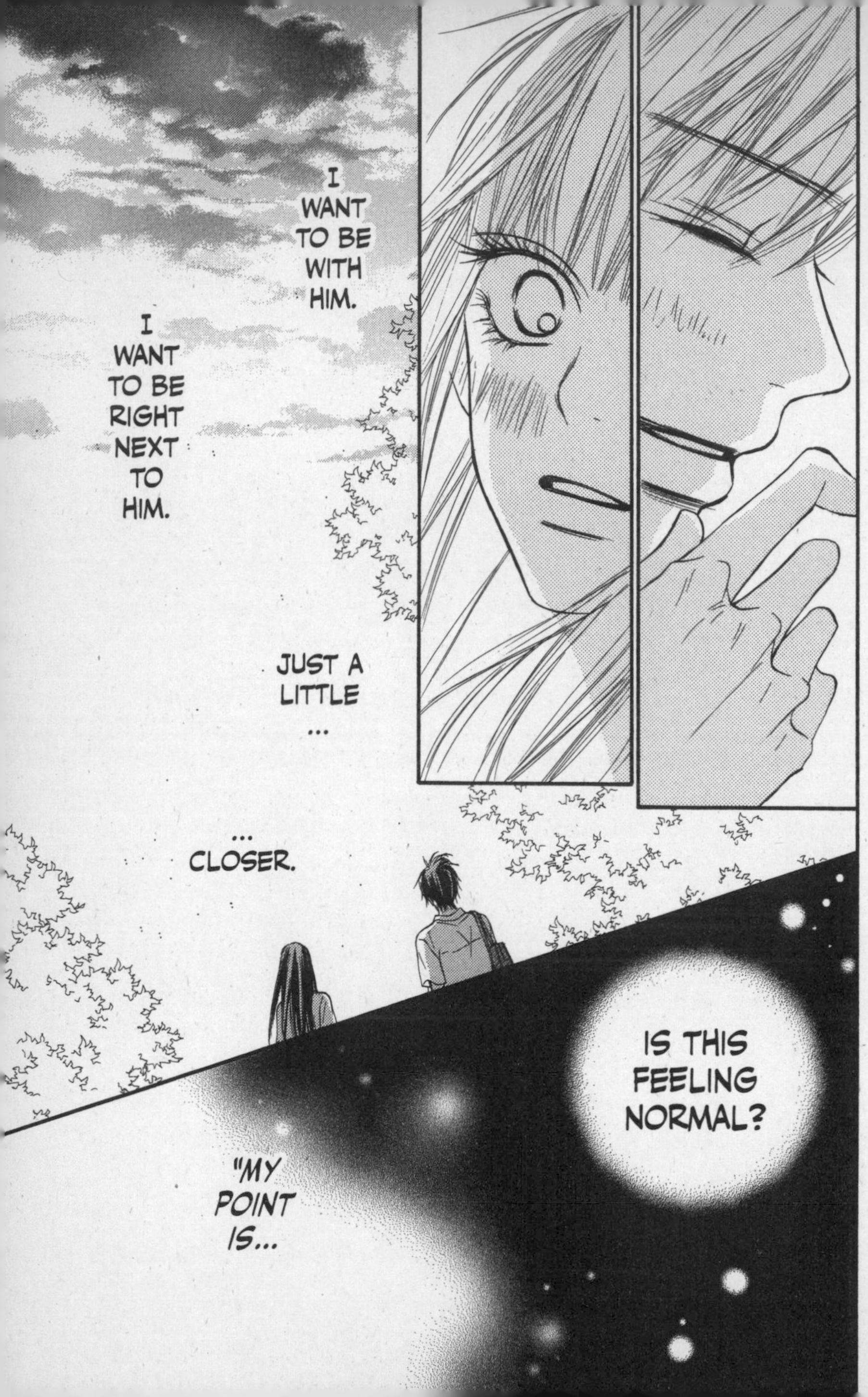
I WANT TO BE WITH HIM.
I WANT TO BE RIGHT NEXT TO HIM.
JUST A LITTLE ...
... CLOSER.
IS THIS FEELING NORMAL?
"MY POINT IS...

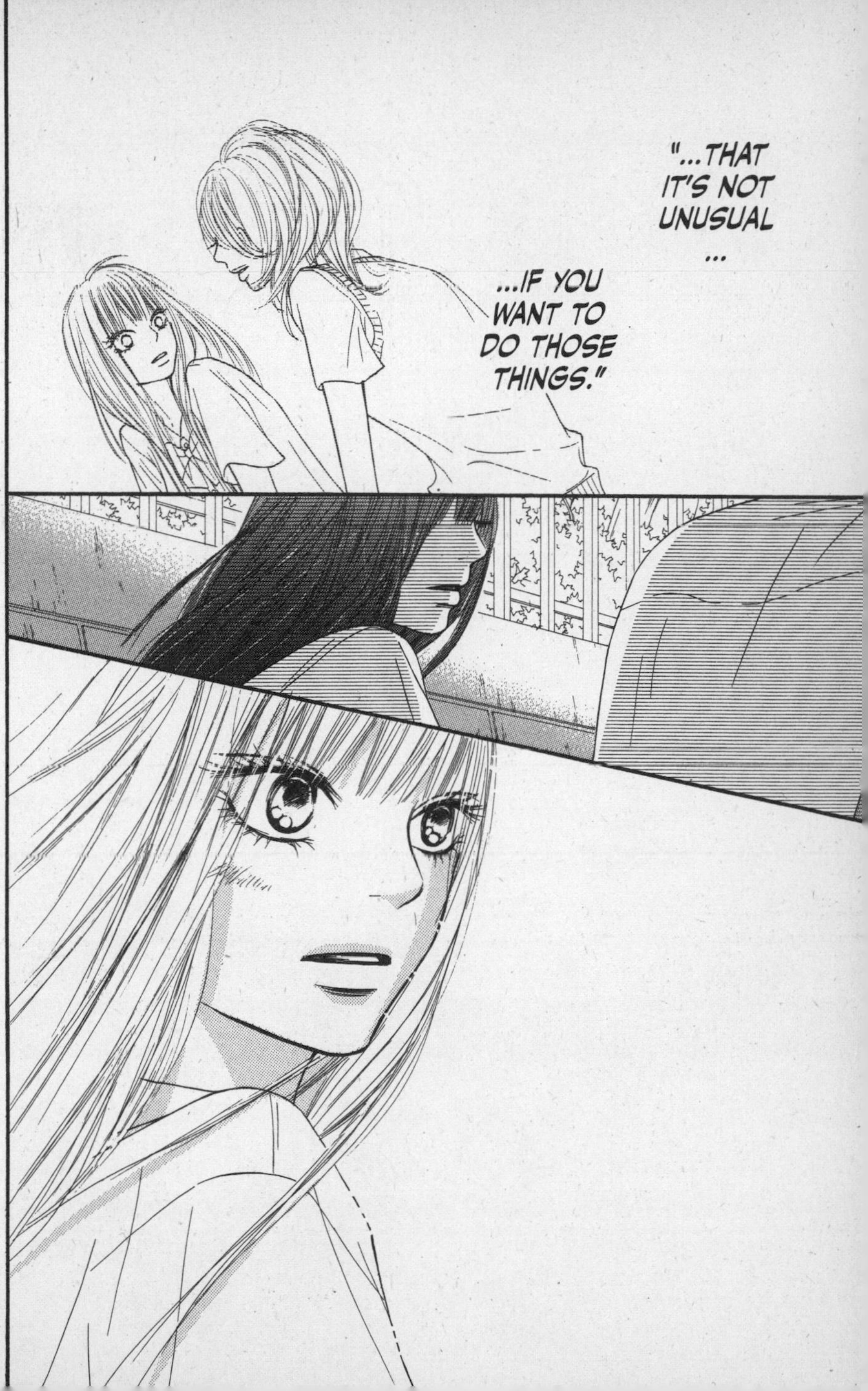
"...THAT IT'S NOT UNUSUAL ...
...IF YOU WANT TO DO THOSE THINGS."

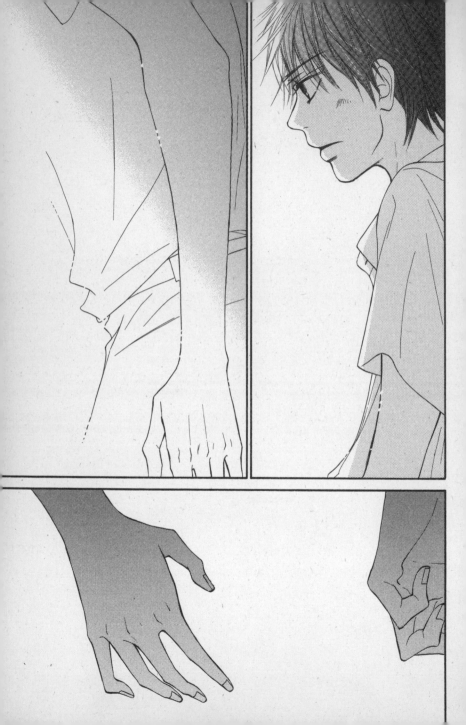

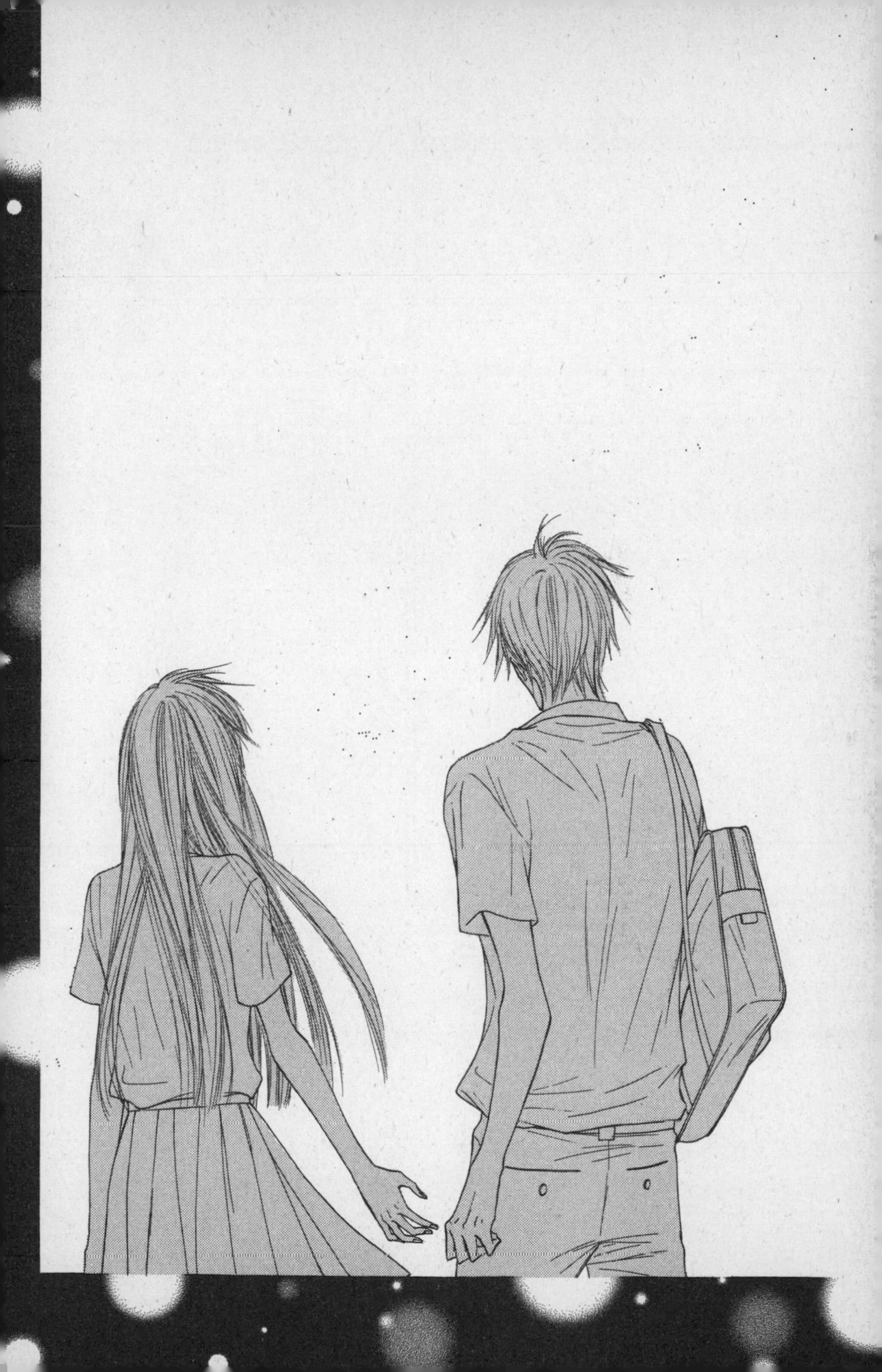

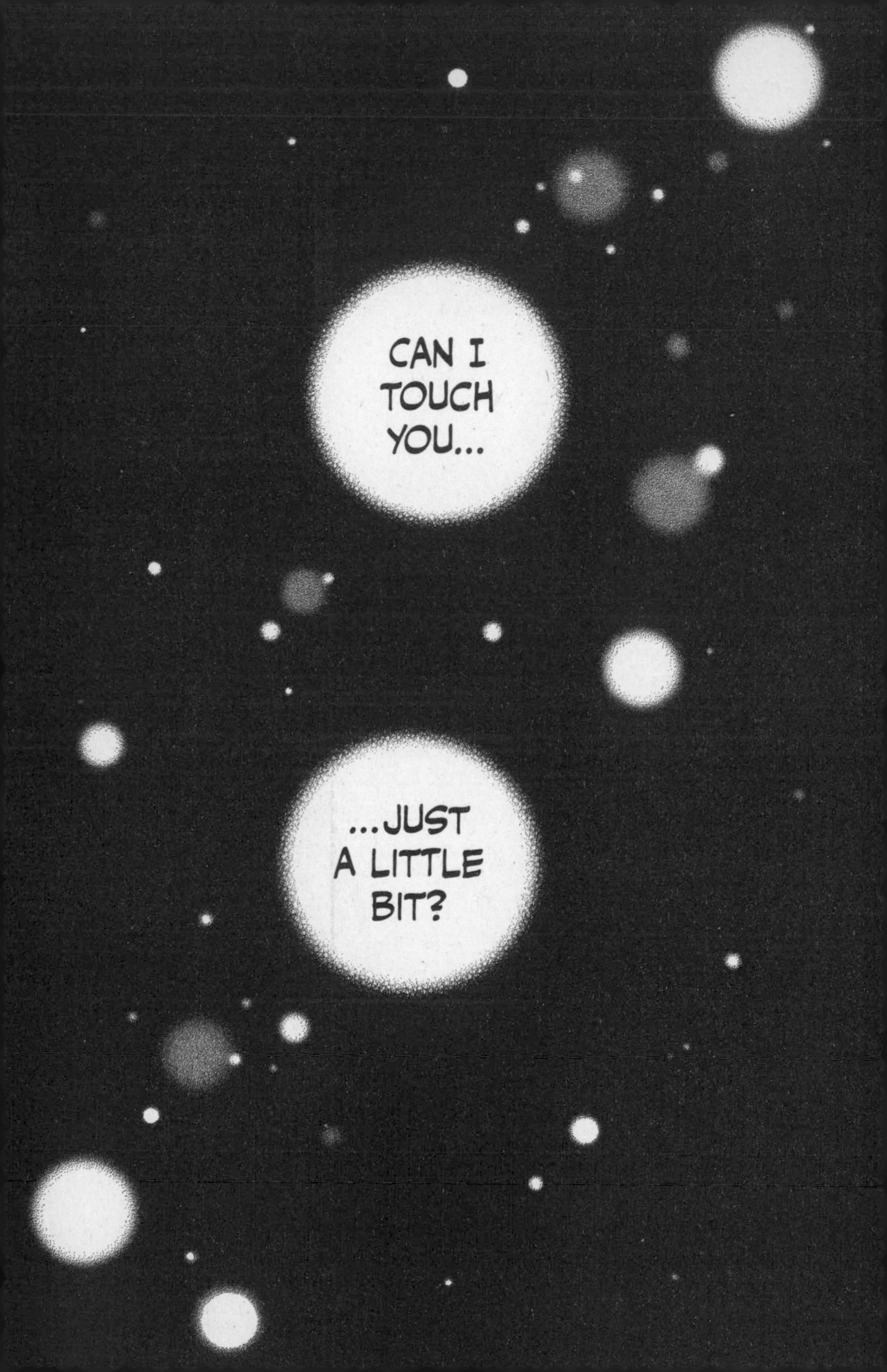
CAN I TOUCH YOU...
...JUST A LITTLE BIT?

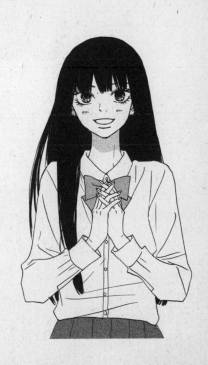

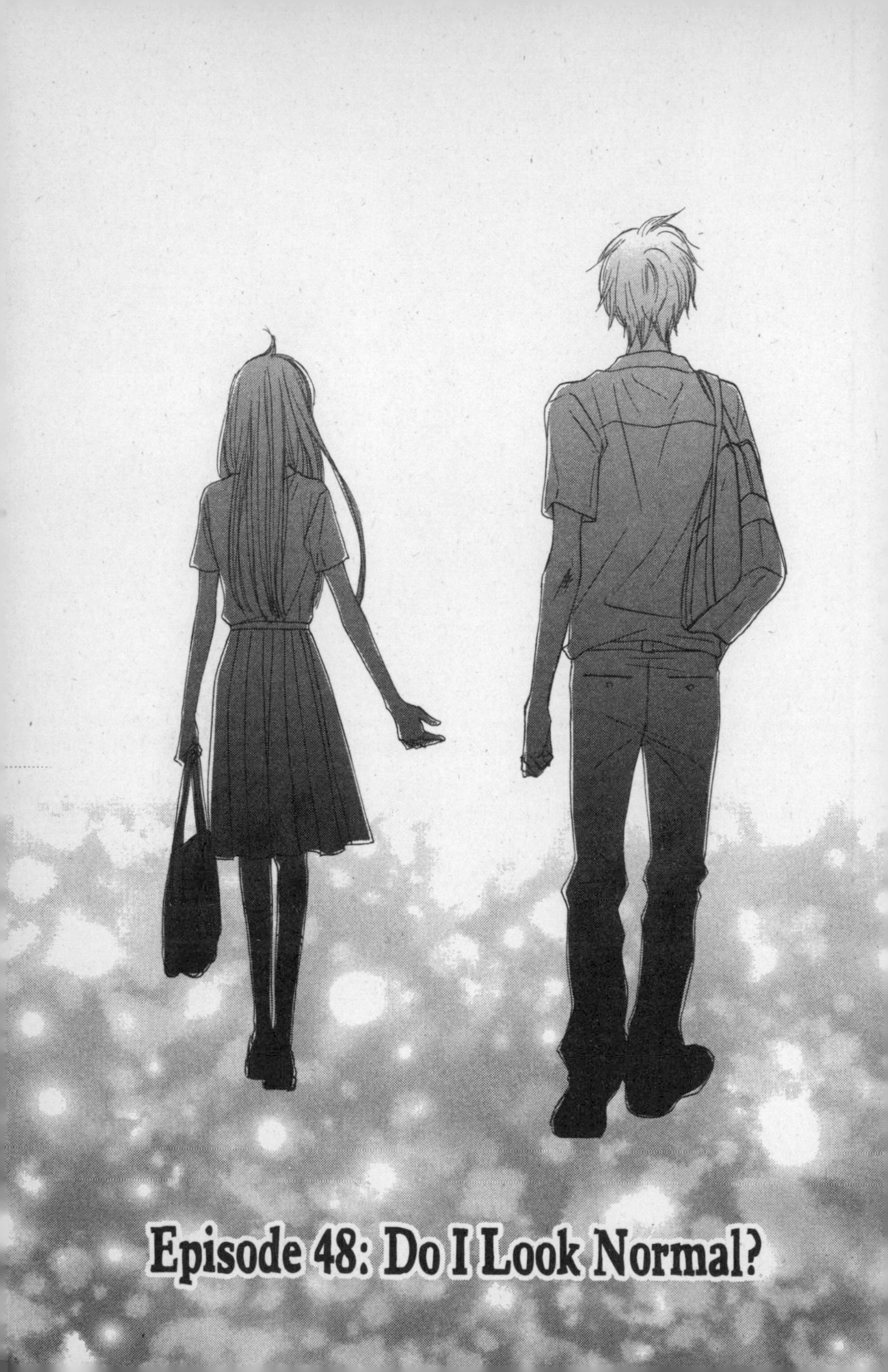

Episode 48: Do I Look Normal?

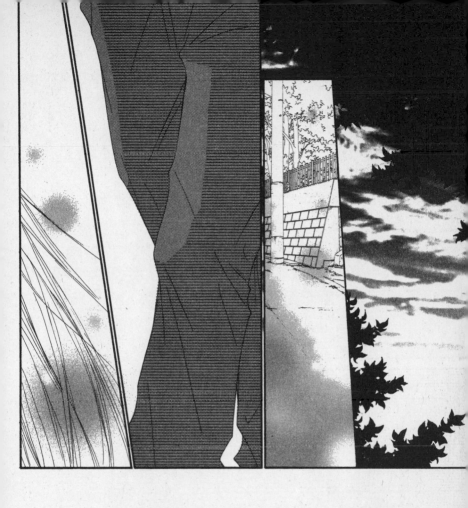
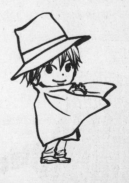

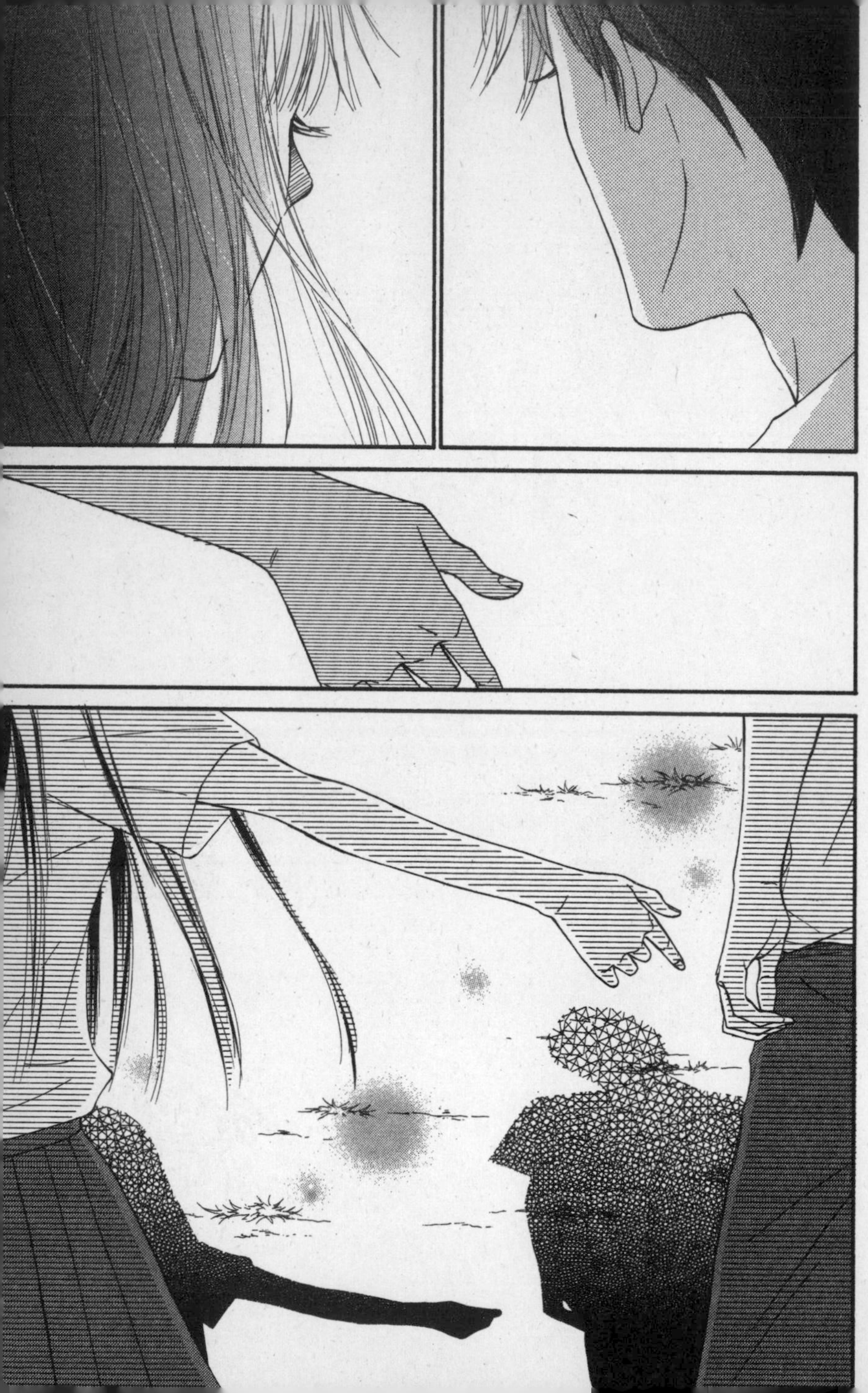

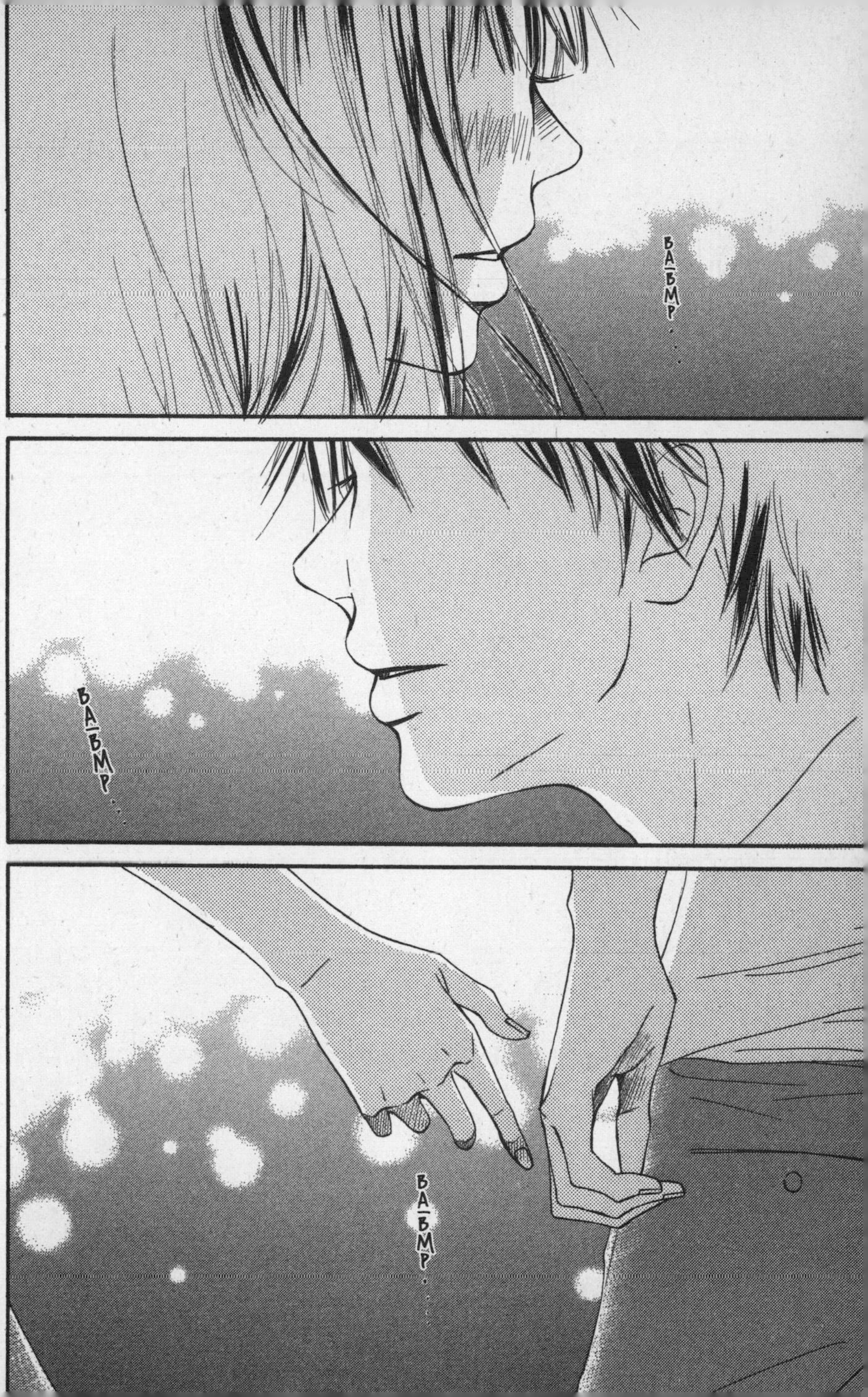
BA-BMP...
BA-BMP...
BA-BMP...

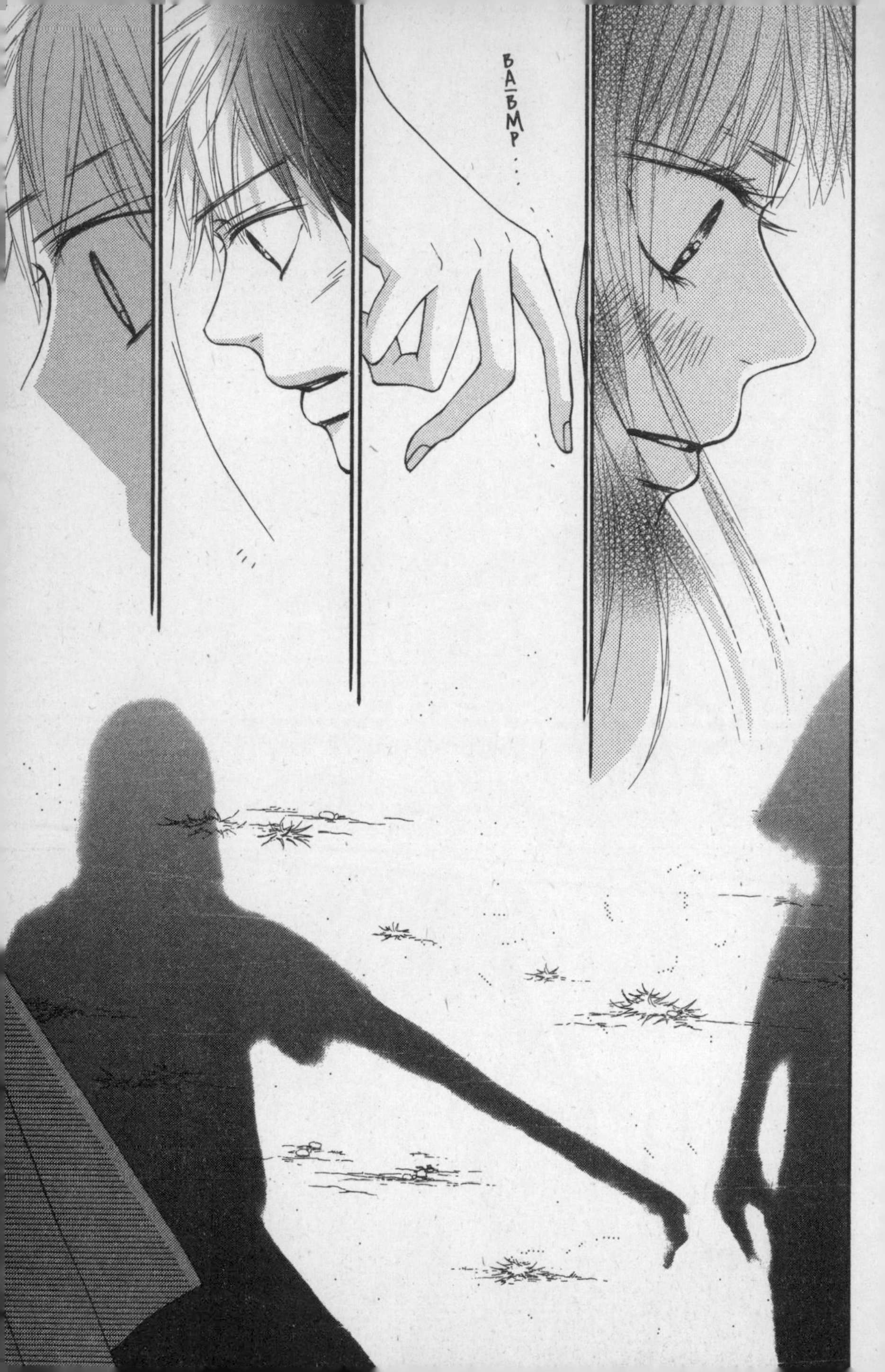
BA-BMP...

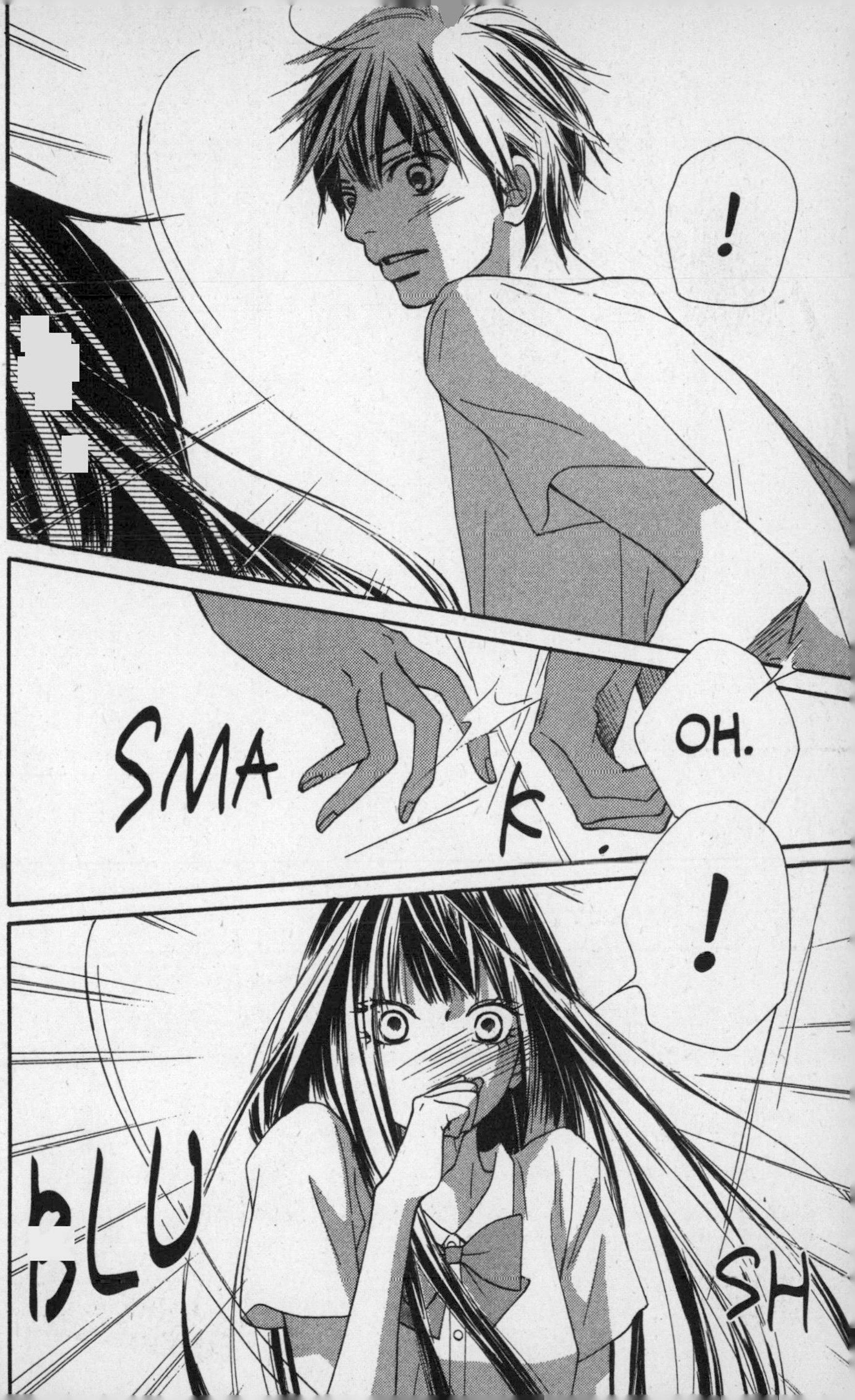
!
OH.
SMA
K
!
BLU
SH

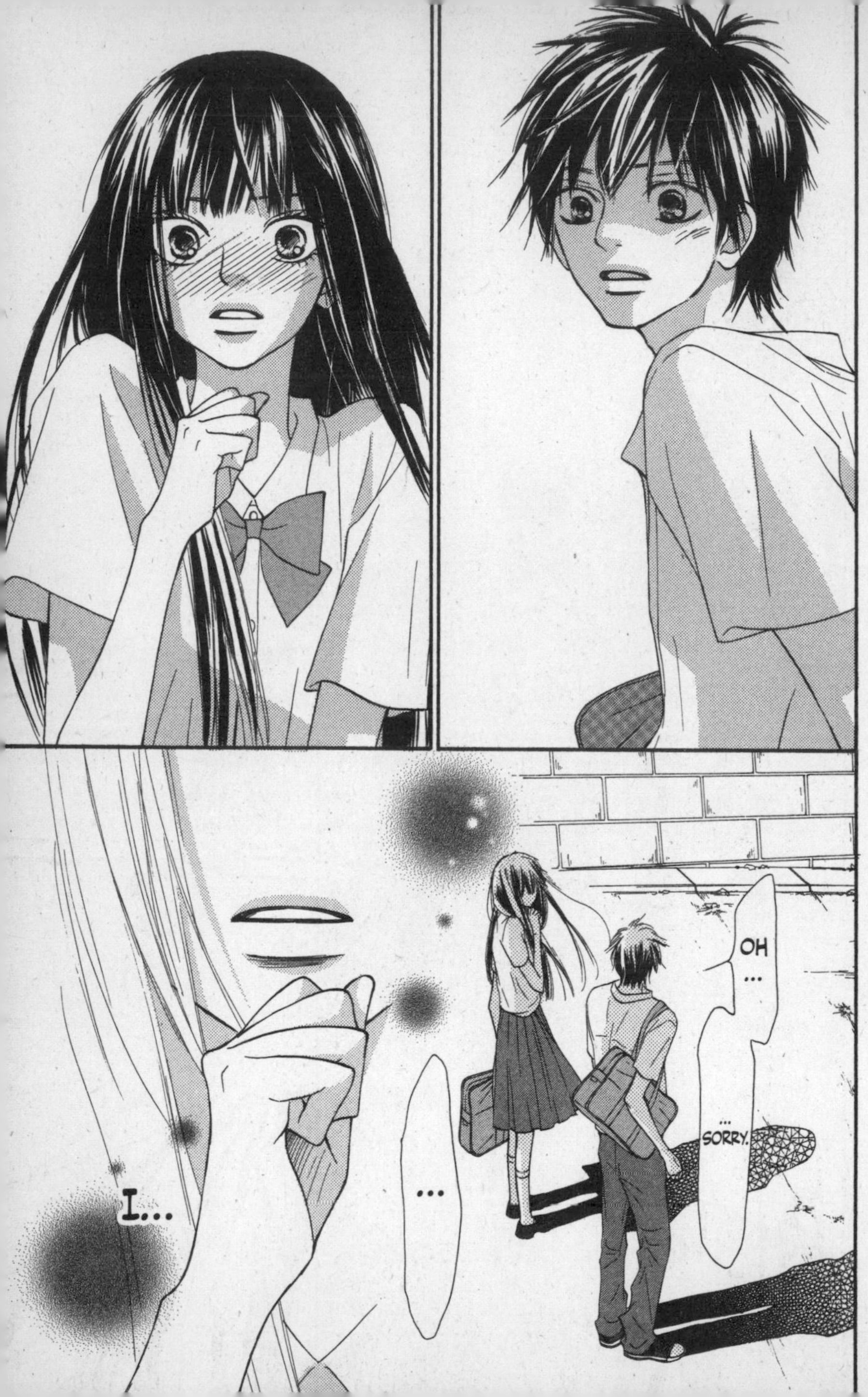
OH ...
... SORRY.
...
I...

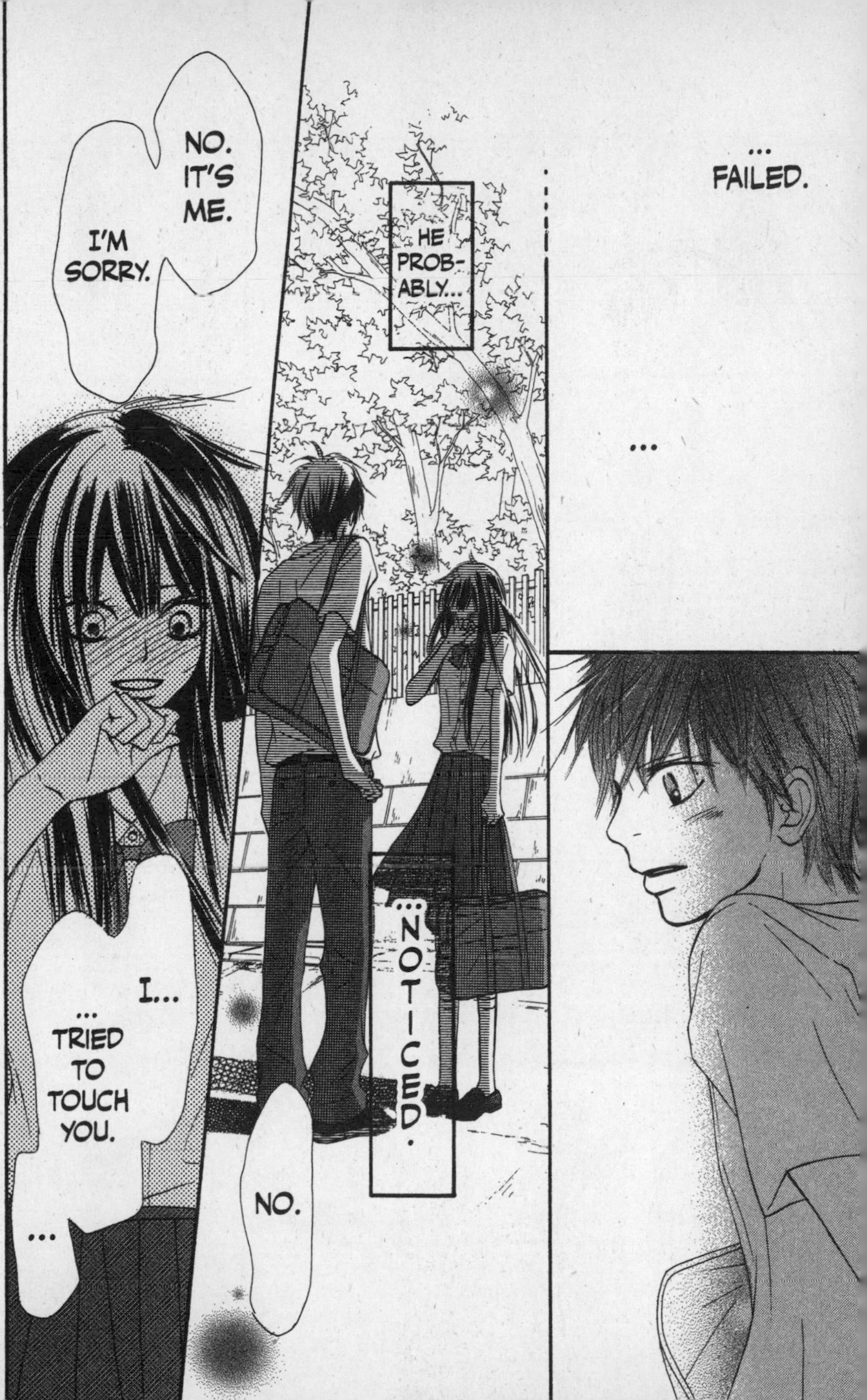
... FAILED.
...
HE PROB-ABLY...
...NOTICED.
NO.
NO. IT'S ME.
I'M SORRY.
I...
... TRIED TO TOUCH YOU.
...

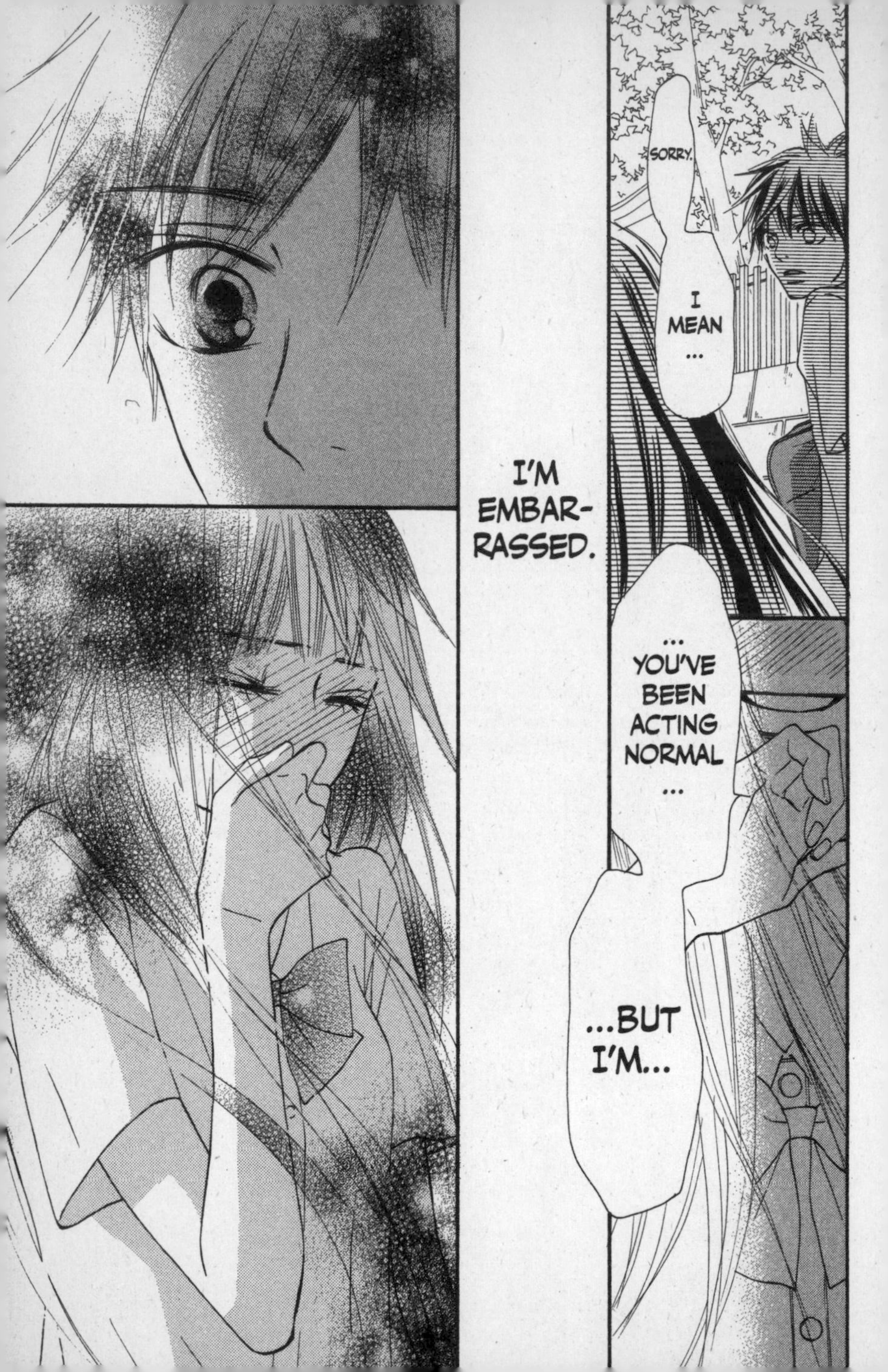
SORRY.
I MEAN ...
... YOU'VE BEEN ACTING NORMAL ...
...BUT I'M...
I'M EMBAR-RASSED.

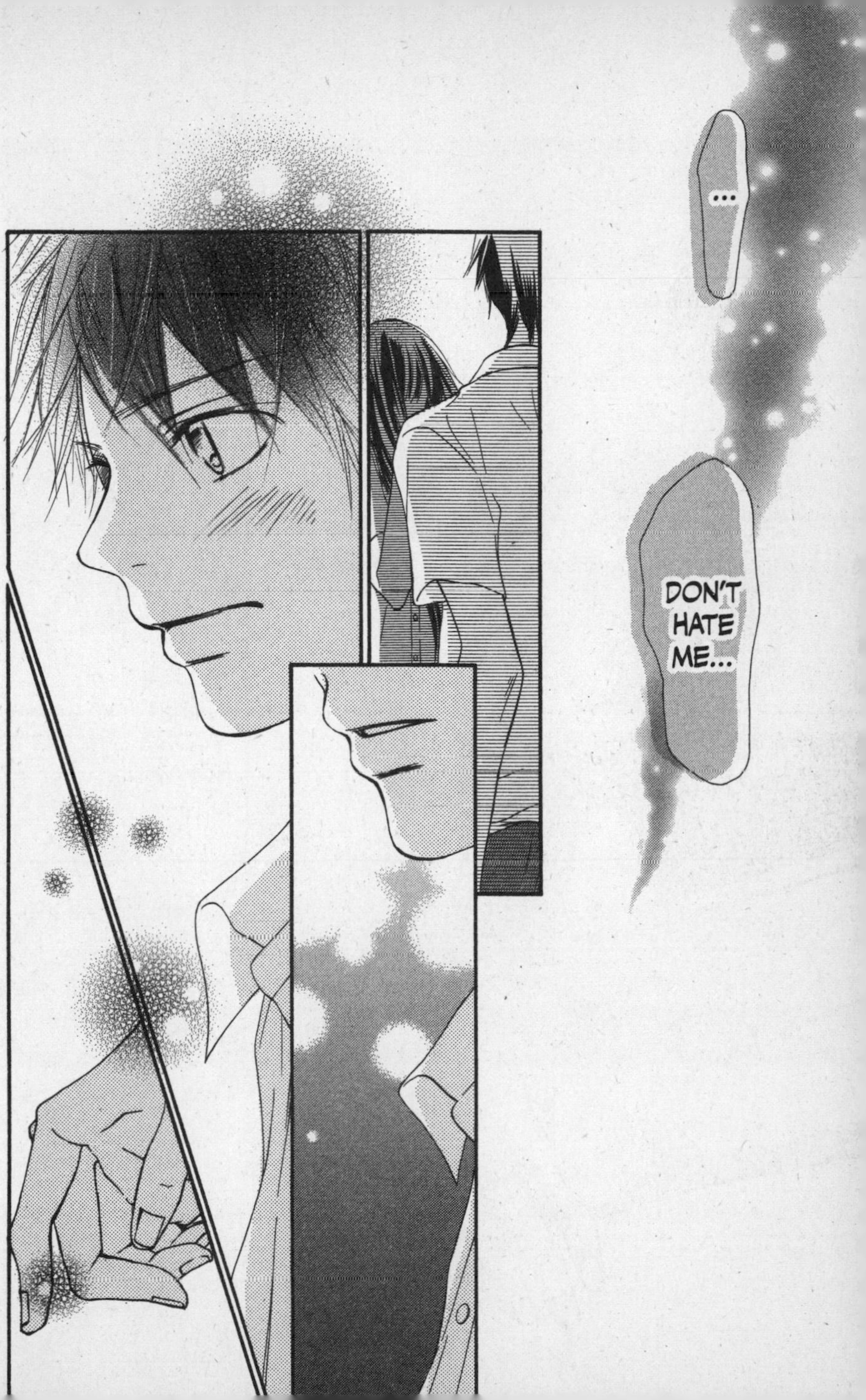
...
DON'T HATE ME...

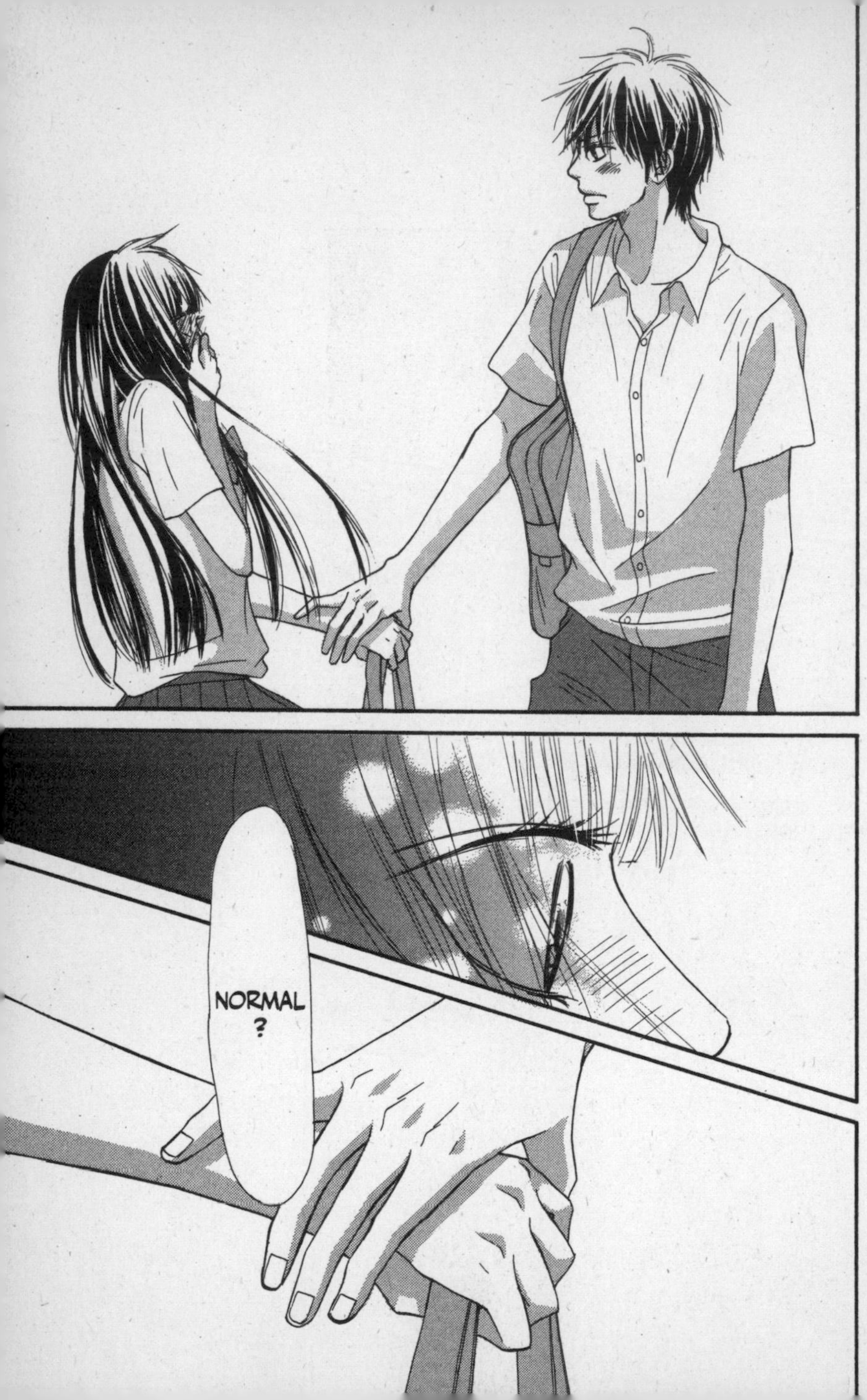
NORMAL
?

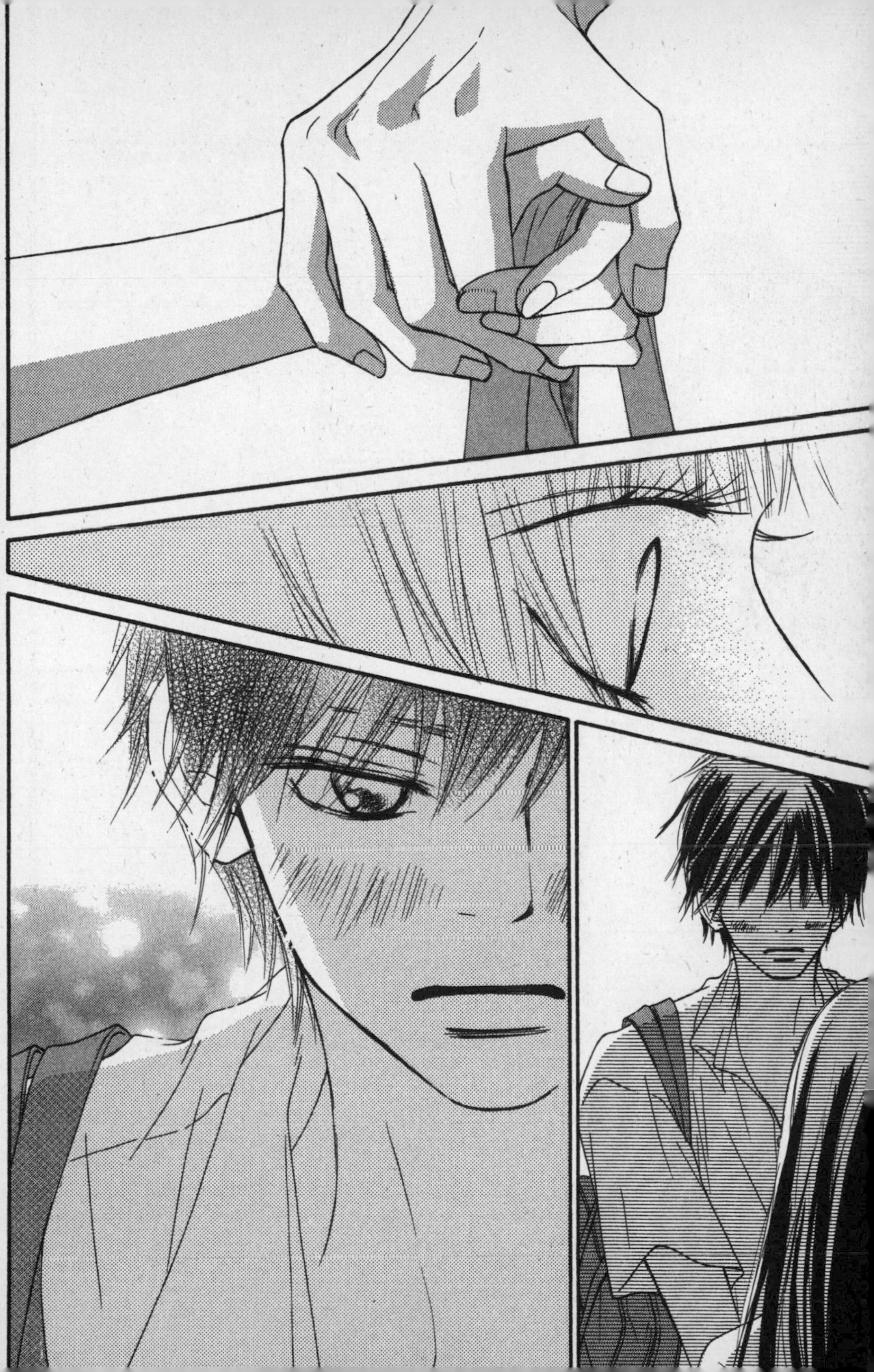

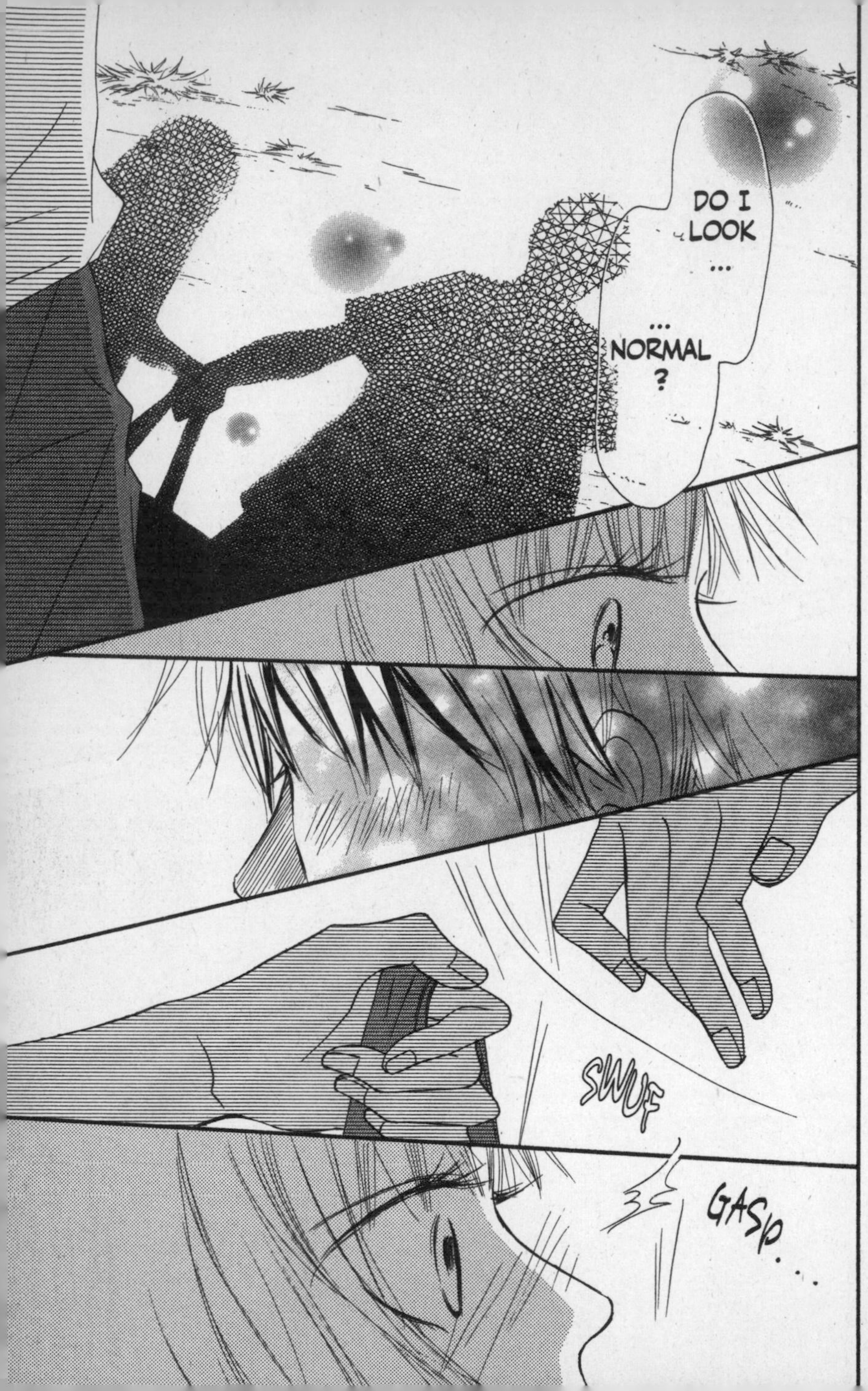
DO I LOOK ... ... NORMAL ?
SWUF
GASP...

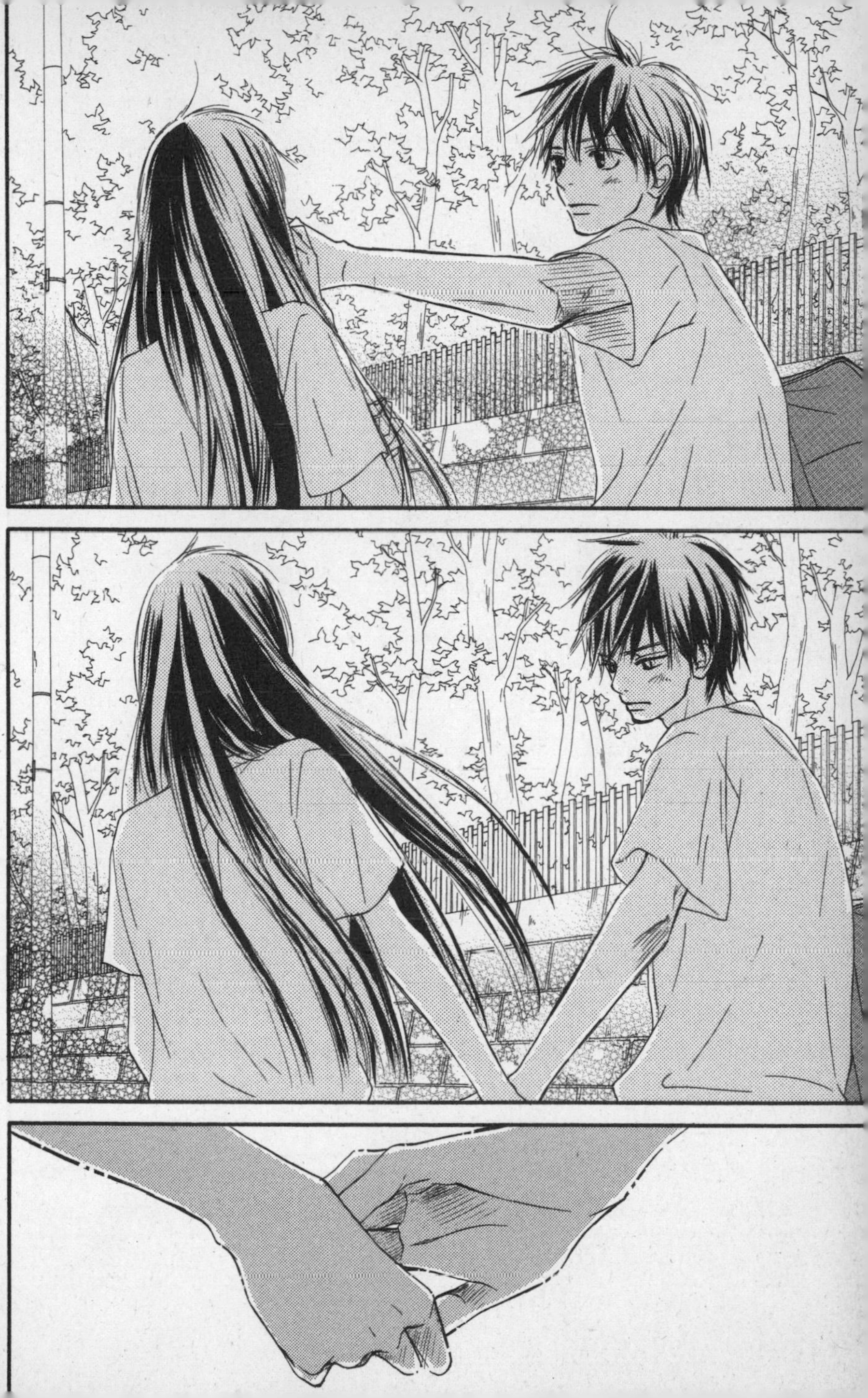

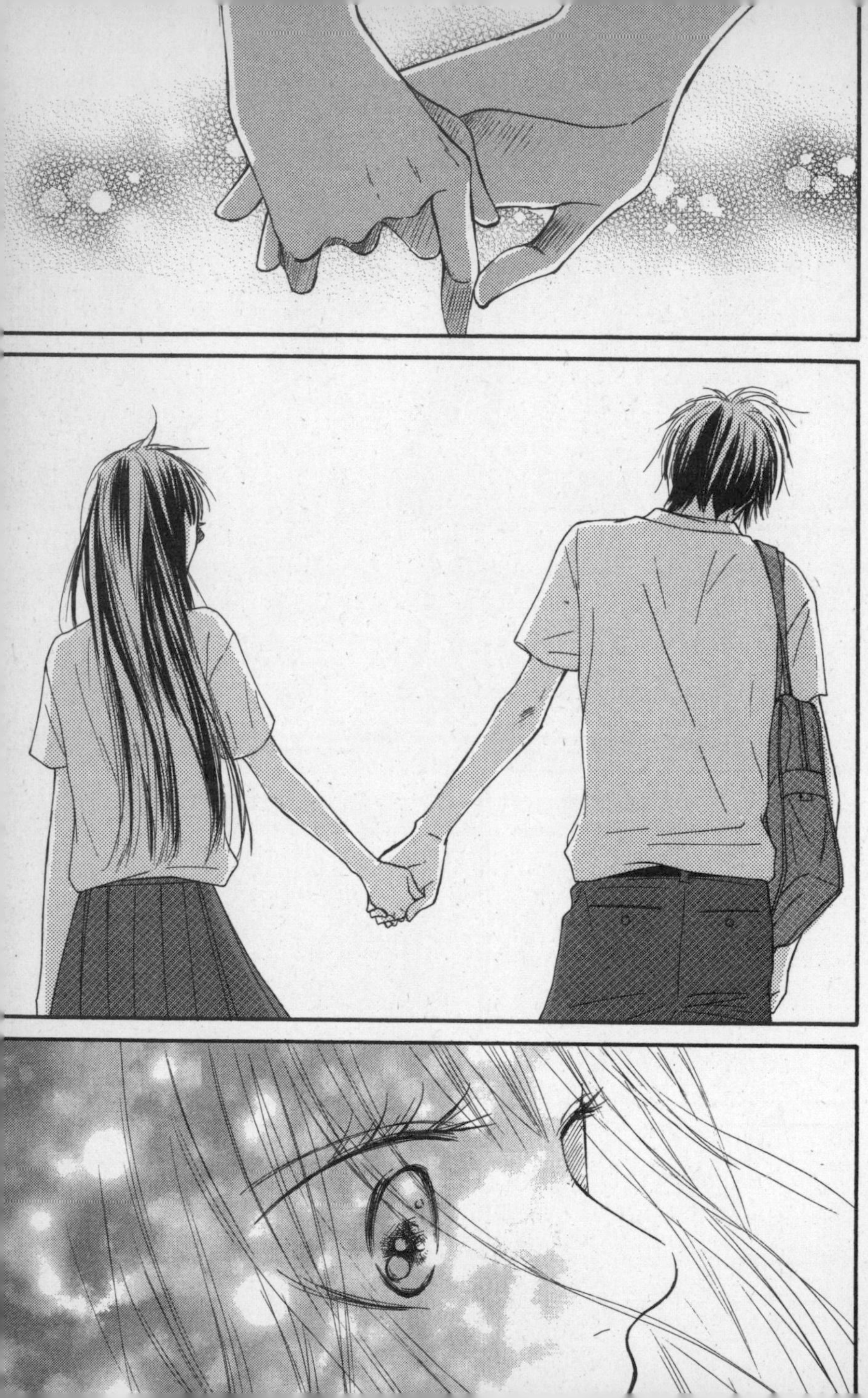

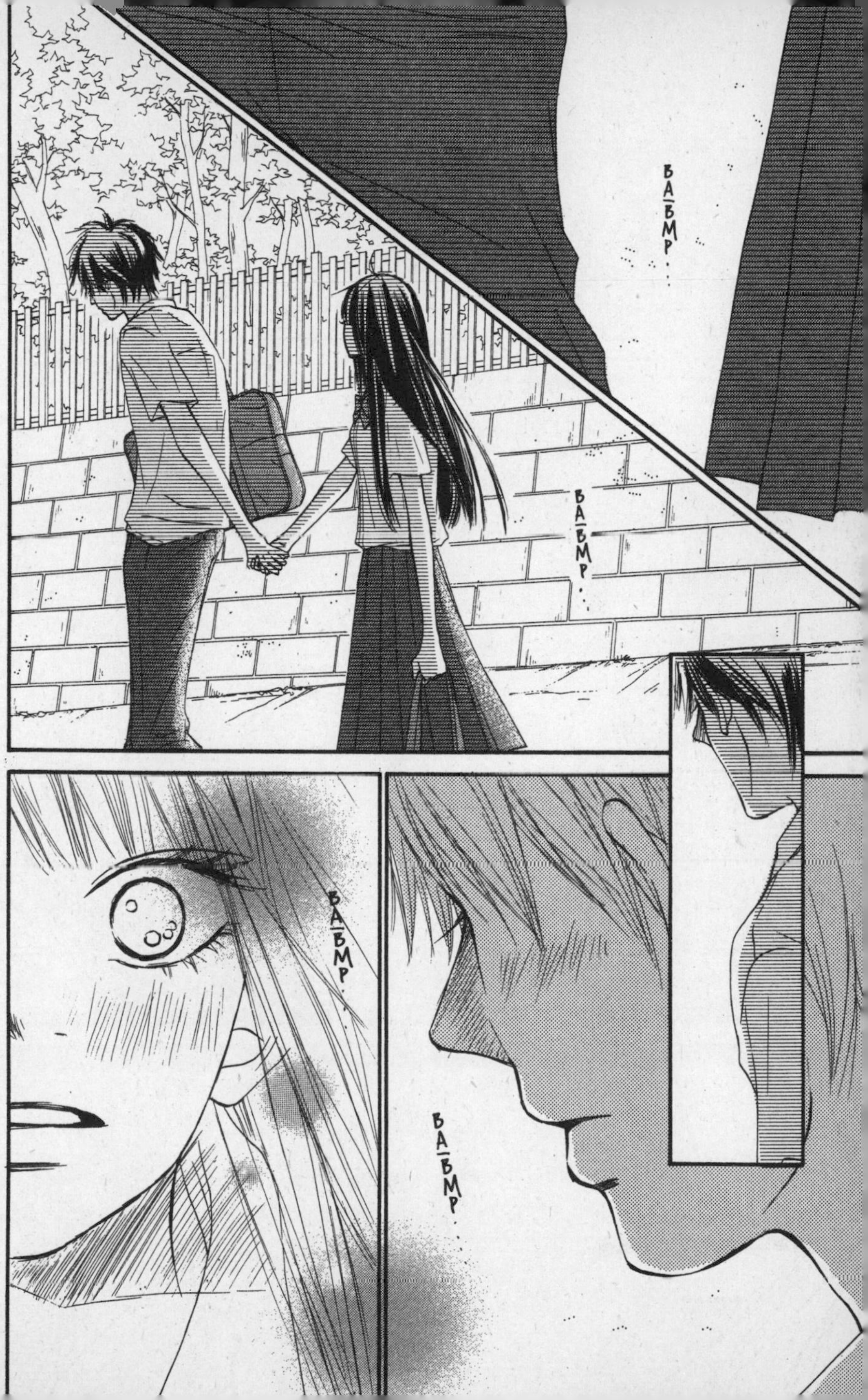

BA-BMP...
BA-BMP...
BA-BMP
BA-BMP

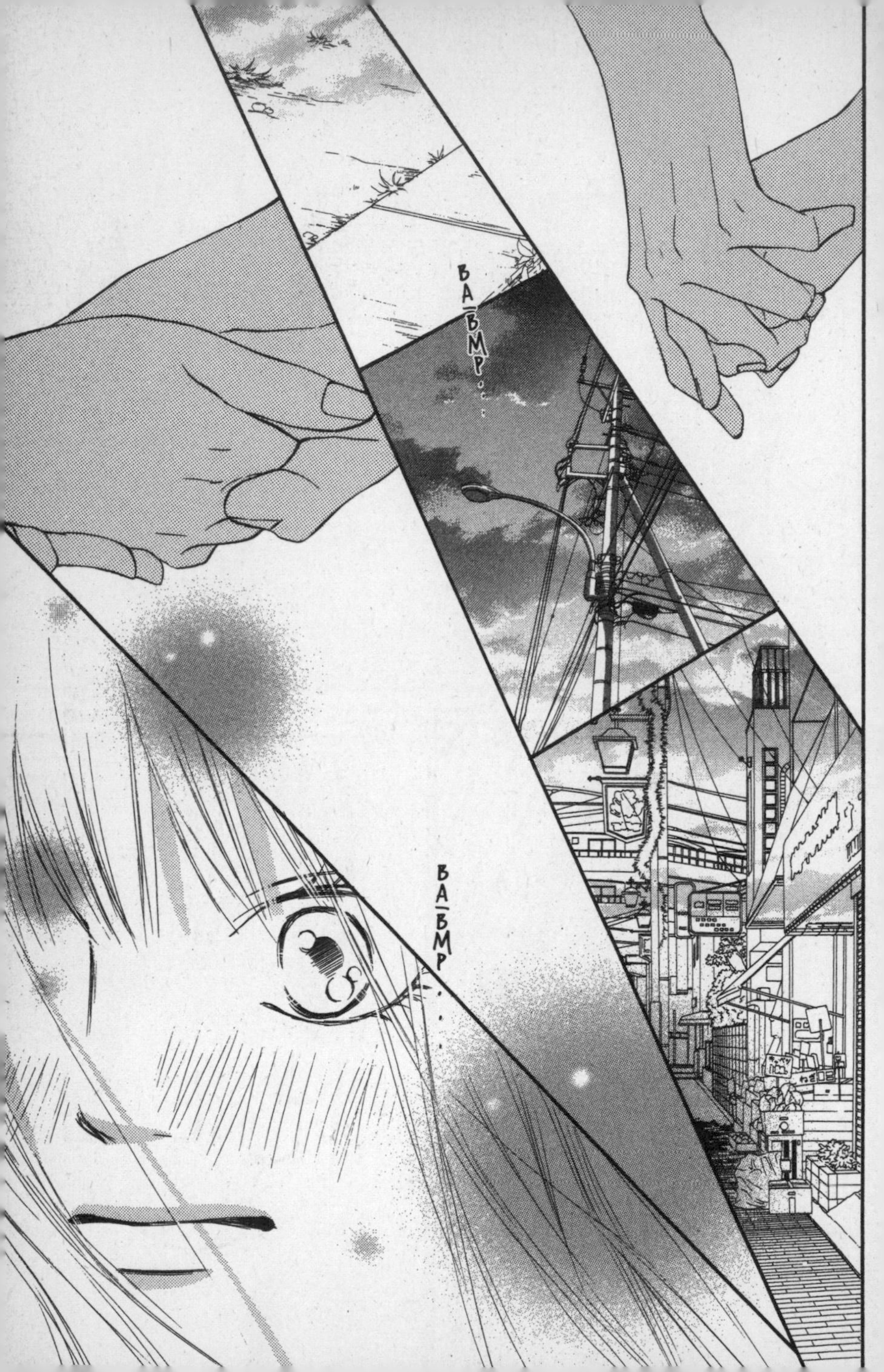
BA-BMP...
BA-BMP...

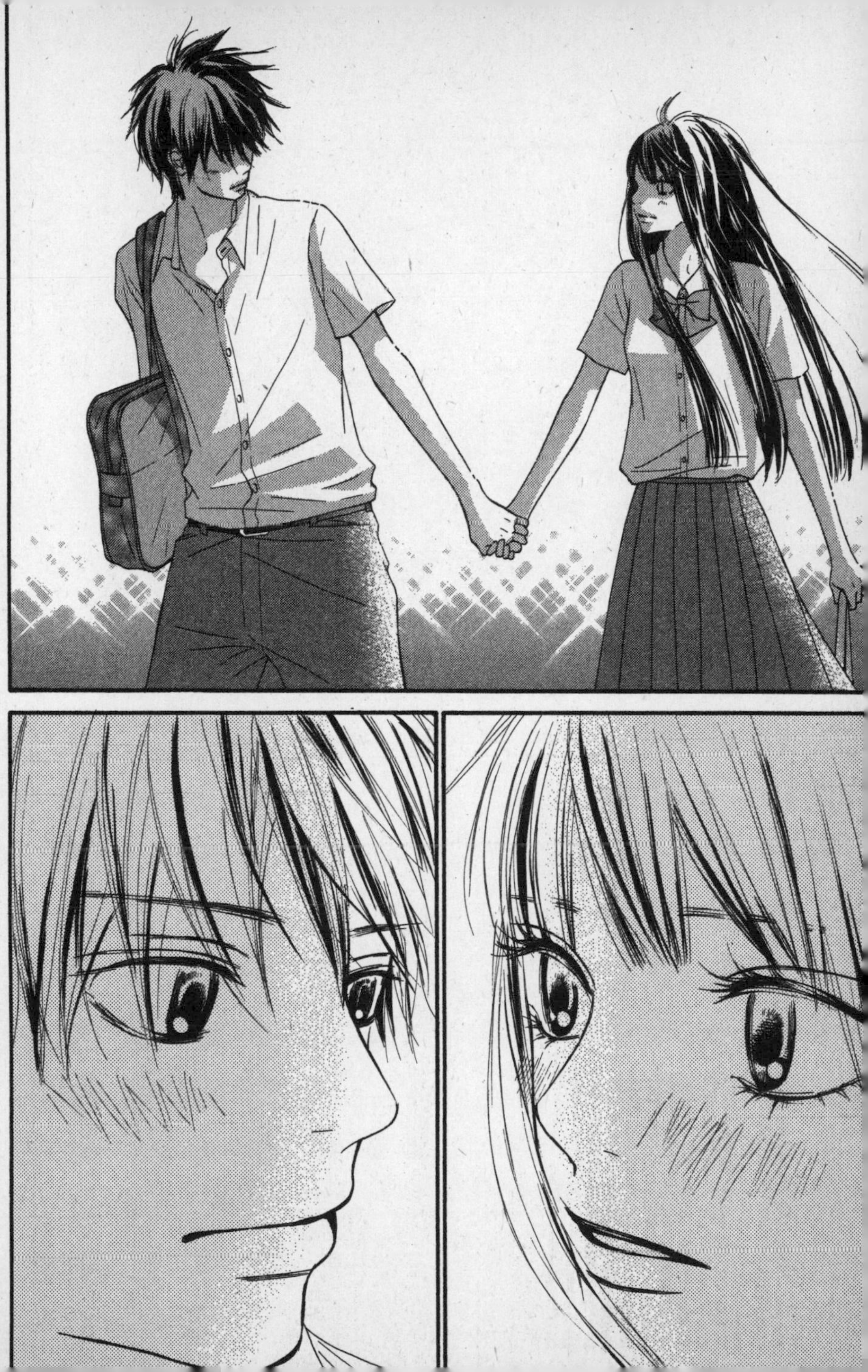

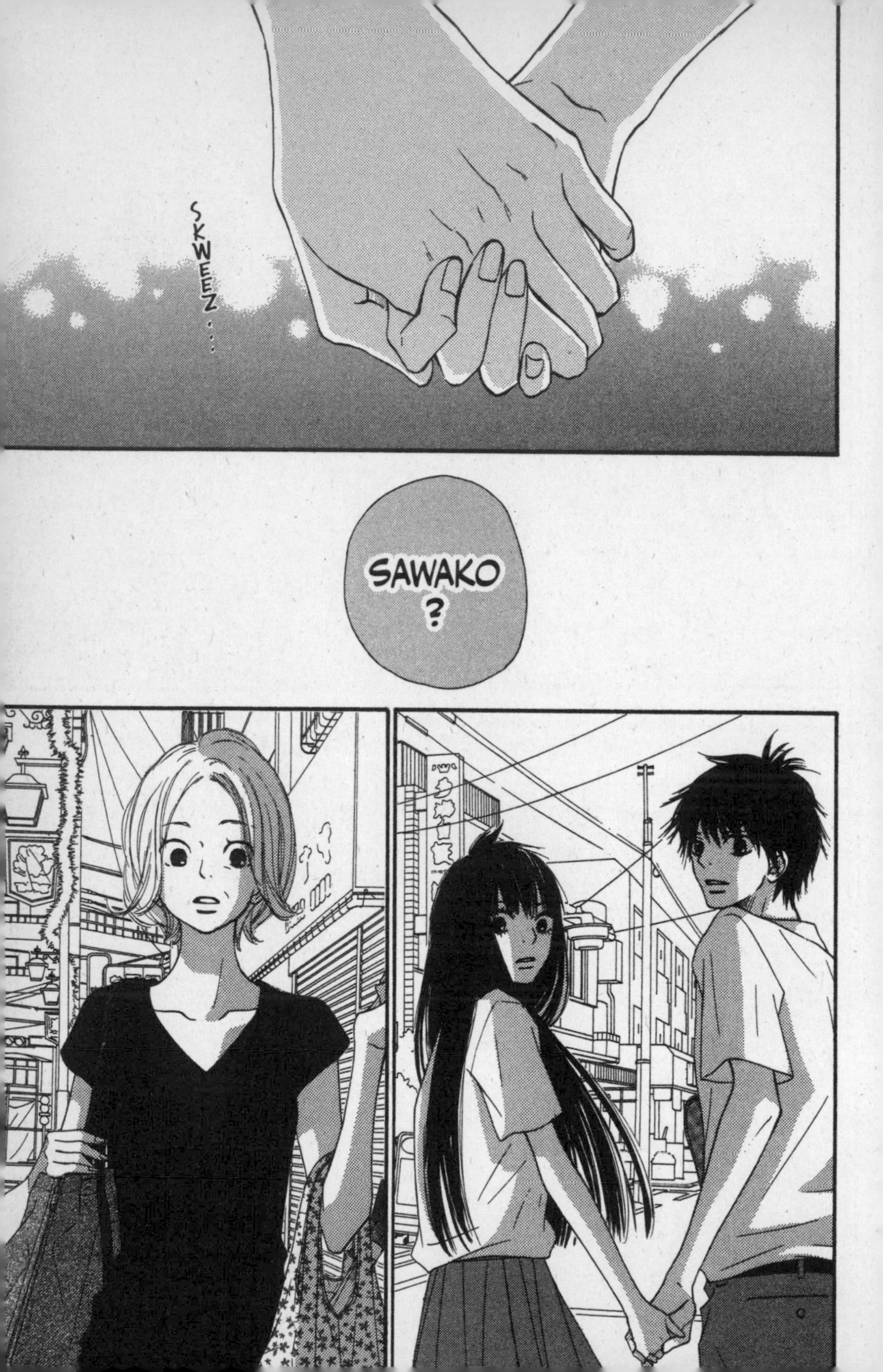
SKWEEZ...
SAWAKO?

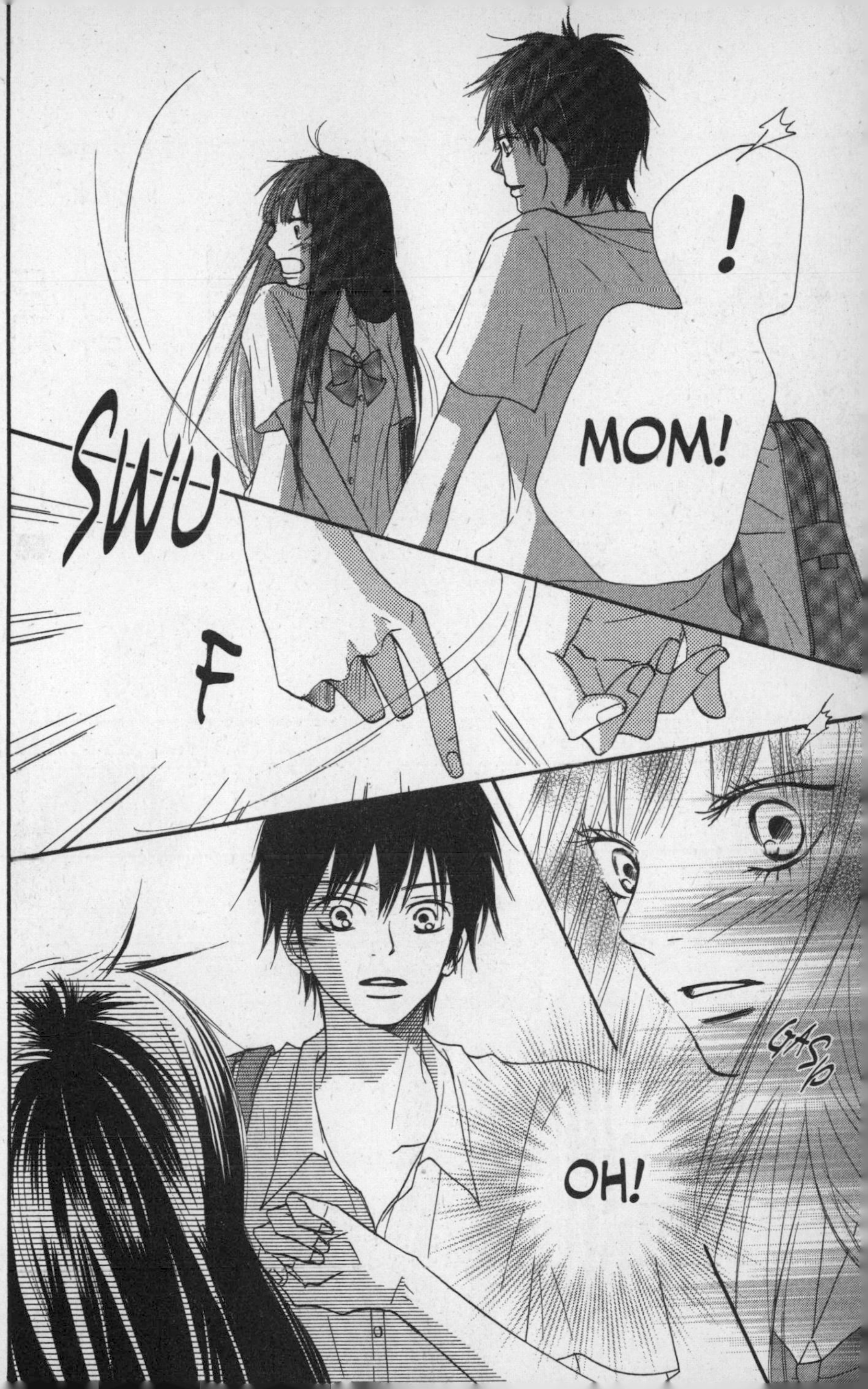
!
MOM!
SWU
F
GASP
OH!

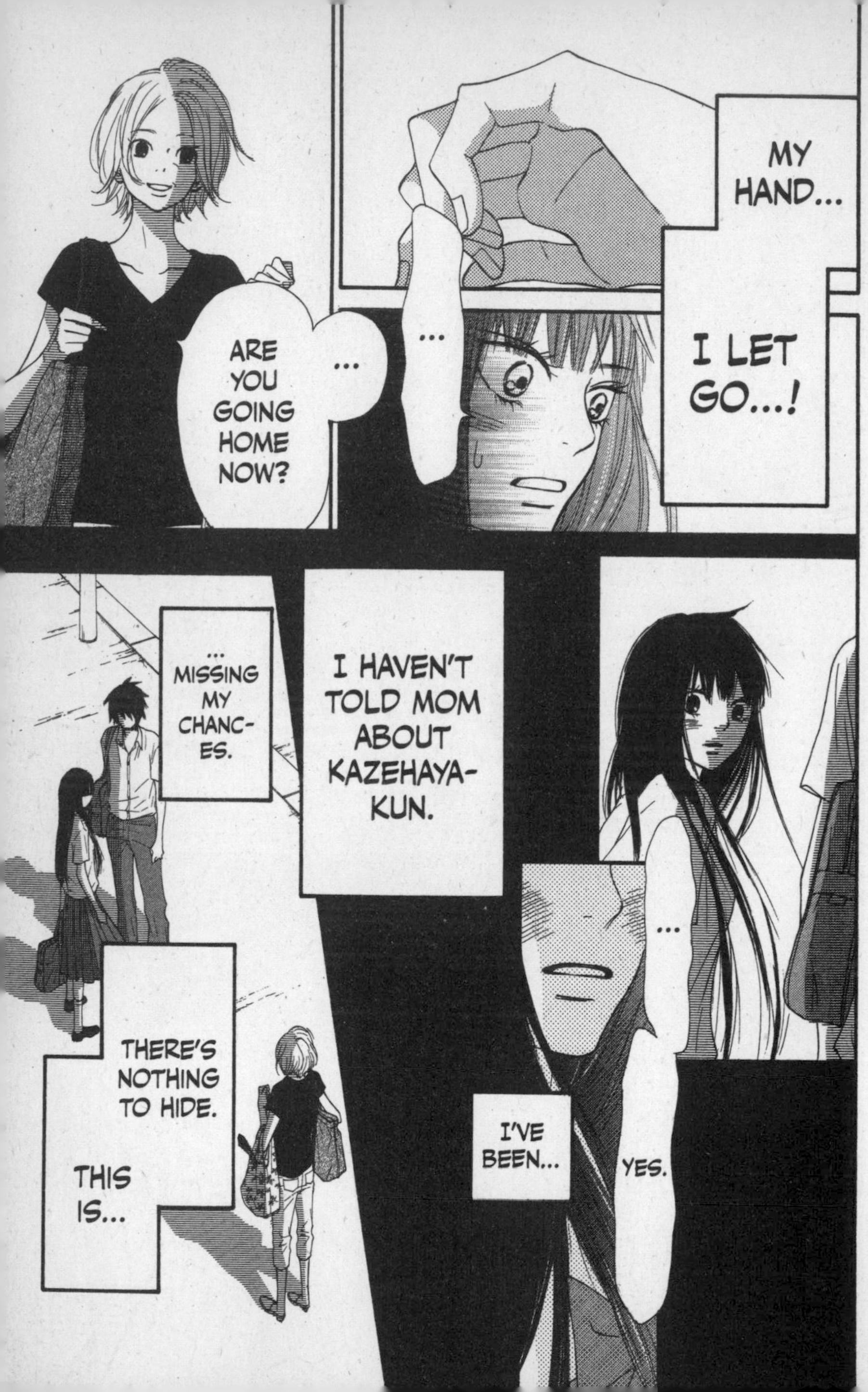
MY HAND...
I LET GO...!
...
...
ARE YOU GOING HOME NOW?
...
YES.
I'VE BEEN...
I HAVEN'T TOLD MOM ABOUT KAZEHAYA-KUN.
... MISSING MY CHANC-ES.
THERE'S NOTHING TO HIDE.
THIS IS...

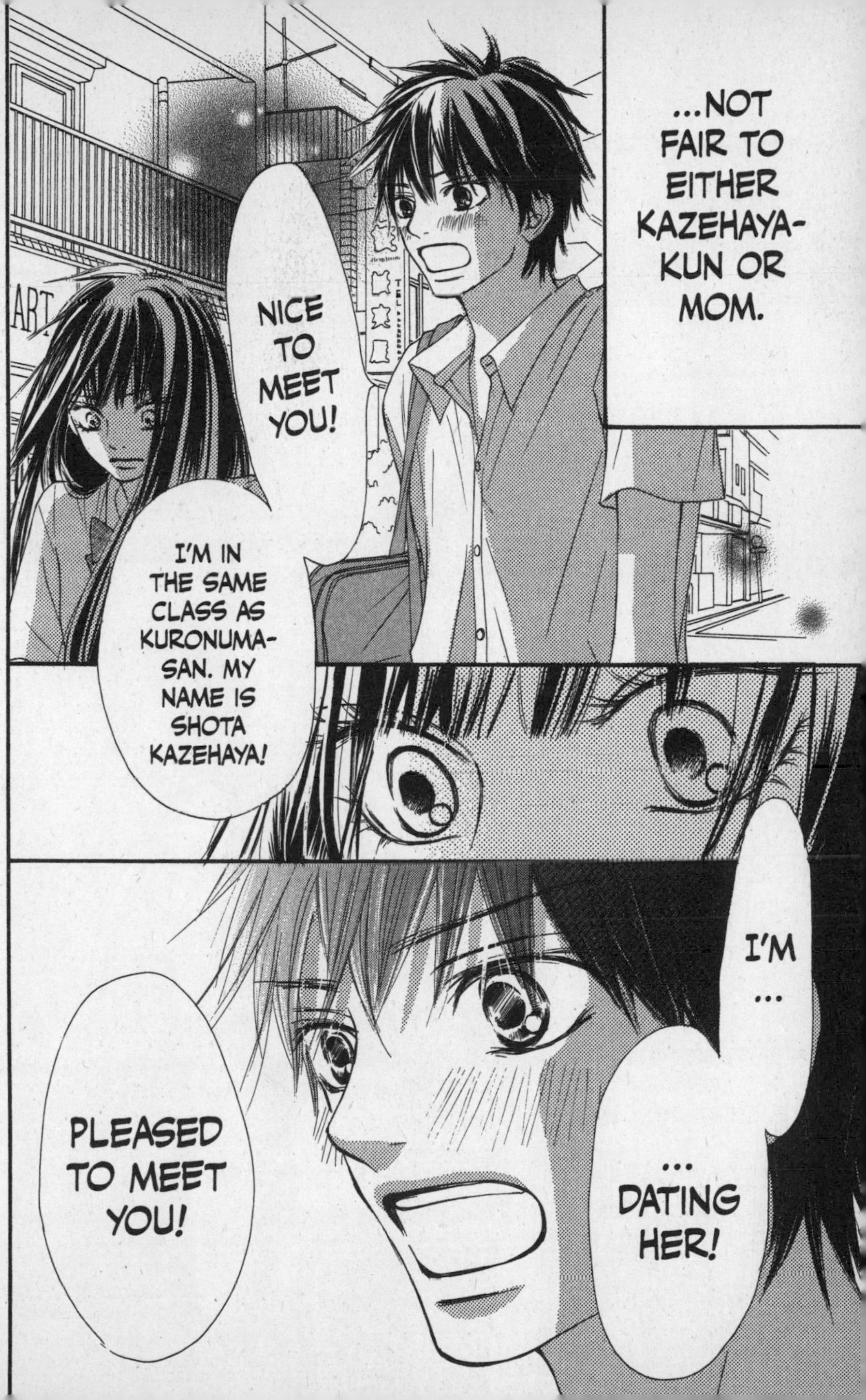
...NOT FAIR TO EITHER KAZEHAYA-KUN OR MOM.
NICE TO MEET YOU!
I'M IN THE SAME CLASS AS KURONUMA-SAN. MY NAME IS SHOTA KAZEHAYA!
I'M ...
... DATING HER!
PLEASED TO MEET YOU!

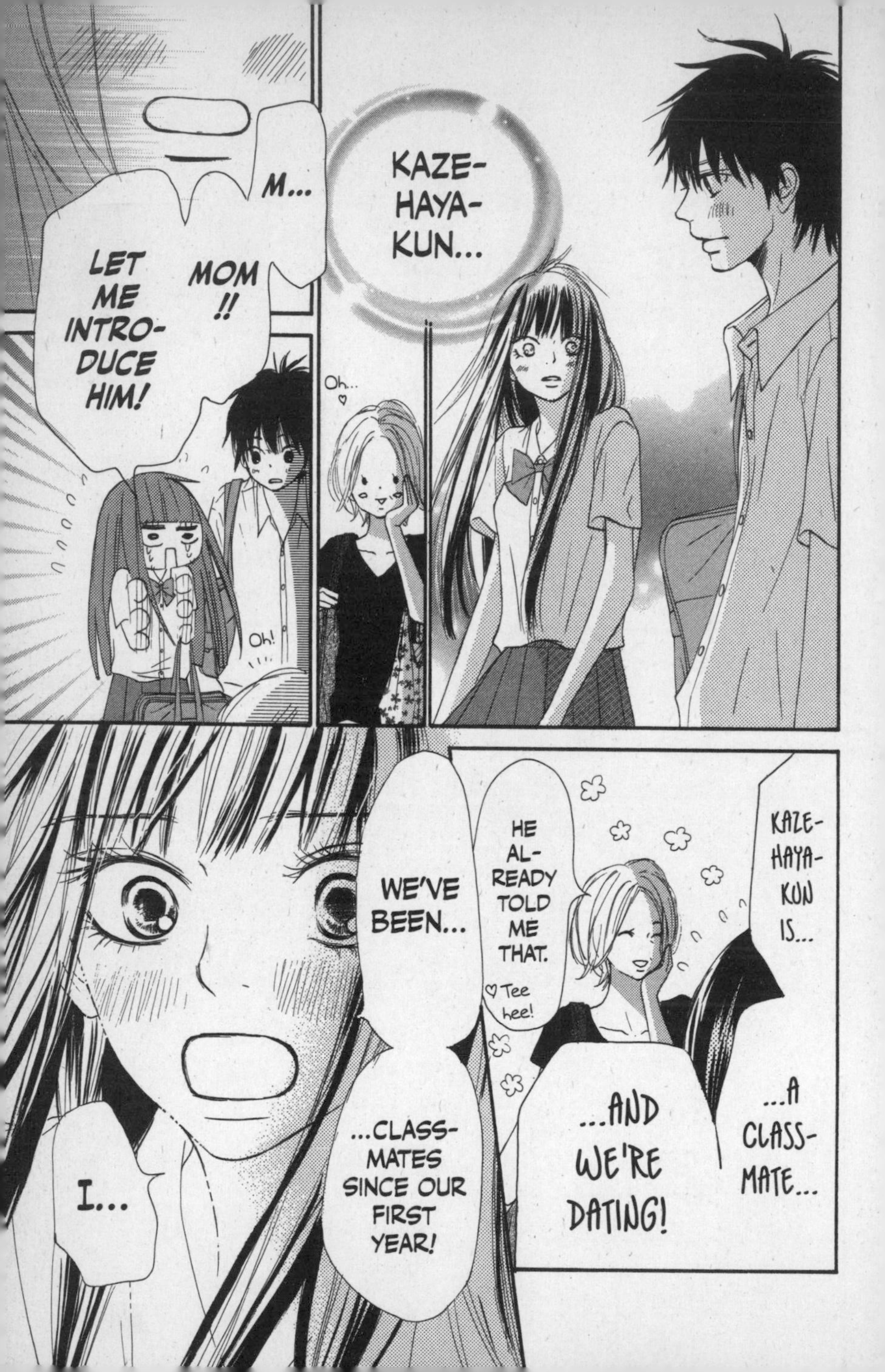
KAZE-HAYA-KUN...
Oh...
M...
MOM!!
LET ME INTRODUCE HIM!
Oh!
KAZE-HAYA-KUN IS...
...A CLASS-MATE...
...AND WE'RE DATING!
HE ALREADY TOLD ME THAT.
Tee hee!
WE'VE BEEN...
...CLASSMATES SINCE OUR FIRST YEAR!
I...

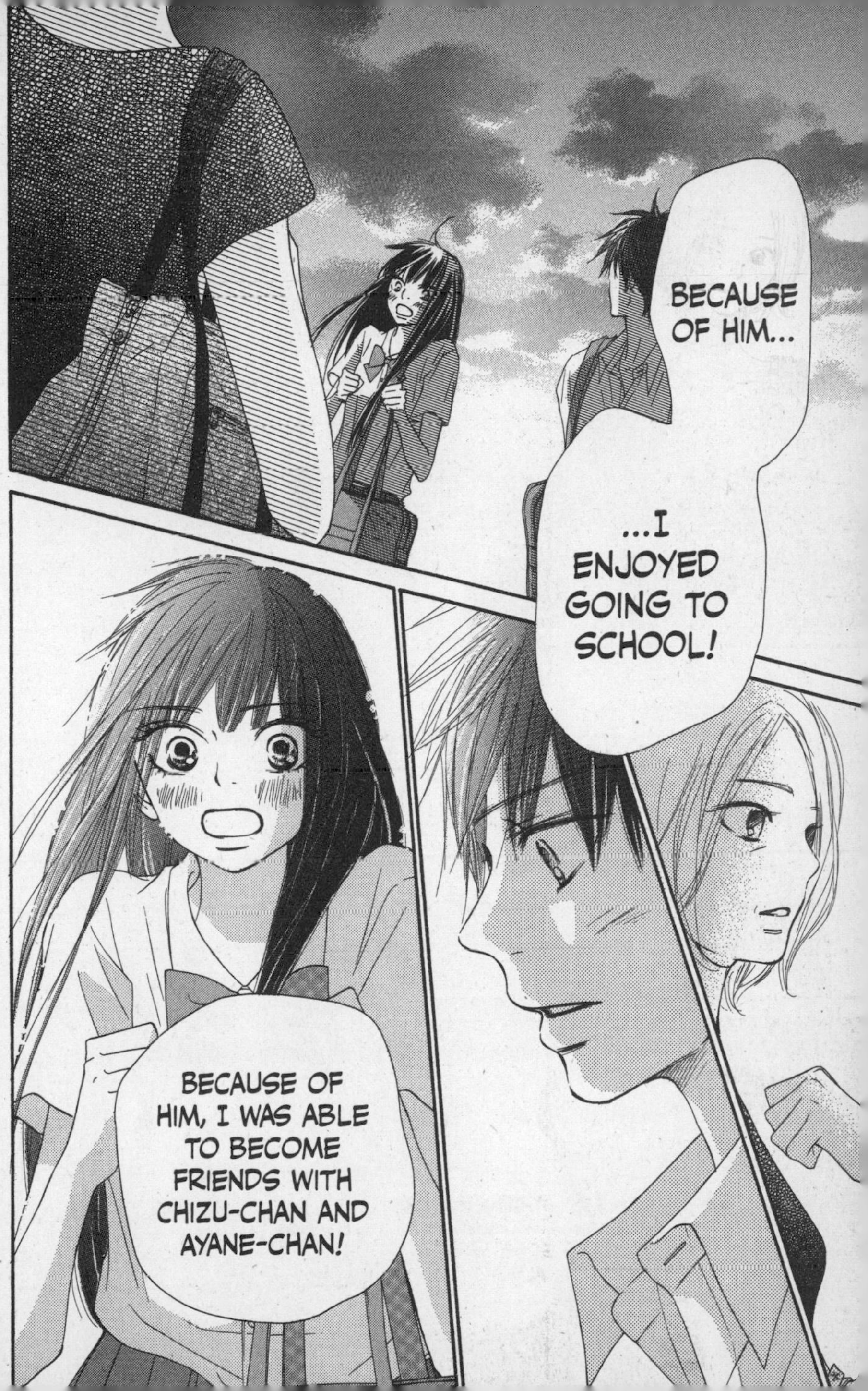
BECAUSE OF HIM...
...I ENJOYED GOING TO SCHOOL!
BECAUSE OF HIM, I WAS ABLE TO BECOME FRIENDS WITH CHIZU-CHAN AND AYANE-CHAN!

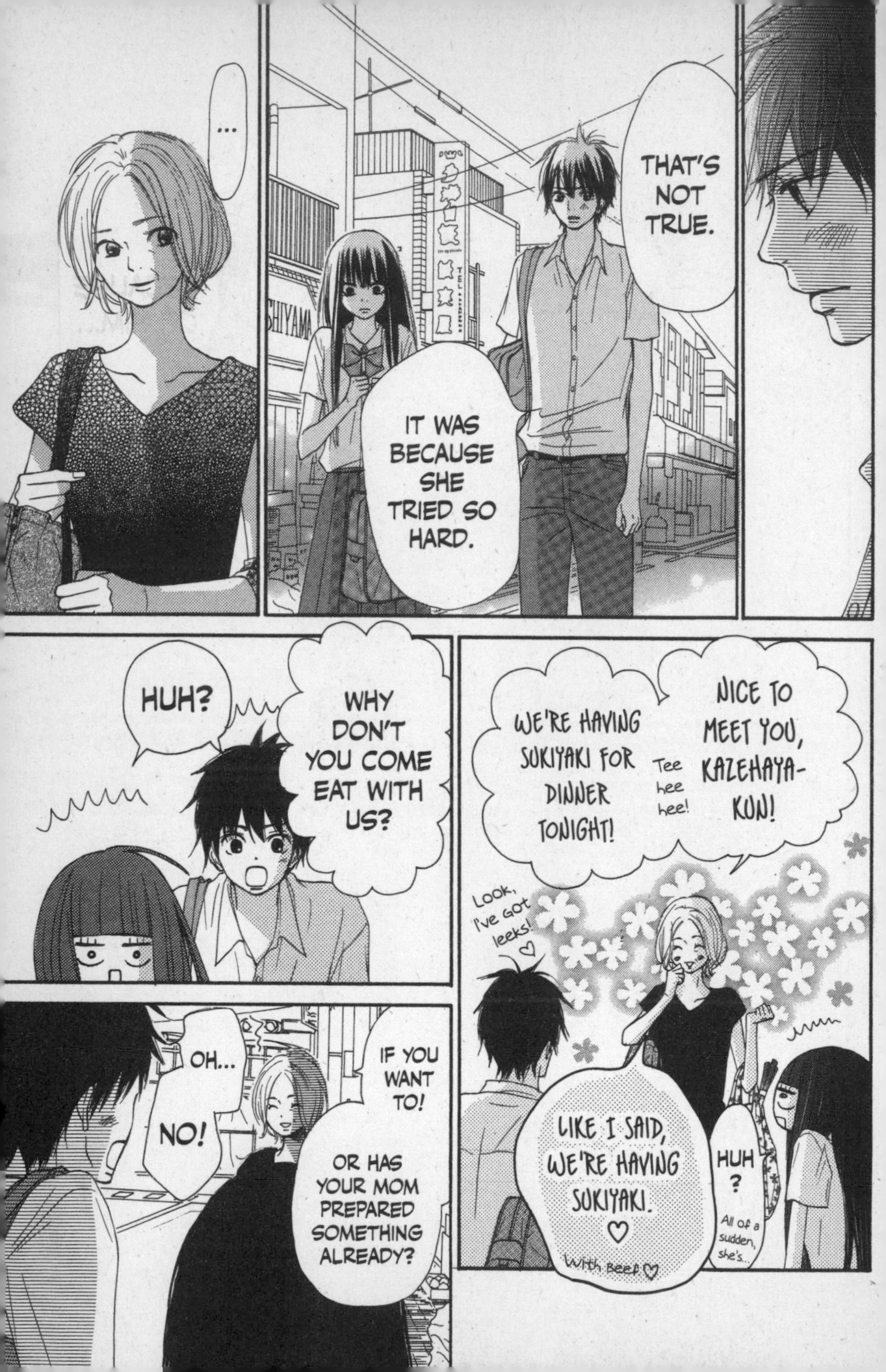
THAT'S NOT TRUE.
IT WAS BECAUSE SHE TRIED SO HARD.
...
NICE TO MEET YOU, KAZEHAYA-KUN!
Tee hee hee!
WE'RE HAVING SUKIYAKI FOR DINNER TONIGHT!
Look, I've got leeks! ♡
LIKE I SAID, WE'RE HAVING SUKIYAKI. ♡
With Beef ♡
HUH?
All of a sudden, she's...
WHY DON'T YOU COME EAT WITH US?
HUH?
IF YOU WANT TO!
OR HAS YOUR MOM PREPARED SOMETHING ALREADY?
OH...
NO!

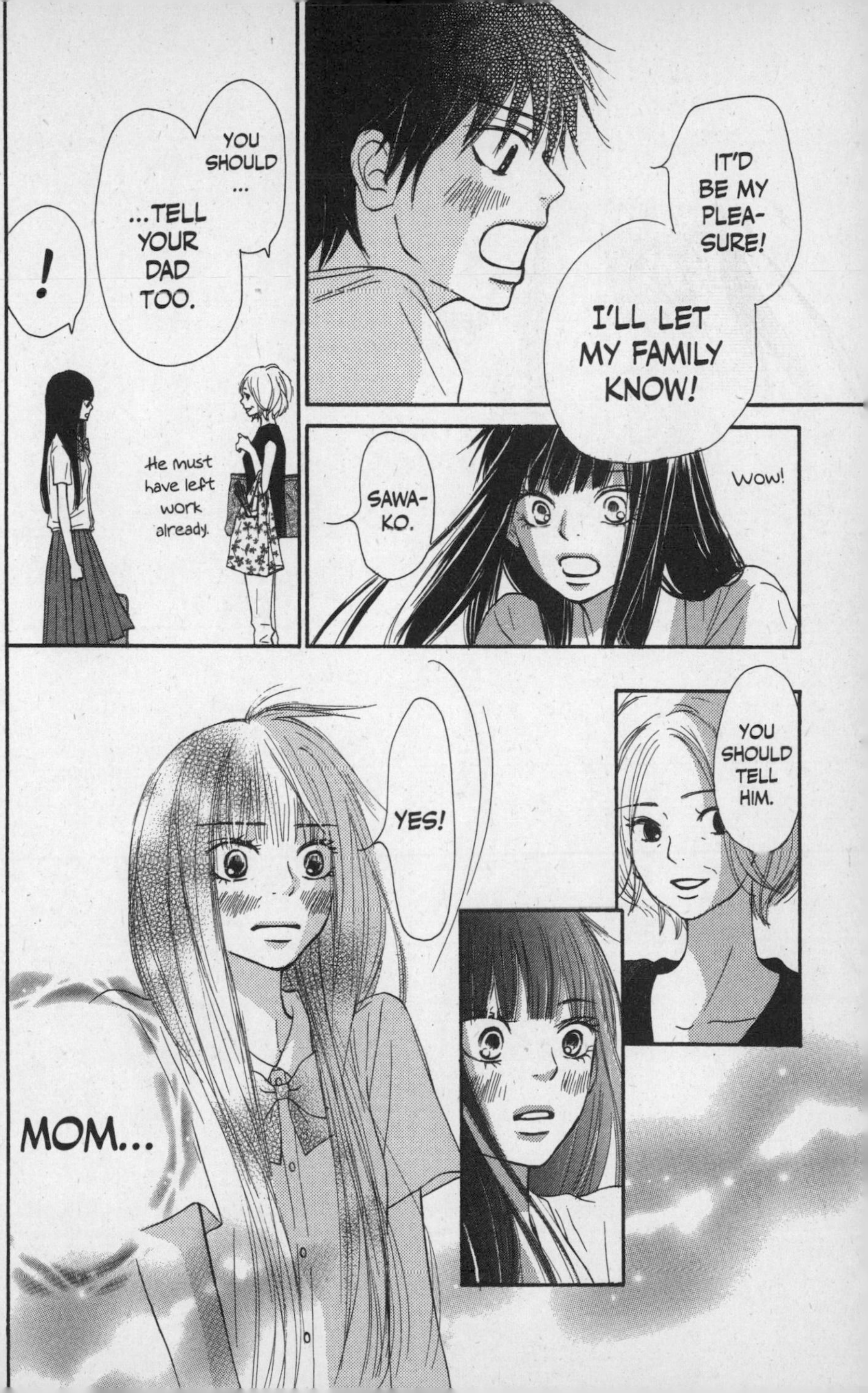
IT'D BE MY PLEASURE!
I'LL LET MY FAMILY KNOW!
Wow!
SAWAKO.
YOU SHOULD ...
...TELL YOUR DAD TOO.
!
He must have left work already.
YOU SHOULD TELL HIM.
YES!
MOM...

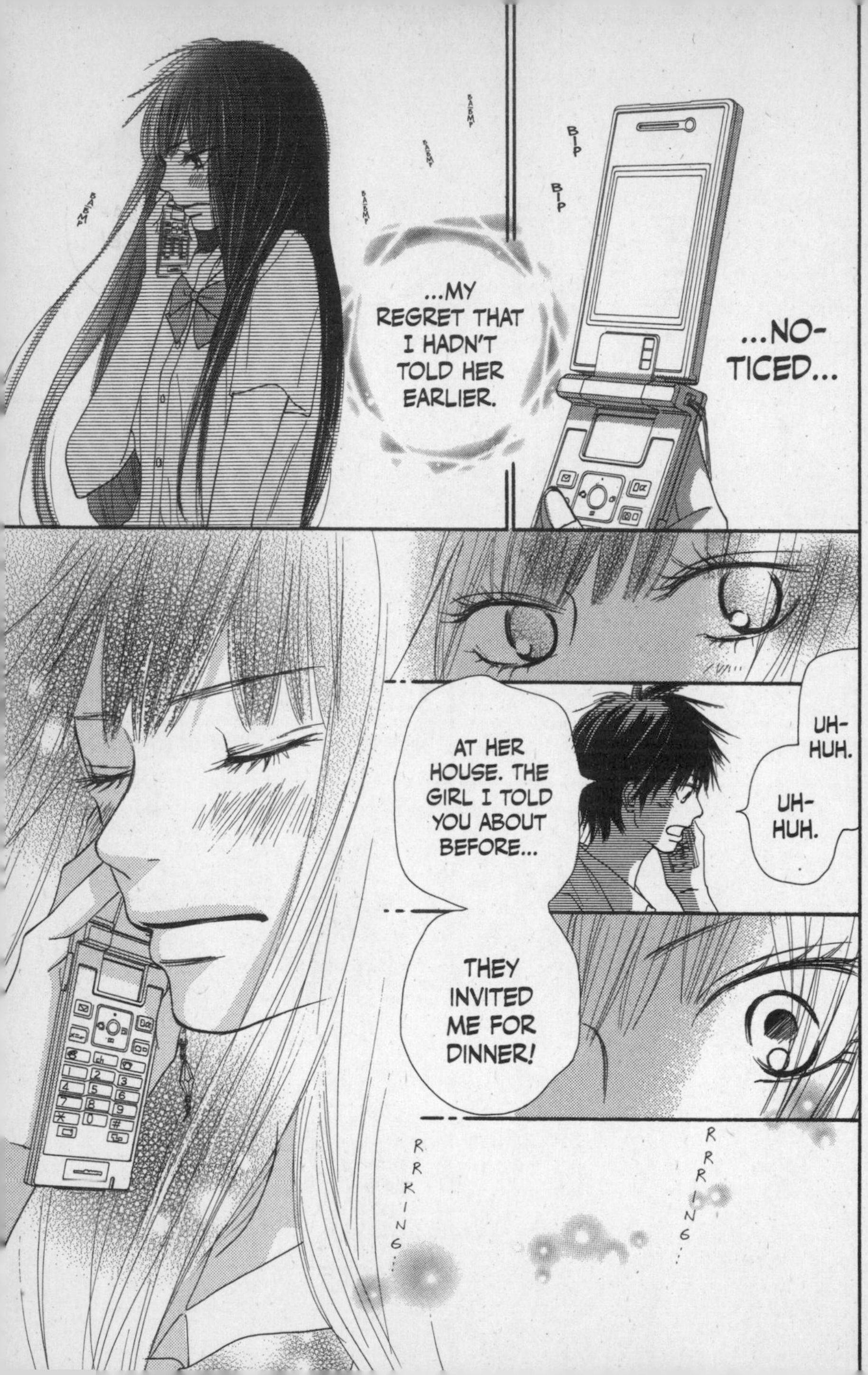
BIP
BIP
...NO-TICED...
...MY REGRET THAT I HADN'T TOLD HER EARLIER.
BA-BUMP
BA-BUMP
BA-BUMP
BA-BUMP
UH-HUH.
UH-HUH.
AT HER HOUSE. THE GIRL I TOLD YOU ABOUT BEFORE...
THEY INVITED ME FOR DINNER!
RRRING...
RRING...

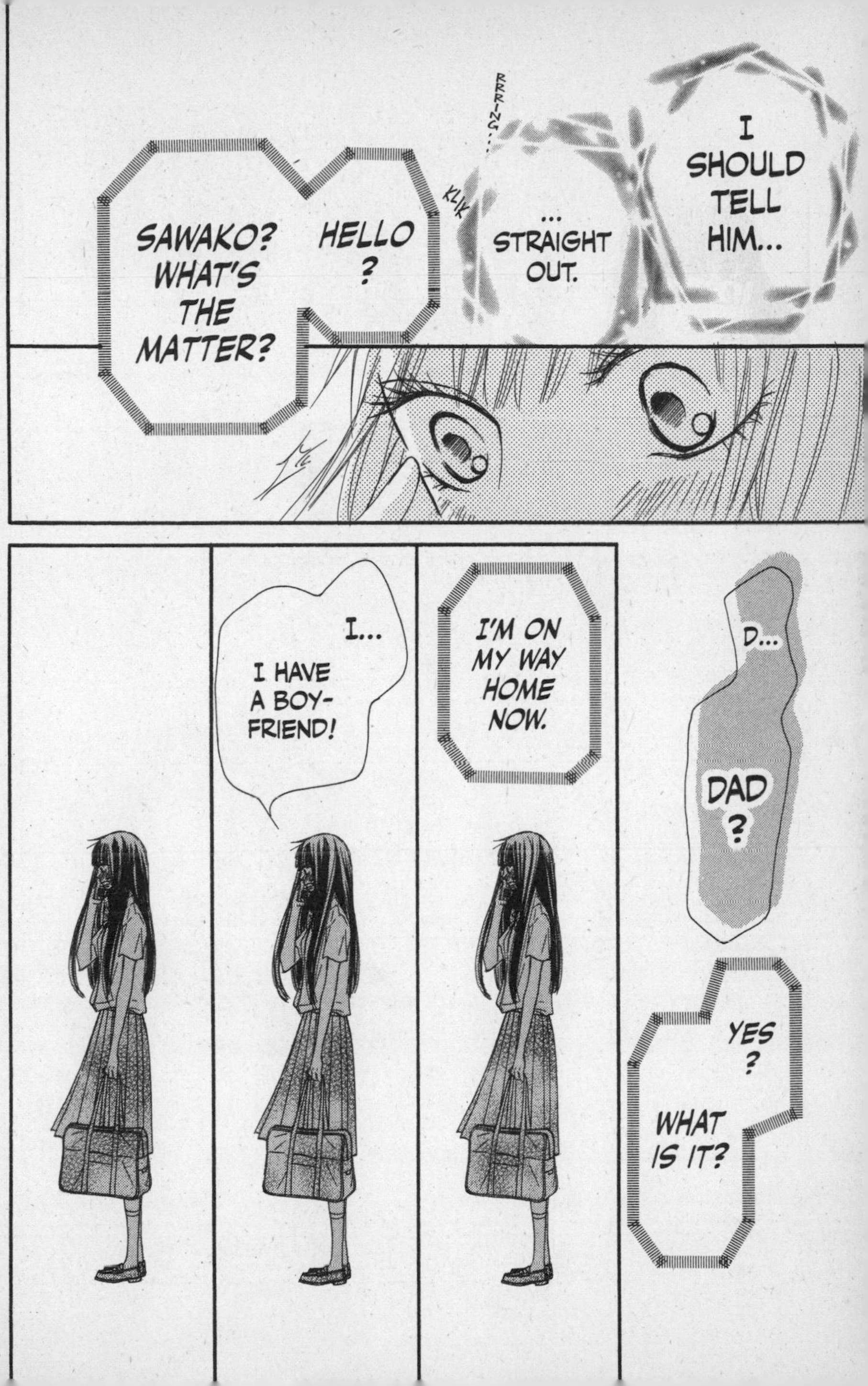
I SHOULD TELL HIM...
... STRAIGHT OUT.
RRRING...
KLIK
HELLO?
SAWAKO? WHAT'S THE MATTER?
D...
DAD?
YES? WHAT IS IT?
I'M ON MY WAY HOME NOW.
I...
I HAVE A BOY-FRIEND!

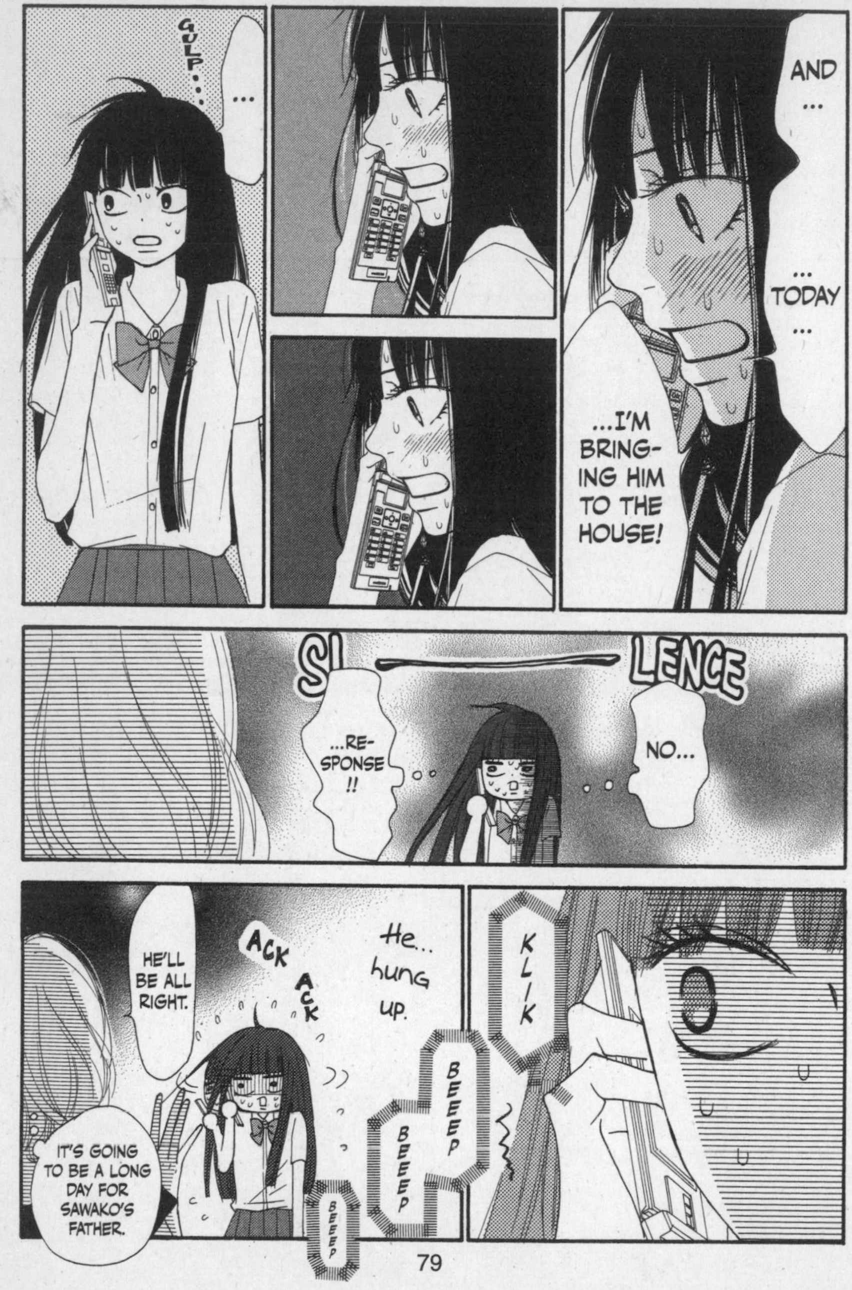
AND ... ... TODAY ...
...I'M BRINGING HIM TO THE HOUSE!
GULP...
...
SI—LENCE
NO...
...RE-SPONSE !!
KLIK
BEEEP
BEEEP
BEEEP
He... hung up.
ACK ACK
HE'LL BE ALL RIGHT.
IT'S GOING TO BE A LONG DAY FOR SAWAKO'S FATHER.

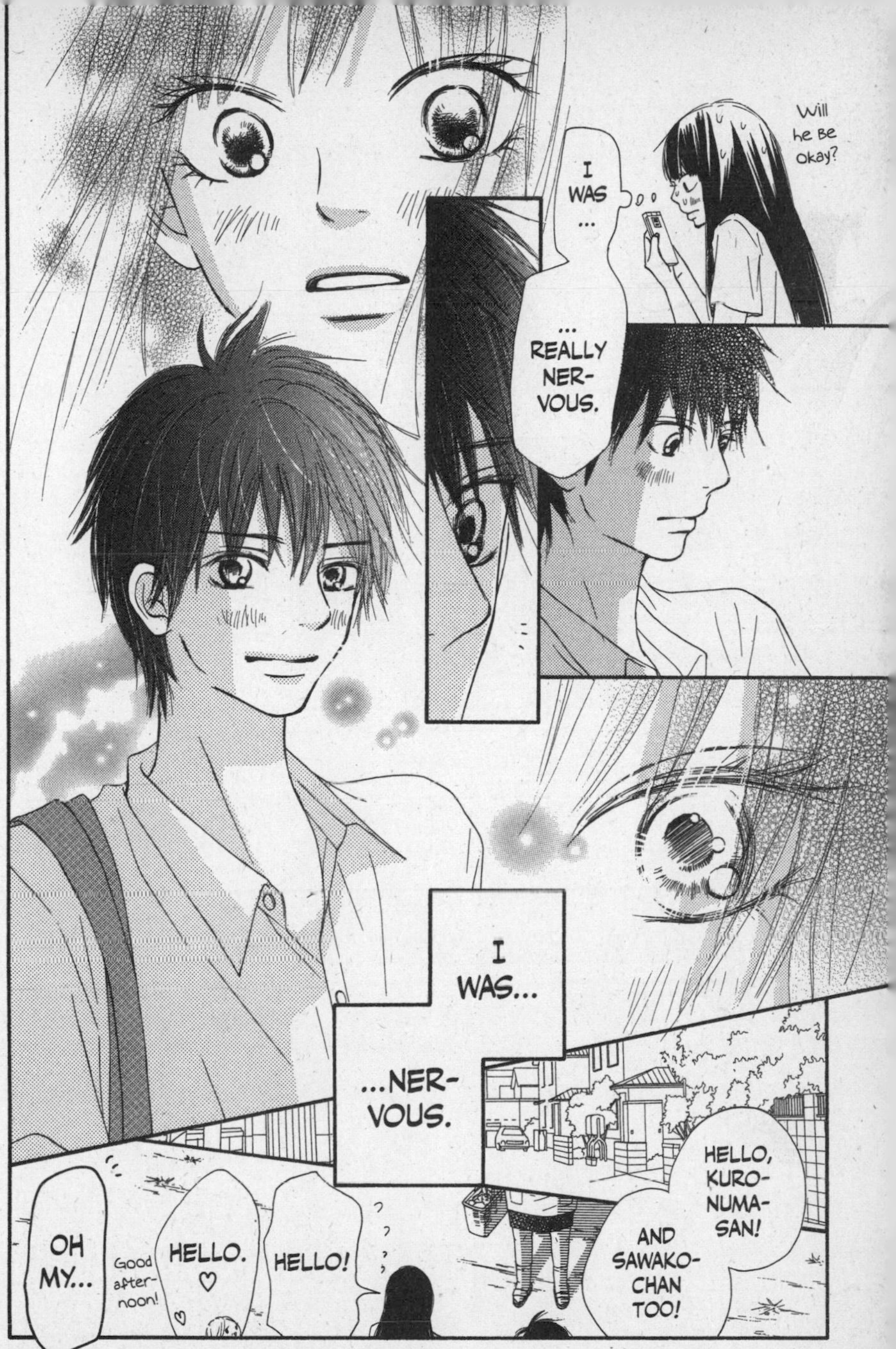
Will he be okay?
I WAS ...
... REALLY NER-VOUS.
I WAS...
...NER-VOUS.
HELLO, KURO-NUMA-SAN!
AND SAWAKO-CHAN TOO!
HELLO!
HELLO. ♡
Good after-noon!
OH MY...

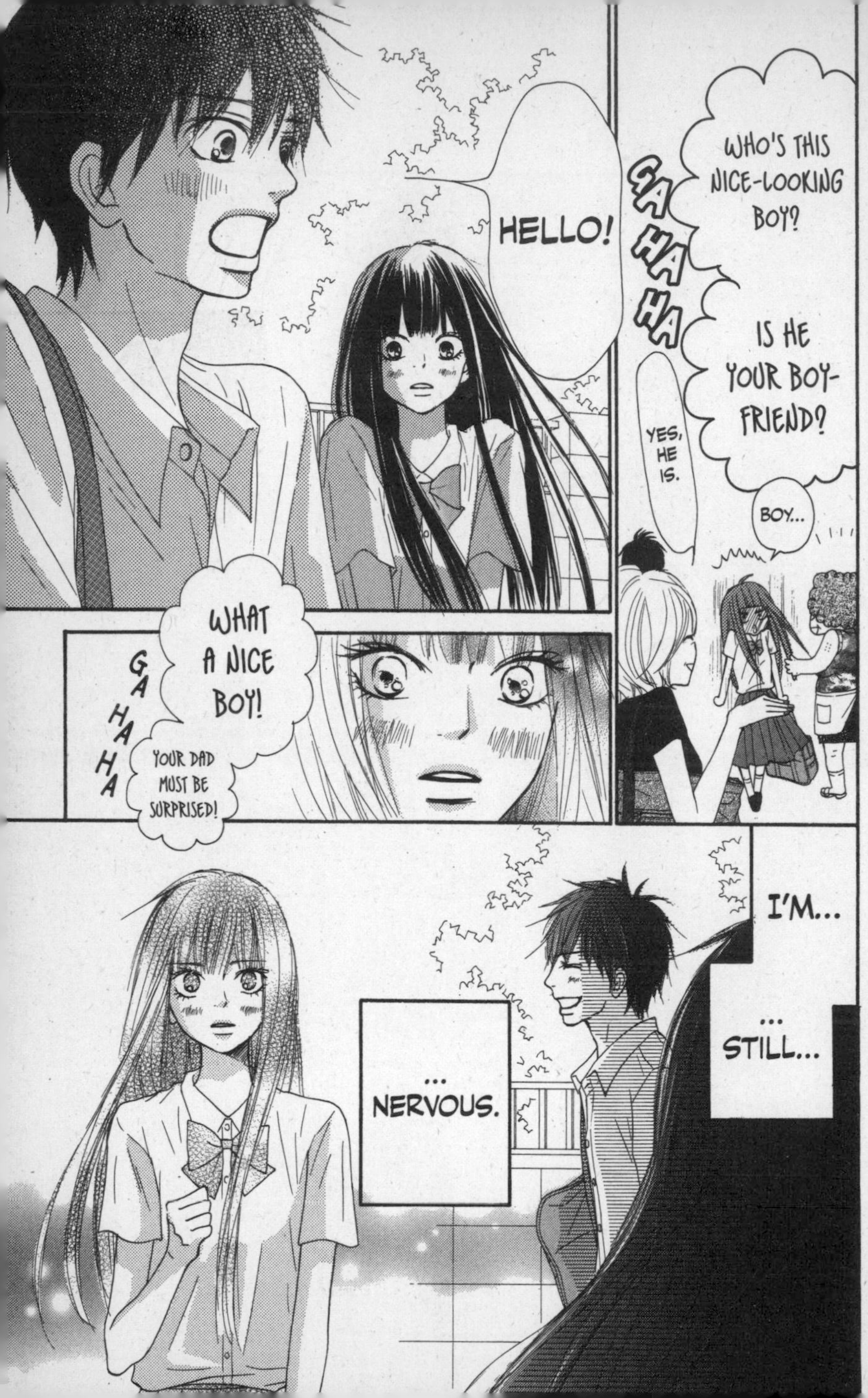
WHO'S THIS NICE-LOOKING BOY?
GA HA HA
IS HE YOUR BOY-FRIEND?
YES, HE IS.
BOY...
HELLO!
WHAT A NICE BOY!
GA HA HA HA
YOUR DAD MUST BE SURPRISED!
I'M...
... STILL...
... NERVOUS.

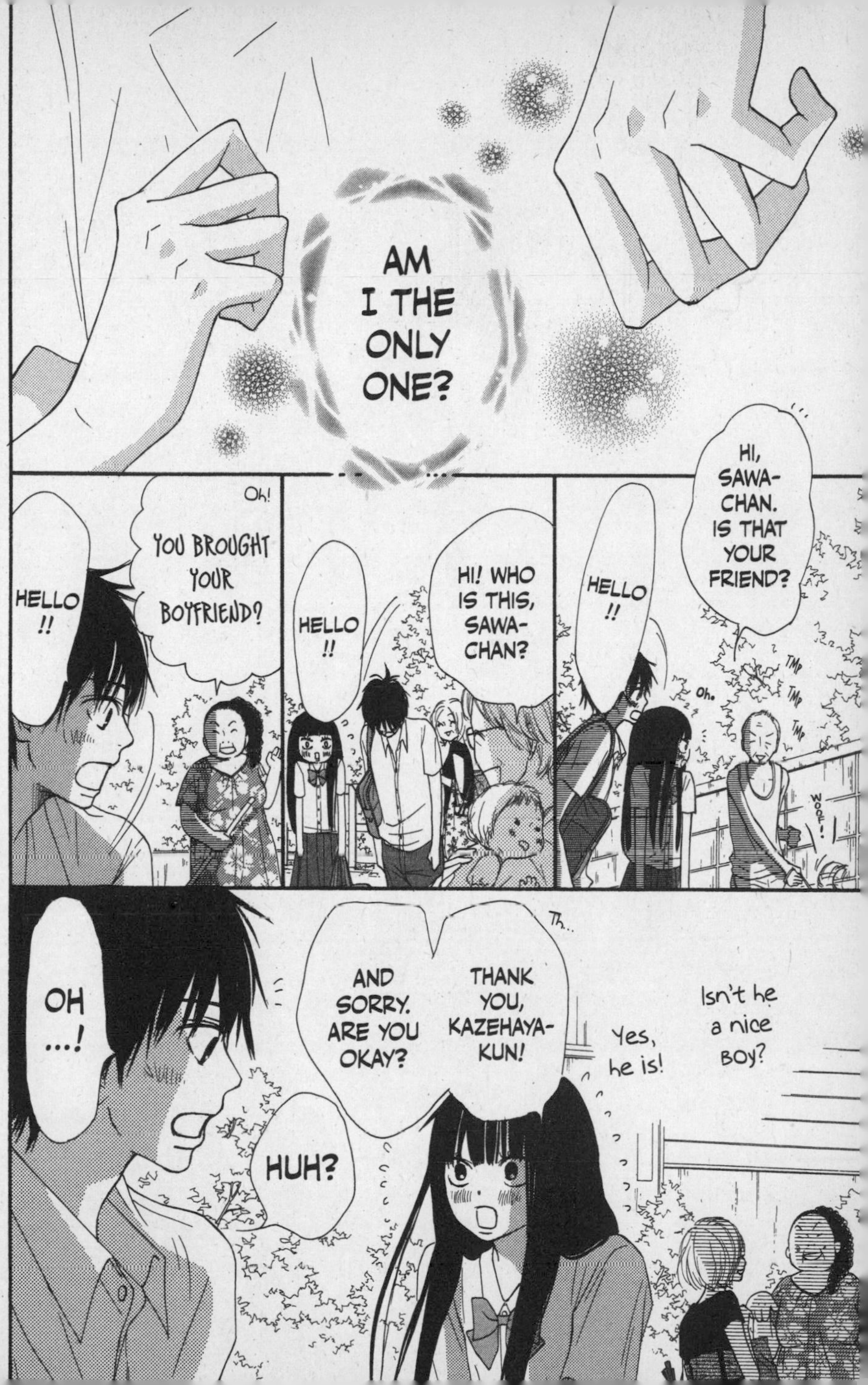
AM I THE ONLY ONE?
HI, SAWA-CHAN. IS THAT YOUR FRIEND?
HELLO !!
Oh.
HI! WHO IS THIS, SAWA-CHAN?
HELLO !!
Oh! YOU BROUGHT YOUR BOYFRIEND?
HELLO !!
Isn't he a nice boy?
Yes, he is!
THANK YOU, KAZEHAYA-KUN!
AND SORRY. ARE YOU OKAY?
HUH?
OH ...!

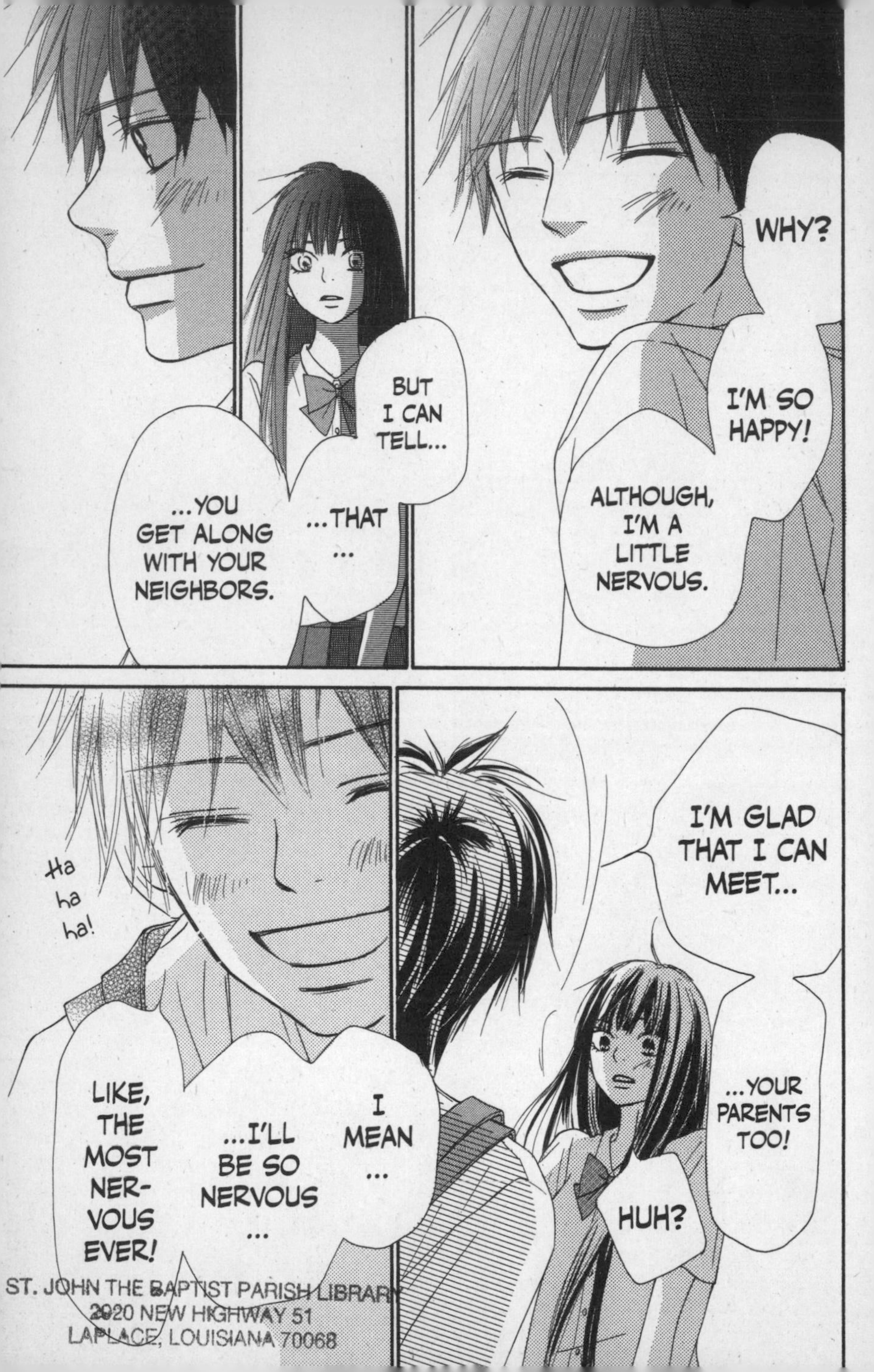
WHY?
I'M SO HAPPY!
ALTHOUGH, I'M A LITTLE NERVOUS.
BUT I CAN TELL...
...THAT ...
...YOU GET ALONG WITH YOUR NEIGHBORS.
I'M GLAD THAT I CAN MEET...
...YOUR PARENTS TOO!
HUH?
I MEAN ...
...I'LL BE SO NERVOUS ...
LIKE, THE MOST NER-VOUS EVER!
Ha ha ha!

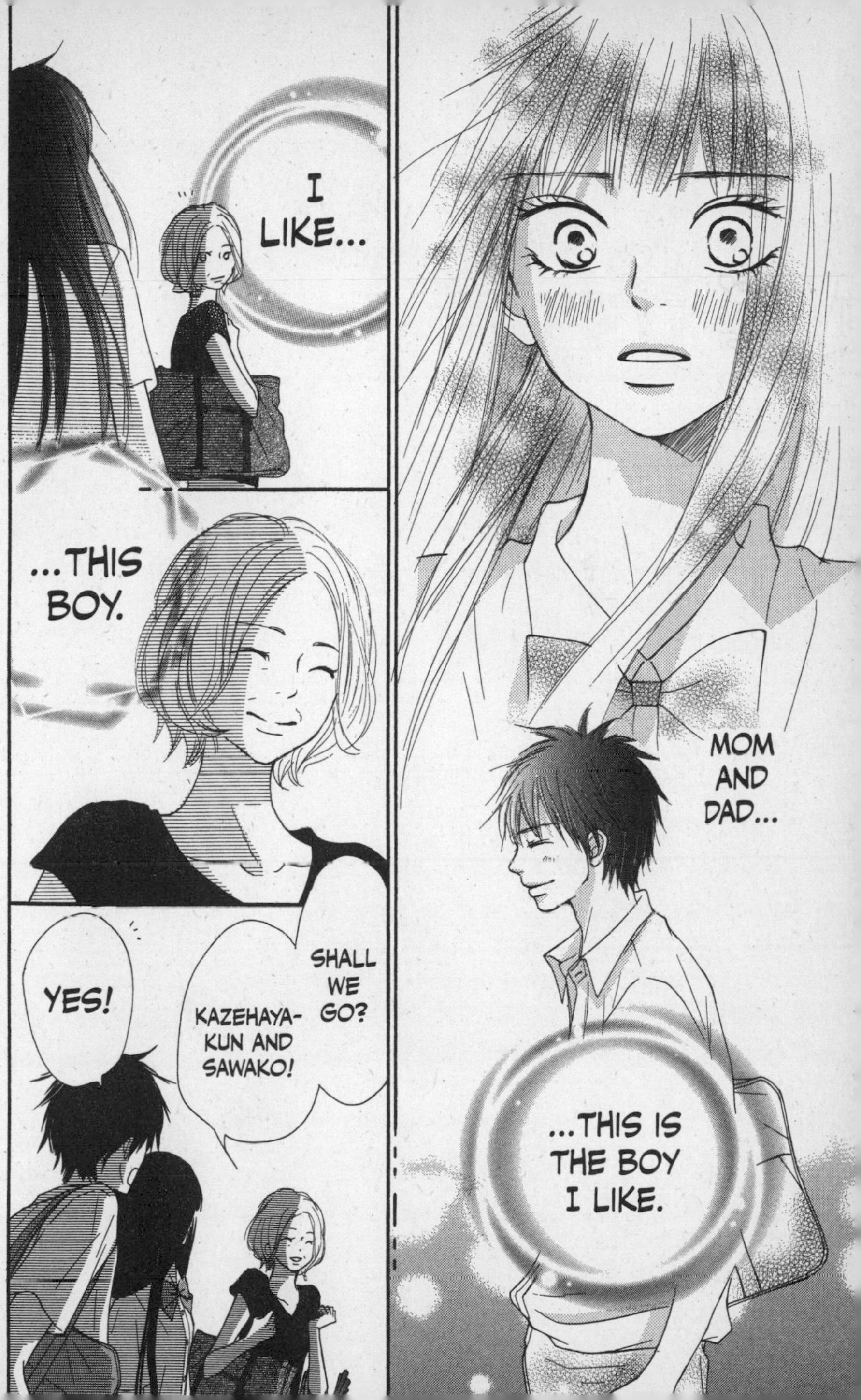
MOM AND DAD...
...THIS IS THE BOY I LIKE.
I LIKE...
...THIS BOY.
SHALL WE GO? KAZEHAYA-KUN AND SAWAKO!
YES!

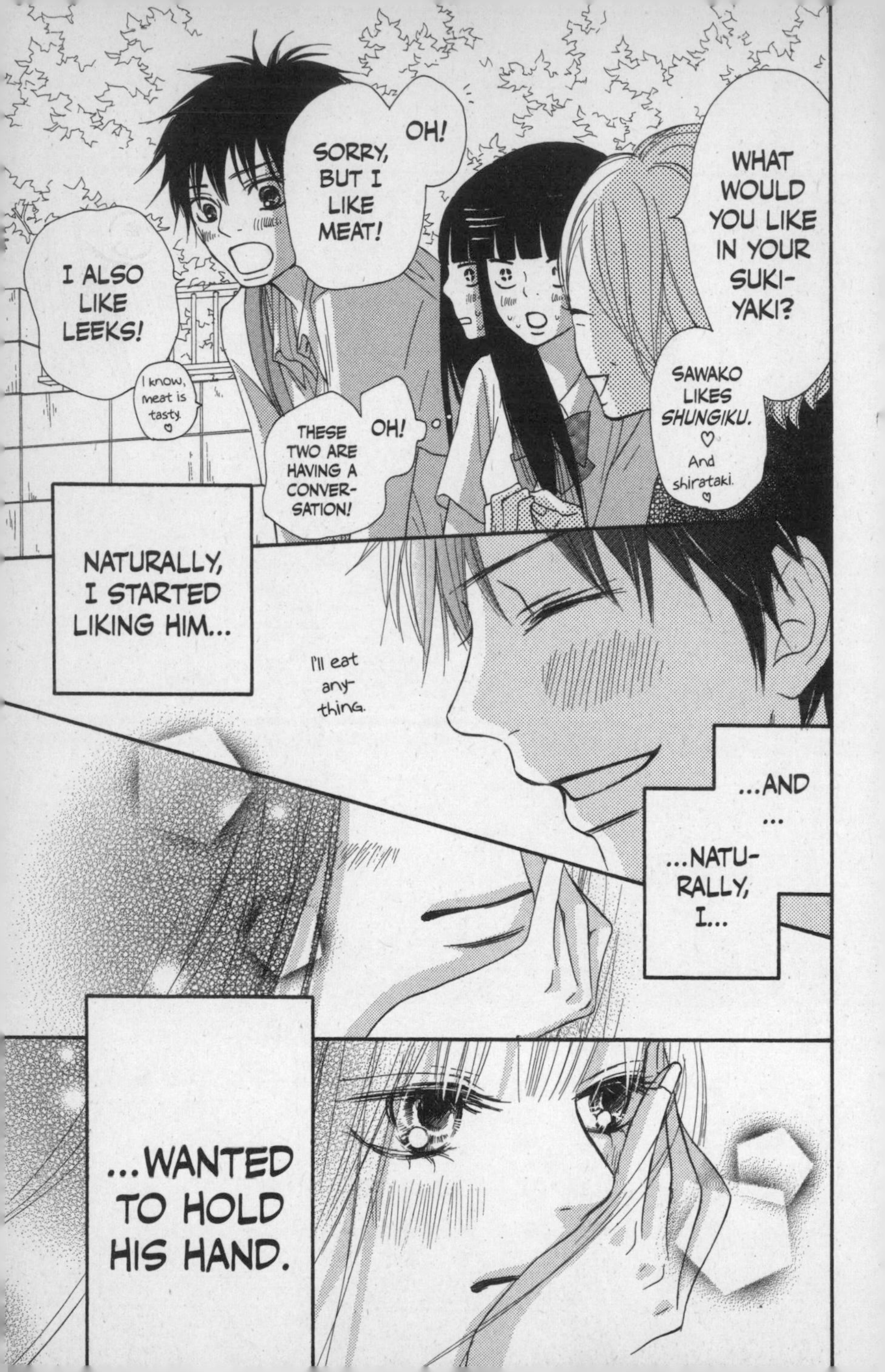
WHAT WOULD YOU LIKE IN YOUR SUKI-YAKI?
SAWAKO LIKES SHUNGIKU. ♡
And shirataki. ♡
OH!
SORRY, BUT I LIKE MEAT!
OH!
THESE TWO ARE HAVING A CONVER-SATION!
I ALSO LIKE LEEKS!
I know, meat is tasty. ♡
I'll eat any-thing.
NATURALLY, I STARTED LIKING HIM...
...AND ... ...NATU-RALLY, I...
...WANTED TO HOLD HIS HAND.

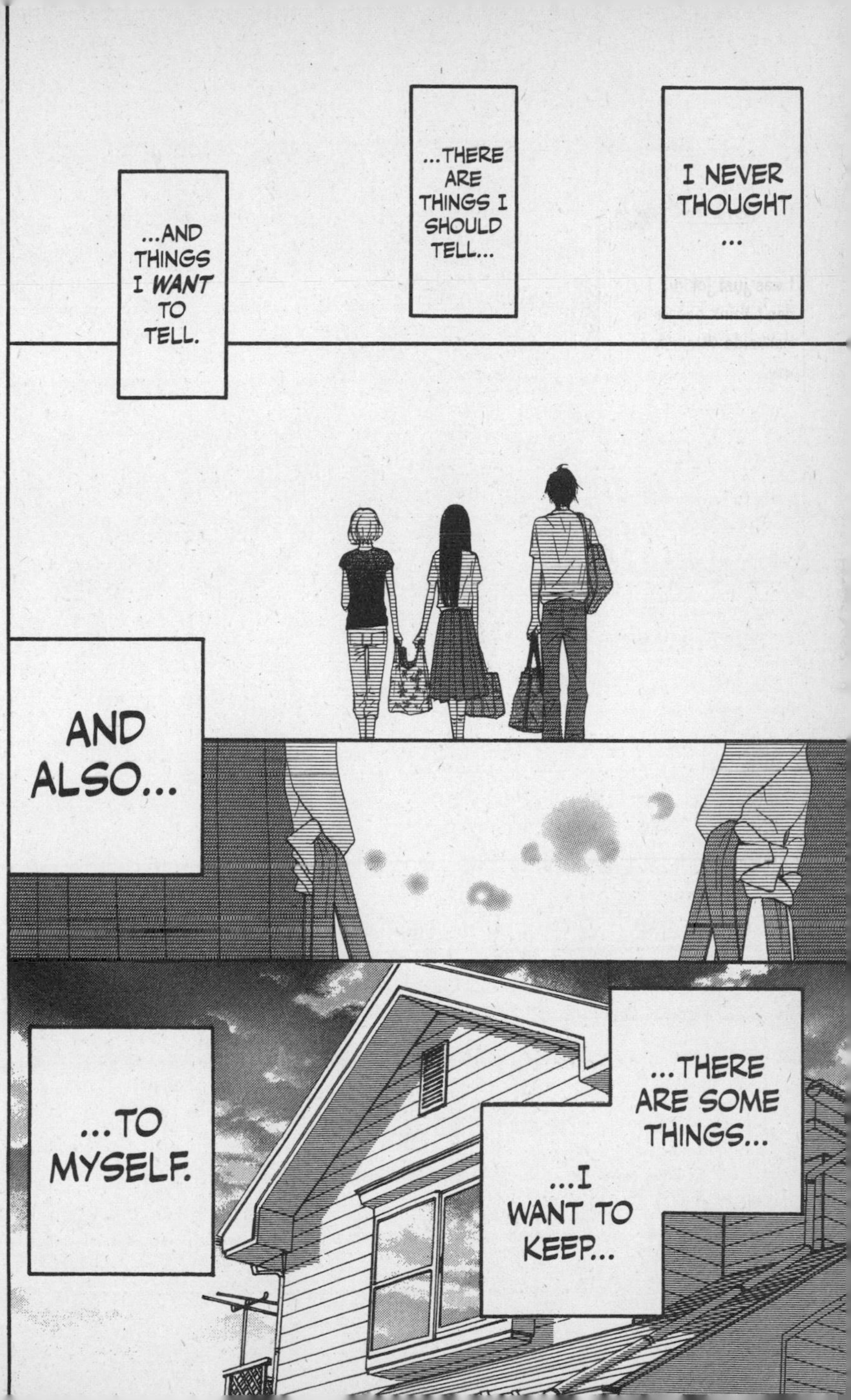

I NEVER THOUGHT ...
...THERE ARE THINGS I SHOULD TELL...
...AND THINGS I *WANT* TO TELL.
AND ALSO...
...THERE ARE SOME THINGS...
...I WANT TO KEEP...
...TO MYSELF.

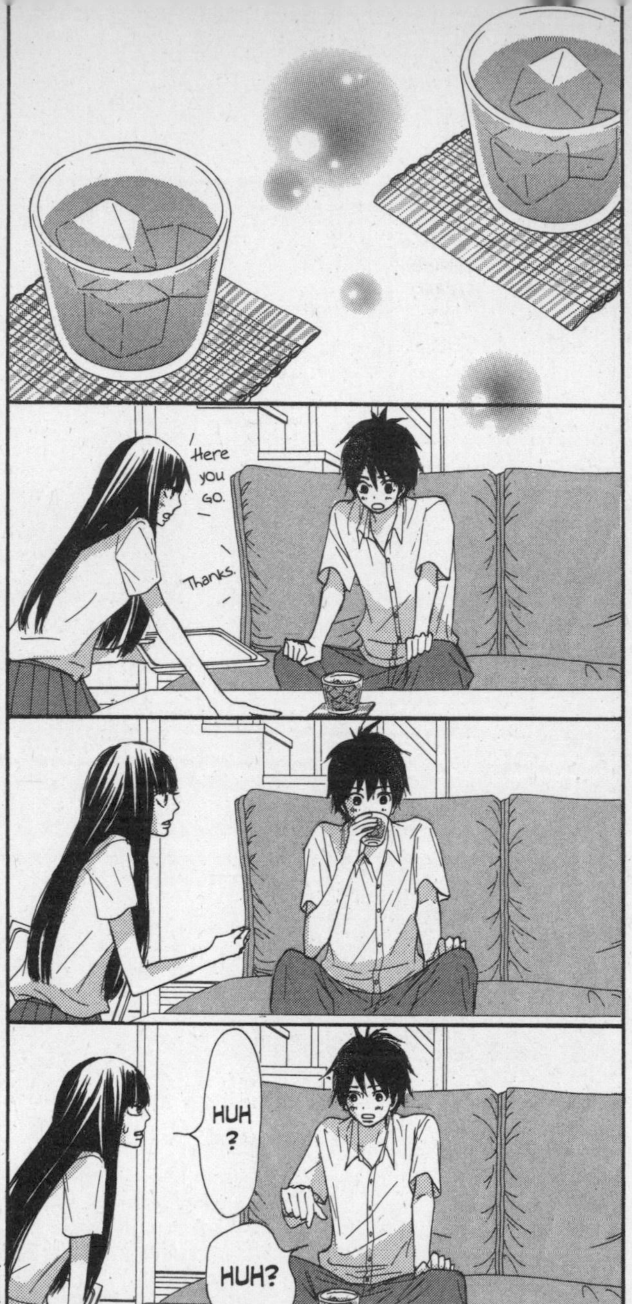
Here you go.
Thanks.
HUH?
HUH?

KARUPIN on JAPAN 2

I was just joking. I don't think people in Hokkaido think that way.

(Let's get back to the real topic.) Finally, the movie will come out!! To tell you the truth, I want to tell you the scenes that are cute or made me scream (in a good way), but I can't. (lol)

I want everyone who likes Tabe-chan and Haruma-kun, or Sawako and Kazehaya, to watch it!

Chizu, Kurumi, Ayane, Ryu, Pin, Joe, Sawako's parents, and little Sawako are also doing a nice job!

Am I doing all right? Really?

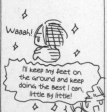

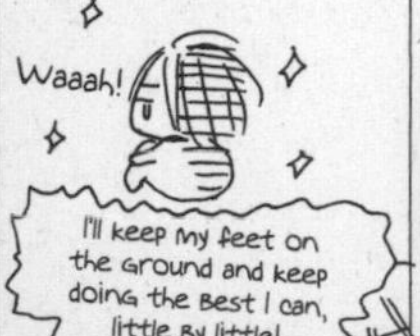
Waaah!
I'll keep my feet on the ground and keep doing the best I can, little by little!

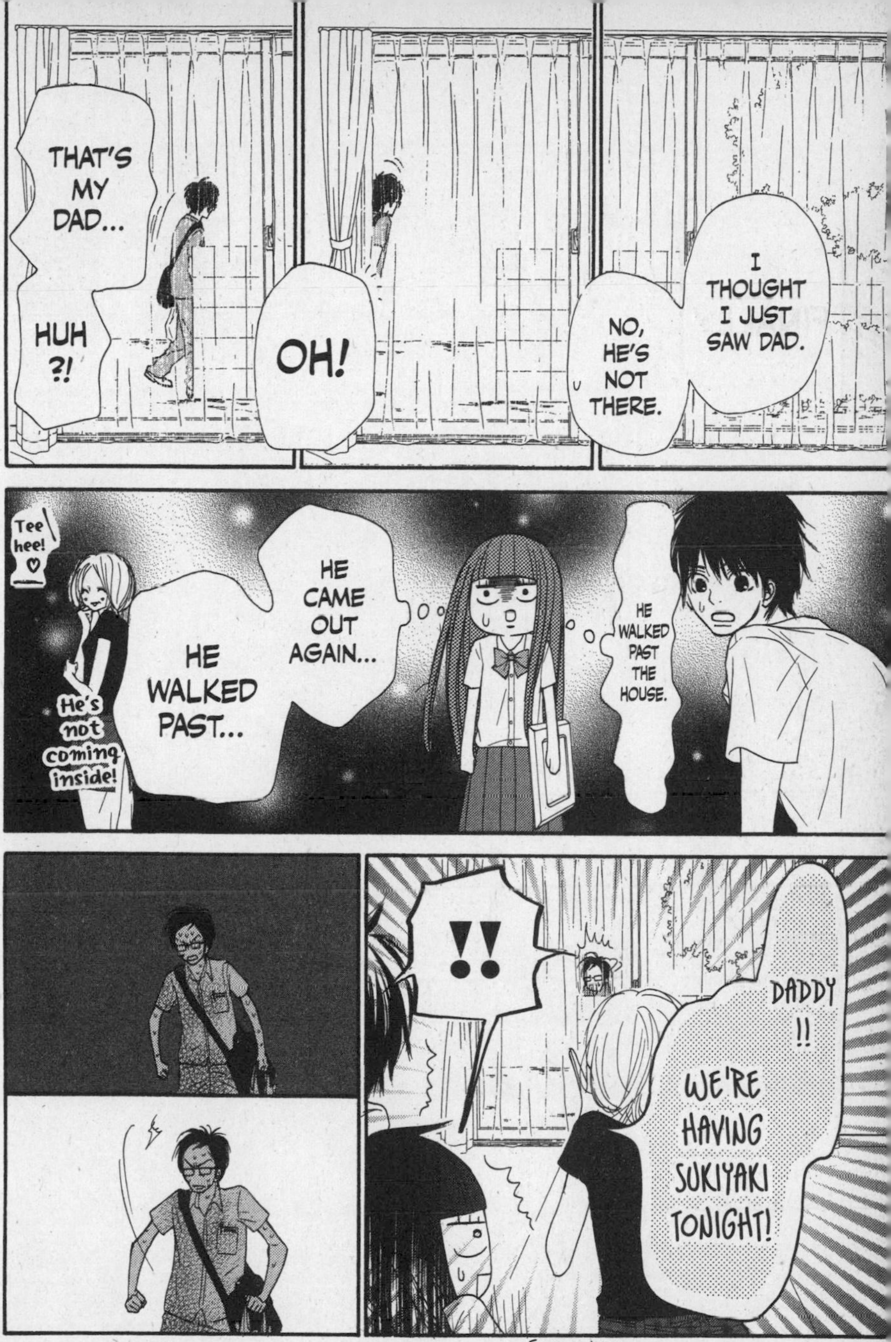
I THOUGHT I JUST SAW DAD.
NO, HE'S NOT THERE.
OH!
THAT'S MY DAD...
HUH ?!
HE WALKED PAST THE HOUSE.
HE CAME OUT AGAIN...
HE WALKED PAST...
Tee hee! ♡
He's not coming inside!
DADDY !!
WE'RE HAVING SUKIYAKI TONIGHT!
!!
Screen door

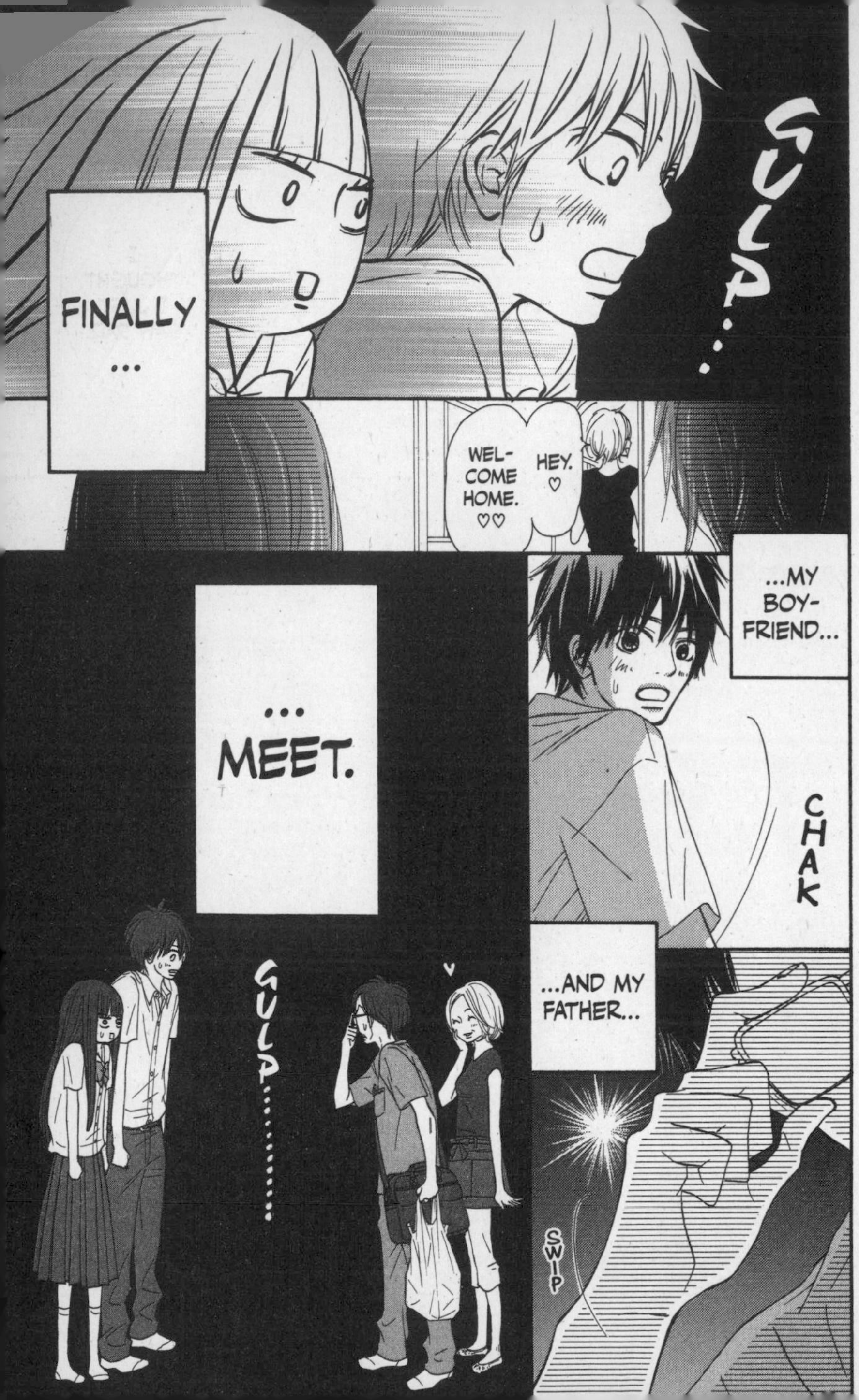
GULP...
FINALLY...
HEY. ♡
WEL-COME HOME. ♡♡
...MY BOY-FRIEND...
CHAK
...AND MY FATHER...
SWIP
... MEET.
GULP......

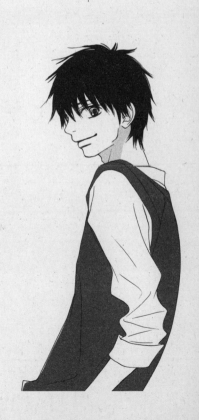

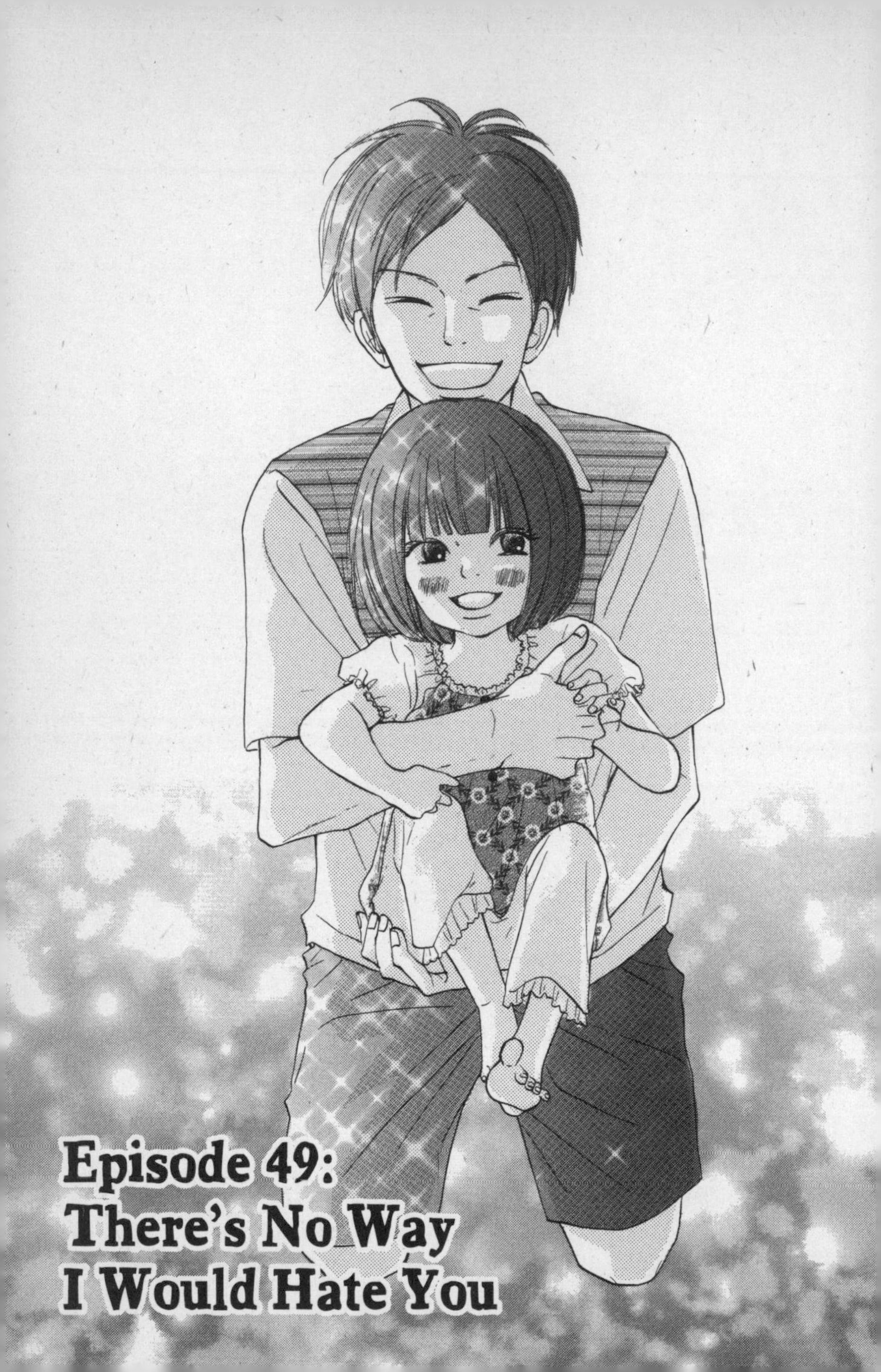

Episode 49: There's No Way I Would Hate You

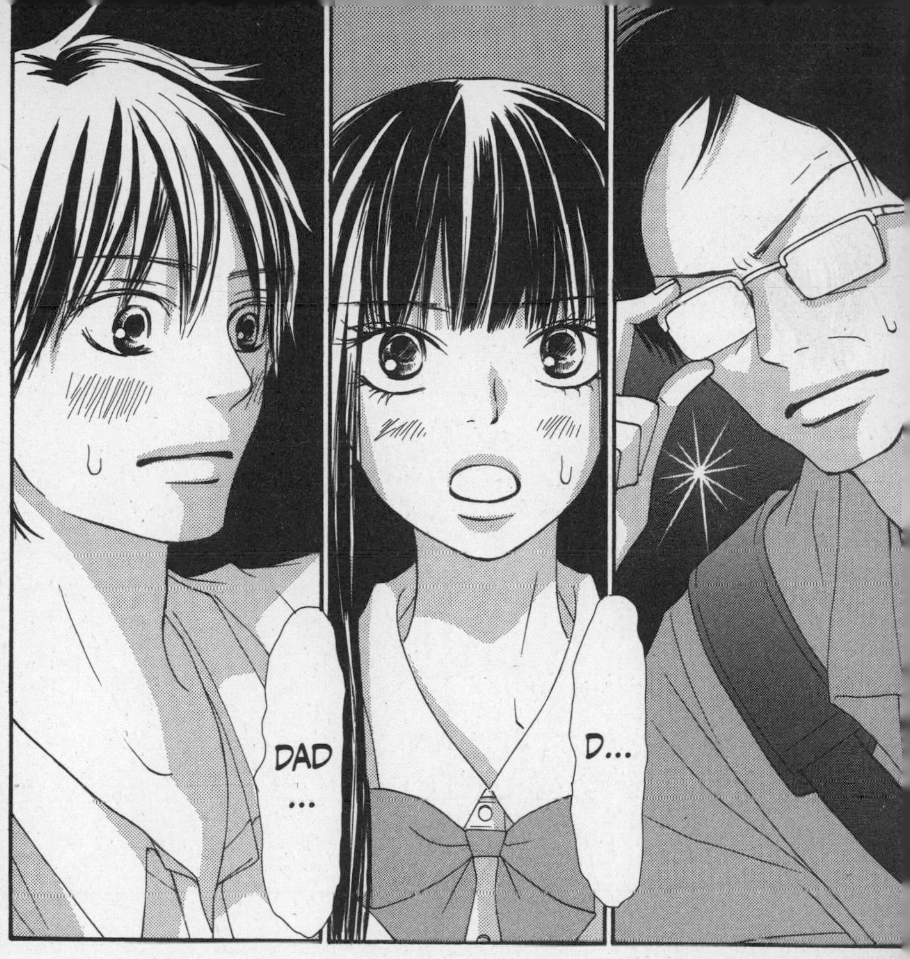
D...
DAD
...

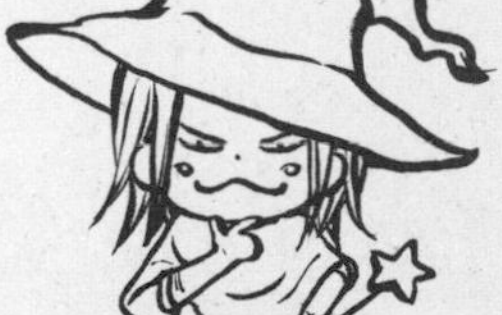

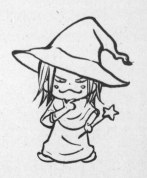

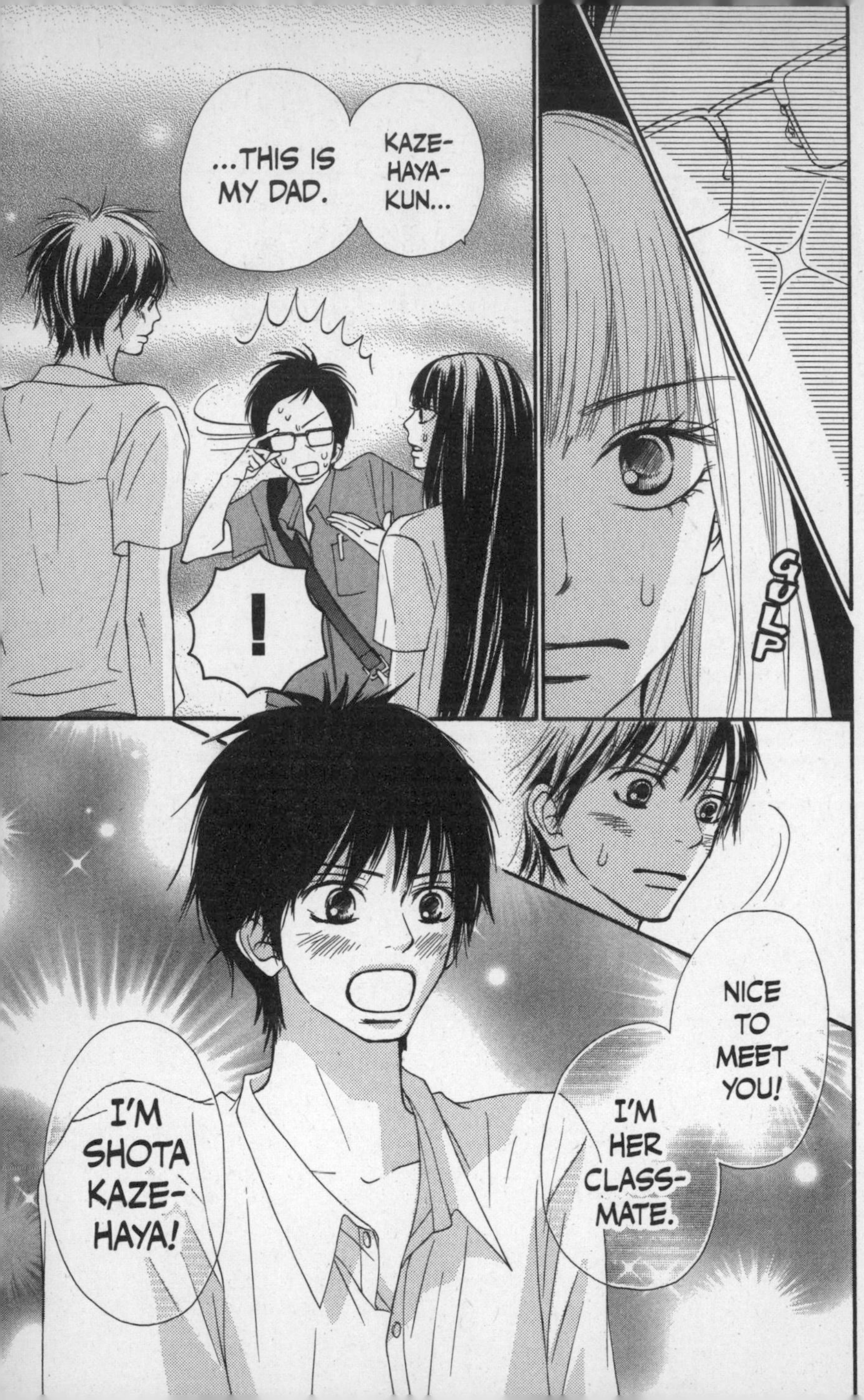
GULP
KAZE-HAYA-KUN...
...THIS IS MY DAD.
!
NICE TO MEET YOU!
I'M HER CLASS-MATE.
I'M SHOTA KAZE-HAYA!

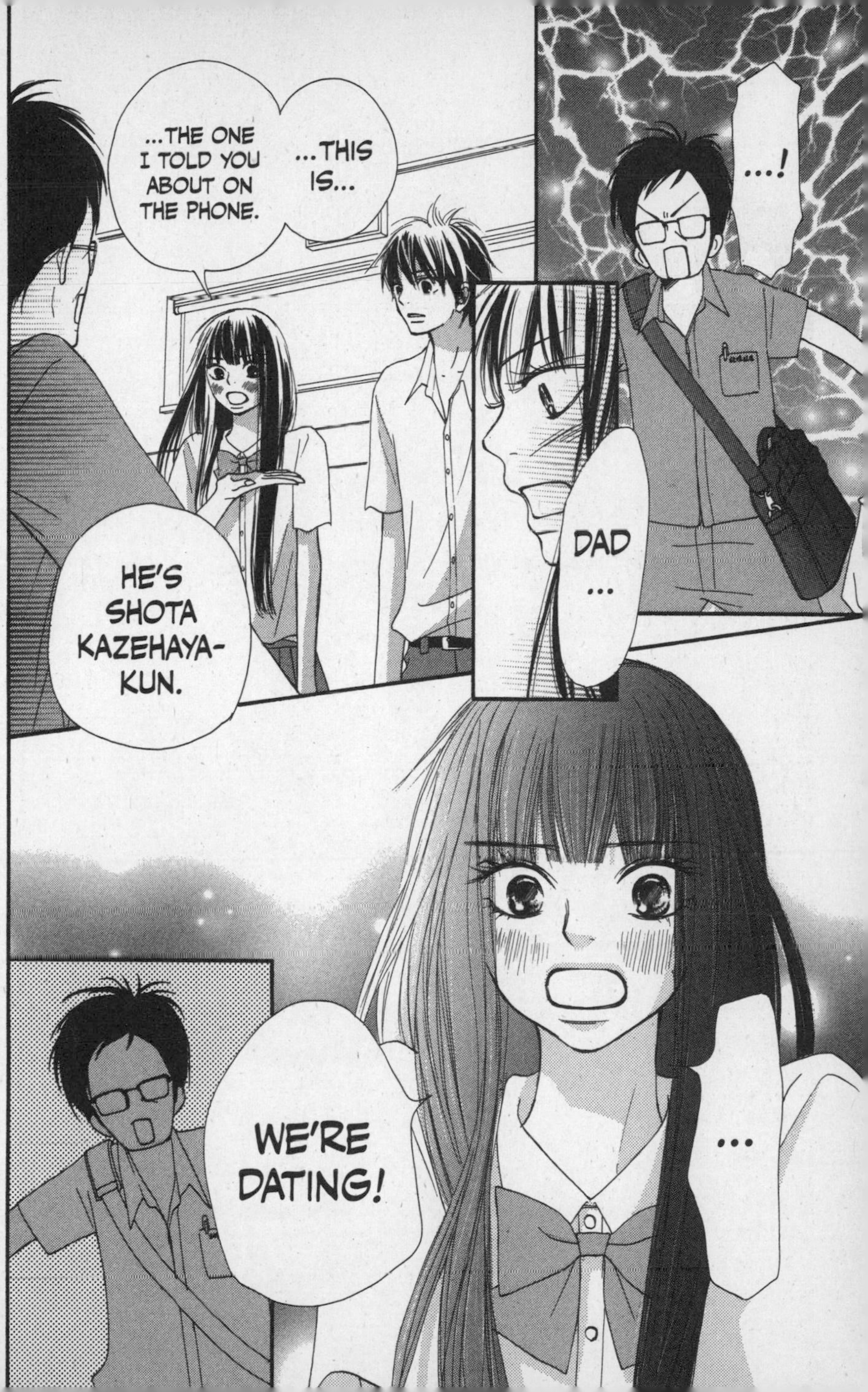
...!
DAD ...
...THIS IS...
...THE ONE I TOLD YOU ABOUT ON THE PHONE.
HE'S SHOTA KAZEHAYA-KUN.
...
WE'RE DATING!

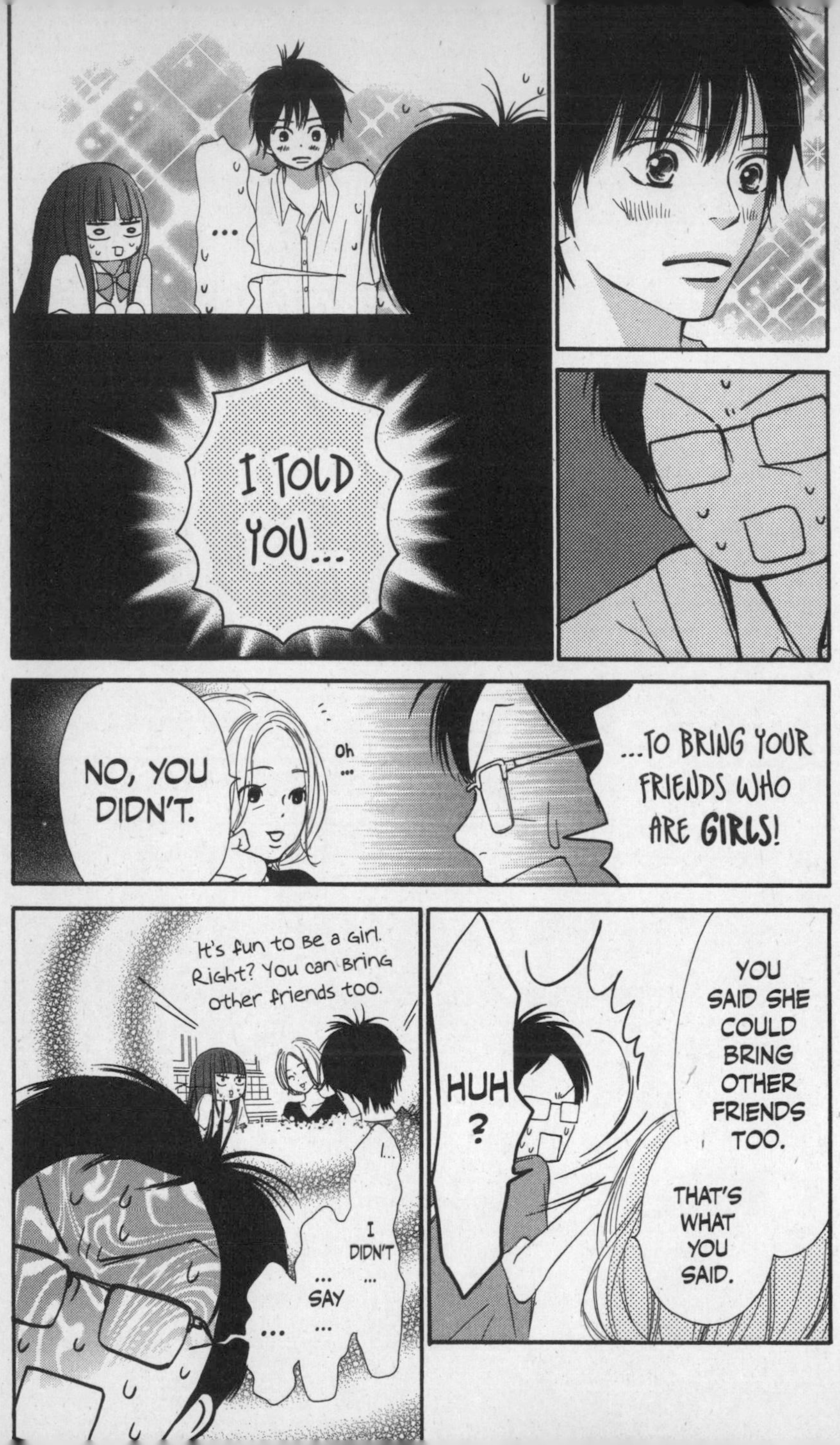
...
I TOLD YOU...
...TO BRING YOUR FRIENDS WHO ARE **GIRLS**!
Oh ...
NO, YOU DIDN'T.
YOU SAID SHE COULD BRING OTHER FRIENDS TOO.
THAT'S WHAT YOU SAID.
HUH?
It's fun to be a Girl. Right? You can bring other friends too.
I...
I DIDN'T ...
... SAY ...
...

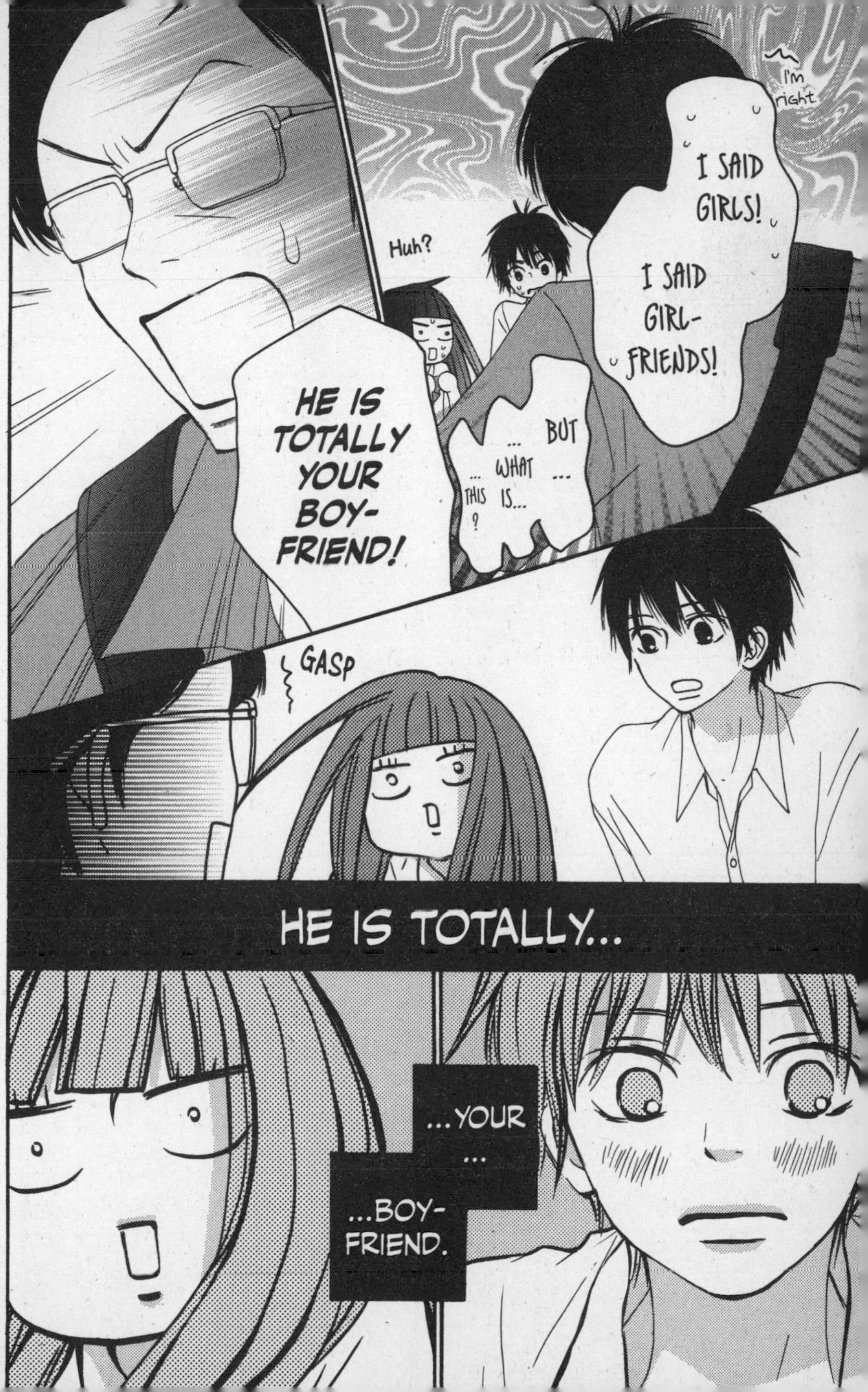
I'm right.
I SAID GIRLS!
I SAID GIRL-FRIENDS!
Huh?
BUT ... WHAT IS... THIS ?
HE IS TOTALLY YOUR BOY-FRIEND!
GASP
HE IS TOTALLY...
...YOUR ...
...BOY-FRIEND.

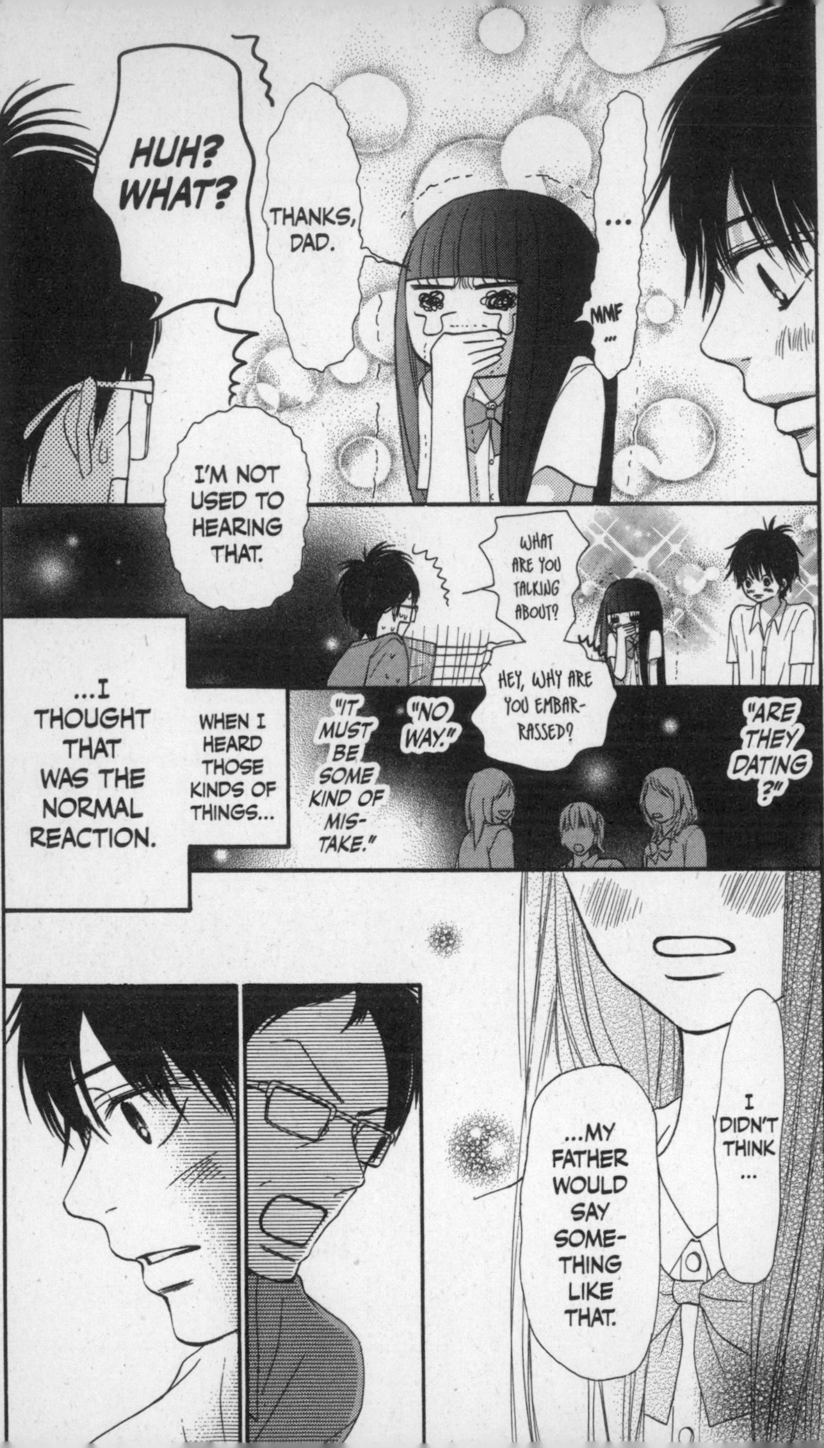
...
MMF ...
THANKS, DAD.
HUH? WHAT?
I'M NOT USED TO HEARING THAT.
WHAT ARE YOU TALKING ABOUT?
HEY, WHY ARE YOU EMBARRASSED?
"ARE THEY DATING?"
"NO WAY."
"IT MUST BE SOME KIND OF MISTAKE."
WHEN I HEARD THOSE KINDS OF THINGS...
...I THOUGHT THAT WAS THE NORMAL REACTION.
I DIDN'T THINK ...
...MY FATHER WOULD SAY SOMETHING LIKE THAT.

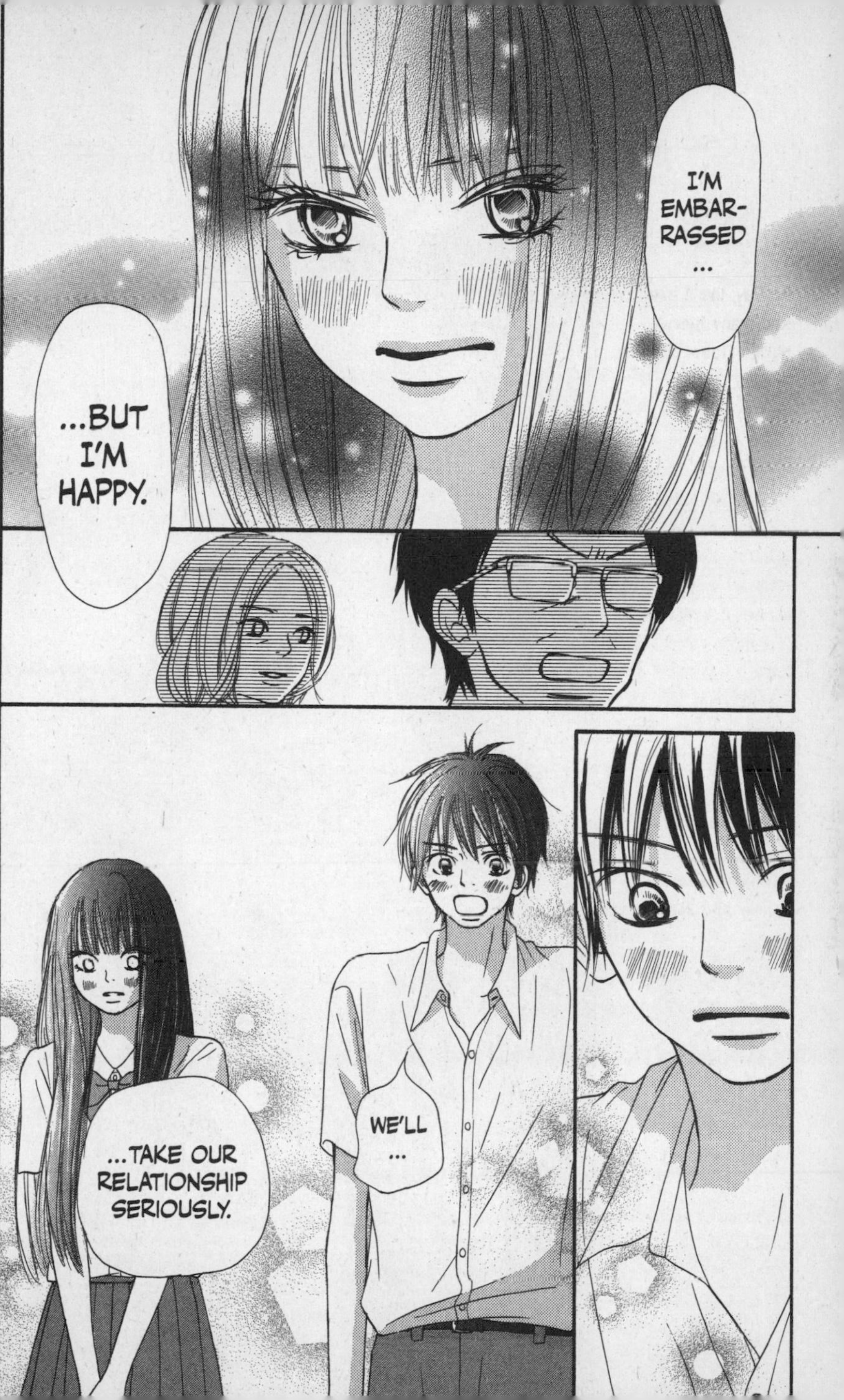
I'M EMBAR-RASSED ...
...BUT I'M HAPPY.
WE'LL ...
...TAKE OUR RELATIONSHIP SERIOUSLY.

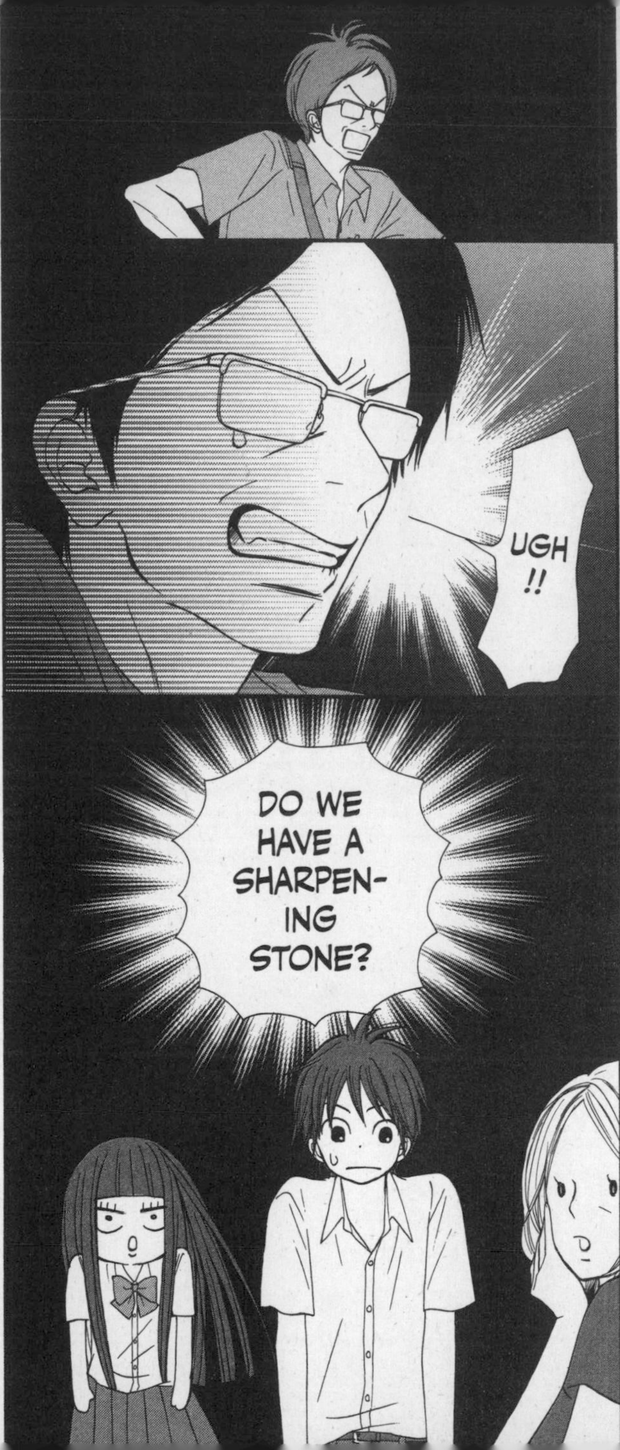
UGH !!
DO WE HAVE A SHARPEN-ING STONE?

KARUPIN on JAPAN 3

Anyway, like I have said many times, Mikako Tabe-chan is so cute that I can't help saying, "What is this cute creature?" And Haruma Miura-kun looks like the character so much that it makes me say, "How could Kazehaya become a real human being?" I know in my heart, though, that they are a girl and a boy from the city.

It's weird to think that those characters don't exist in reality. I'm impressed by the actors' and actresses' work!

Also, I want to thank the director, who understood and cared about aspects of the story that aren't written in the words.

Please go see the movie *Kimi ni Todoke!* It made the author really cry!

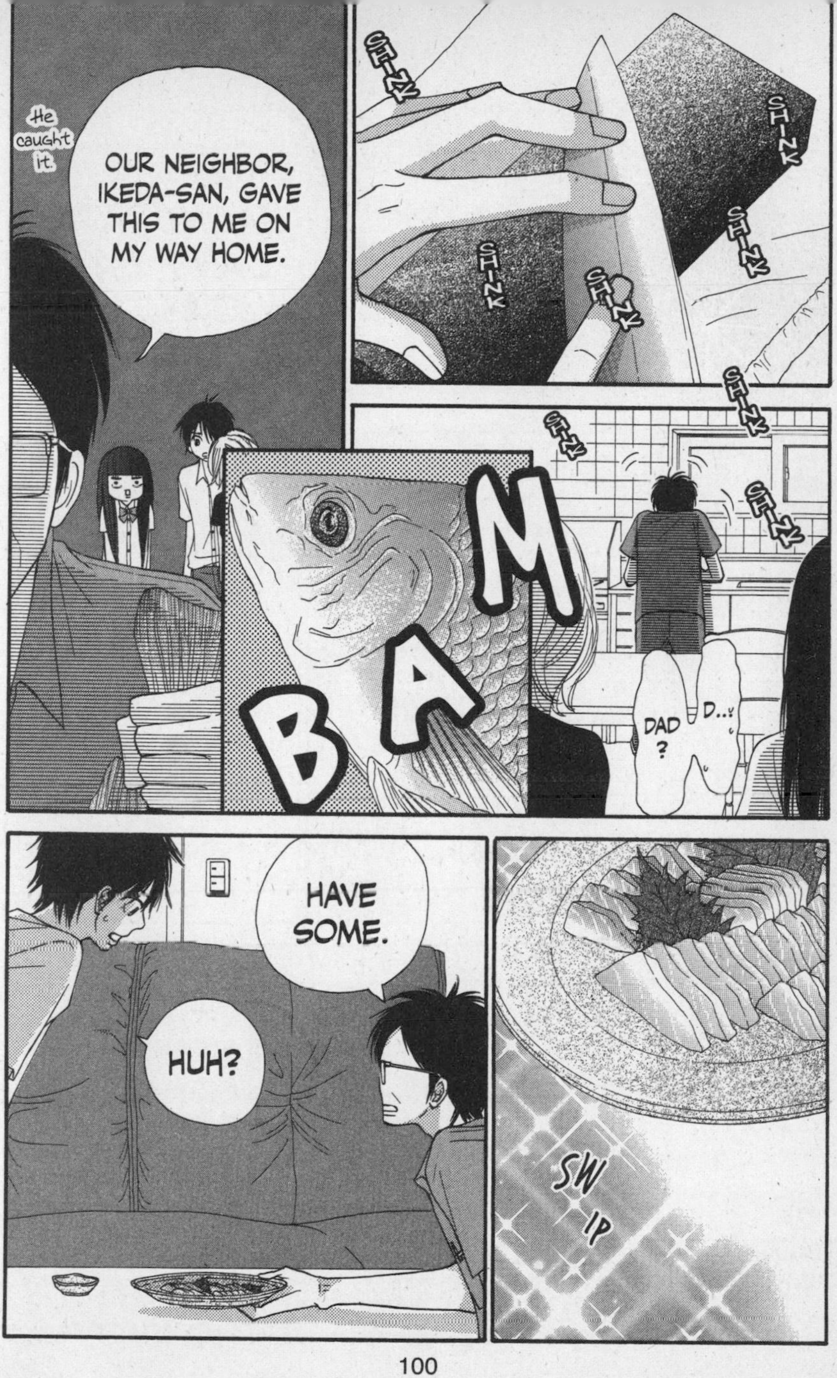
SHINK
SHINK
SHINK
SHINK
SHINK
SHINK
SHINK
SHINK
D...
DAD?
He caught it.
OUR NEIGHBOR, IKEDA-SAN, GAVE THIS TO ME ON MY WAY HOME.
BAM
SWIP
HAVE SOME.
HUH?

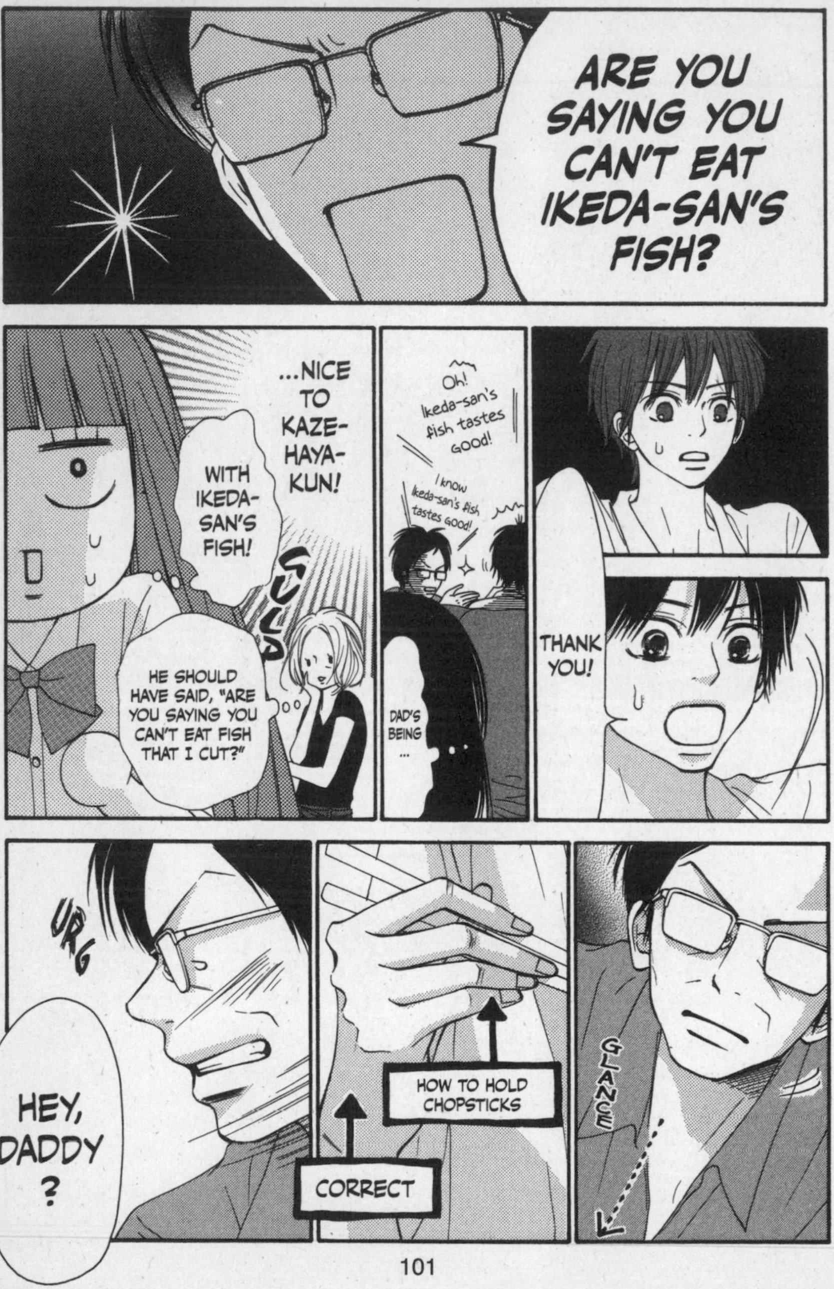
ARE YOU SAYING YOU CAN'T EAT IKEDA-SAN'S FISH?
THANK YOU!
Oh! Ikeda-san's fish tastes good!
I know Ikeda-san's fish tastes good!
DAD'S BEING ...
...NICE TO KAZE-HAYA-KUN!
WITH IKEDA-SAN'S FISH!
SULA
HE SHOULD HAVE SAID, "ARE YOU SAYING YOU CAN'T EAT FISH THAT I CUT?"
GLANCE
HOW TO HOLD CHOPSTICKS
CORRECT
URG
HEY, DADDY?

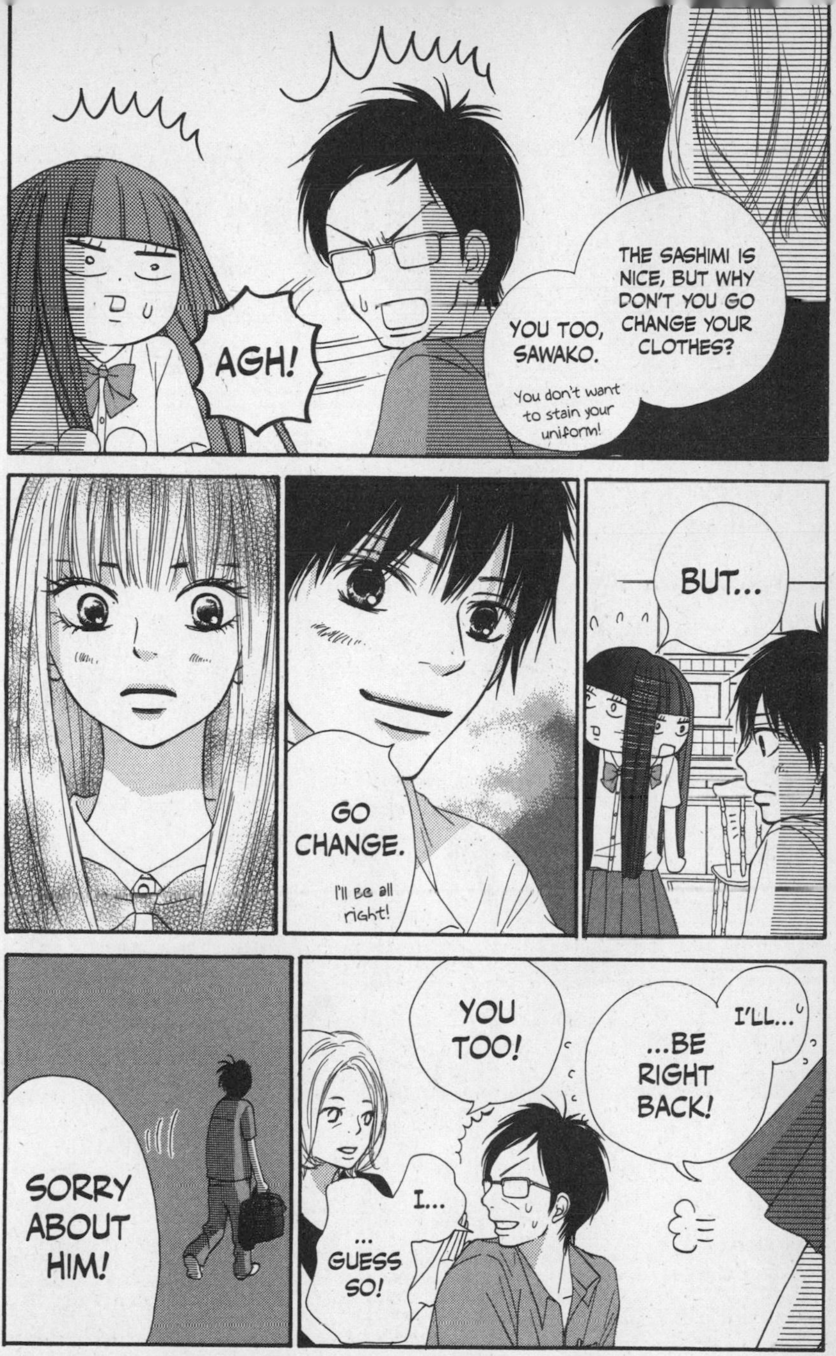
THE SASHIMI IS NICE, BUT WHY DON'T YOU GO CHANGE YOUR CLOTHES?
YOU TOO, SAWAKO.
You don't want to stain your uniform!
AGH!
BUT...
GO CHANGE.
I'll be all right!
I'LL...
...BE RIGHT BACK!
YOU TOO!
I...
...GUESS SO!
SORRY ABOUT HIM!

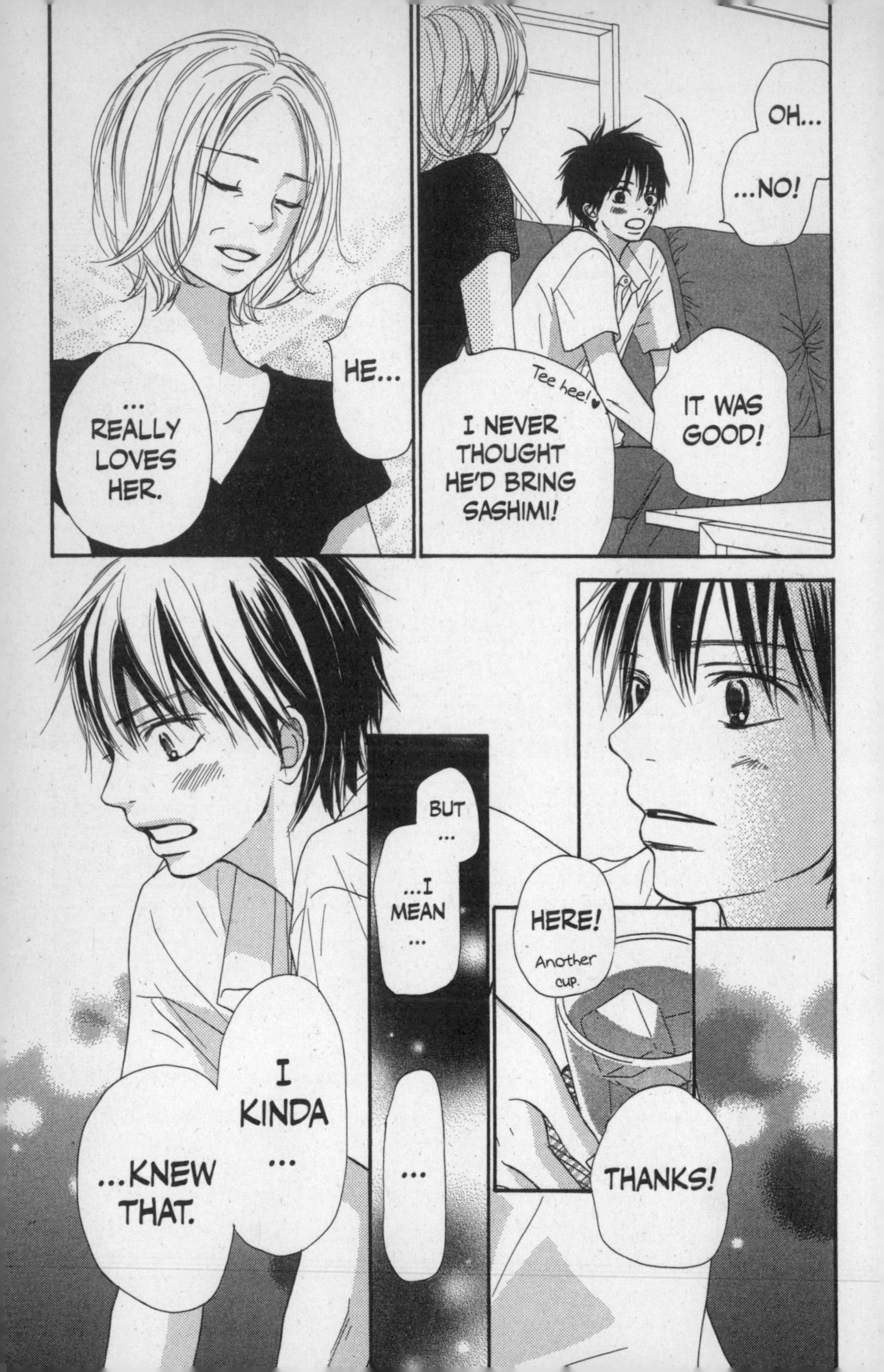
OH...
...NO!
IT WAS GOOD!
Tee hee!
I NEVER THOUGHT HE'D BRING SASHIMI!
HE...
...REALLY LOVES HER.
HERE!
Another cup.
THANKS!
BUT...
...I MEAN...
...
I KINDA...
...KNEW THAT.

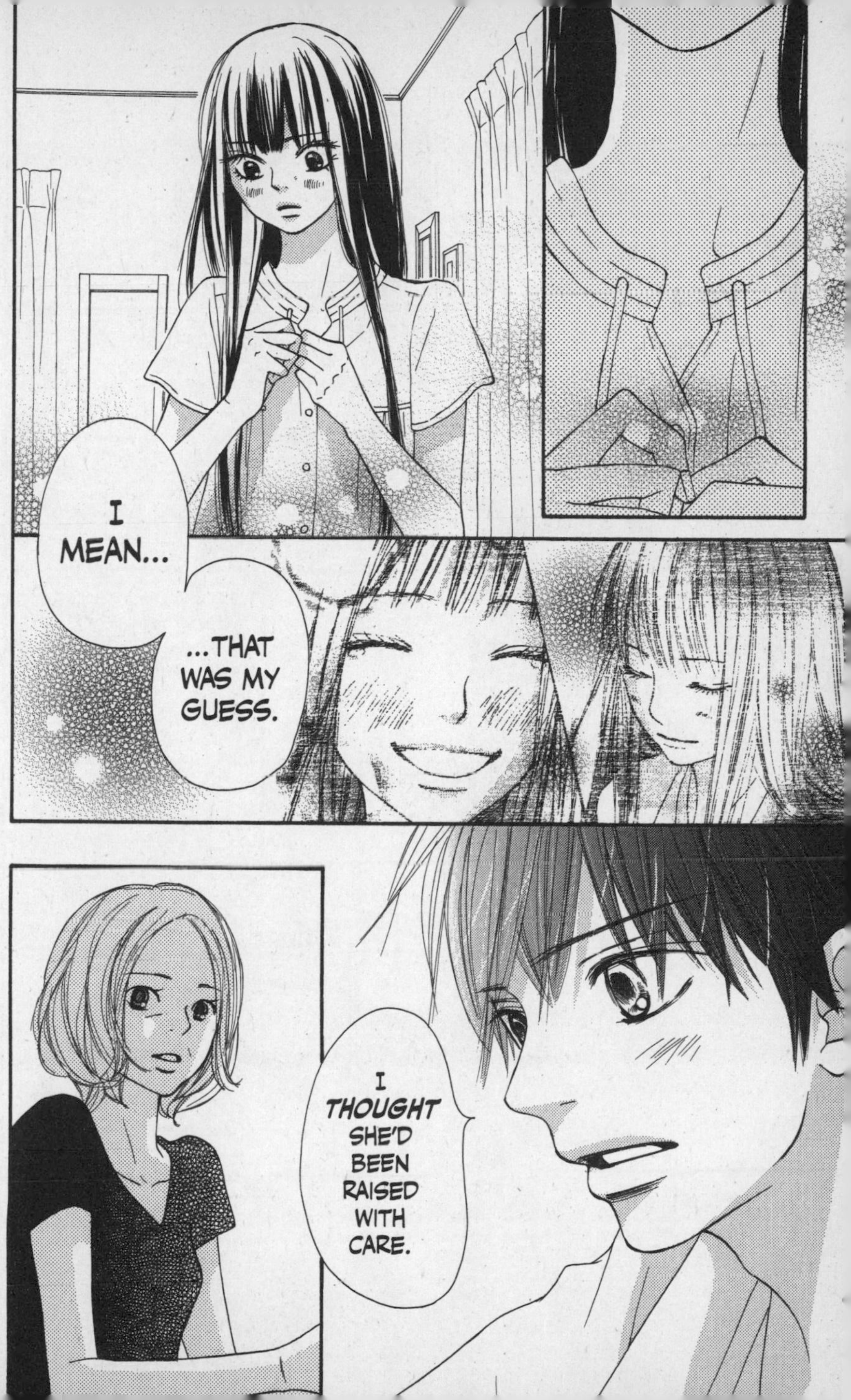
I MEAN...
...THAT WAS MY GUESS.
I THOUGHT SHE'D BEEN RAISED WITH CARE.

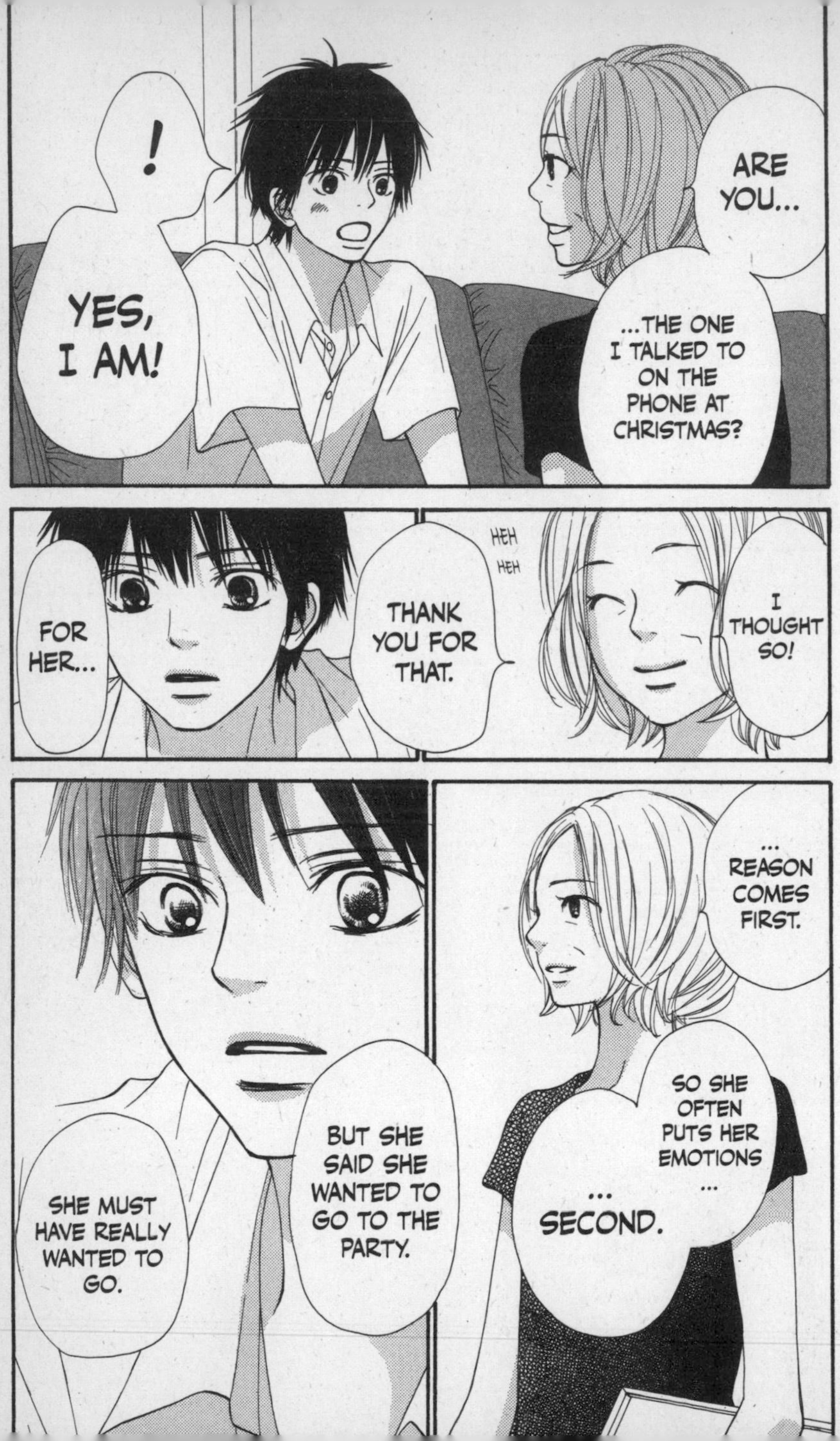
ARE YOU...
...THE ONE I TALKED TO ON THE PHONE AT CHRISTMAS?
!
YES, I AM!
I THOUGHT SO!
HEH HEH
THANK YOU FOR THAT.
FOR HER...
... REASON COMES FIRST.
SO SHE OFTEN PUTS HER EMOTIONS ... ... SECOND.
BUT SHE SAID SHE WANTED TO GO TO THE PARTY.
SHE MUST HAVE REALLY WANTED TO GO.

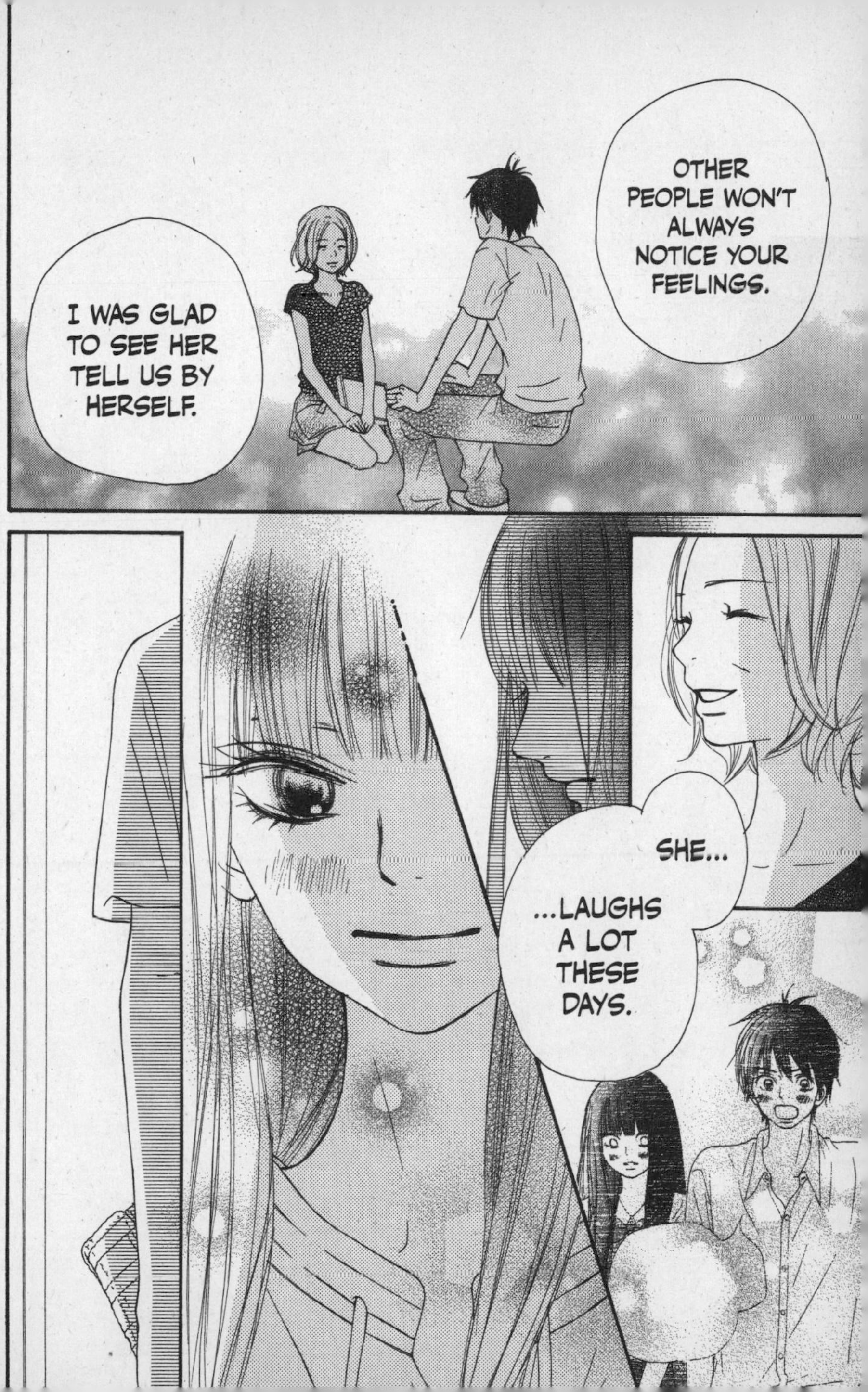
OTHER PEOPLE WON'T ALWAYS NOTICE YOUR FEELINGS.
I WAS GLAD TO SEE HER TELL US BY HERSELF.
SHE...
...LAUGHS A LOT THESE DAYS.

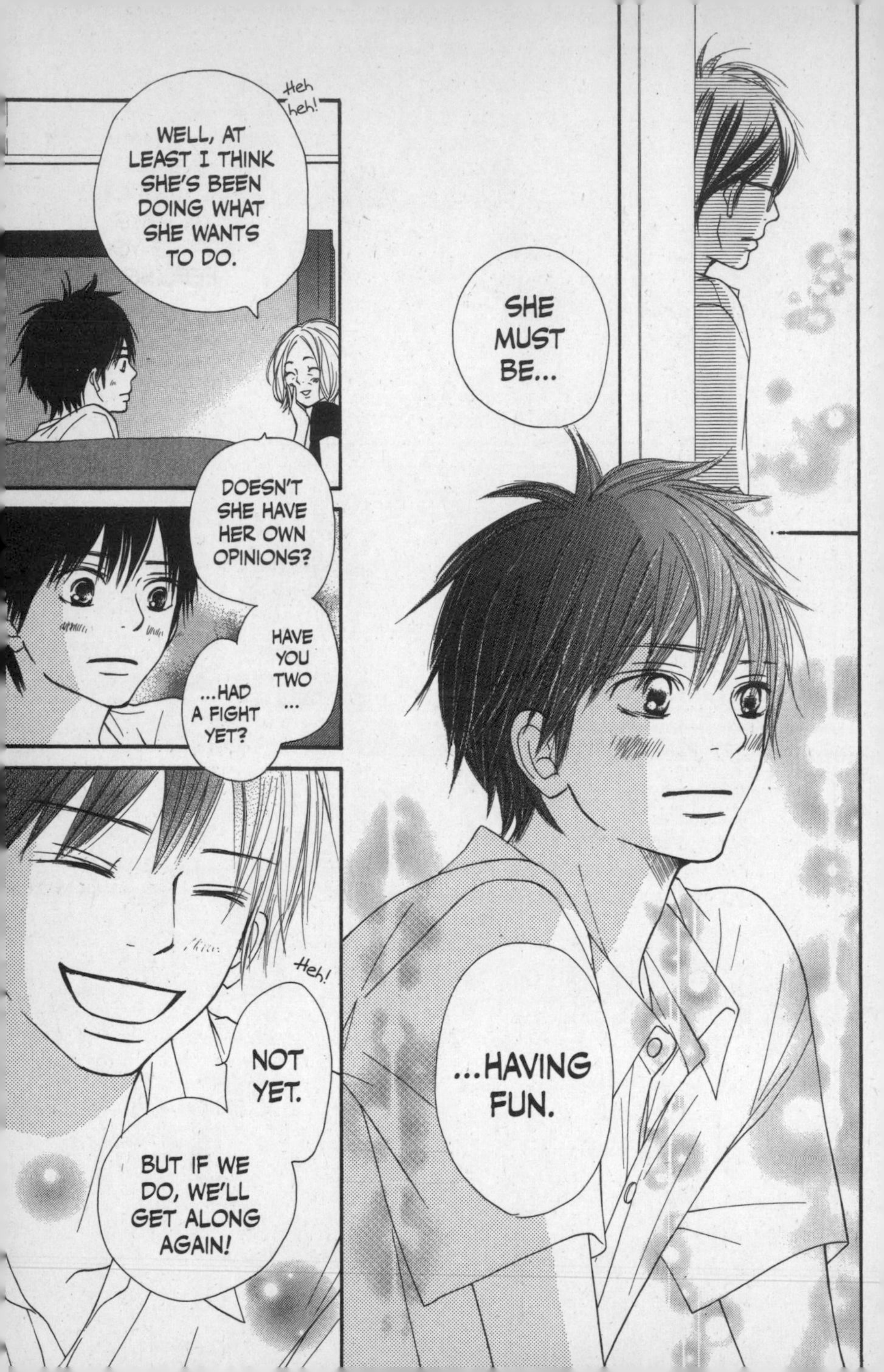
SHE MUST BE...
...HAVING FUN.
Heh heh!
WELL, AT LEAST I THINK SHE'S BEEN DOING WHAT SHE WANTS TO DO.
DOESN'T SHE HAVE HER OWN OPINIONS?
HAVE YOU TWO...
...HAD A FIGHT YET?
Heh!
NOT YET.
BUT IF WE DO, WE'LL GET ALONG AGAIN!

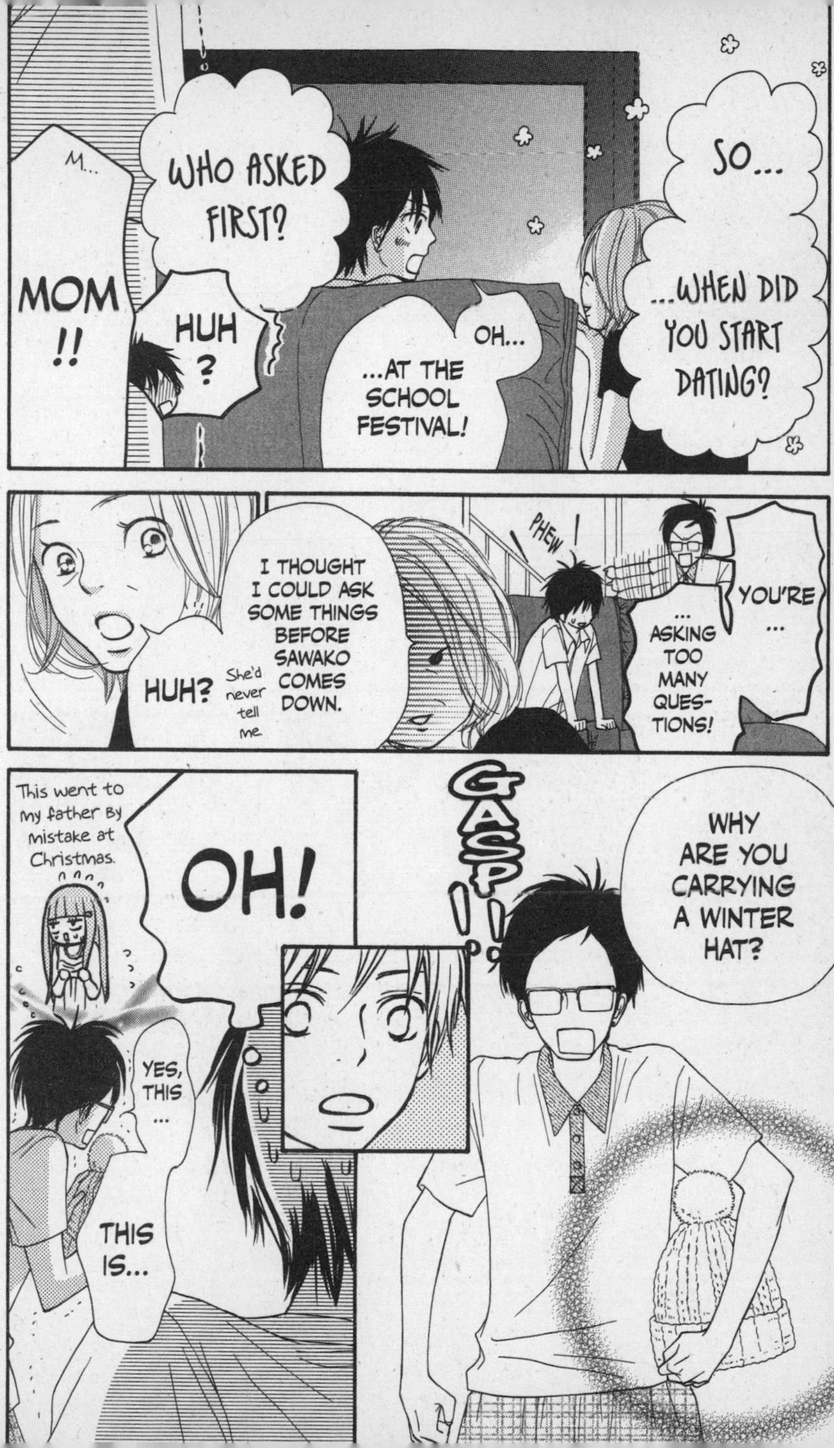
SO...
...WHEN DID YOU START DATING?
OH...
...AT THE SCHOOL FESTIVAL!
HUH ?
WHO ASKED FIRST?
M...
MOM !!
YOU'RE ...
... ASKING TOO MANY QUES-TIONS!
PHEW !
I THOUGHT I COULD ASK SOME THINGS BEFORE SAWAKO COMES DOWN.
She'd never tell me.
HUH?
WHY ARE YOU CARRYING A WINTER HAT?
GASP !!
OH!
This went to my father By mistake at Christmas.
YES, THIS ...
THIS IS...

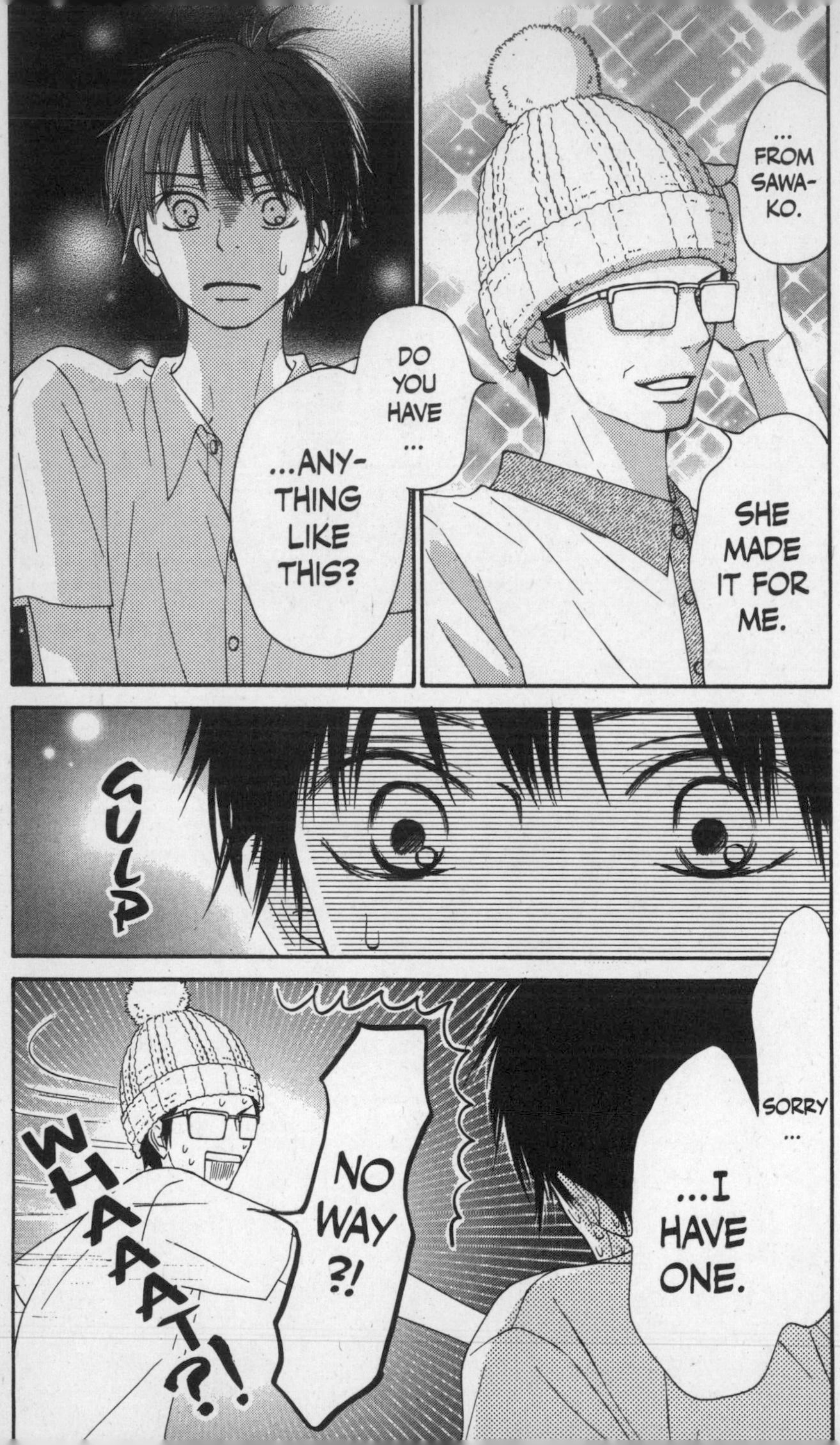
... FROM SAWA-KO.
SHE MADE IT FOR ME.
DO YOU HAVE ...
...ANY-THING LIKE THIS?
GULP
SORRY ...
...I HAVE ONE.
NO WAY ?!
WHAAAT?!

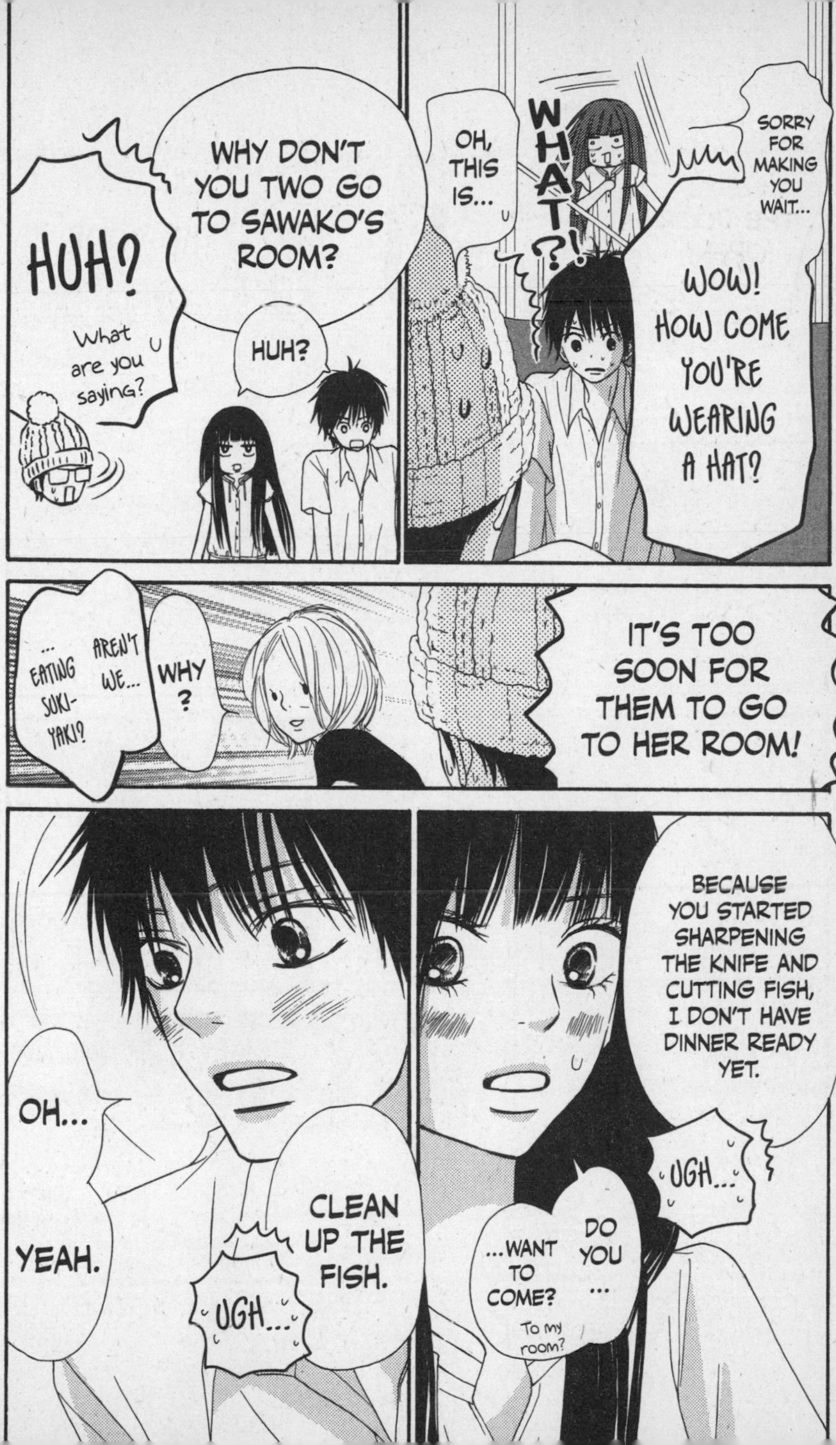
SORRY FOR MAKING YOU WAIT...
WOW! HOW COME YOU'RE WEARING A HAT?
WHAT?!
OH, THIS IS...
WHY DON'T YOU TWO GO TO SAWAKO'S ROOM?
HUH?
What are you saying?
HUH?
IT'S TOO SOON FOR THEM TO GO TO HER ROOM!
WHY?
AREN'T WE... ...EATING SUKI-YAKI?
BECAUSE YOU STARTED SHARPENING THE KNIFE AND CUTTING FISH, I DON'T HAVE DINNER READY YET.
UGH...
DO YOU ...
...WANT TO COME?
To my room?
OH...
YEAH.
CLEAN UP THE FISH.
UGH...

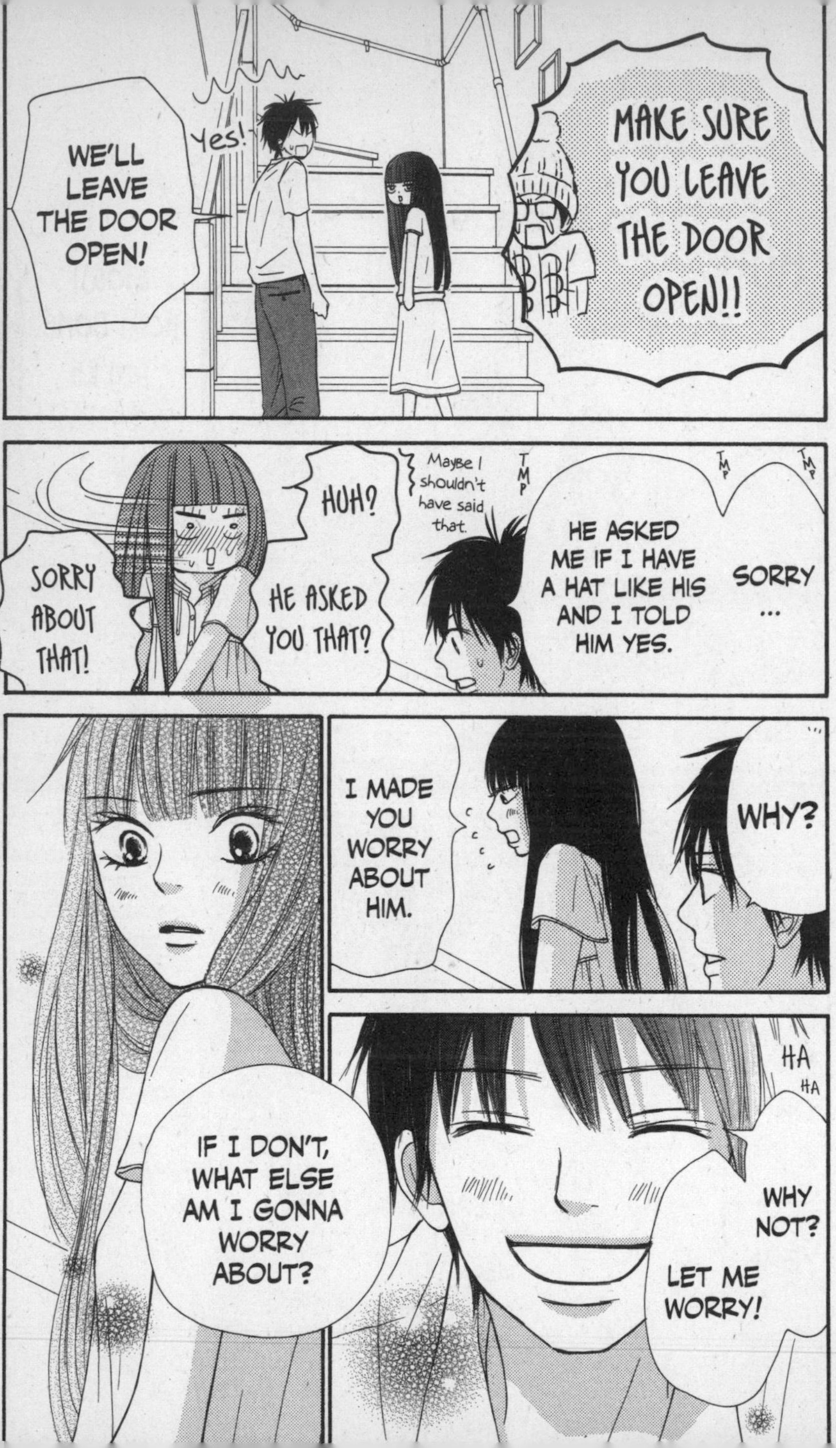
MAKE SURE YOU LEAVE THE DOOR OPEN!!
Yes!
WE'LL LEAVE THE DOOR OPEN!
TMP
TMP
SORRY ...
HE ASKED ME IF I HAVE A HAT LIKE HIS AND I TOLD HIM YES.
TMP
Maybe I shouldn't have said that.
HUH?
HE ASKED YOU THAT?
SORRY ABOUT THAT!
...
WHY?
I MADE YOU WORRY ABOUT HIM.
HA
HA
WHY NOT?
LET ME WORRY!
IF I DON'T, WHAT ELSE AM I GONNA WORRY ABOUT?

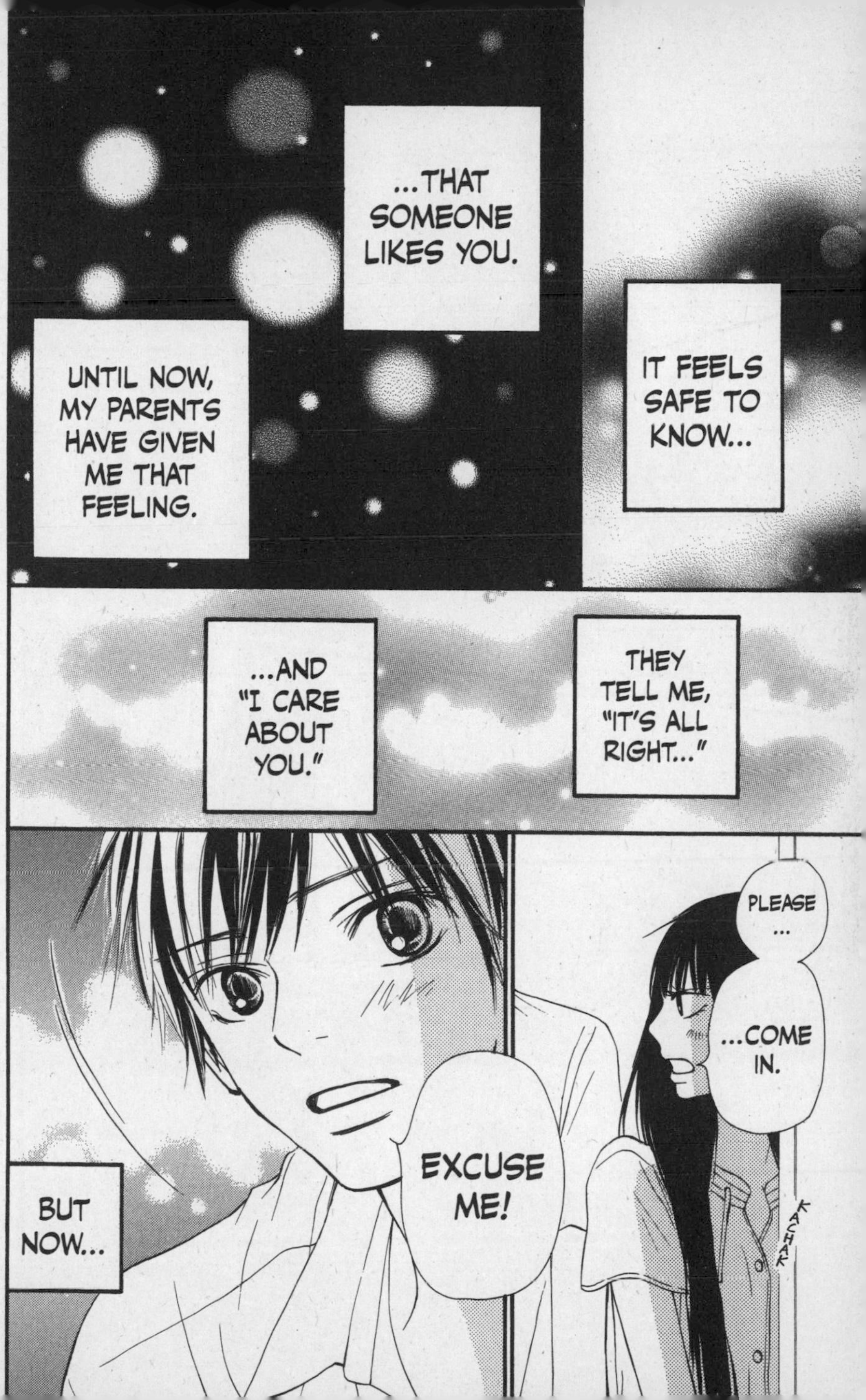
IT FEELS SAFE TO KNOW...
...THAT SOMEONE LIKES YOU.
UNTIL NOW, MY PARENTS HAVE GIVEN ME THAT FEELING.
THEY TELL ME, "IT'S ALL RIGHT..."
...AND "I CARE ABOUT YOU."
PLEASE...
...COME IN.
KACHAK
EXCUSE ME!
BUT NOW...

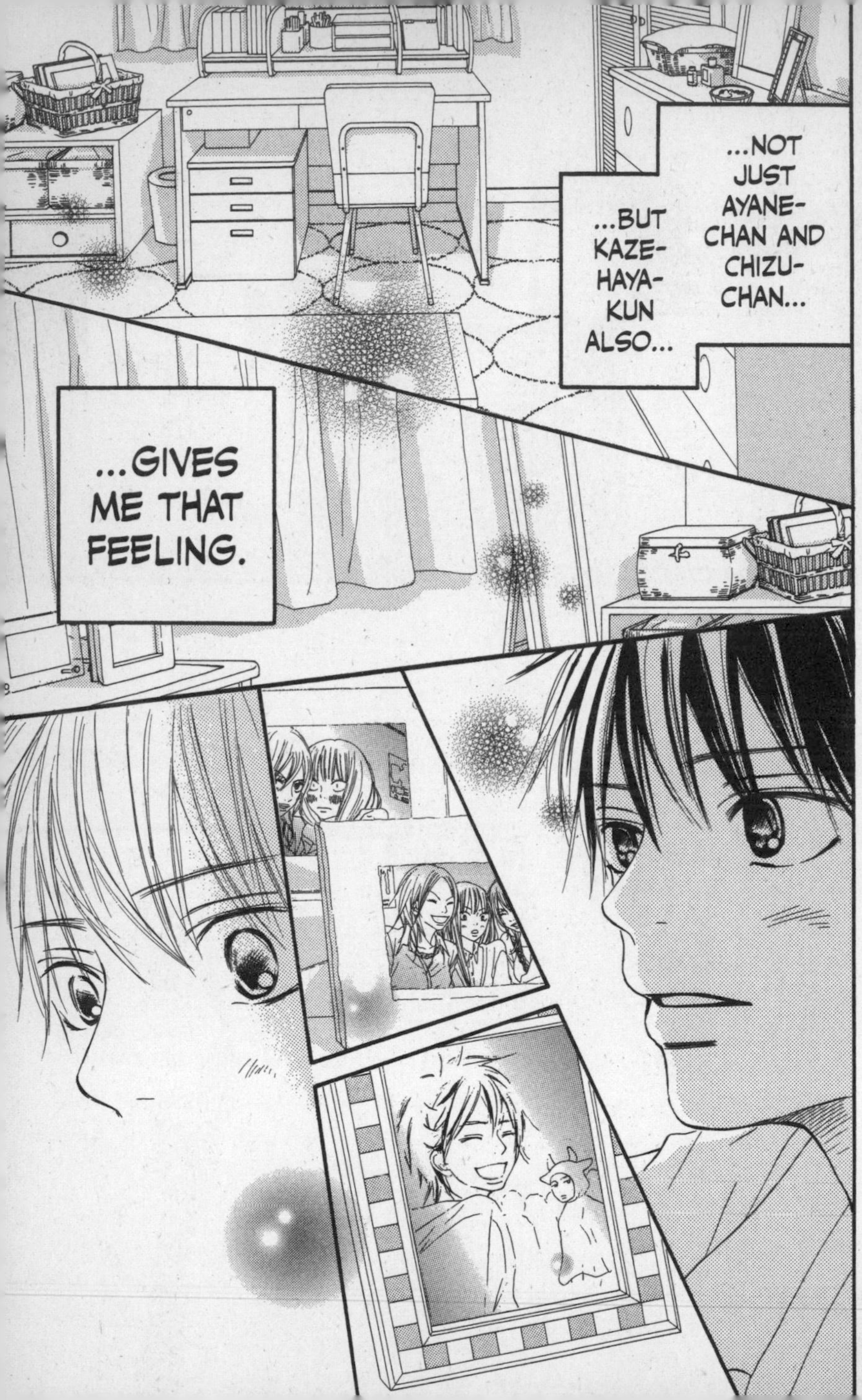
...NOT JUST AYANE-CHAN AND CHIZU-CHAN...
...BUT KAZE-HAYA-KUN ALSO...
...GIVES ME THAT FEELING.

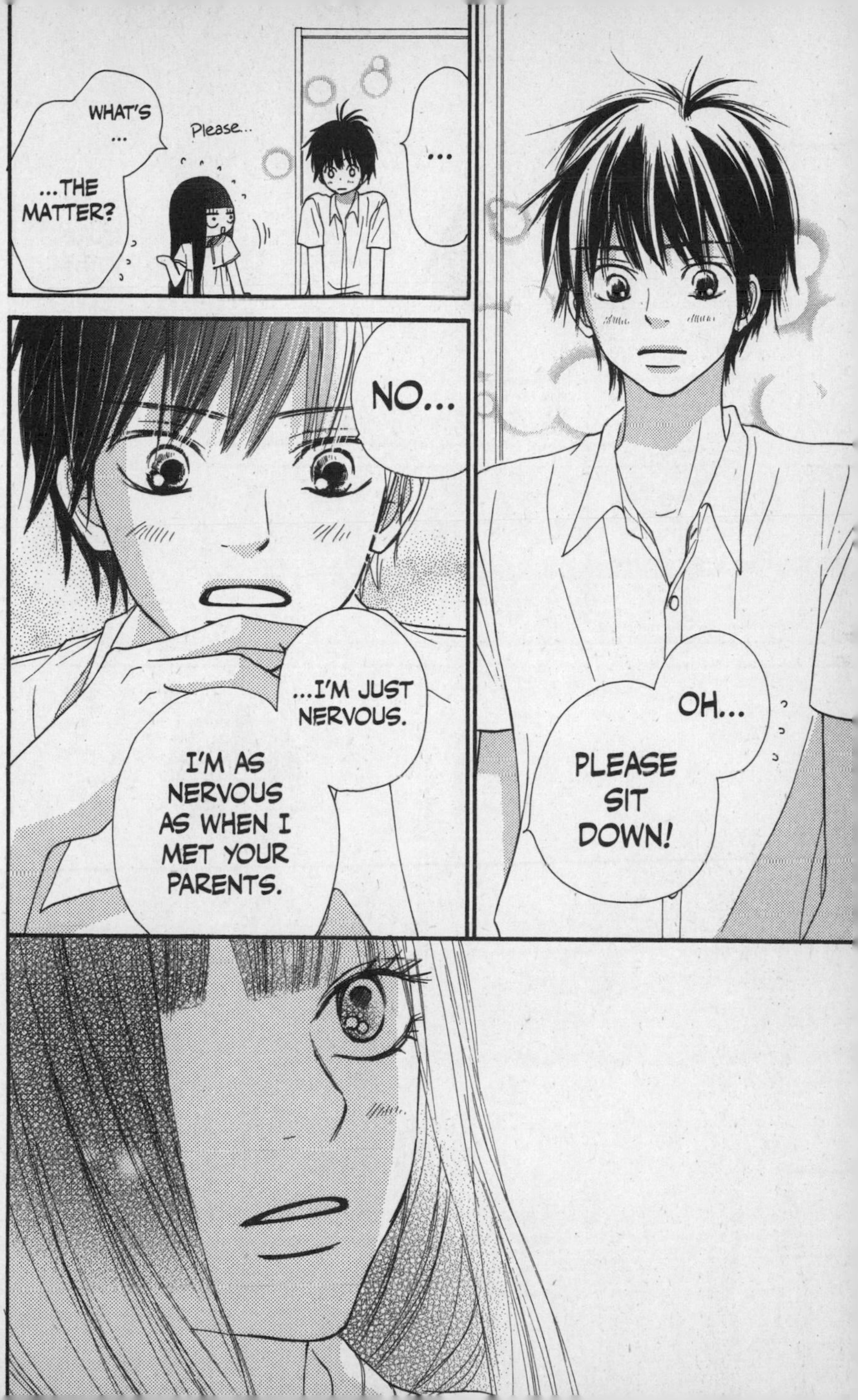
OH...
PLEASE SIT DOWN!
...
Please...
WHAT'S ...
...THE MATTER?
NO...
...I'M JUST NERVOUS.
I'M AS NERVOUS AS WHEN I MET YOUR PARENTS.

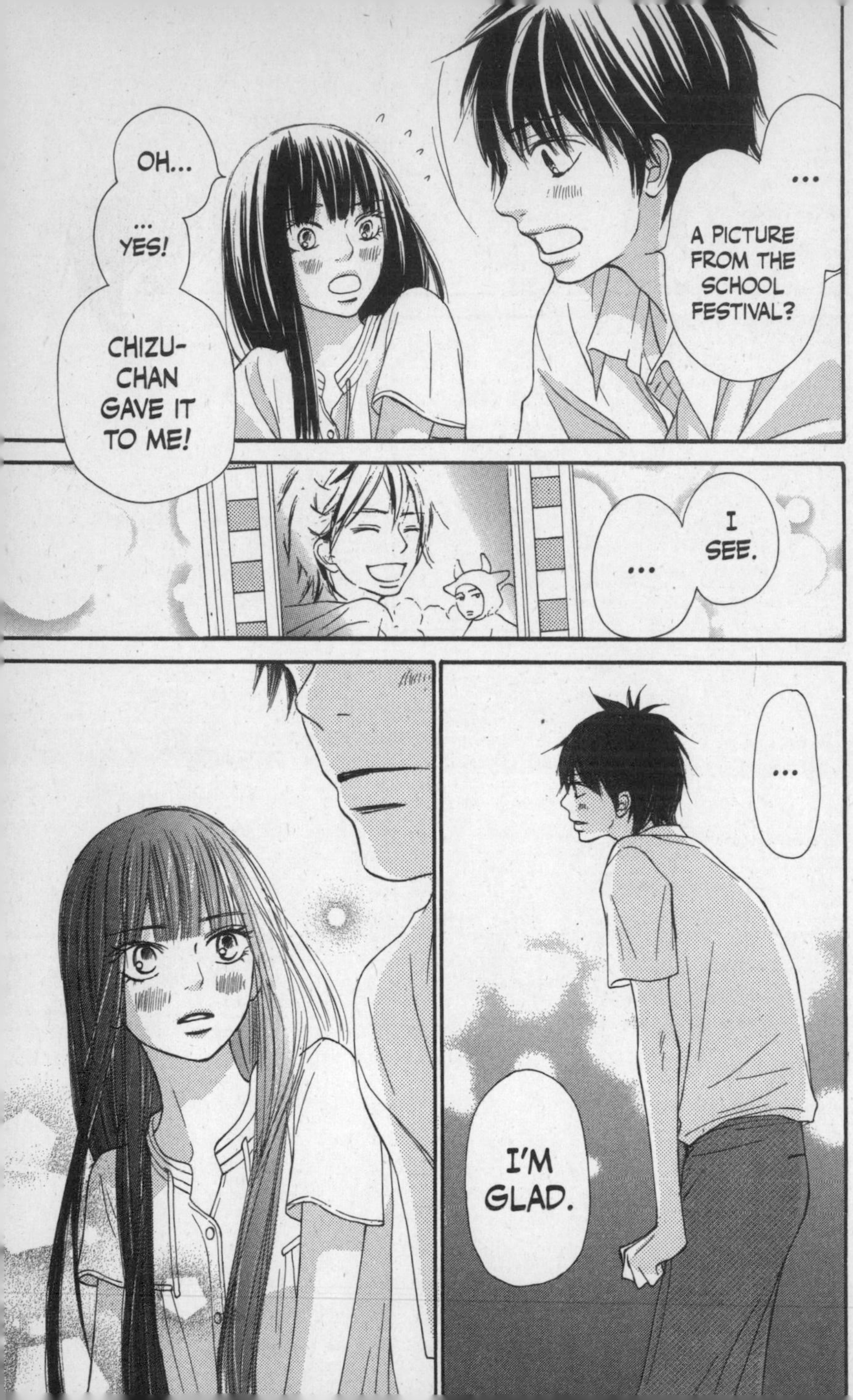
... A PICTURE FROM THE SCHOOL FESTIVAL?
OH...
... YES!
CHIZU-CHAN GAVE IT TO ME!
... I SEE.
...
I'M GLAD.

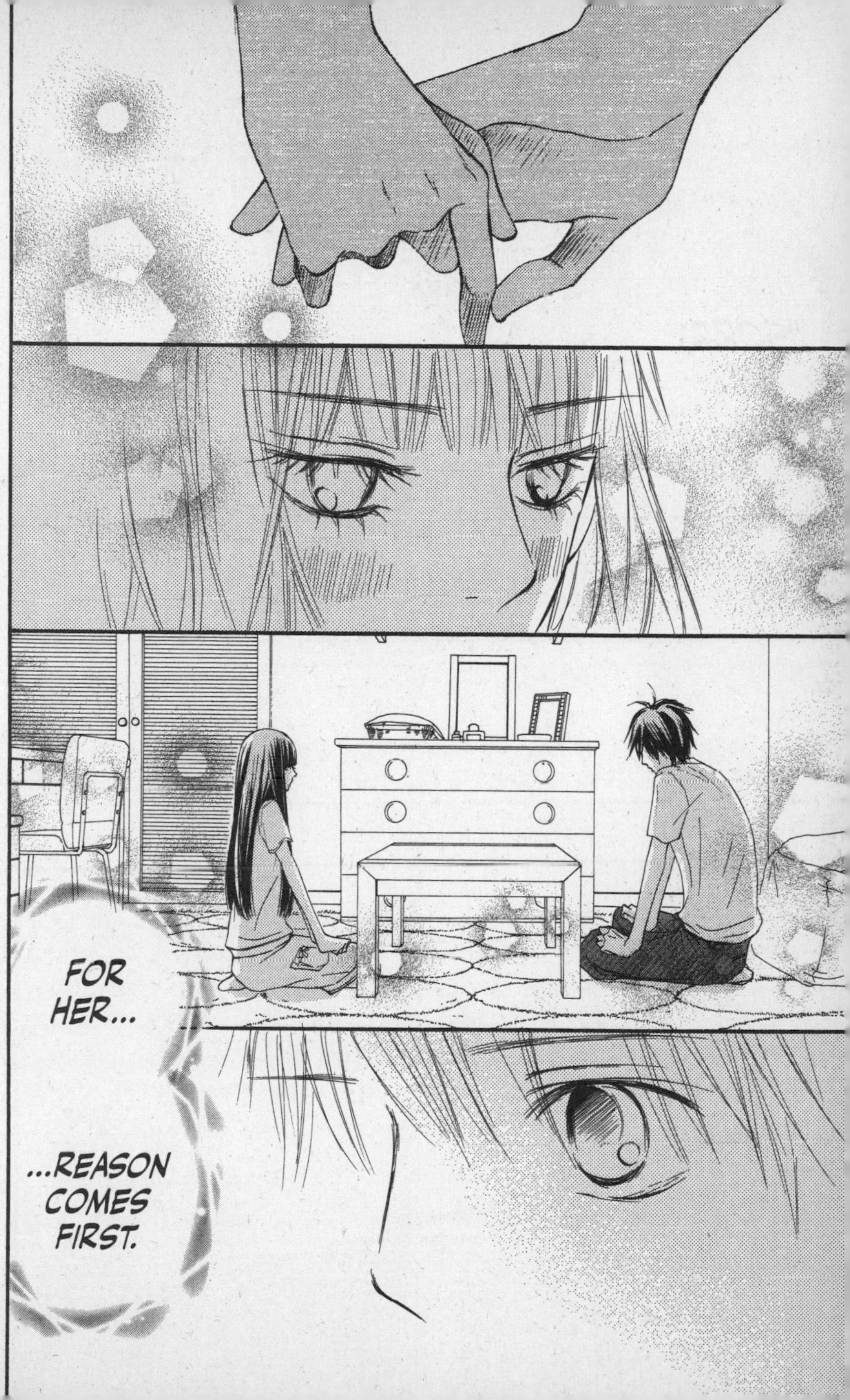
FOR HER...
...REASON COMES FIRST.

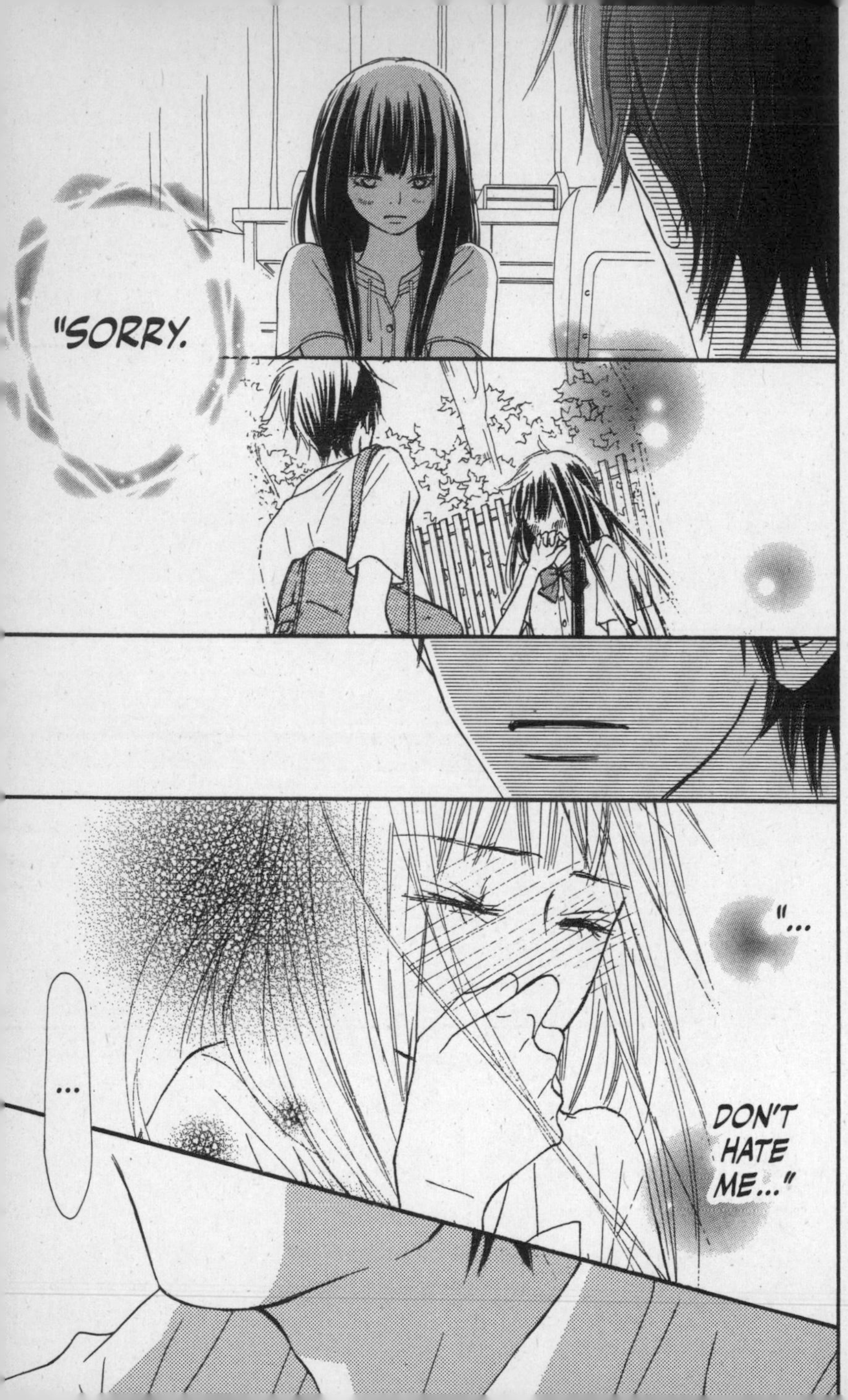
"SORRY.
"...
DON'T HATE ME..."
...

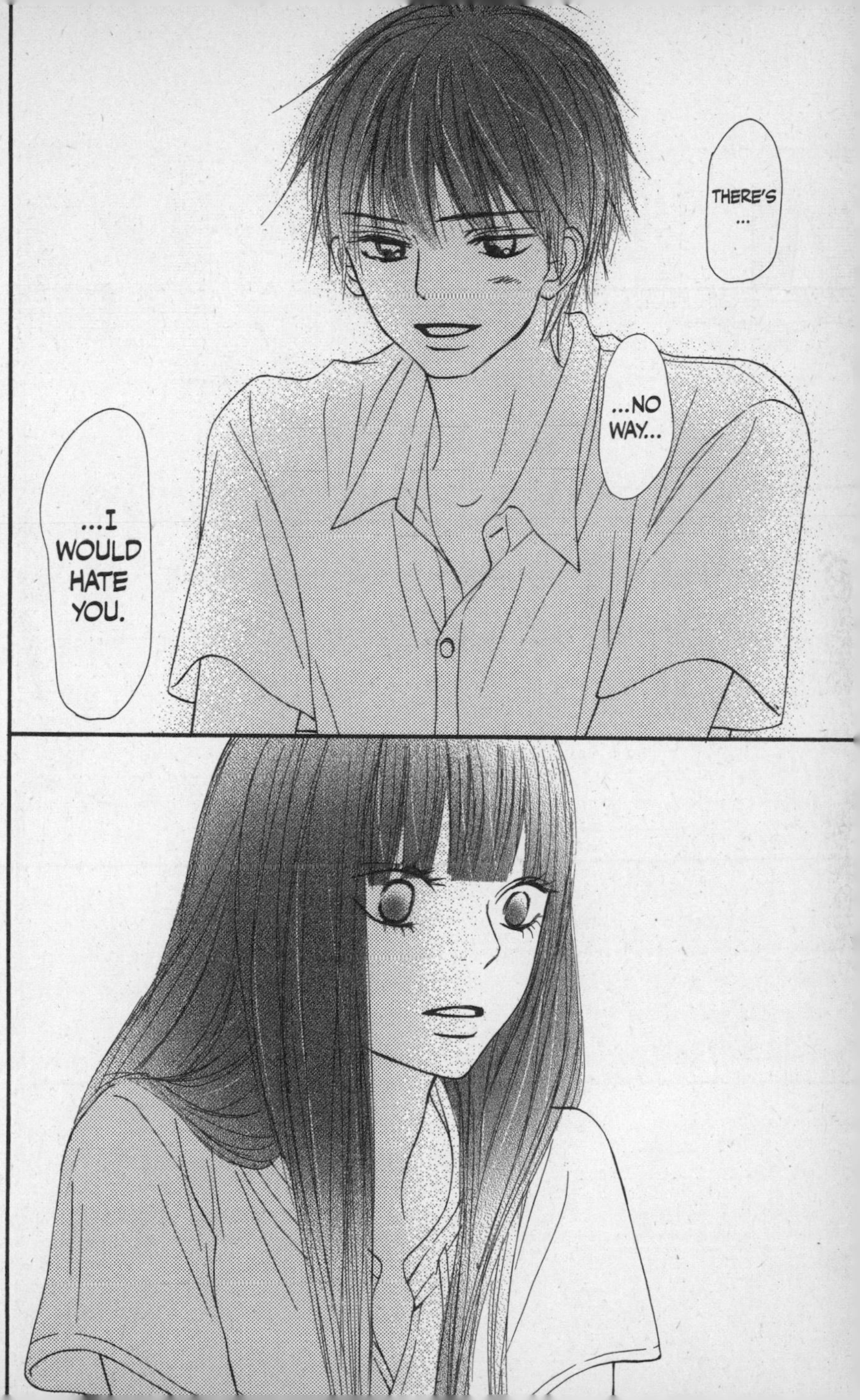
THERE'S ...
...NO WAY...
...I WOULD HATE YOU.

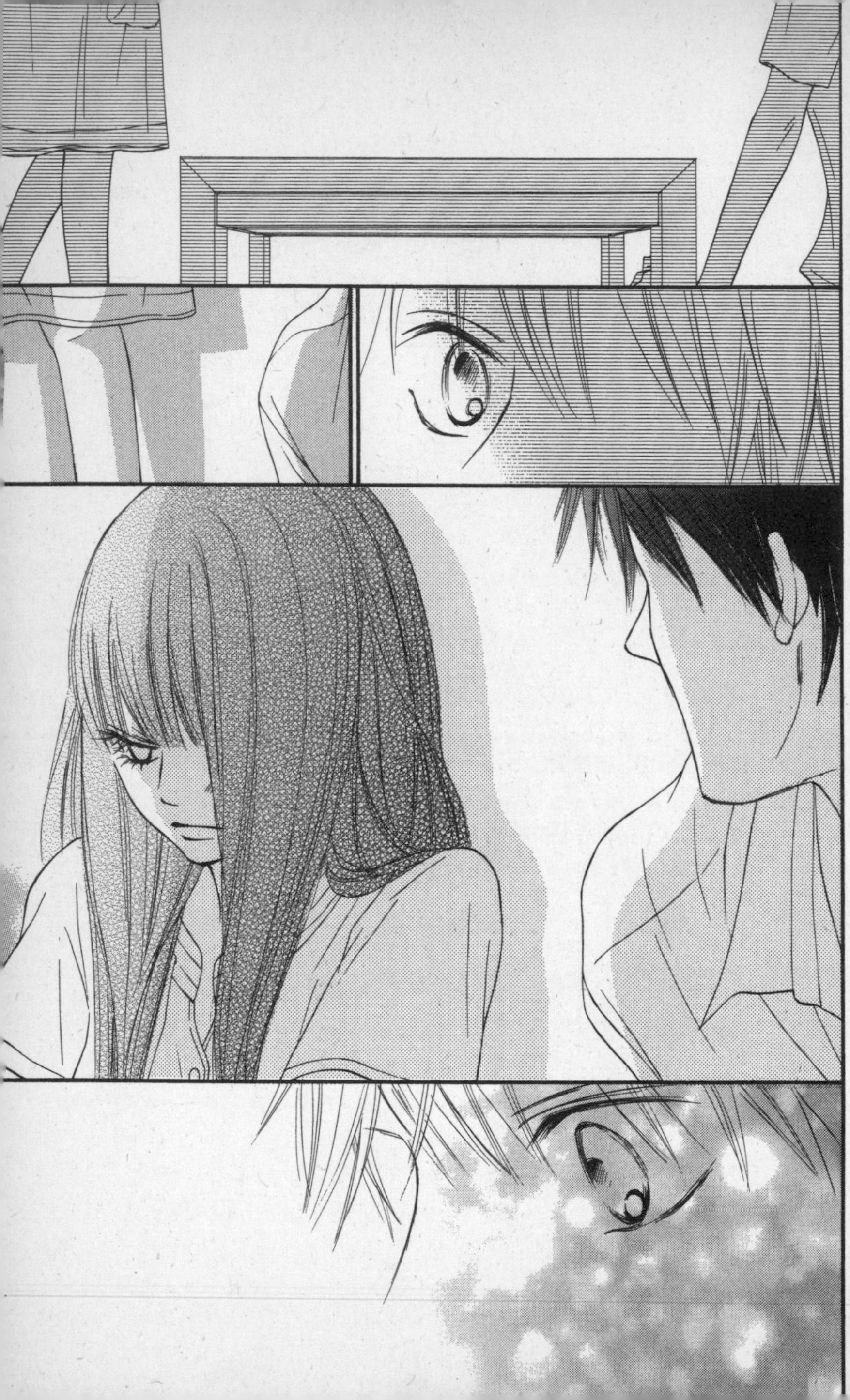

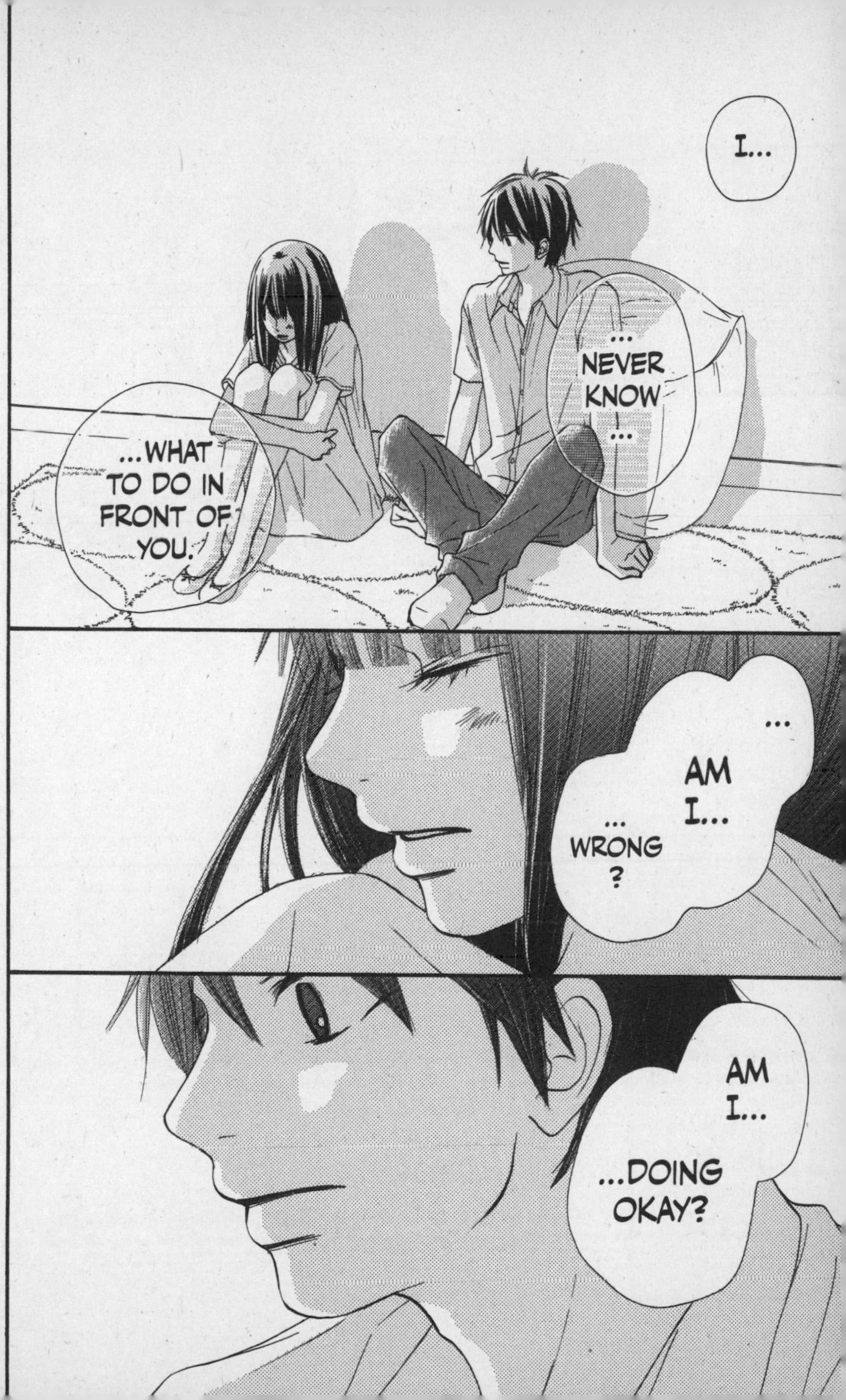
I...
...NEVER KNOW...
...WHAT TO DO IN FRONT OF YOU.
... AM I...
...WRONG?
AM I...
...DOING OKAY?

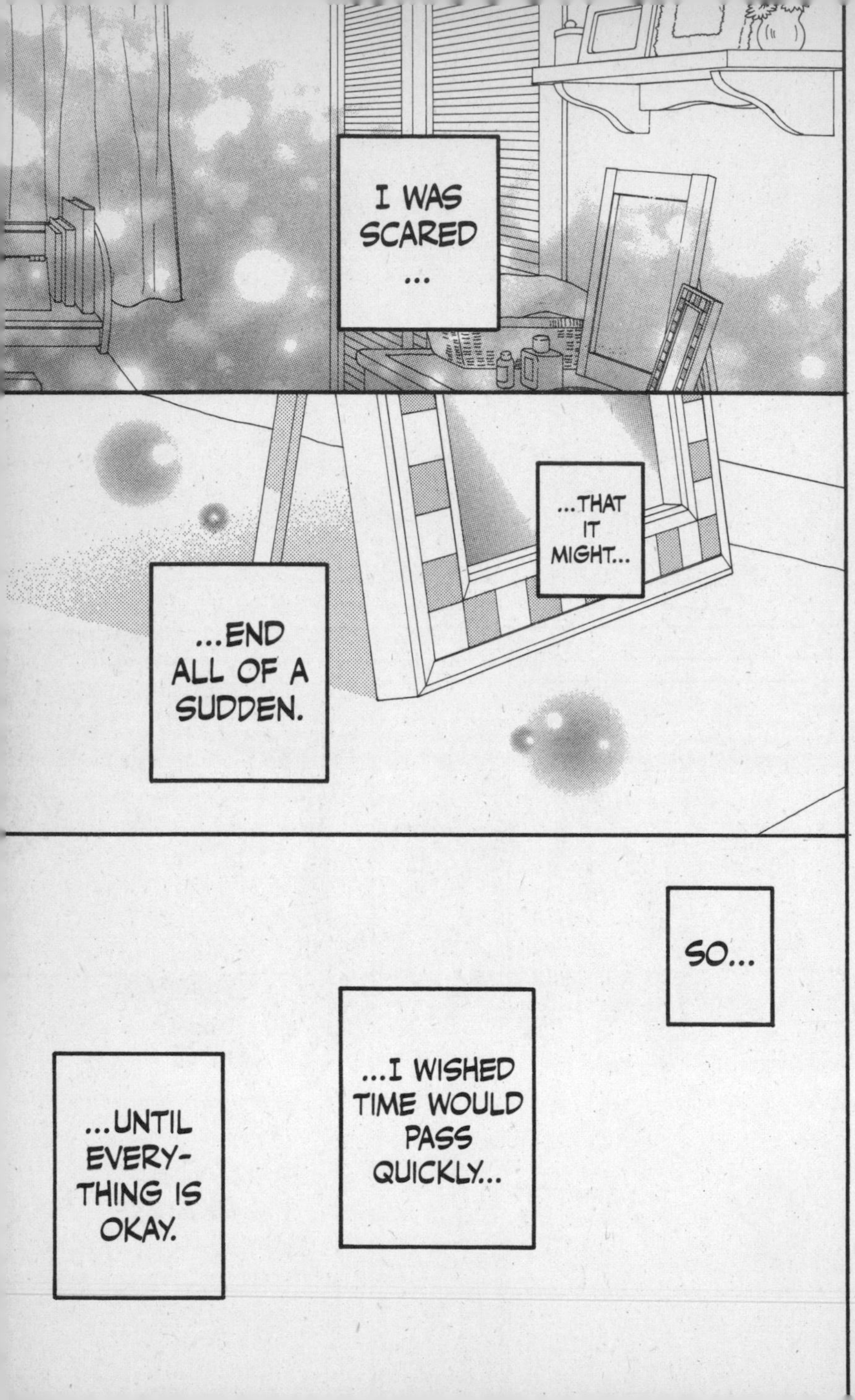
I WAS SCARED ...
...THAT IT MIGHT...
...END ALL OF A SUDDEN.
SO...
...I WISHED TIME WOULD PASS QUICKLY...
...UNTIL EVERY-THING IS OKAY.

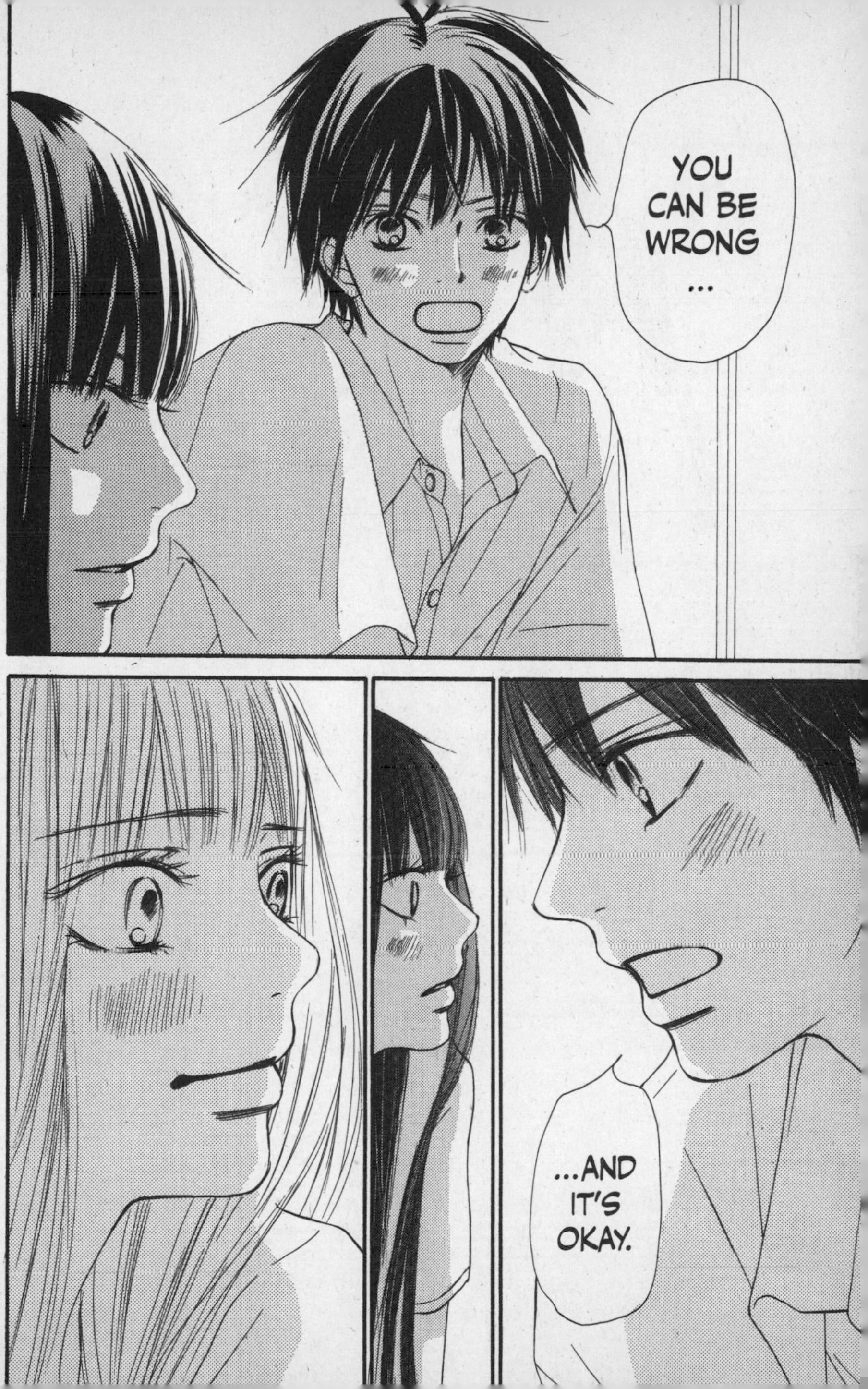
YOU CAN BE WRONG ...
...AND IT'S OKAY.

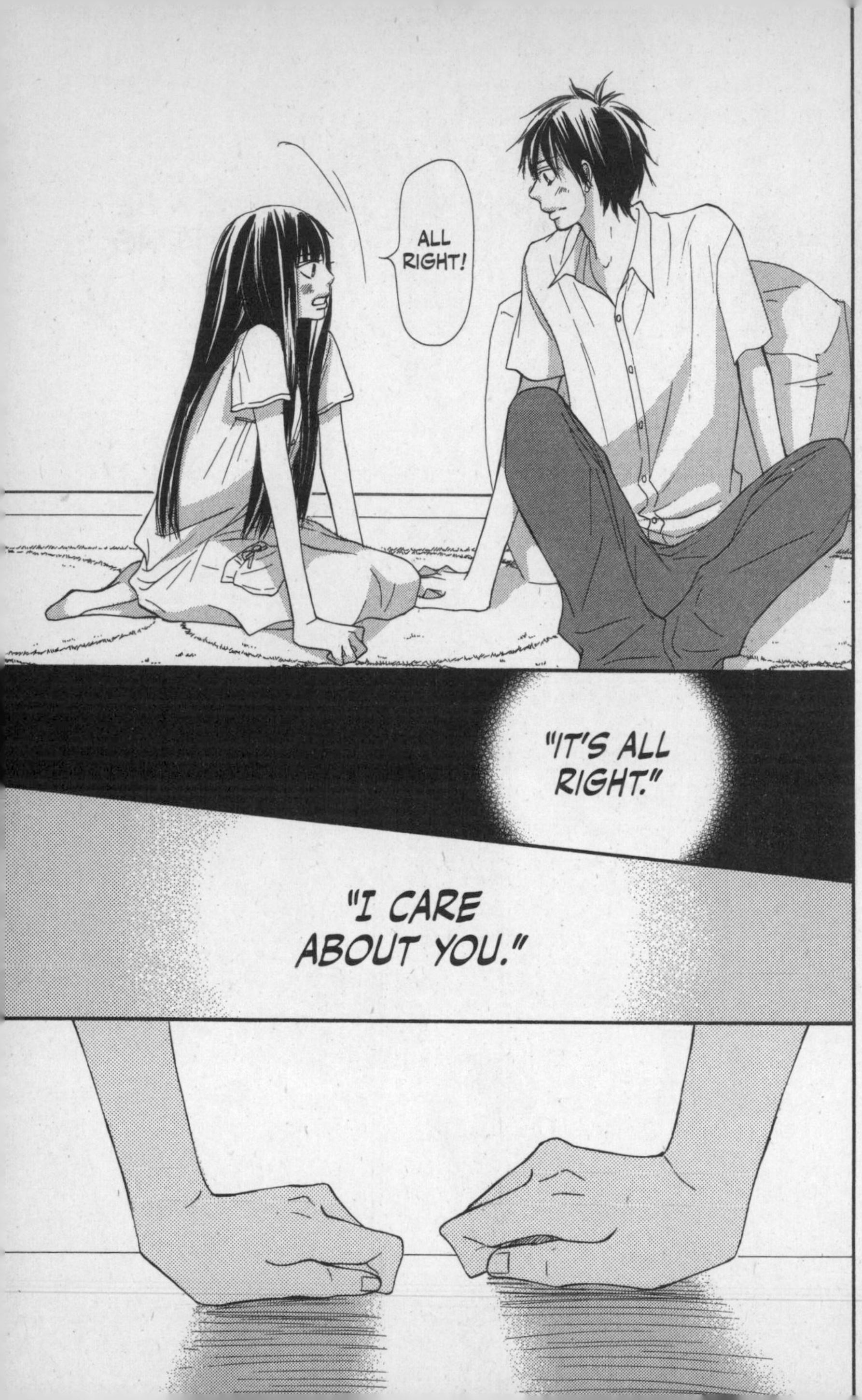
ALL RIGHT!
"IT'S ALL RIGHT."
"I CARE ABOUT YOU."

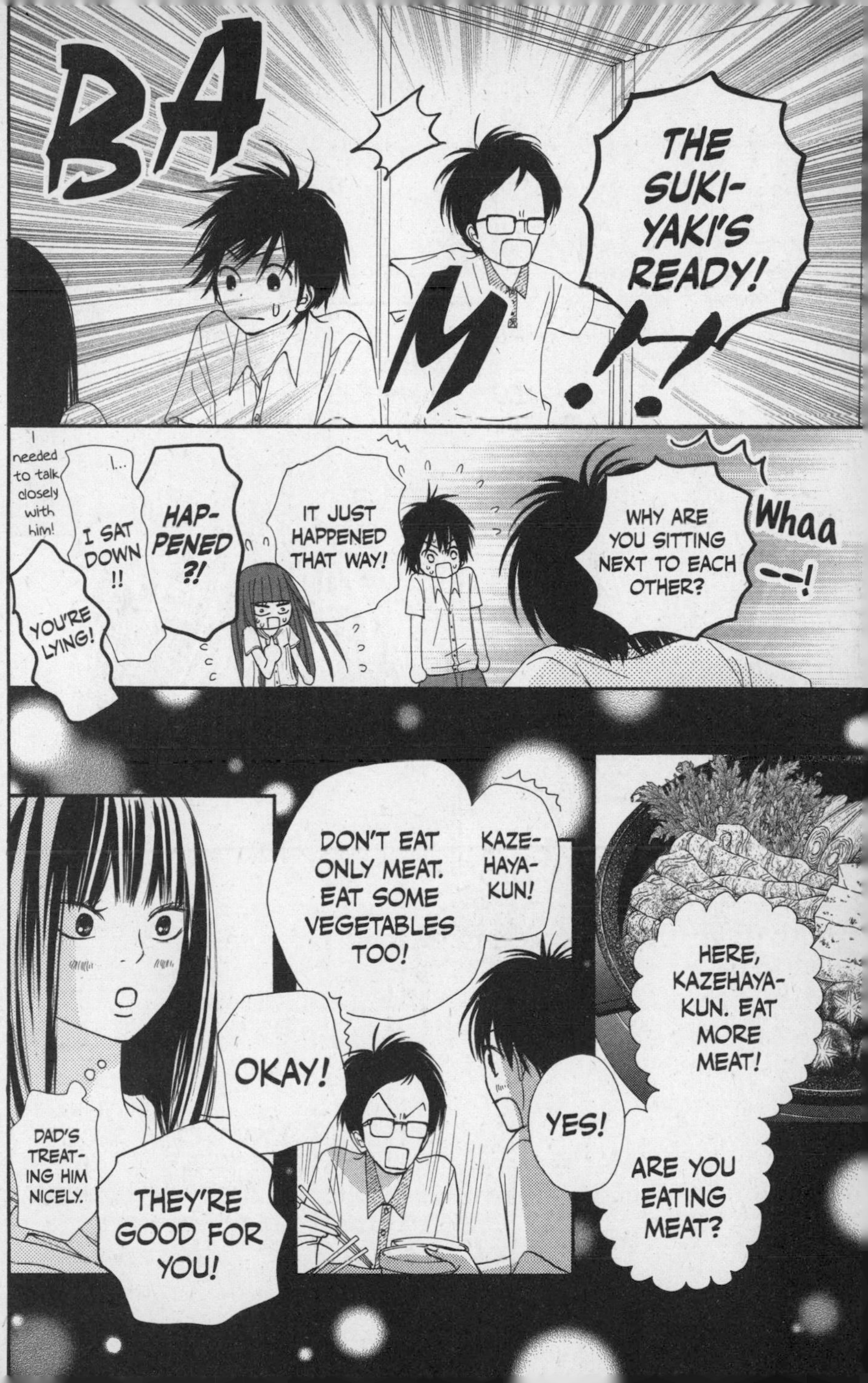
THE SUKI-YAKI'S READY!
BAM!!
Whaa--!
WHY ARE YOU SITTING NEXT TO EACH OTHER?
IT JUST HAPPENED THAT WAY!
HAP-PENED?!
I SAT DOWN!!
I...
I needed to talk closely with him!
YOU'RE LYING!
HERE, KAZEHAYA-KUN. EAT MORE MEAT!
YES!
ARE YOU EATING MEAT?
KAZE-HAYA-KUN!
DON'T EAT ONLY MEAT. EAT SOME VEGETABLES TOO!
OKAY!
THEY'RE GOOD FOR YOU!
DAD'S TREAT-ING HIM NICELY.

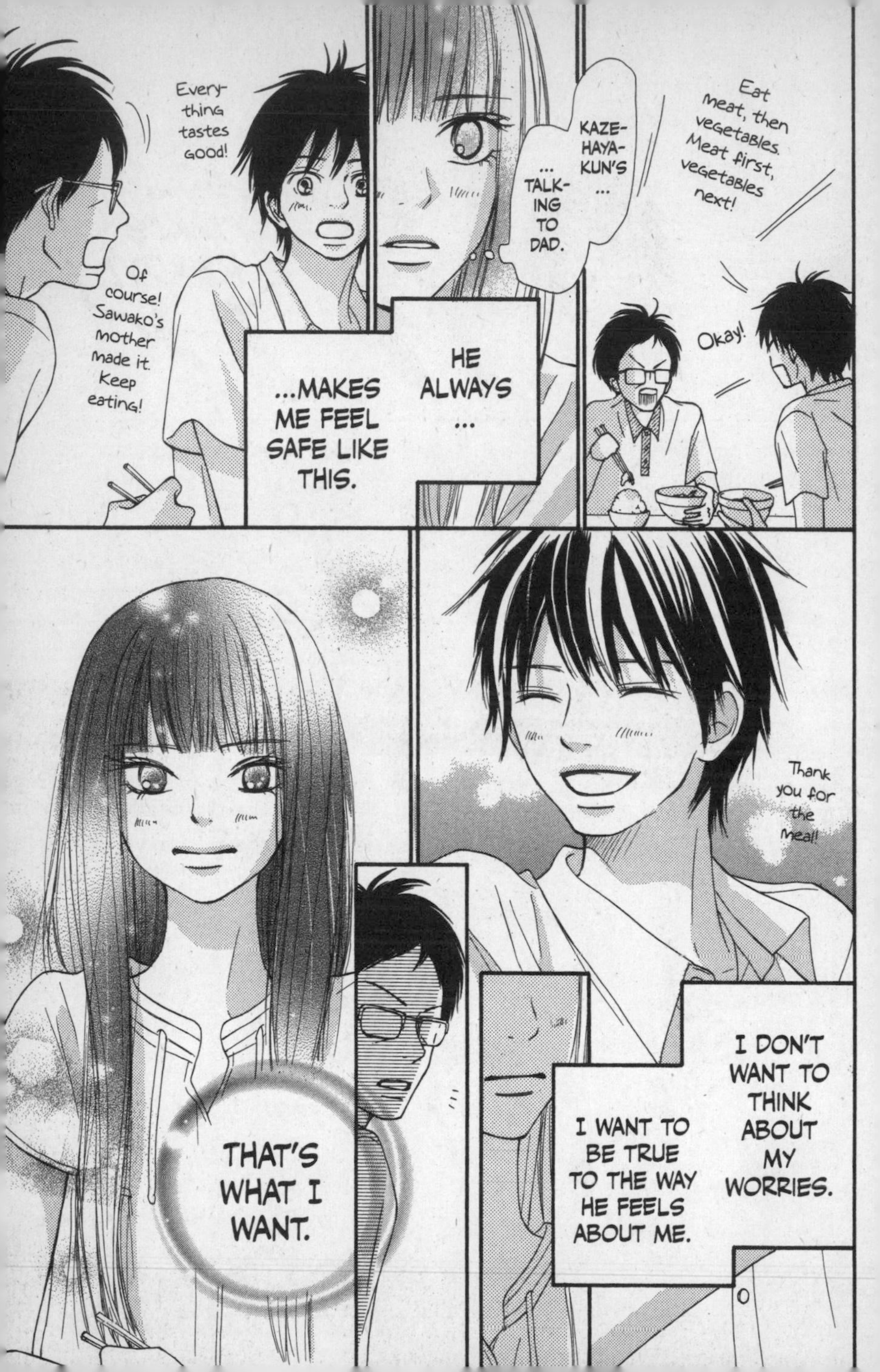
Eat meat, then vegetables. Meat first, vegetables next!
Okay!
KAZEHAYA-KUN'S ... TALKING TO DAD.
HE ALWAYS ...
...MAKES ME FEEL SAFE LIKE THIS.
Everything tastes good!
Of course! Sawako's mother made it. Keep eating!
Thank you for the meal!
I DON'T WANT TO THINK ABOUT MY WORRIES.
I WANT TO BE TRUE TO THE WAY HE FEELS ABOUT ME.
THAT'S WHAT I WANT.

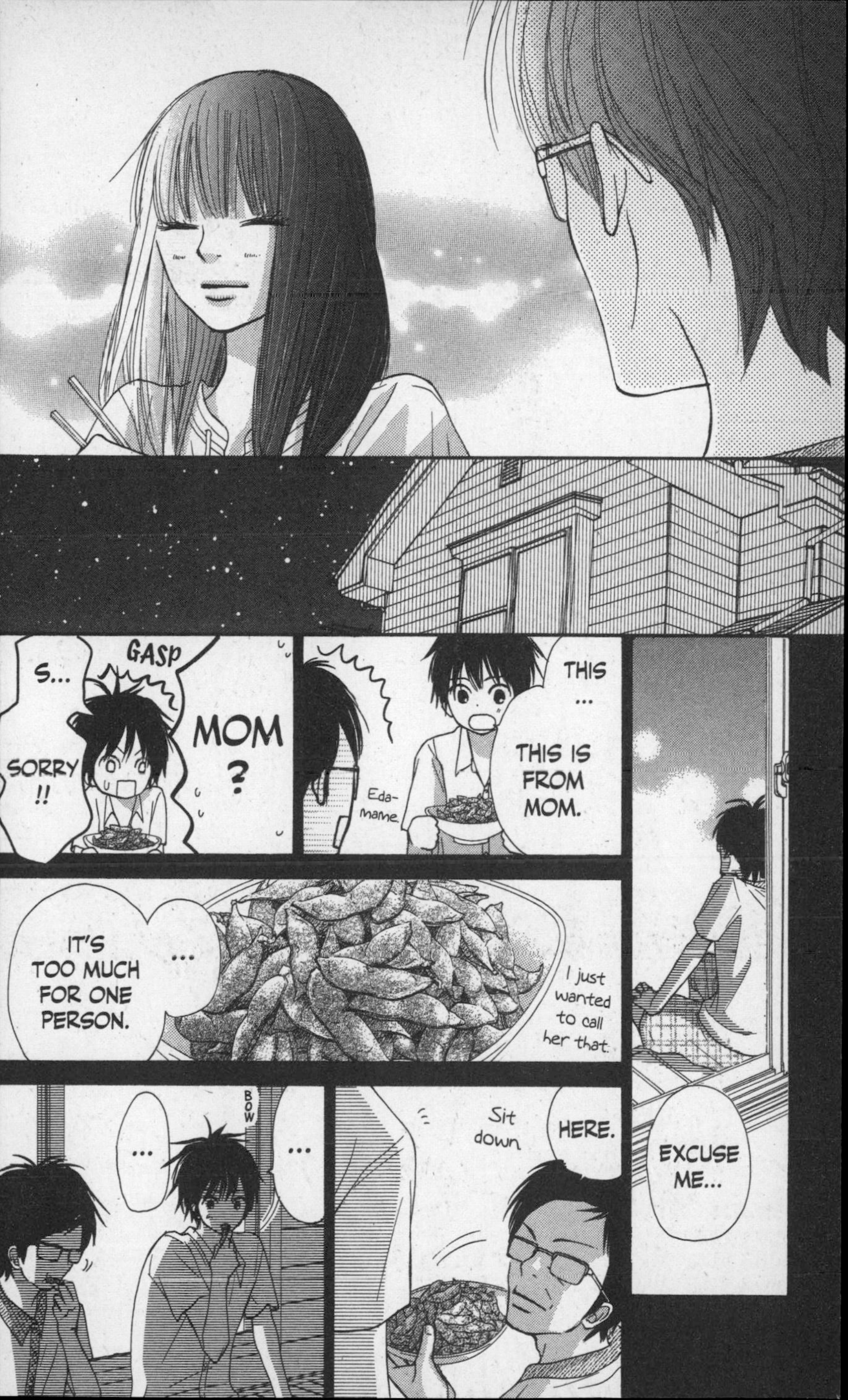
EXCUSE ME...
THIS ... THIS IS FROM MOM.
Eda-mame.
MOM ?
GASP
S... SORRY !!
I just wanted to call her that.
...
IT'S TOO MUCH FOR ONE PERSON.
HERE.
Sit down
...
BOW
...

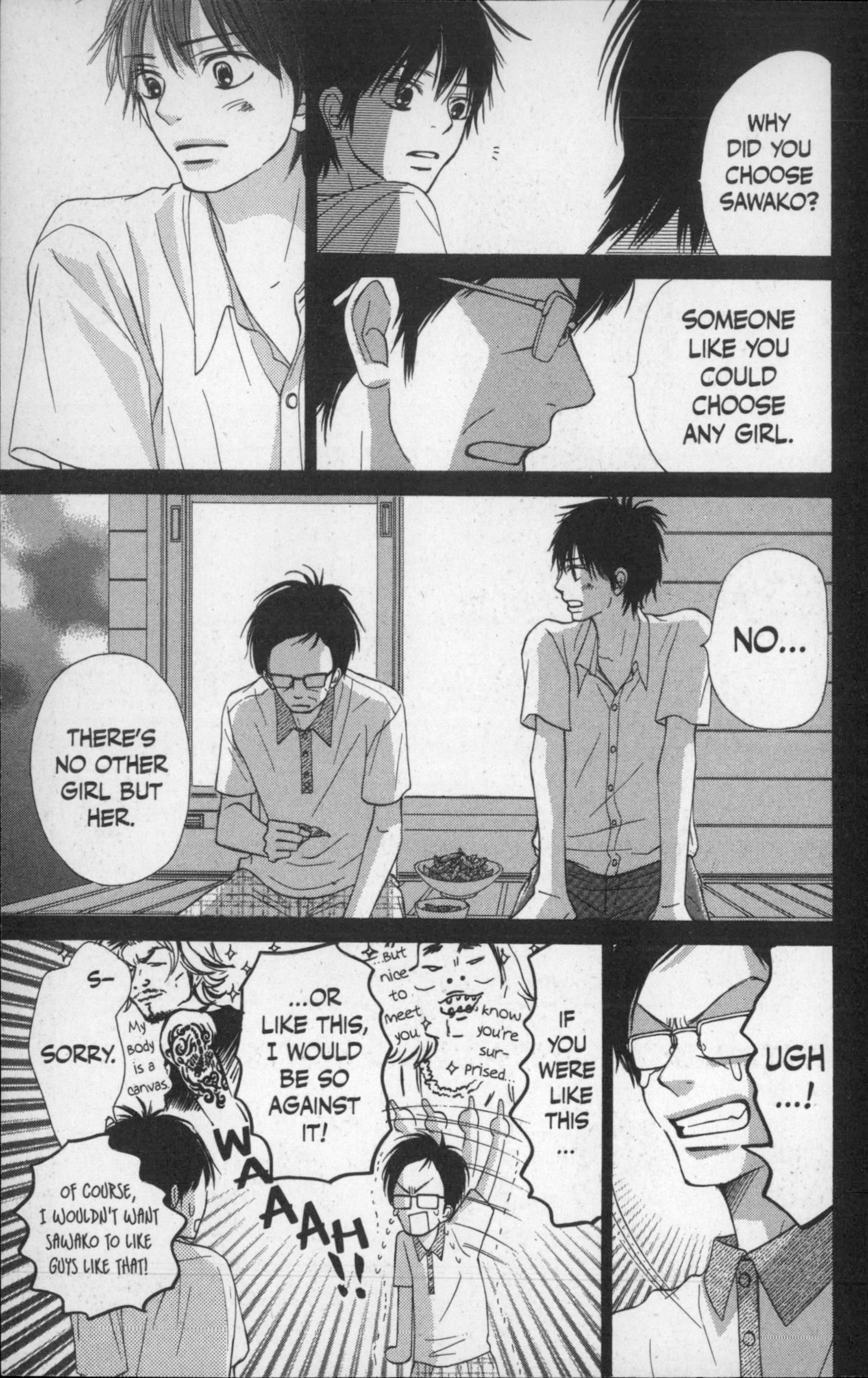
WHY DID YOU CHOOSE SAWAKO?
SOMEONE LIKE YOU COULD CHOOSE ANY GIRL.
NO...
THERE'S NO OTHER GIRL BUT HER.
UGH ...!
IF YOU WERE LIKE THIS ...
...But nice to meet you
know you're sur-prised...
...OR LIKE THIS, I WOULD BE SO AGAINST IT!
S- SORRY.
My body is a canvas.
WAAAAH!!
OF COURSE, I WOULDN'T WANT SAWAKO TO LIKE GUYS LIKE THAT!

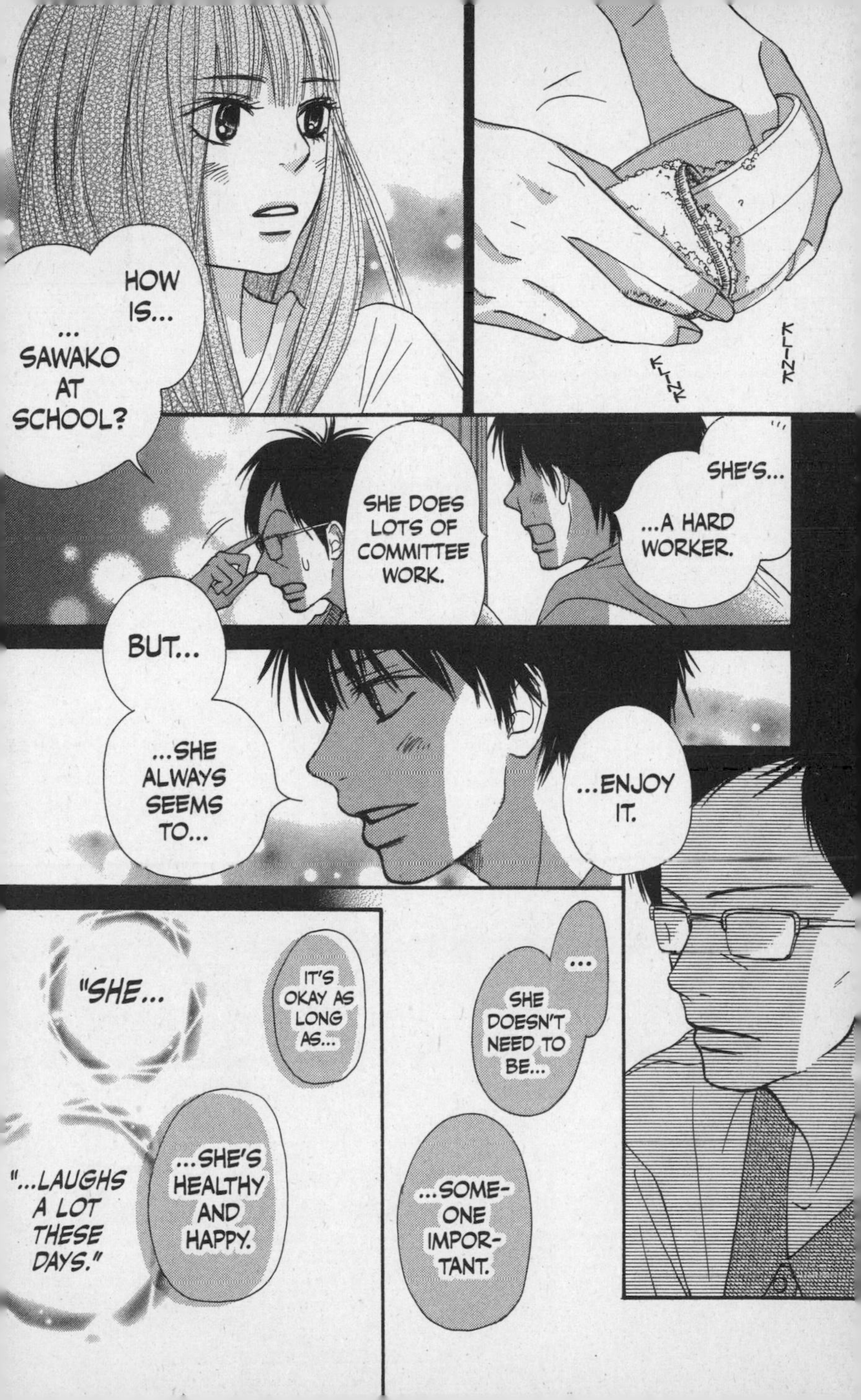
KLINK
KLINK
HOW IS...
...SAWAKO AT SCHOOL?
SHE'S...
...A HARD WORKER.
SHE DOES LOTS OF COMMITTEE WORK.
BUT...
...SHE ALWAYS SEEMS TO...
...ENJOY IT.
...
SHE DOESN'T NEED TO BE...
...SOME-ONE IMPOR-TANT.
IT'S OKAY AS LONG AS...
"SHE...
...SHE'S HEALTHY AND HAPPY.
"...LAUGHS A LOT THESE DAYS."

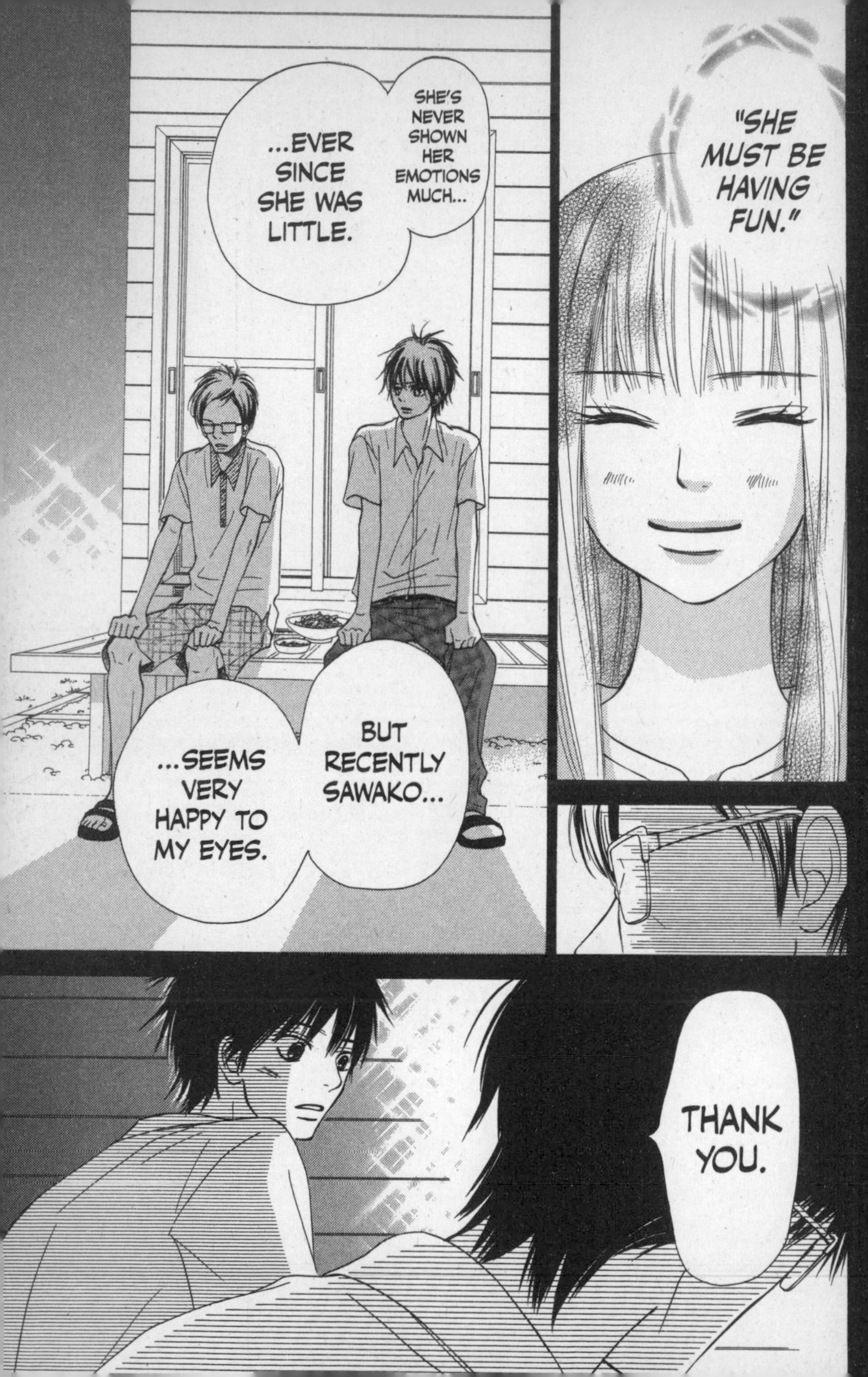
"SHE MUST BE HAVING FUN."
SHE'S NEVER SHOWN HER EMOTIONS MUCH...
...EVER SINCE SHE WAS LITTLE.
BUT RECENTLY SAWAKO...
...SEEMS VERY HAPPY TO MY EYES.
THANK YOU.

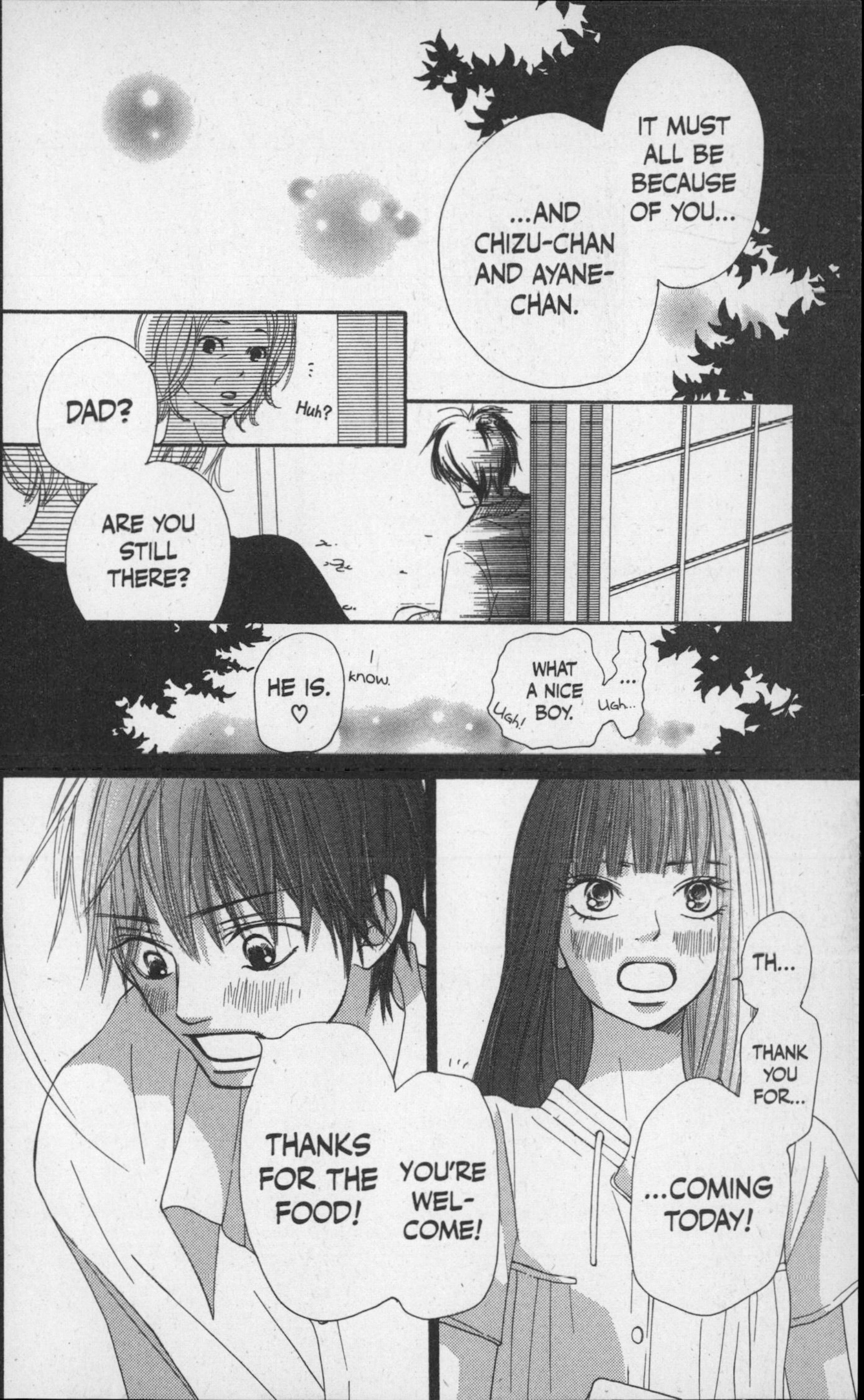
IT MUST ALL BE BECAUSE OF YOU...
...AND CHIZU-CHAN AND AYANE-CHAN.
...
Huh?
DAD?
ARE YOU STILL THERE?
WHAT A NICE BOY.
...
Ugh...
Ugh!
HE IS. ♡
I know.
TH...
THANK YOU FOR...
...COMING TODAY!
THANKS FOR THE FOOD!
YOU'RE WEL-COME!

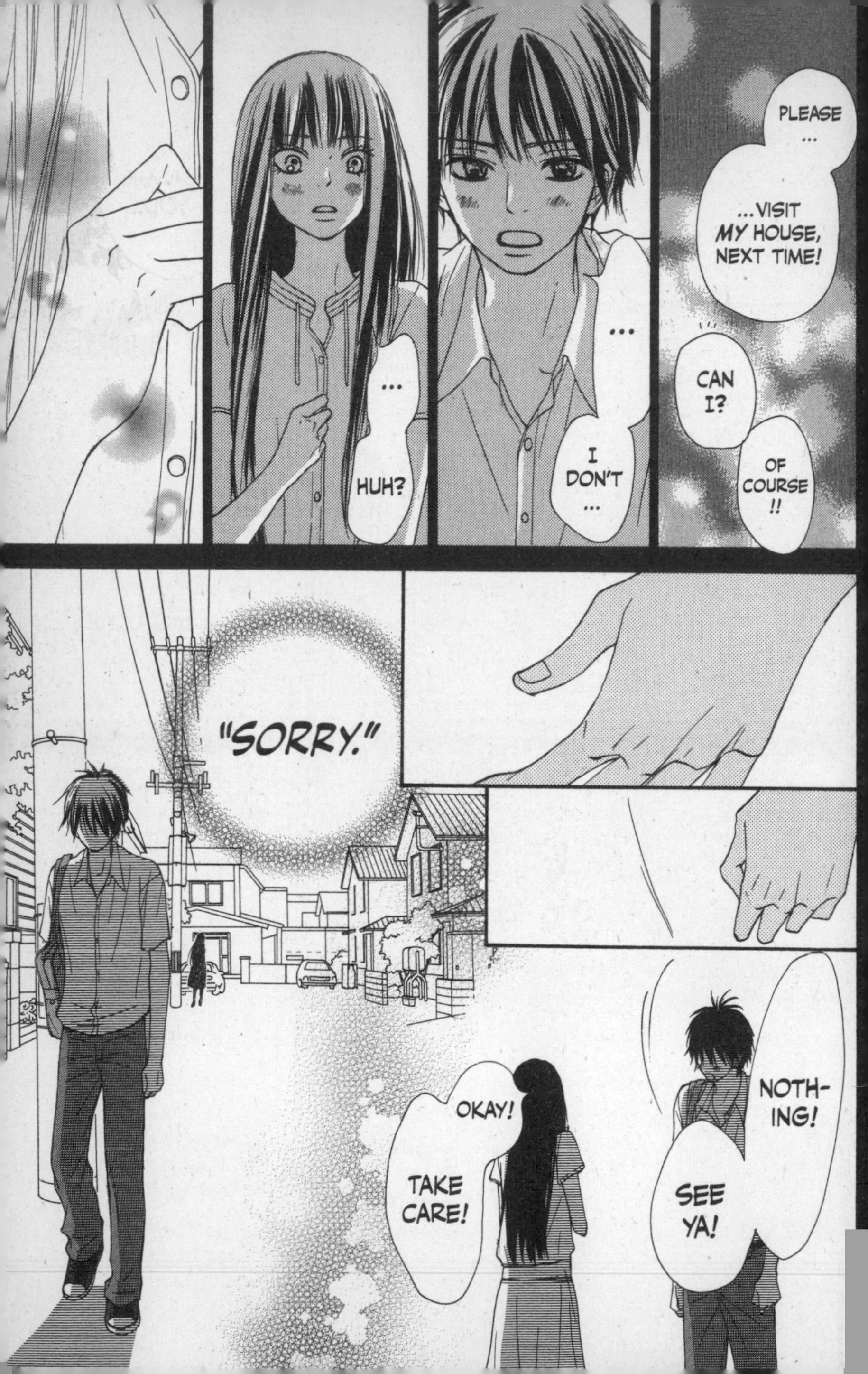
PLEASE ...
...VISIT *MY* HOUSE, NEXT TIME!
CAN I?
OF COURSE !!
...
I DON'T ...
...
HUH?
NOTH-ING!
SEE YA!
OKAY!
TAKE CARE!
"SORRY."

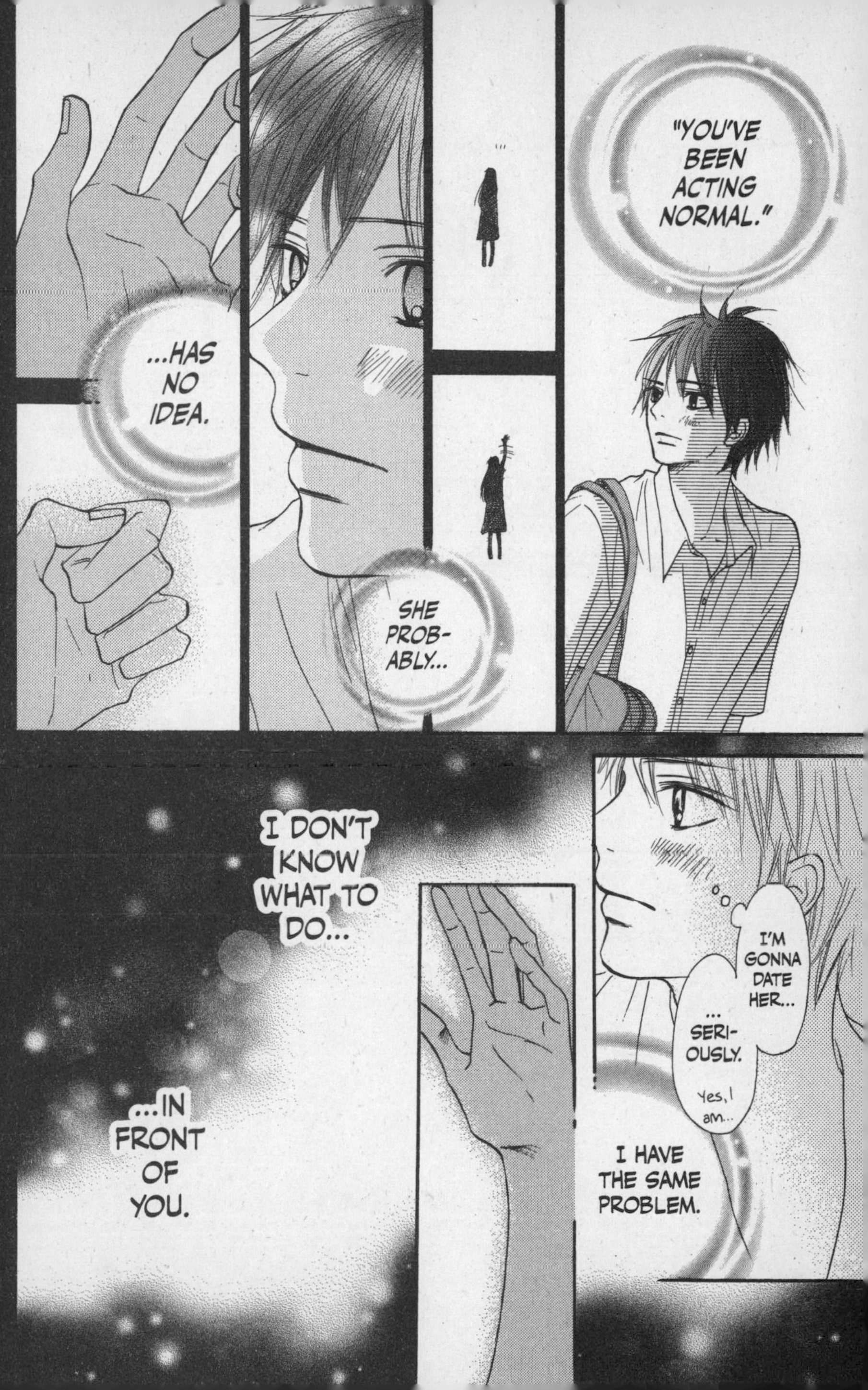
"YOU'VE BEEN ACTING NORMAL."
SHE PROBABLY...
...HAS NO IDEA.
I'M GONNA DATE HER...
... SERIOUSLY.
Yes, I am...
I HAVE THE SAME PROBLEM.
I DON'T KNOW WHAT TO DO...
...IN FRONT OF YOU.

♥Episode 50: You're Too Loud

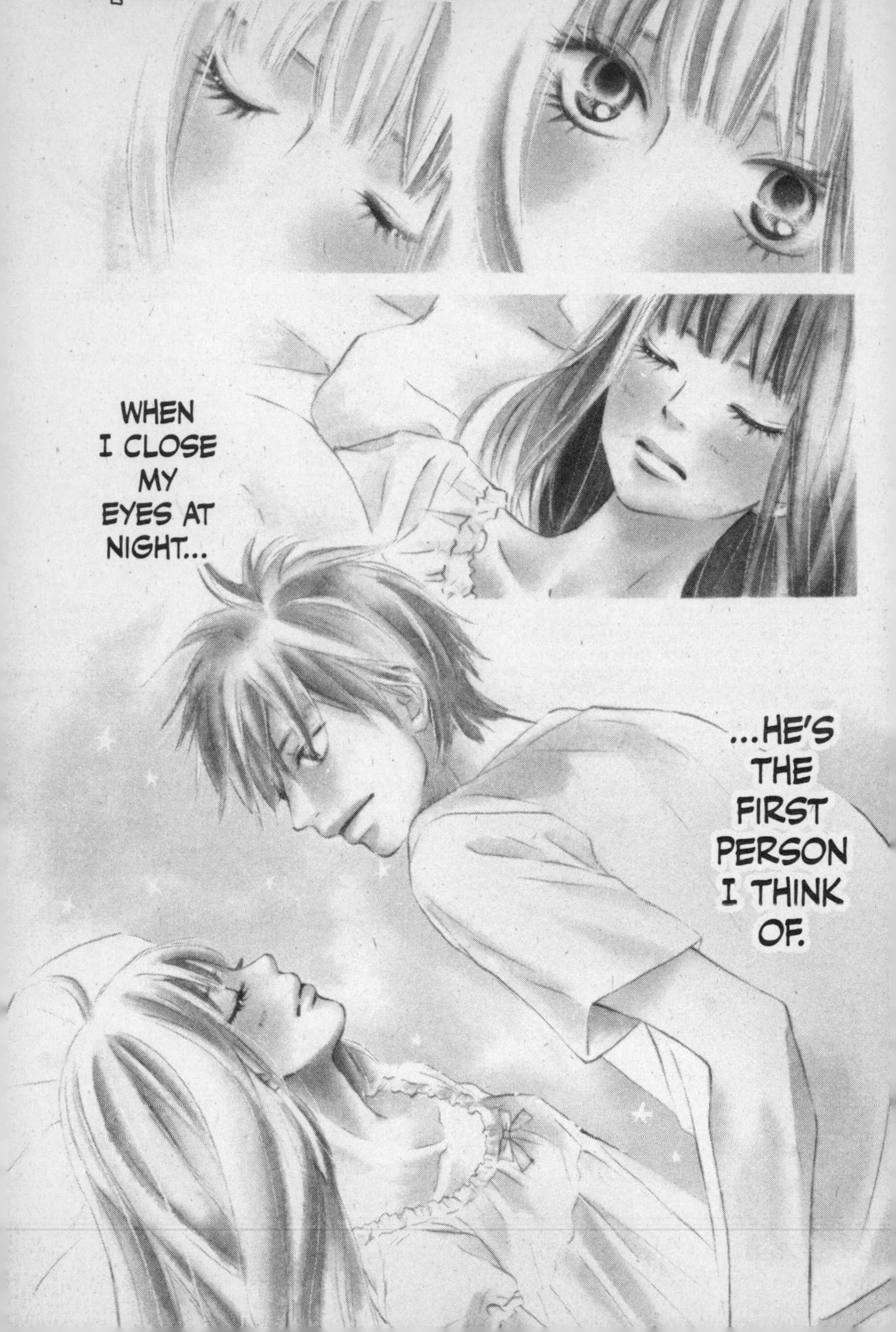
WHEN I CLOSE MY EYES AT NIGHT...
...HE'S THE FIRST PERSON I THINK OF.

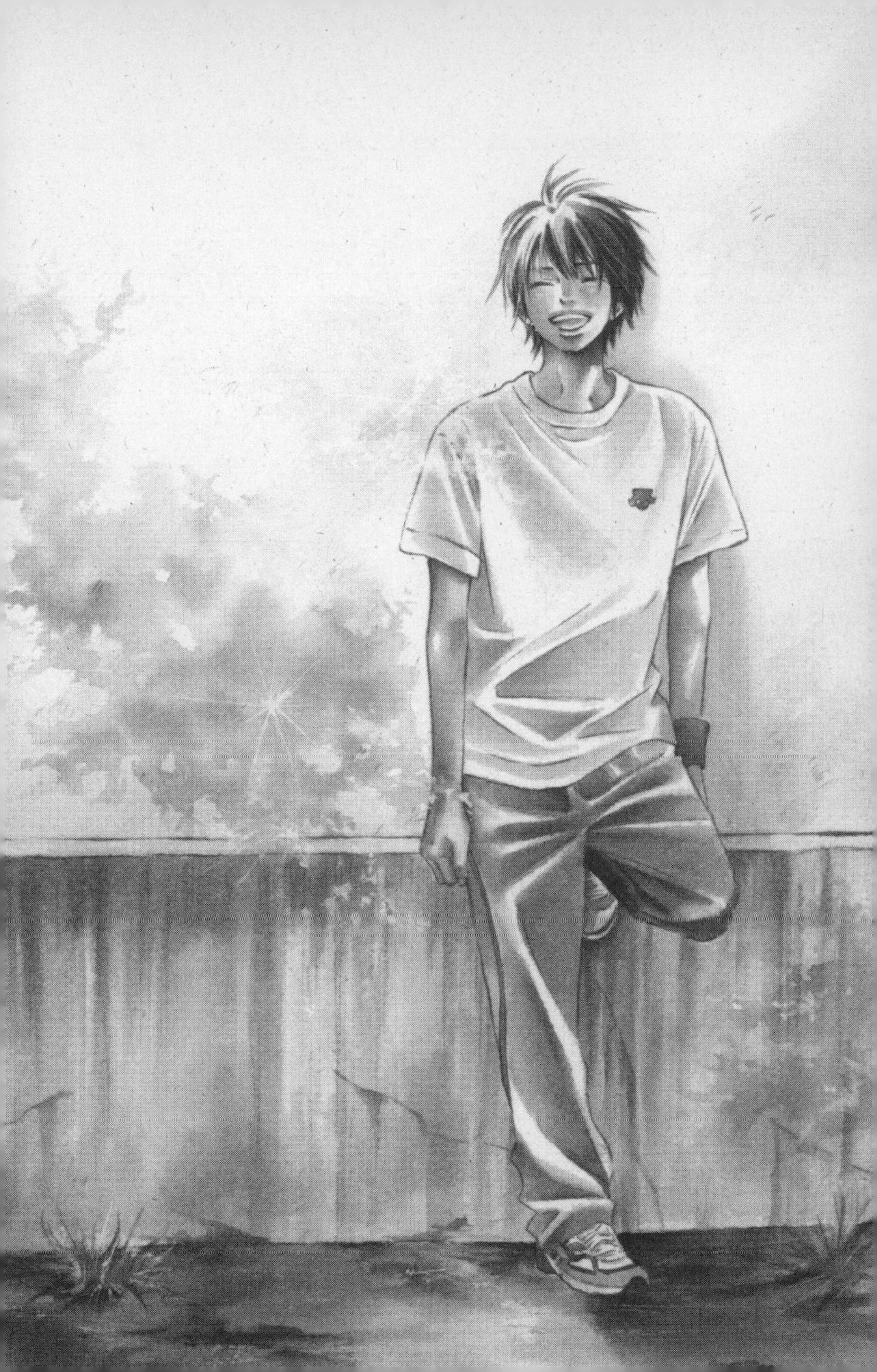

Episode 50: You're Too Loud

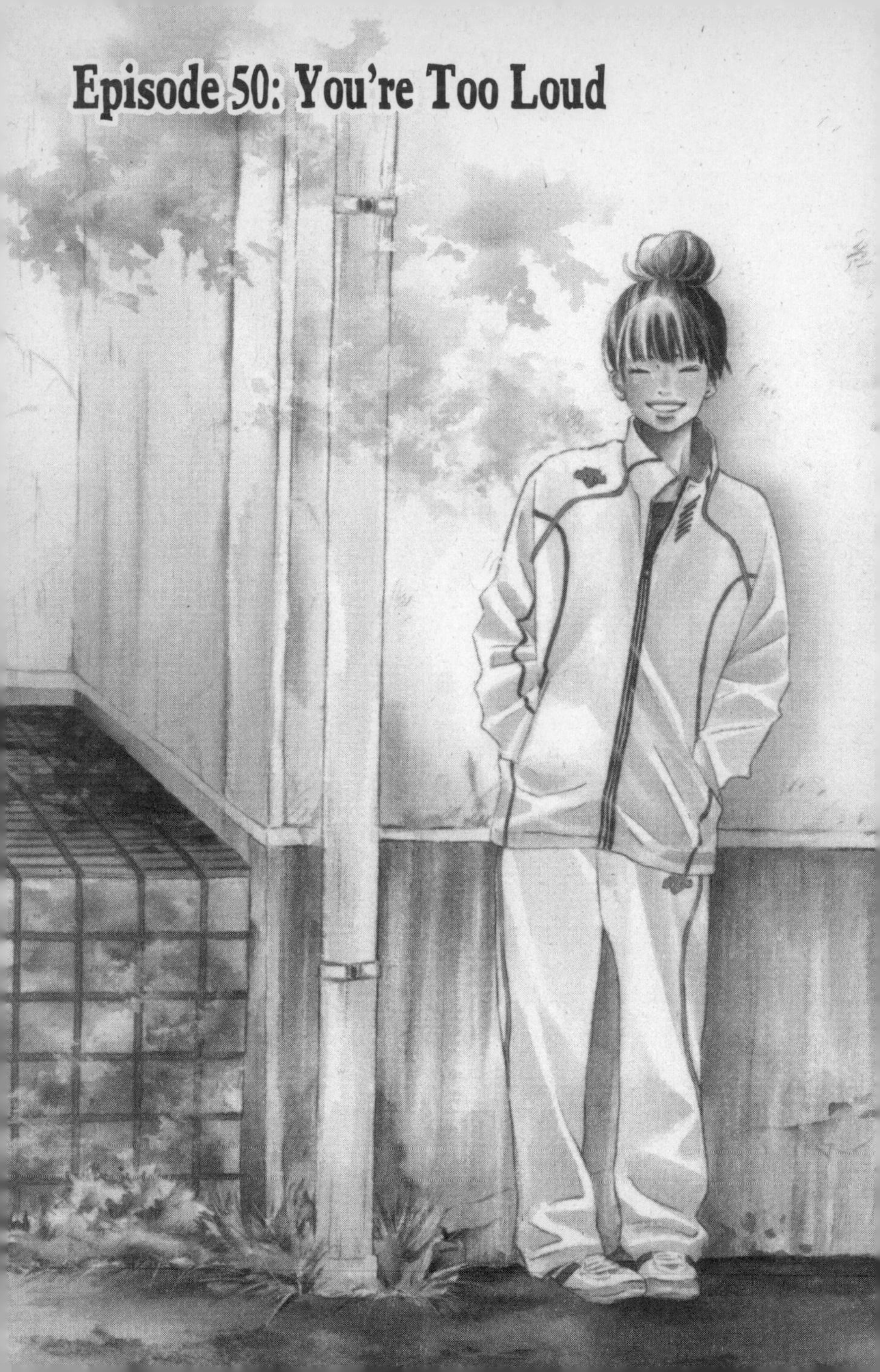

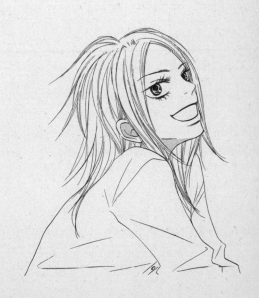

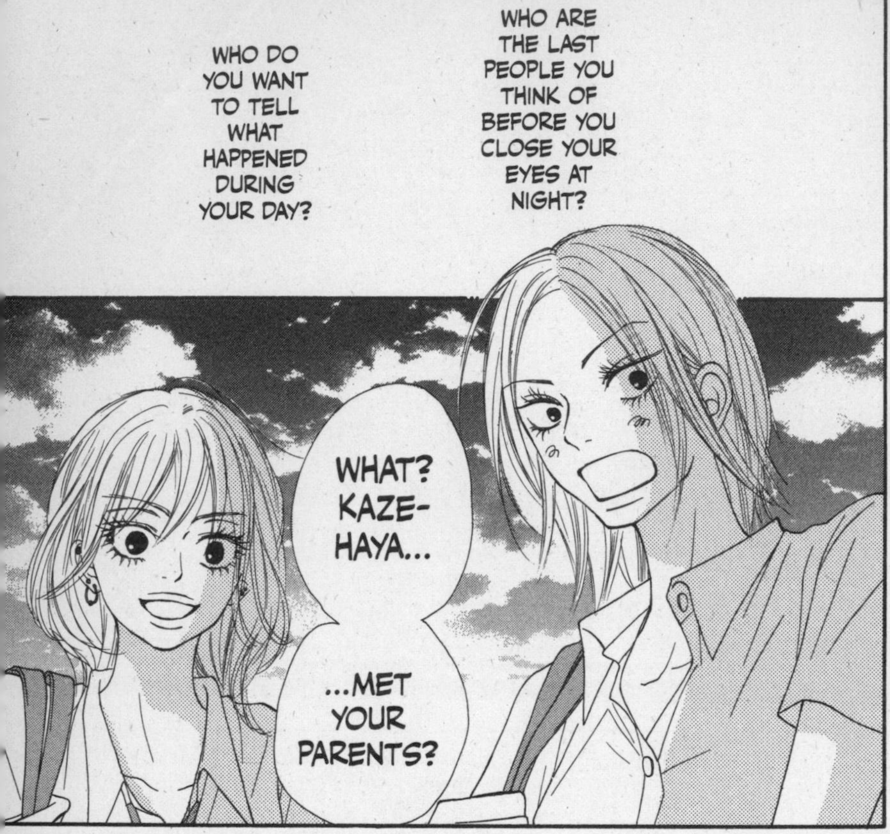
WHO ARE THE LAST PEOPLE YOU THINK OF BEFORE YOU CLOSE YOUR EYES AT NIGHT?
WHO DO YOU WANT TO TELL WHAT HAPPENED DURING YOUR DAY?
WHAT? KAZE-HAYA...
...MET YOUR PARENTS?

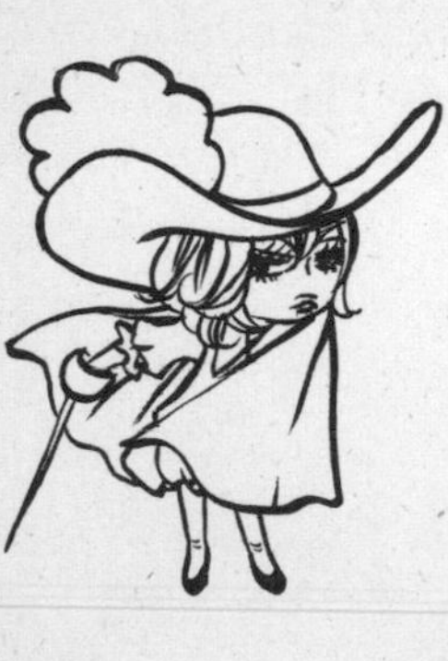

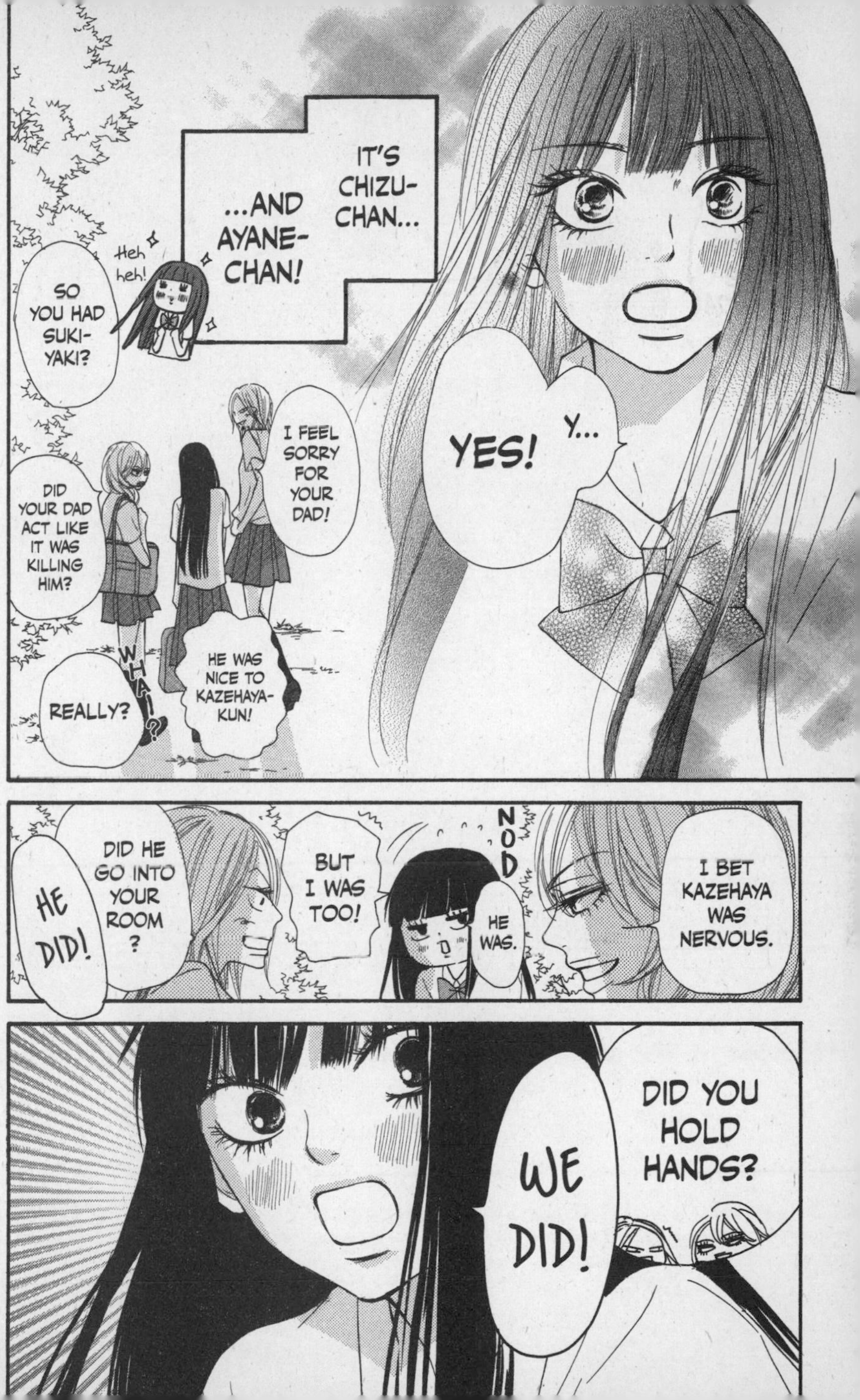
IT'S CHIZU-CHAN...
...AND AYANE-CHAN!
Y... YES!
Heh heh!
SO YOU HAD SUKI-YAKI?
I FEEL SORRY FOR YOUR DAD!
DID YOUR DAD ACT LIKE IT WAS KILLING HIM?
HE WAS NICE TO KAZEHAYA-KUN!
WHA!?
REALLY?
I BET KAZEHAYA WAS NERVOUS.
NOD
HE WAS.
BUT I WAS TOO!
DID HE GO INTO YOUR ROOM?
HE DID!
DID YOU HOLD HANDS?
WE DID!

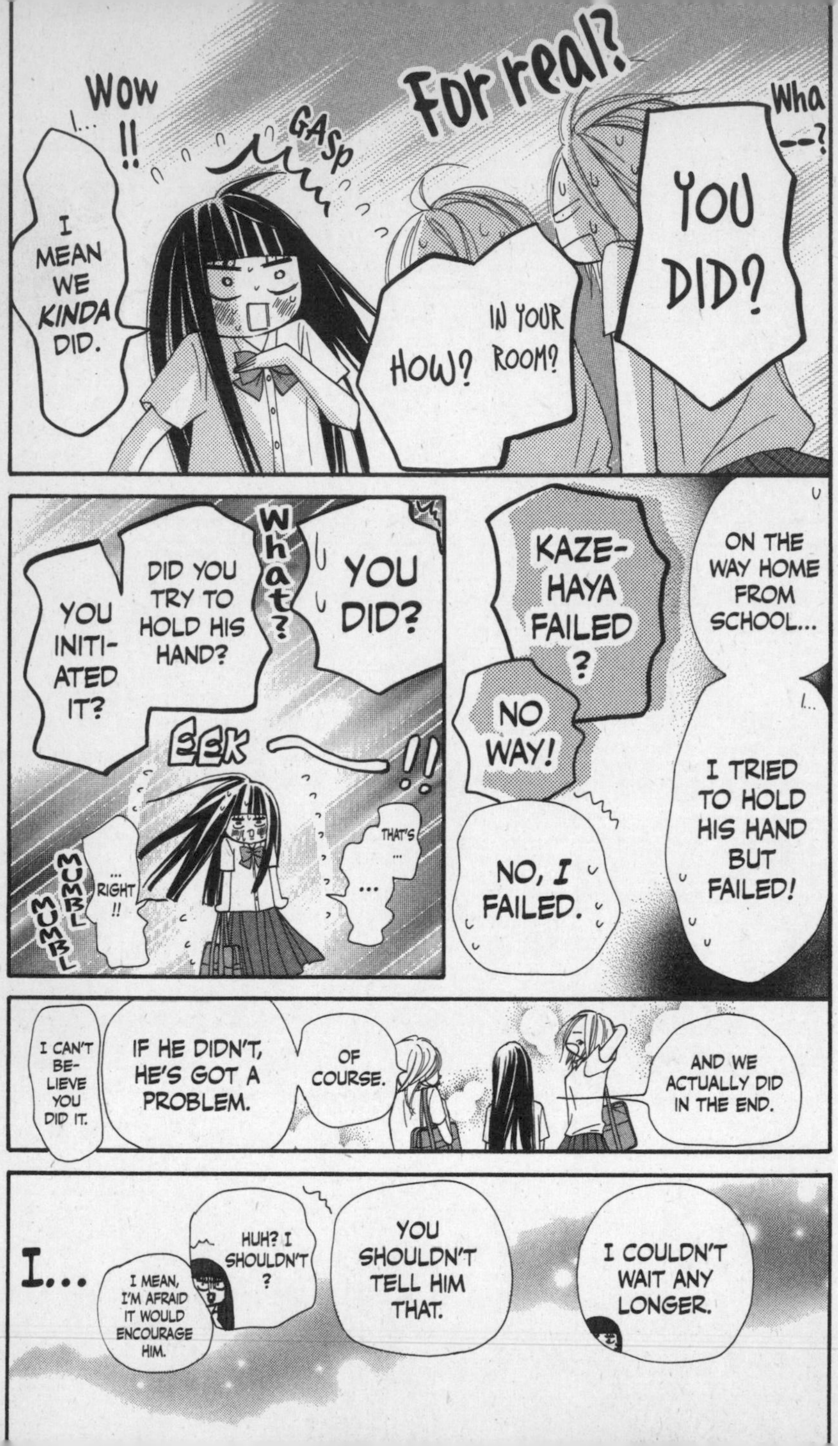
Wha--?
YOU DID?
For real?
IN YOUR ROOM?
HOW?
GASp
WOW!!
I...
I MEAN WE KINDA DID.
ON THE WAY HOME FROM SCHOOL...
I...
I TRIED TO HOLD HIS HAND BUT FAILED!
KAZE-HAYA FAILED?
NO WAY!
NO, I FAILED.
YOU DID?
What?
DID YOU TRY TO HOLD HIS HAND?
YOU INITI-ATED IT?
EEK!!
THAT'S... ...
...RIGHT!!
MUMBL MUMBL
AND WE ACTUALLY DID IN THE END.
OF COURSE.
IF HE DIDN'T, HE'S GOT A PROBLEM.
I CAN'T BE-LIEVE YOU DID IT.
I COULDN'T WAIT ANY LONGER.
YOU SHOULDN'T TELL HIM THAT.
HUH? I SHOULDN'T?
I MEAN, I'M AFRAID IT WOULD ENCOURAGE HIM.
I...

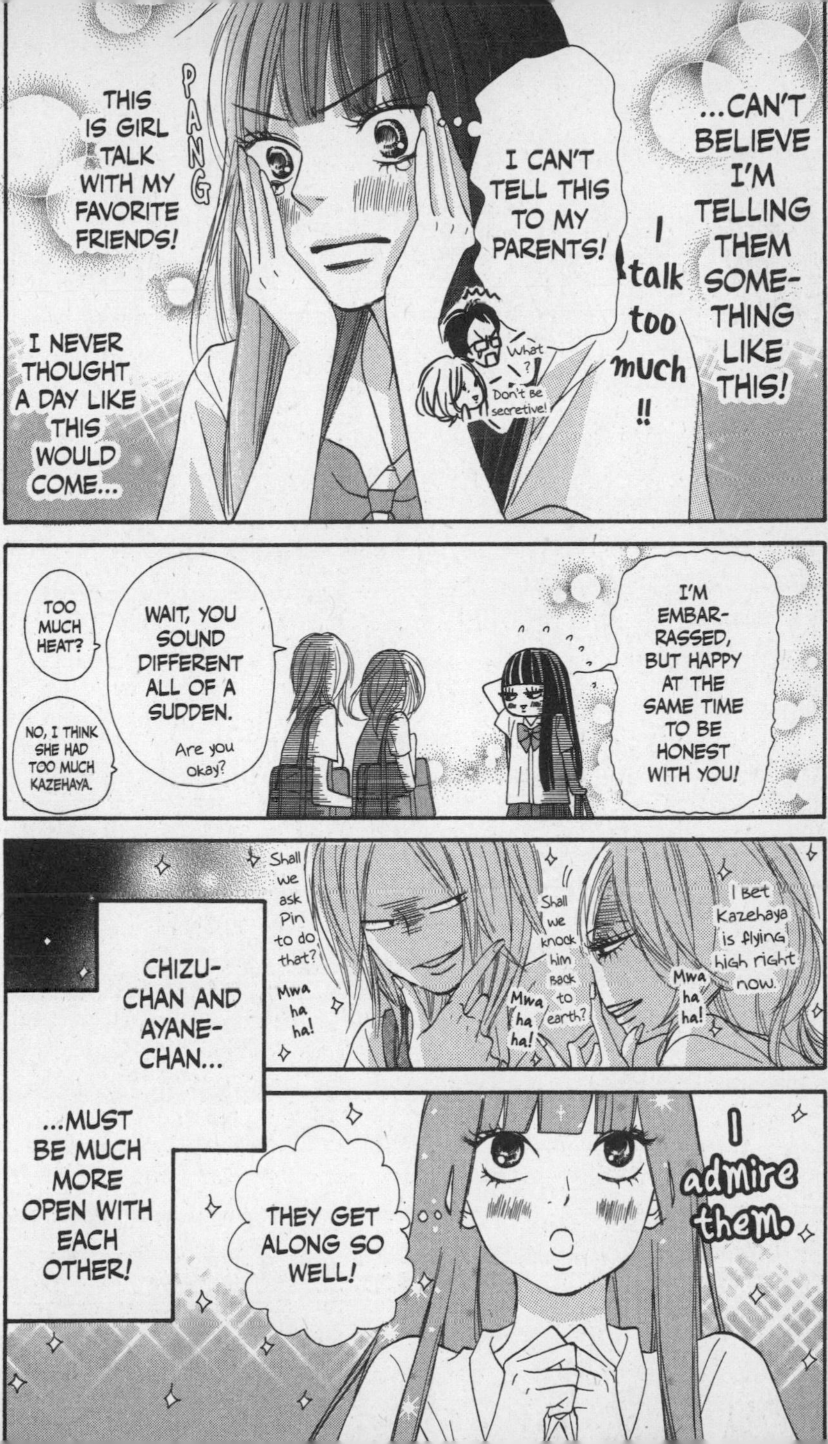
...CAN'T BELIEVE I'M TELLING THEM SOMETHING LIKE THIS!
I talk too much!!
I CAN'T TELL THIS TO MY PARENTS!
What?
Don't be secretive!
PANG
THIS IS GIRL TALK WITH MY FAVORITE FRIENDS!
I NEVER THOUGHT A DAY LIKE THIS WOULD COME...
I'M EMBARRASSED, BUT HAPPY AT THE SAME TIME TO BE HONEST WITH YOU!
WAIT, YOU SOUND DIFFERENT ALL OF A SUDDEN.
Are you okay?
TOO MUCH HEAT?
NO, I THINK SHE HAD TOO MUCH KAZEHAYA.
I bet Kazehaya is flying high right now.
Mwa ha ha!
Shall we knock him back to earth?
Mwa ha ha!
Shall we ask Pin to do that?
Mwa ha ha!
CHIZU-CHAN AND AYANE-CHAN...
I admire them.
THEY GET ALONG SO WELL!
...MUST BE MUCH MORE OPEN WITH EACH OTHER!

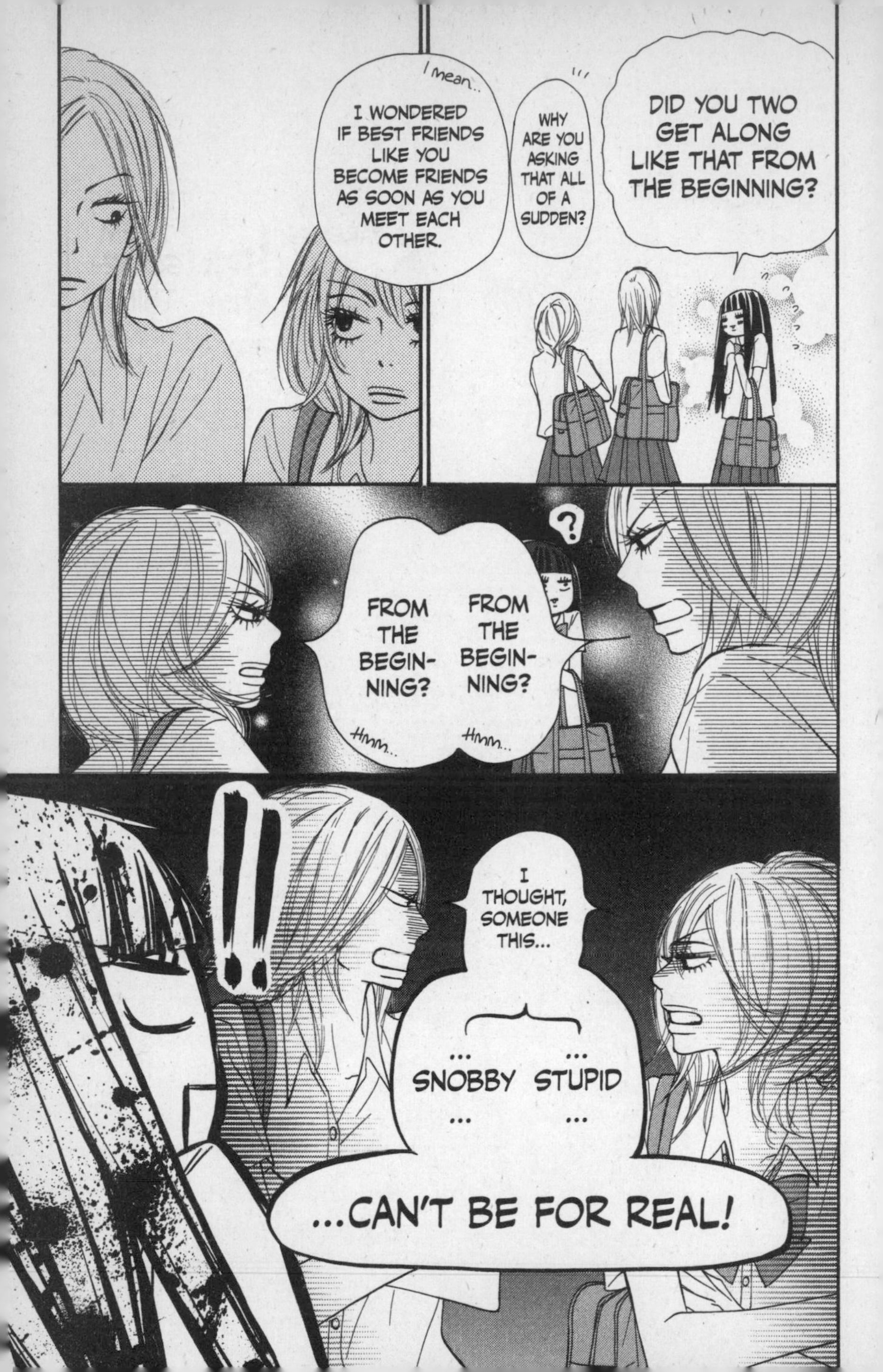
DID YOU TWO GET ALONG LIKE THAT FROM THE BEGINNING?
WHY ARE YOU ASKING THAT ALL OF A SUDDEN?
I mean..
I WONDERED IF BEST FRIENDS LIKE YOU BECOME FRIENDS AS SOON AS YOU MEET EACH OTHER.
?
FROM THE BEGIN-NING?
Hmm..
FROM THE BEGIN-NING?
Hmm..
!!
I THOUGHT, SOMEONE THIS...
... STUPID ...
... SNOBBY ...
...CAN'T BE FOR REAL!

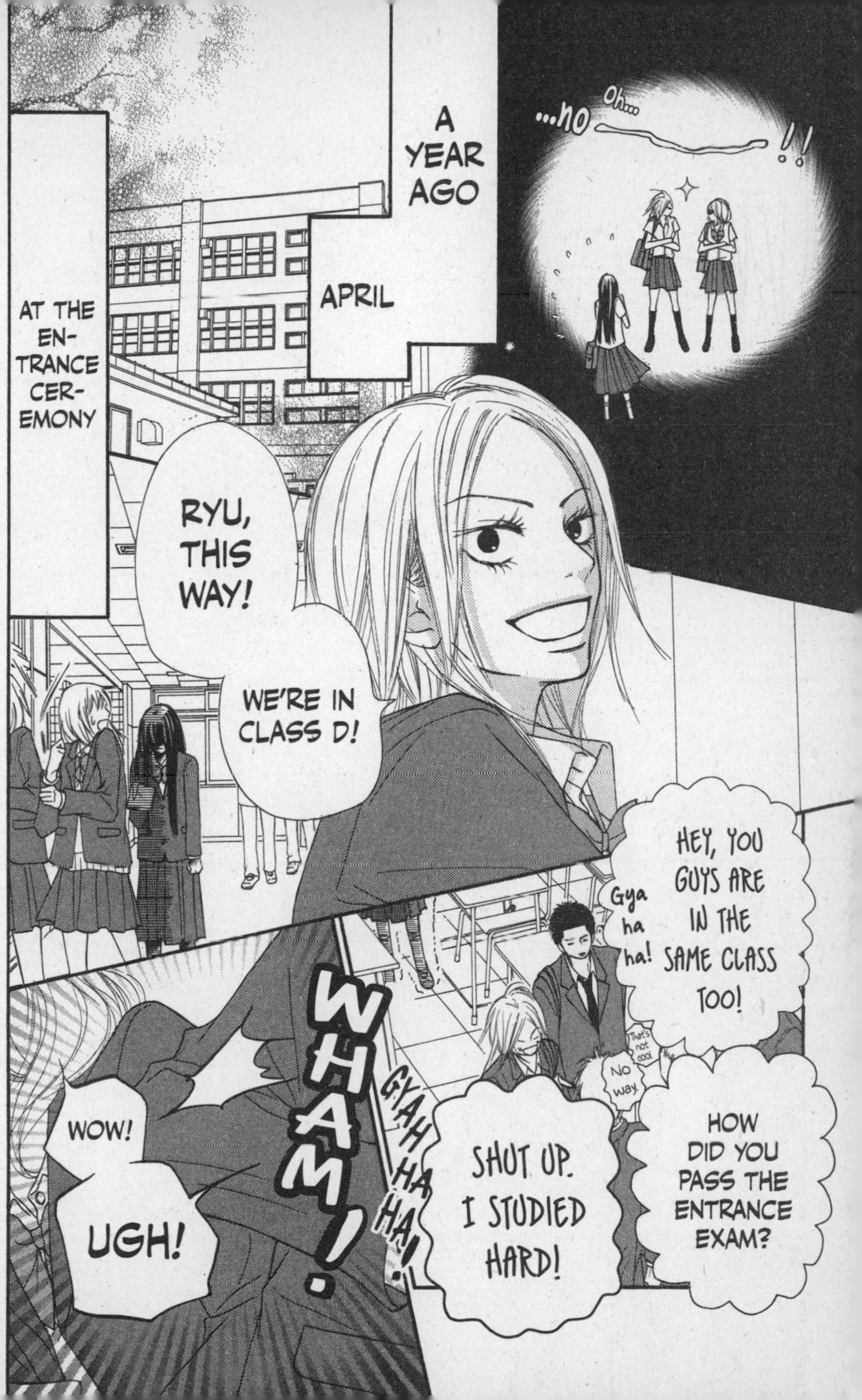
Oh... ...no —!!
A YEAR AGO
APRIL
AT THE EN-TRANCE CER-EMONY
RYU, THIS WAY!
WE'RE IN CLASS D!
HEY, YOU GUYS ARE IN THE SAME CLASS TOO!
Gya ha ha!
That's not cool.
No way.
HOW DID YOU PASS THE ENTRANCE EXAM?
SHUT UP. I STUDIED HARD!
GYAH HA HA!
WHAM!
WOW!
UGH!

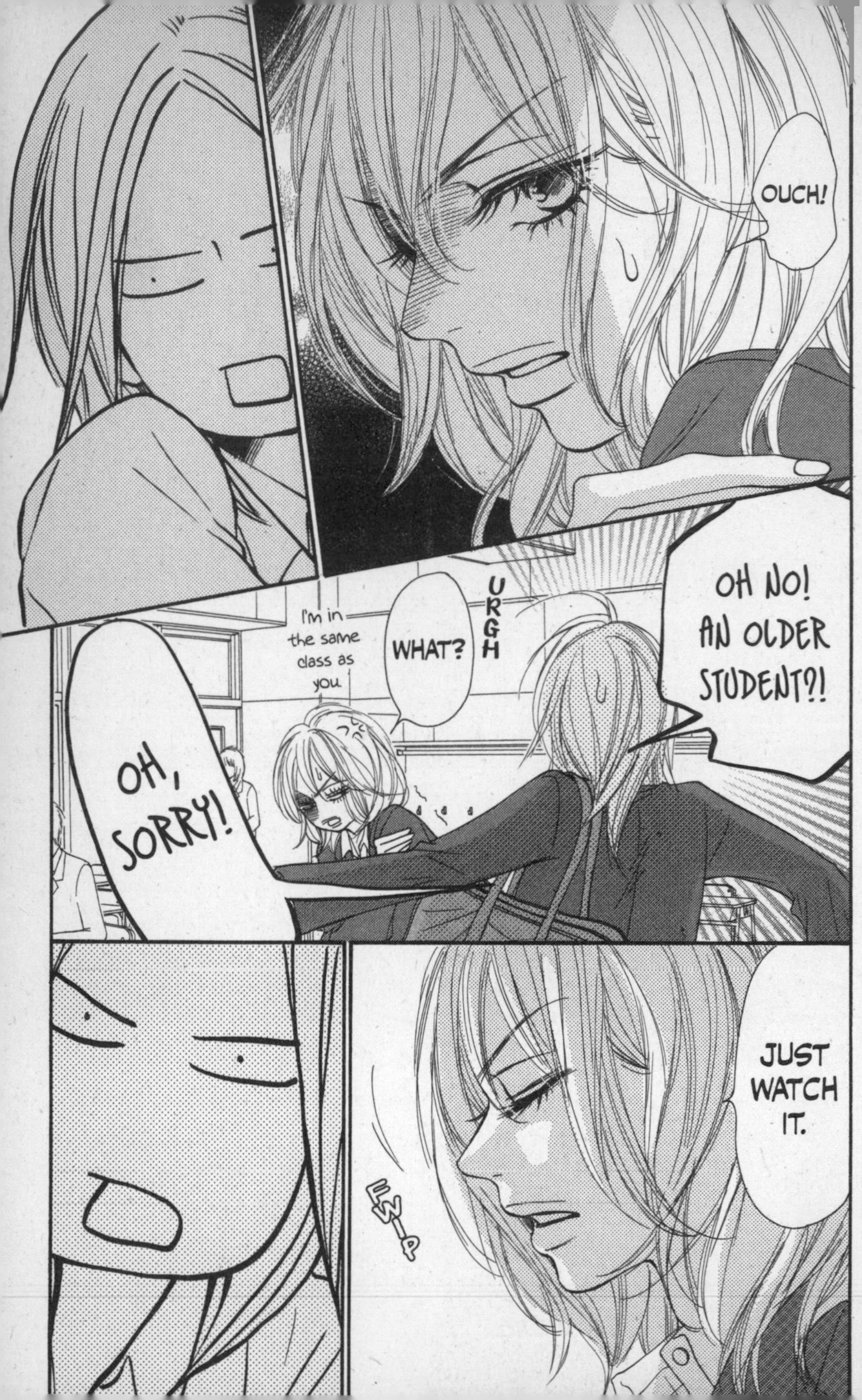
OUCH!
OH NO! AN OLDER STUDENT?!
URGH
WHAT?
I'm in the same class as you.
OH, SORRY!
JUST WATCH IT.
FWIP

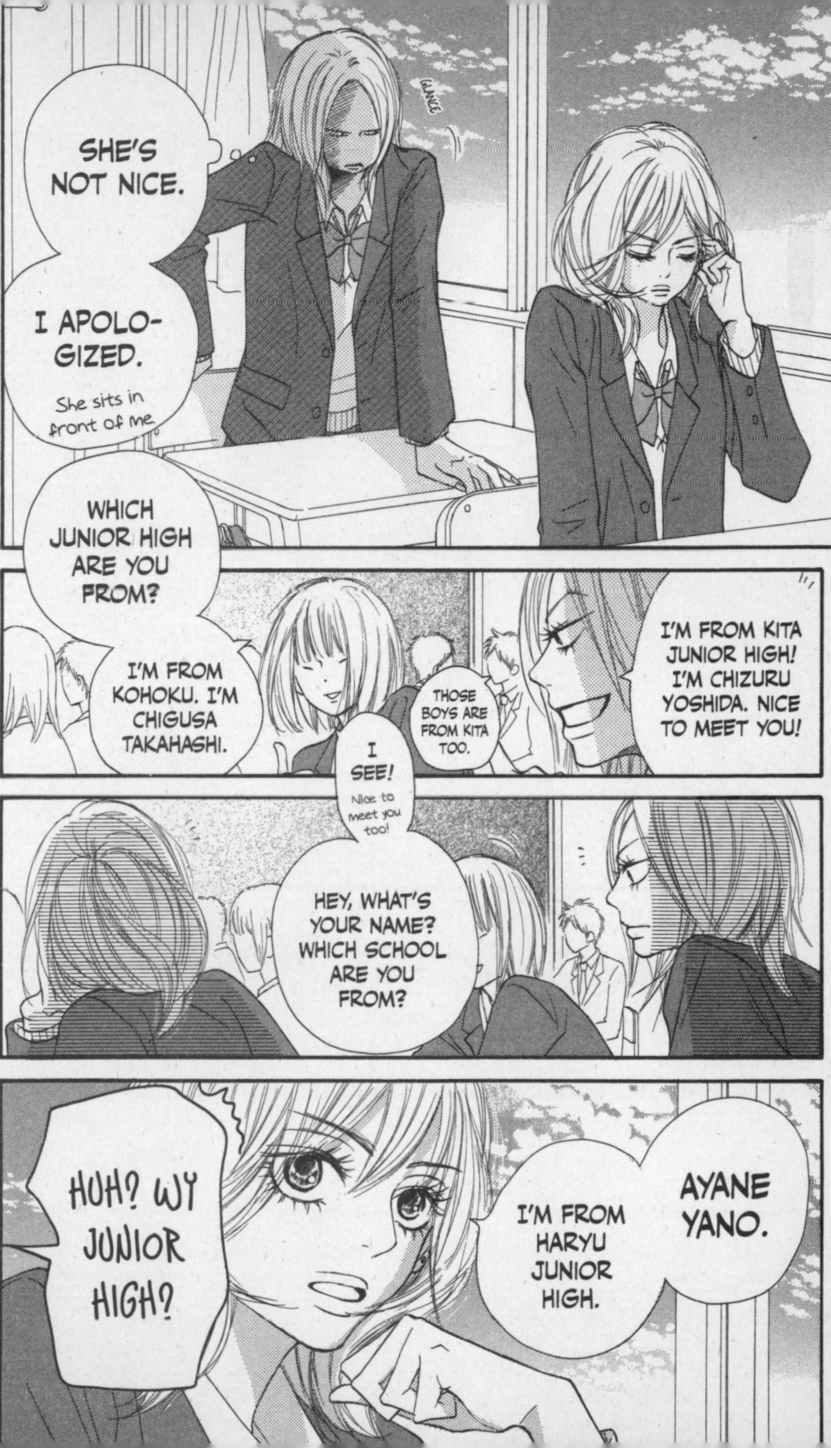
GLANCE
SHE'S NOT NICE.
I APOLOGIZED.
She sits in front of me.
WHICH JUNIOR HIGH ARE YOU FROM?
I'M FROM KITA JUNIOR HIGH! I'M CHIZURU YOSHIDA. NICE TO MEET YOU!
THOSE BOYS ARE FROM KITA TOO.
I'M FROM KOHOKU. I'M CHIGUSA TAKAHASHI.
I SEE!
Nice to meet you too!
HEY, WHAT'S YOUR NAME? WHICH SCHOOL ARE YOU FROM?
AYANE YANO.
I'M FROM HARYU JUNIOR HIGH.
HUH? WY JUNIOR HIGH?

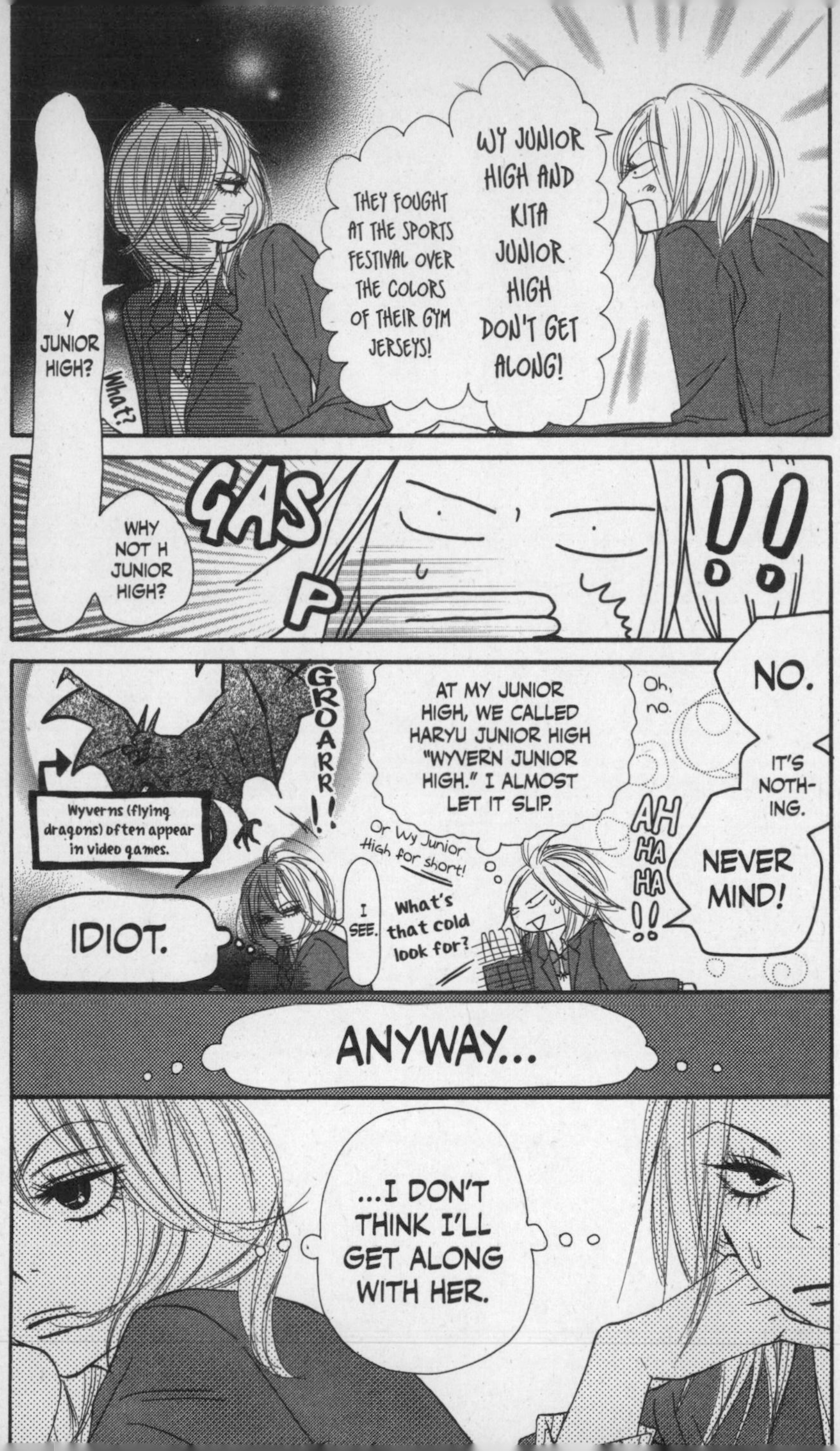
WY JUNIOR HIGH AND KITA JUNIOR HIGH DON'T GET ALONG!
THEY FOUGHT AT THE SPORTS FESTIVAL OVER THE COLORS OF THEIR GYM JERSEYS!
What?
Y JUNIOR HIGH?
WHY NOT H JUNIOR HIGH?
!!
GASP
NO.
IT'S NOTHING.
NEVER MIND!
AH HA HA!!
Oh, no.
AT MY JUNIOR HIGH, WE CALLED HARYU JUNIOR HIGH "WYVERN JUNIOR HIGH." I ALMOST LET IT SLIP.
Or Wy Junior High for short!
GROARR!!
Wyverns (flying dragons) often appear in video games.
What's that cold look for?
I SEE.
IDIOT.
ANYWAY...
...I DON'T THINK I'LL GET ALONG WITH HER.

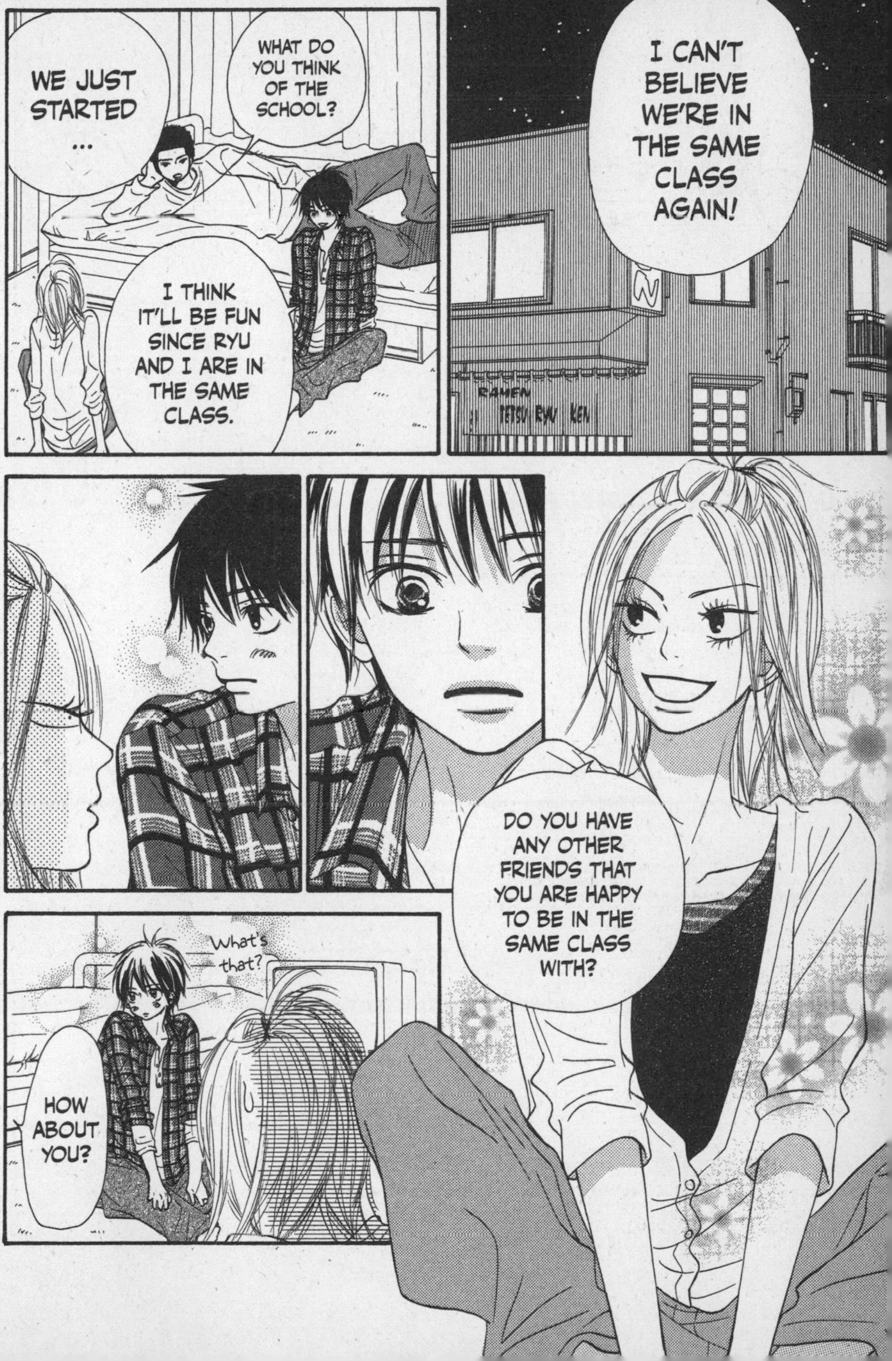
I CAN'T BELIEVE WE'RE IN THE SAME CLASS AGAIN!
RAMEN TETSU RYU KEN
WHAT DO YOU THINK OF THE SCHOOL?
WE JUST STARTED ...
I THINK IT'LL BE FUN SINCE RYU AND I ARE IN THE SAME CLASS.
DO YOU HAVE ANY OTHER FRIENDS THAT YOU ARE HAPPY TO BE IN THE SAME CLASS WITH?
What's that?
HOW ABOUT YOU?

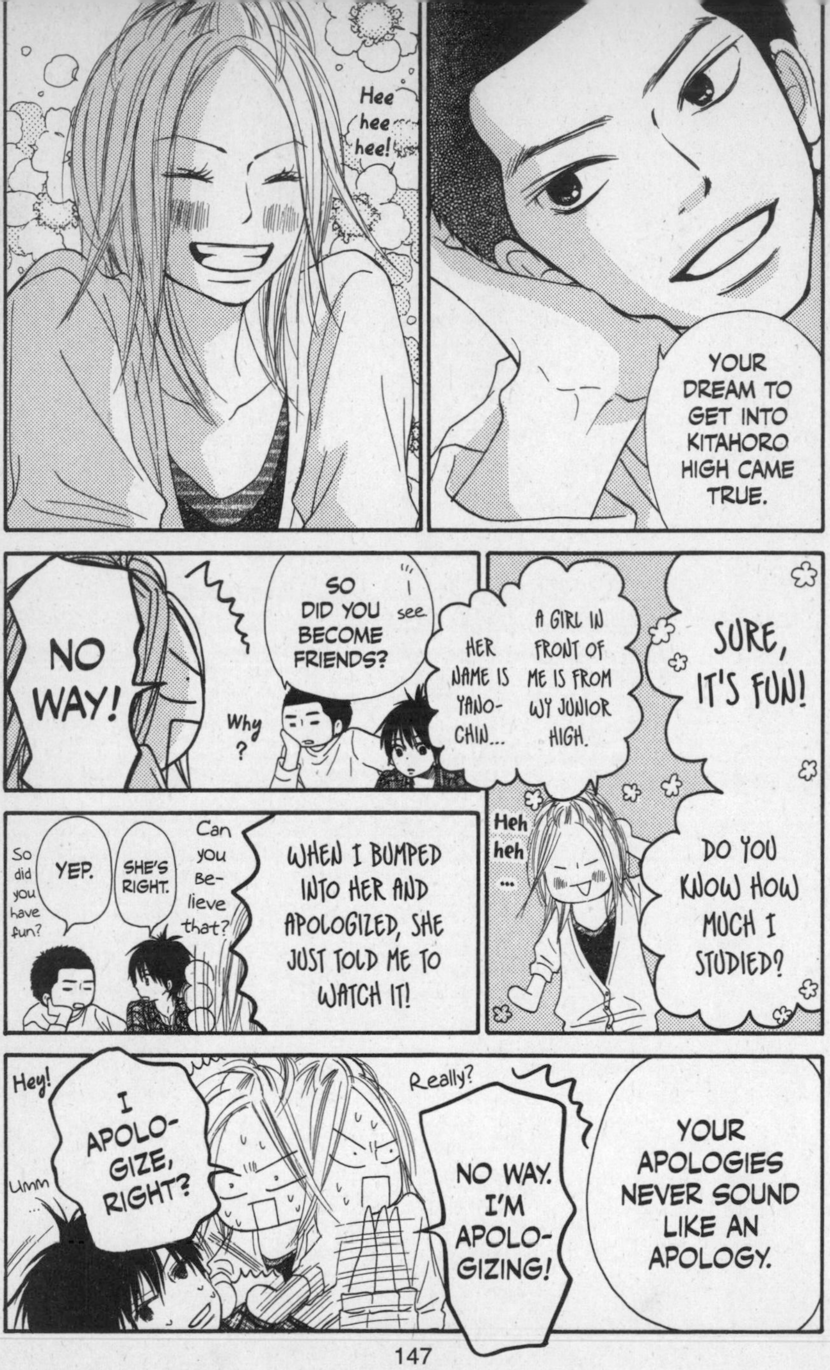
YOUR DREAM TO GET INTO KITAHORO HIGH CAME TRUE.
Hee hee hee!
SURE, IT'S FUN!
A GIRL IN FRONT OF ME IS FROM MY JUNIOR HIGH.
HER NAME IS YANO-CHIN...
Heh heh...
DO YOU KNOW HOW MUCH I STUDIED?
I see.
SO DID YOU BECOME FRIENDS?
NO WAY!
Why?
WHEN I BUMPED INTO HER AND APOLOGIZED, SHE JUST TOLD ME TO WATCH IT!
Can you be-lieve that?
SHE'S RIGHT.
YEP.
So did you have fun?
YOUR APOLOGIES NEVER SOUND LIKE AN APOLOGY.
Really?
NO WAY. I'M APOLO-GIZING!
I APOLO-GIZE, RIGHT?
Hey!
Umm...

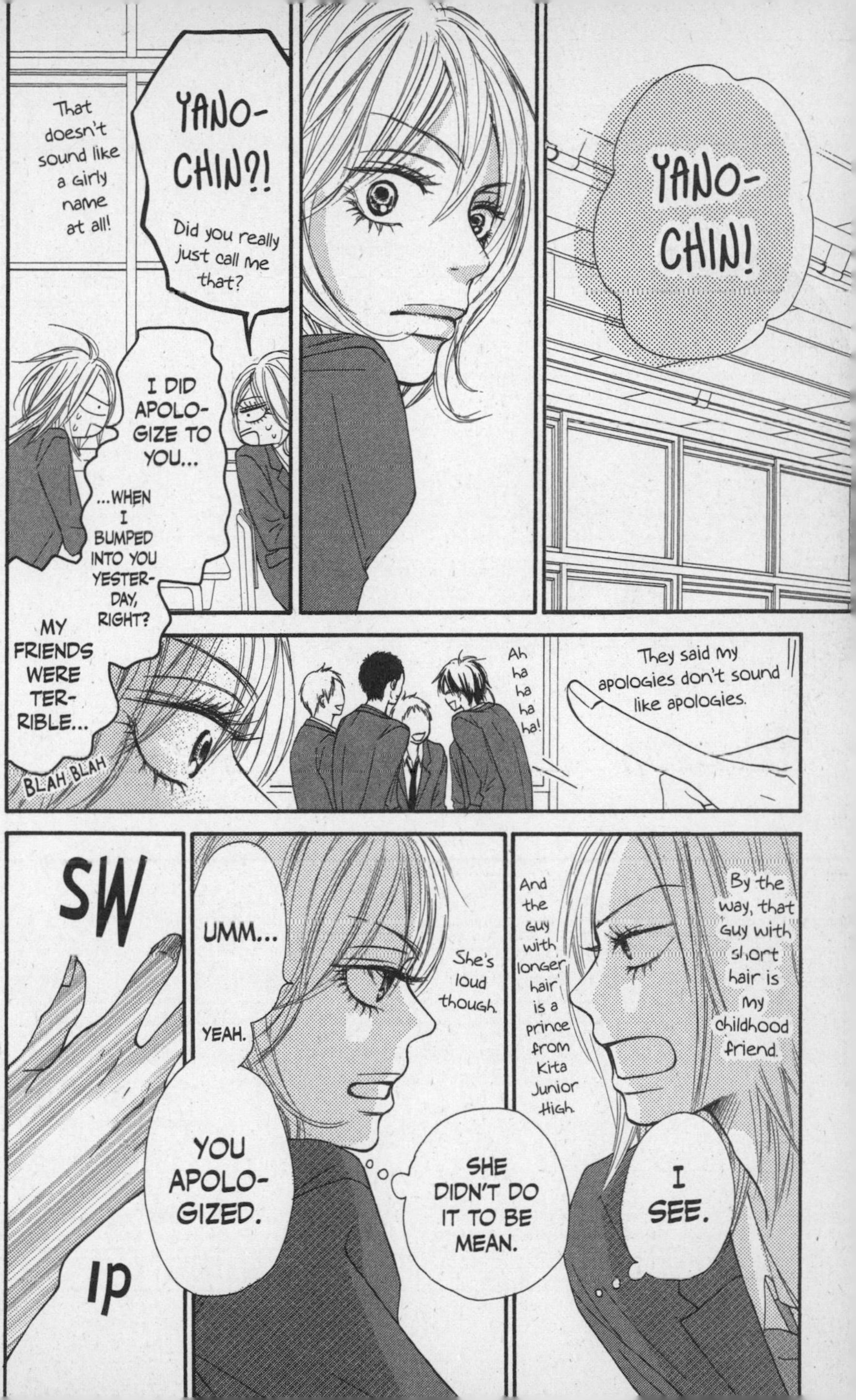
YANO-CHIN!
YANO-CHIN?!
Did you really just call me that?
That doesn't sound like a girly name at all!
I DID APOLOGIZE TO YOU...
...WHEN I BUMPED INTO YOU YESTERDAY, RIGHT?
They said my apologies don't sound like apologies.
Ah ha ha ha ha!
MY FRIENDS WERE TERRIBLE...
BLAH BLAH
By the way, that guy with short hair is my childhood friend.
And the guy with longer hair is a prince from Kita Junior High.
I SEE.
She's loud though.
UMM...
YEAH.
SHE DIDN'T DO IT TO BE MEAN.
YOU APOLOGIZED.
SW
IP

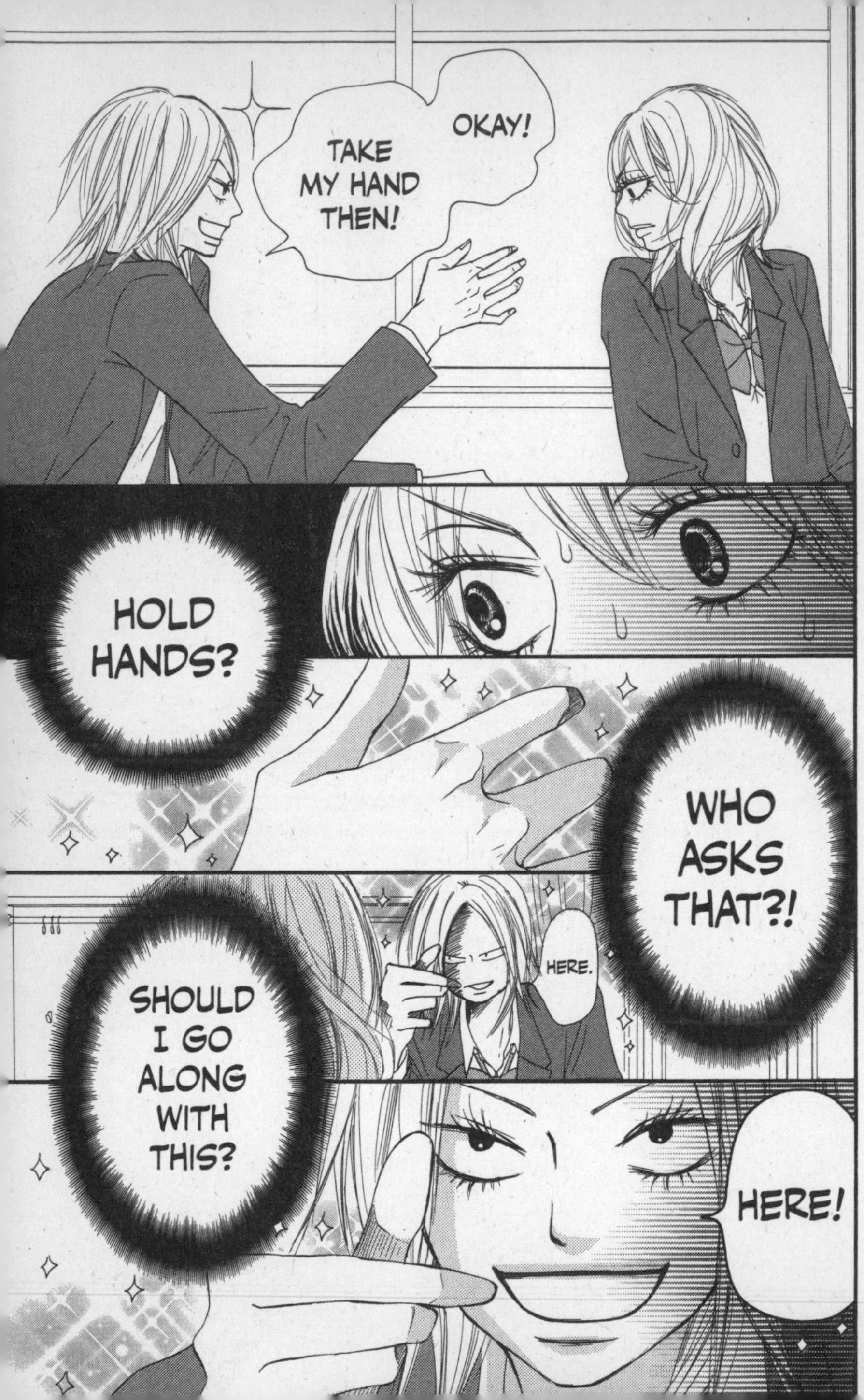
OKAY!
TAKE MY HAND THEN!
HOLD HANDS?
WHO ASKS THAT?!
HERE.
SHOULD I GO ALONG WITH THIS?
HERE!

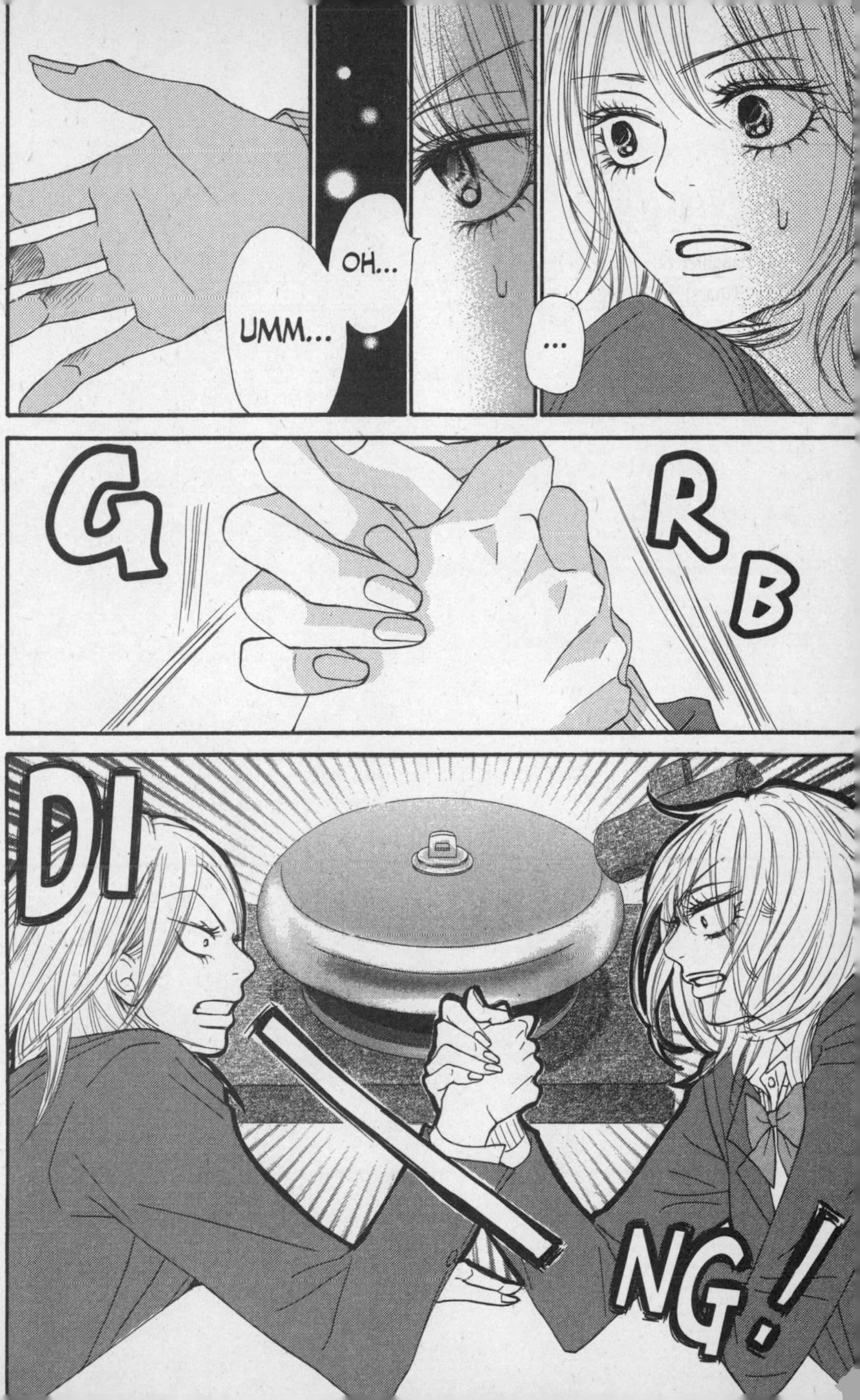
...
OH...
UMM...
G
R
B
DI
NG!

KARUPIN on JAPAN 4

My Daughter Now (Diary)

[Assistants]

Ami-chan

Am ...

Hanna-chan

Hanna...

Yoko-san

Yo ...

Yoko-chan

Yan-yan ...

Yo (pronouncing it) seems to be hard for her. Yoko-chan got a new nickname: Yan-yan. Even after everyone's left for home, she keeps calling their names every now and then.

When she wakes up... Hanna...

Am ... At the stairs...

She likes everyone! See you in Volume 13!

See ☆ ya!

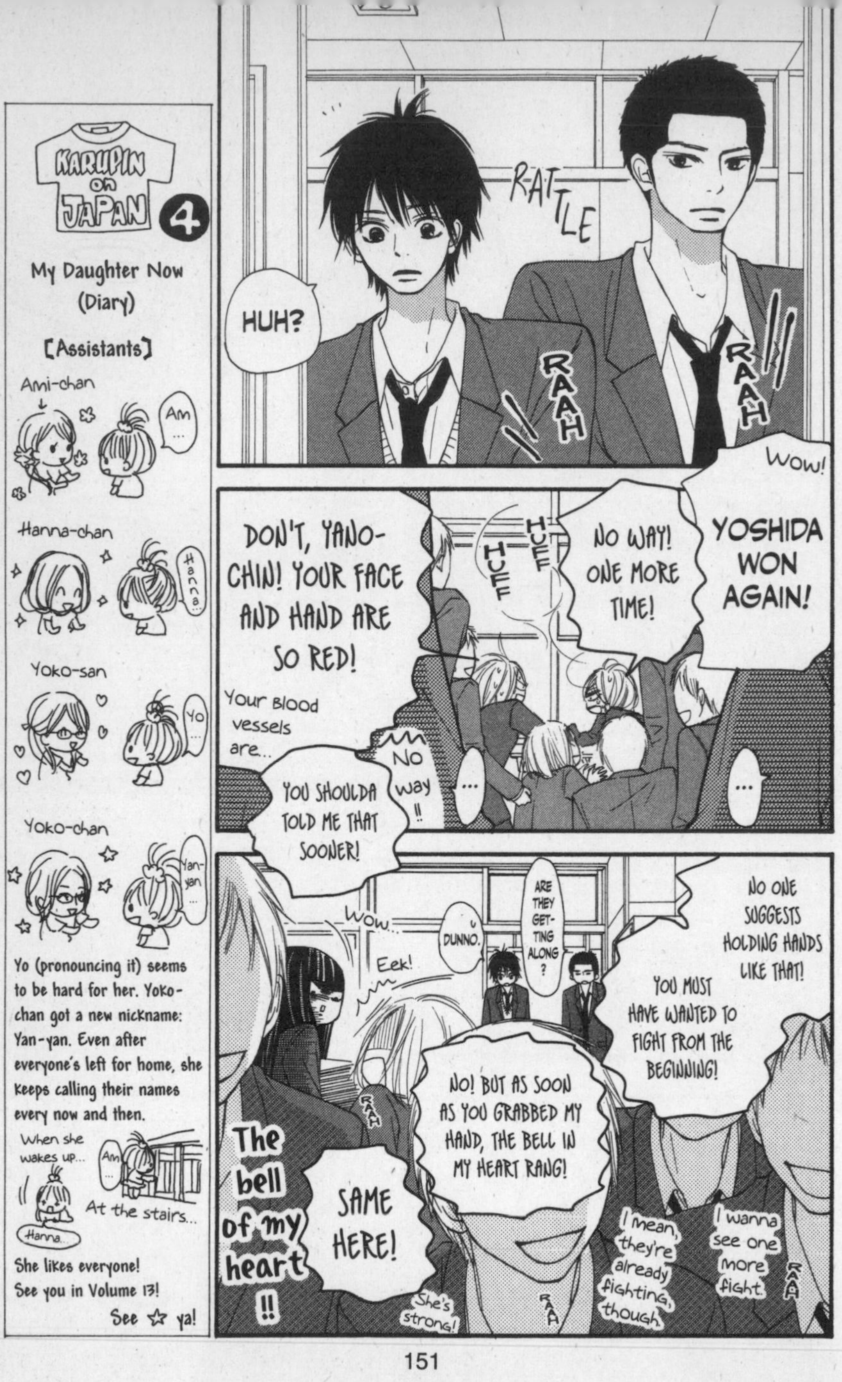

RAAH
RATTLE
HUH?
RAAH
Wow!
YOSHIDA WON AGAIN!
NO WAY! ONE MORE TIME!
HUFF HUFF
DON'T, YANO-CHIN! YOUR FACE AND HAND ARE SO RED!
Your blood vessels are...
...
No way!!
YOU SHOULDA TOLD ME THAT SOONER!
...
NO ONE SUGGESTS HOLDING HANDS LIKE THAT!
YOU MUST HAVE WANTED TO FIGHT FROM THE BEGINNING!
ARE THEY GETTING ALONG?
DUNNO.
Wow...
Eek!
NO! BUT AS SOON AS YOU GRABBED MY HAND, THE BELL IN MY HEART RANG!
I wanna see one more fight.
RAAH
I mean, they're already fighting, though.
RAAH
SAME HERE!
The bell of my heart!!
RAAH
She's strong!

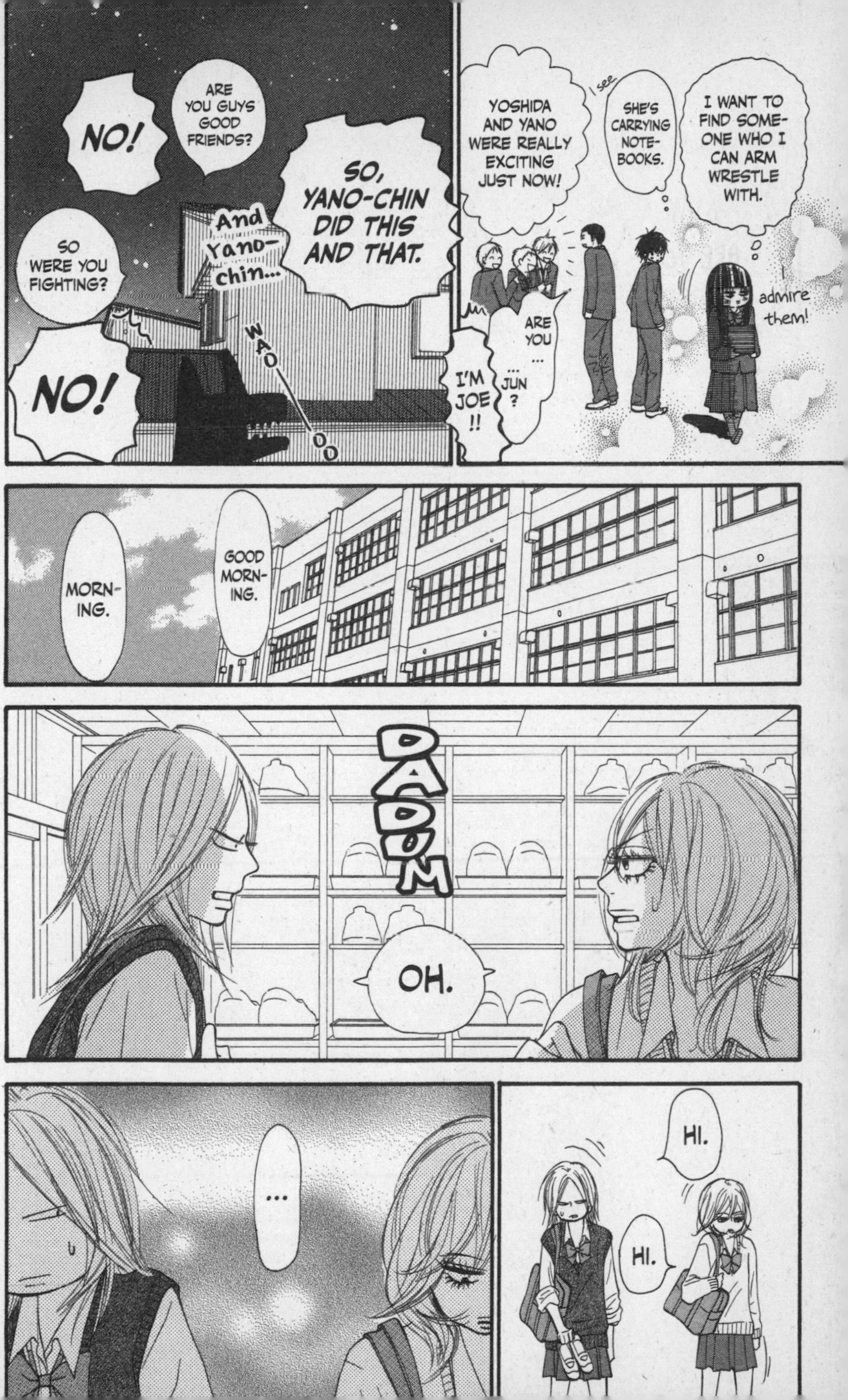
I WANT TO FIND SOME-ONE WHO I CAN ARM WRESTLE WITH.
I admire them!
SHE'S CARRYING NOTE-BOOKS.
I see
YOSHIDA AND YANO WERE REALLY EXCITING JUST NOW!
ARE YOU ... ... JUN?
I'M JOE!!
SO, YANO-CHIN DID THIS AND THAT.
ARE YOU GUYS GOOD FRIENDS?
NO!
And Yano-chin...
SO WERE YOU FIGHTING?
NO!
WAO—OO
GOOD MORN-ING.
MORN-ING.
DADUM
OH.
HI.
HI.
...

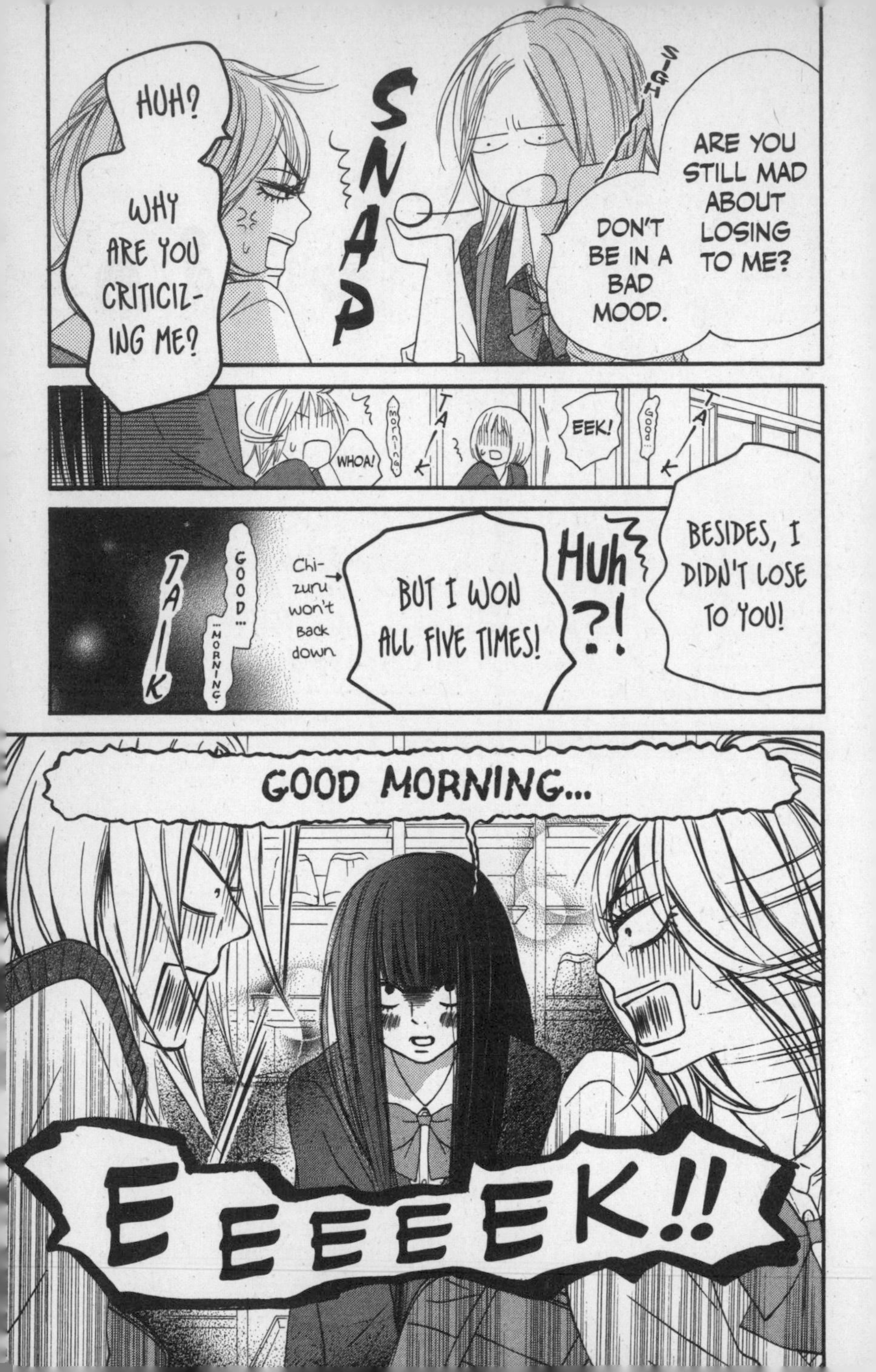
SIGH
ARE YOU STILL MAD ABOUT LOSING TO ME?
DON'T BE IN A BAD MOOD.
SNAP
HUH?
WHY ARE YOU CRITICIZ-ING ME?
TAIK
Good...
EEK!
TAIK
...morning.
WHOA!
BESIDES, I DIDN'T LOSE TO YOU!
Huh?!
BUT I WON ALL FIVE TIMES!
Chi-zuru won't back down
GOOD...
...MORNING.
TAIK
GOOD MORNING...
EEEEEK!!

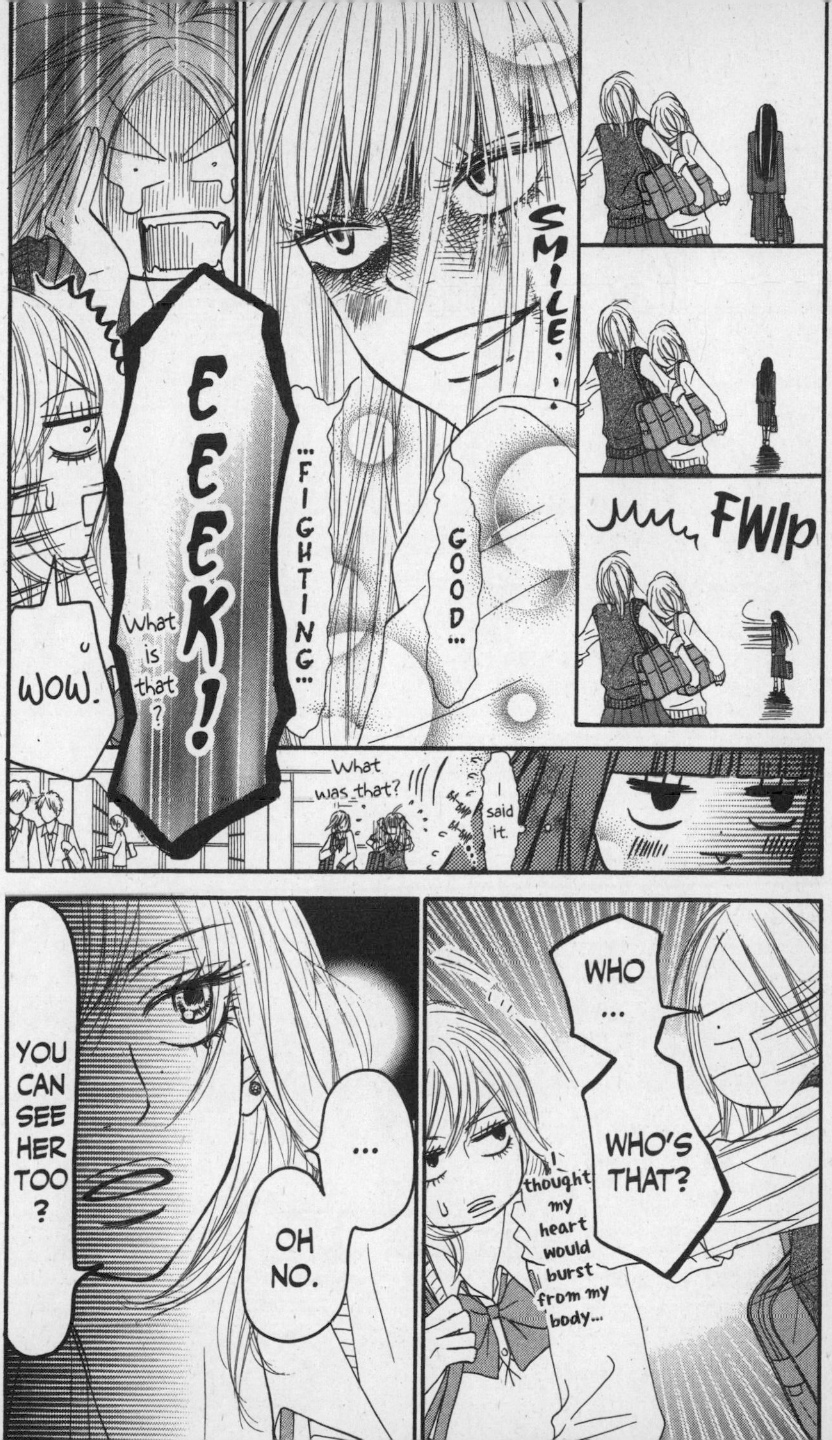
FWIP
SMILE...
...FIGHTING...
GOOD...
EEEK!
What is that?
WOW.
I said it.
What was that?
WHO... WHO'S THAT?
I thought my heart would burst from my body...
...
OH NO.
YOU CAN SEE HER TOO?

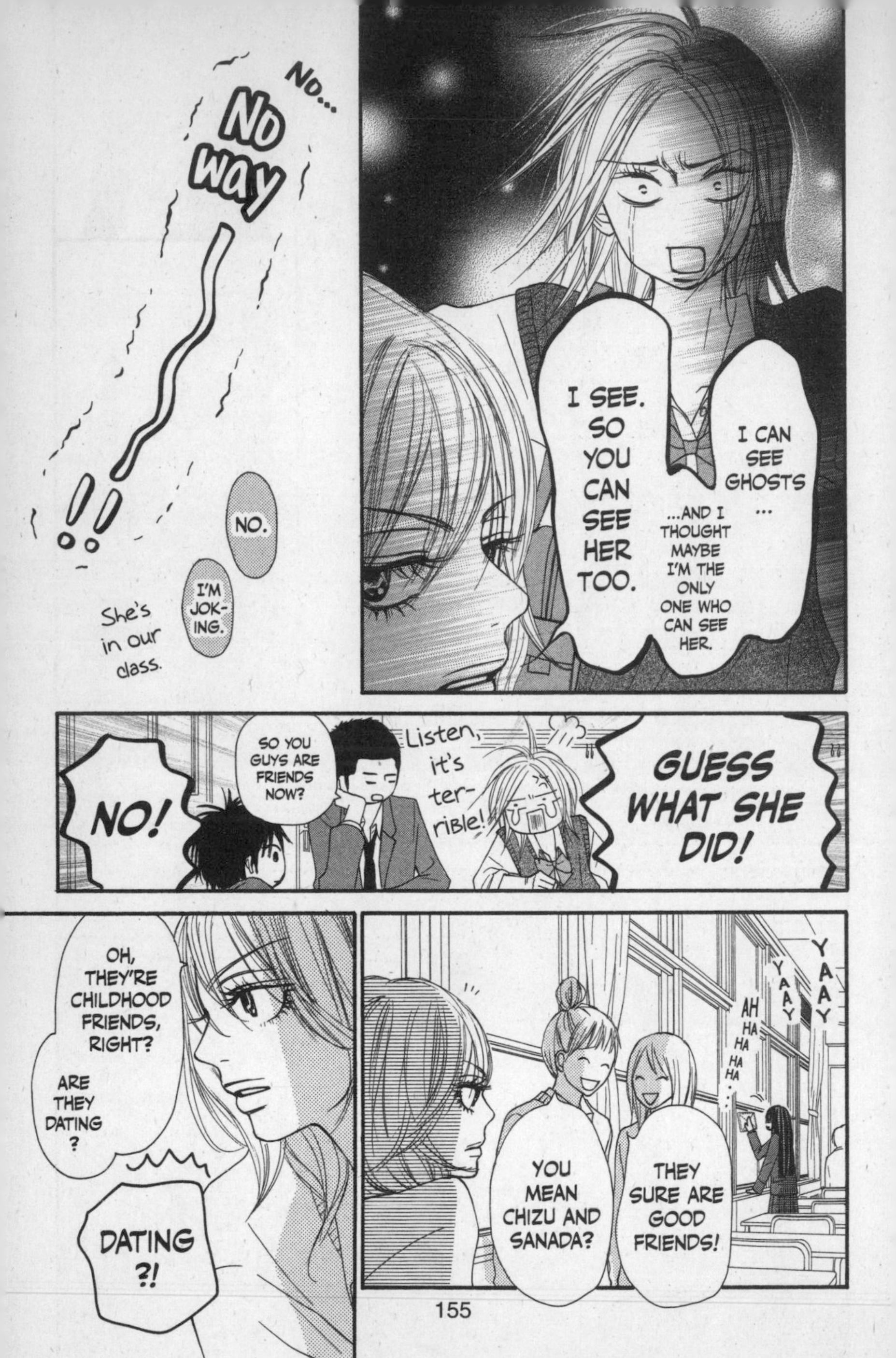
I CAN SEE GHOSTS...
...AND I THOUGHT MAYBE I'M THE ONLY ONE WHO CAN SEE HER.
I SEE. SO YOU CAN SEE HER TOO.
No...
No way
!!
NO.
I'M JOK-ING.
She's in our class.
GUESS WHAT SHE DID!
Listen, it's ter-rible!
SO YOU GUYS ARE FRIENDS NOW?
NO!
YAAY
YAAY
AH HA HA HA HA...
THEY SURE ARE GOOD FRIENDS!
YOU MEAN CHIZU AND SANADA?
OH, THEY'RE CHILDHOOD FRIENDS, RIGHT?
ARE THEY DATING?
DATING?!

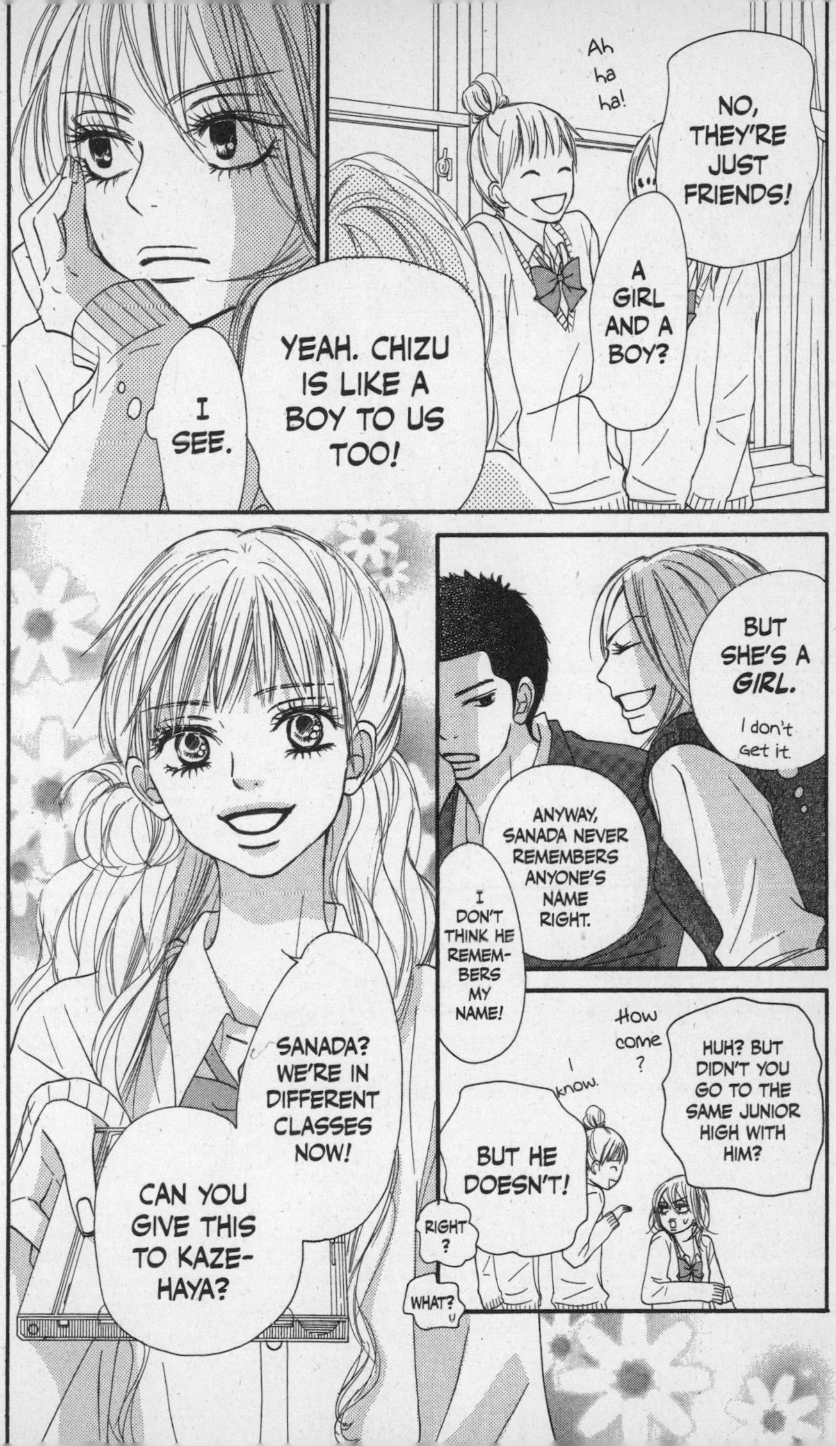
NO, THEY'RE JUST FRIENDS!
Ah ha ha!
A GIRL AND A BOY?
YEAH. CHIZU IS LIKE A BOY TO US TOO!
I SEE.
BUT SHE'S A GIRL.
I don't get it.
ANYWAY, SANADA NEVER REMEMBERS ANYONE'S NAME RIGHT.
I DON'T THINK HE REMEMBERS MY NAME!
HUH? BUT DIDN'T YOU GO TO THE SAME JUNIOR HIGH WITH HIM?
How come?
I know.
BUT HE DOESN'T!
RIGHT?
WHAT?
SANADA? WE'RE IN DIFFERENT CLASSES NOW!
CAN YOU GIVE THIS TO KAZE-HAYA?

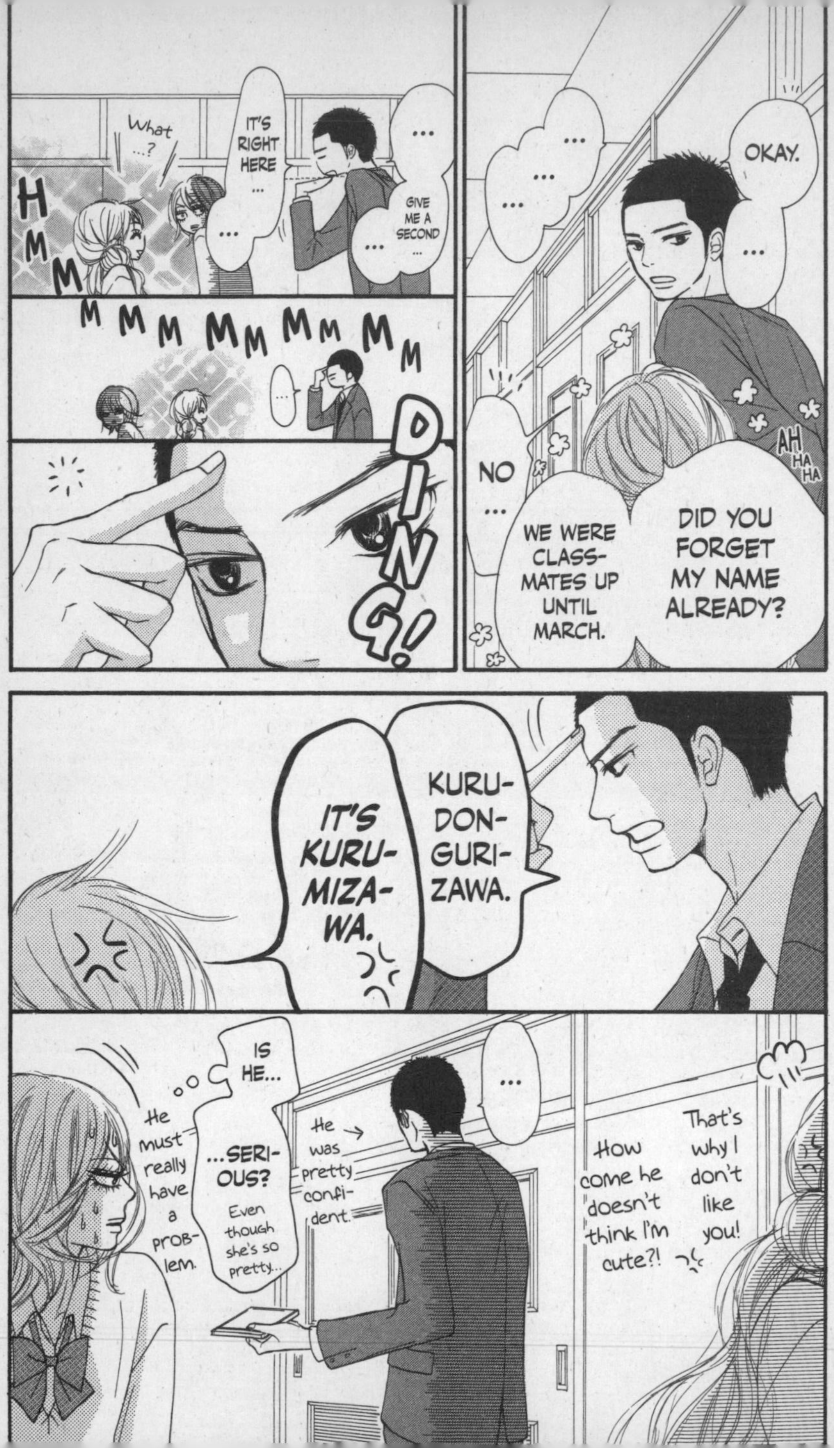
OKAY.
...
...
...
...
DID YOU FORGET MY NAME ALREADY?
AH HA HA
WE WERE CLASSMATES UP UNTIL MARCH.
NO ...
...
GIVE ME A SECOND ...
IT'S RIGHT HERE ...
...
What ...?
HMMMMMMMMMMMMM
...
DING!
KURU-DON-GURI-ZAWA.
IT'S KURU-MIZA-WA.
That's why I don't like you!
How come he doesn't think I'm cute?!
...
He was pretty confident.
IS HE... ...SERIOUS?
Even though she's so pretty...
He must really have a problem.

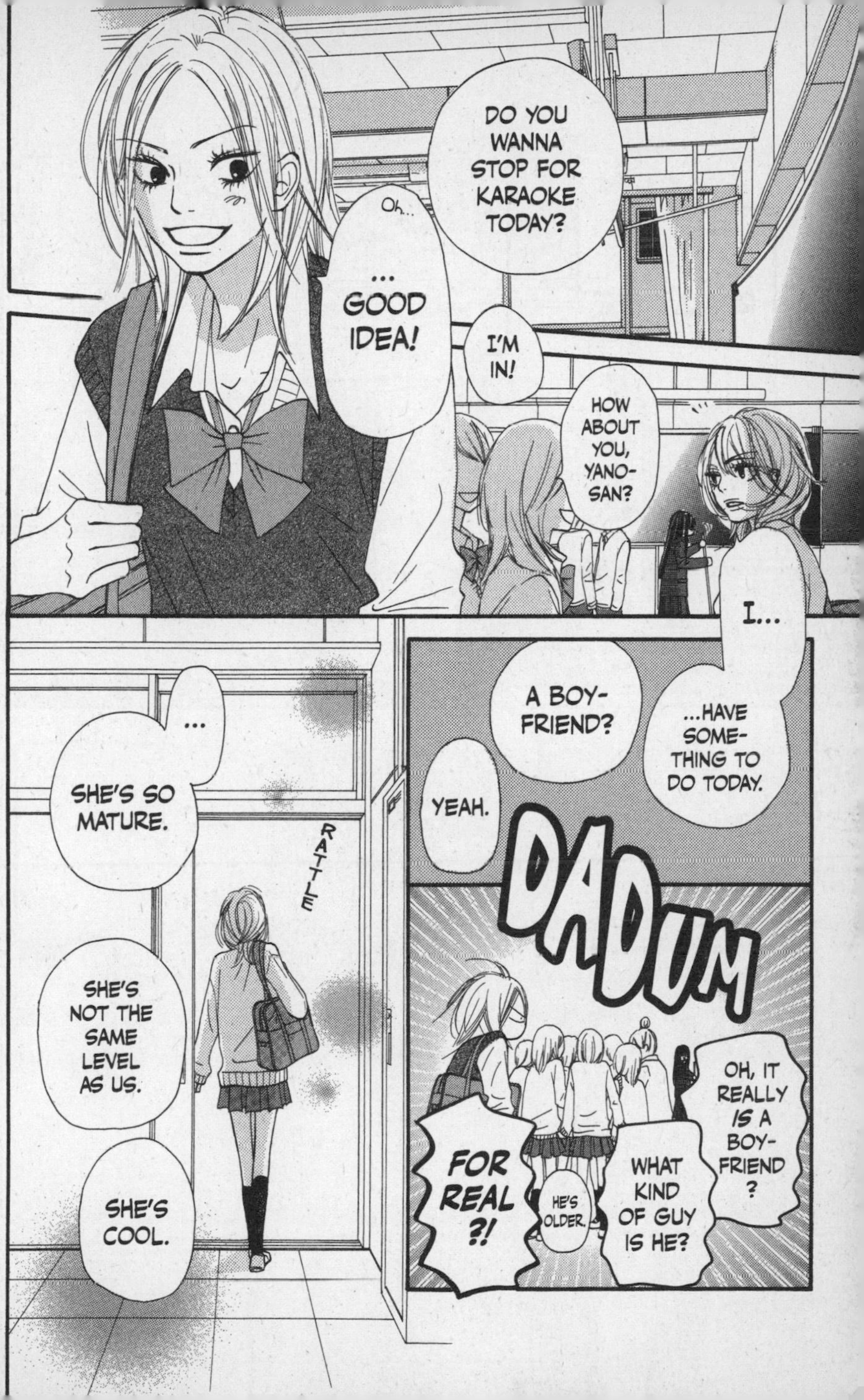
DO YOU WANNA STOP FOR KARAOKE TODAY?
Oh... ...GOOD IDEA!
I'M IN!
HOW ABOUT YOU, YANO-SAN?
I... ...HAVE SOMETHING TO DO TODAY.
A BOY-FRIEND?
YEAH.
DADUM
OH, IT REALLY IS A BOY-FRIEND?
WHAT KIND OF GUY IS HE?
HE'S OLDER.
FOR REAL?!
...
SHE'S SO MATURE.
RATTLE
SHE'S NOT THE SAME LEVEL AS US.
SHE'S COOL.

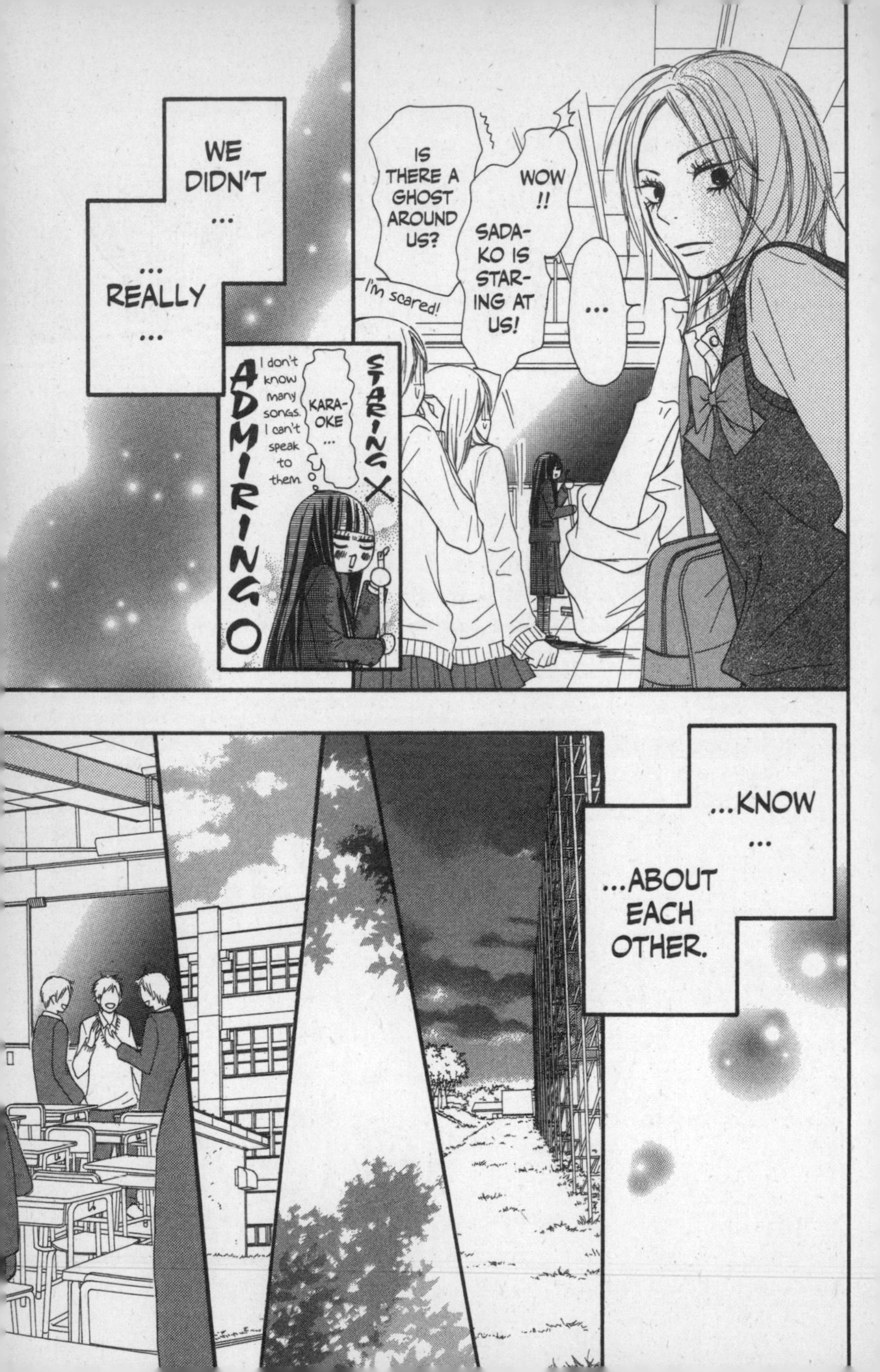
WOW!! SADAKO IS STARING AT US!
IS THERE A GHOST AROUND US?
I'm scared!
...
STARING ✕
KARAOKE...
I don't know many songs. I can't speak to them.
ADMIRING ○
WE DIDN'T ... ... REALLY ...
...KNOW ... ...ABOUT EACH OTHER.

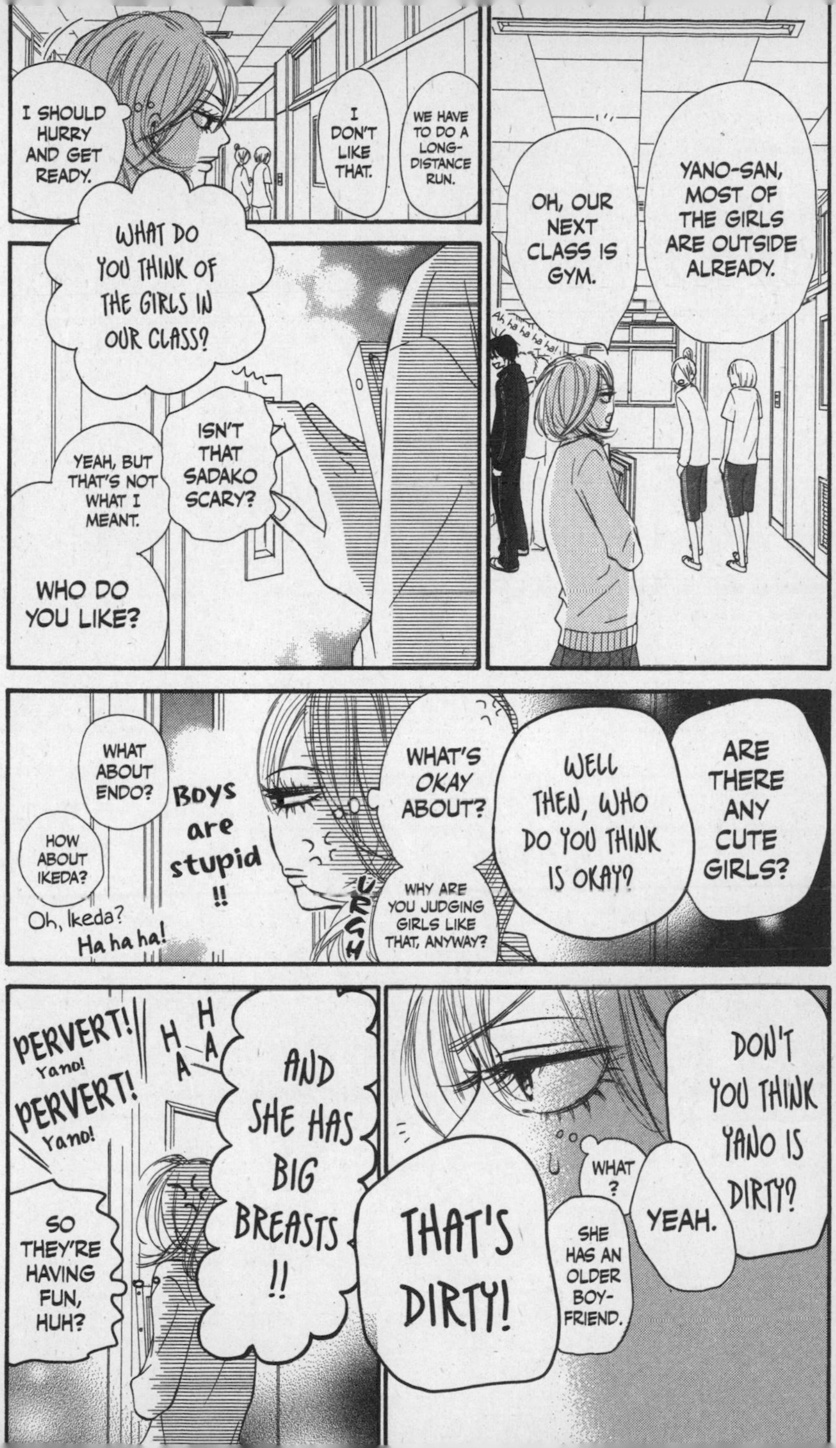
YANO-SAN, MOST OF THE GIRLS ARE OUTSIDE ALREADY.
OH, OUR NEXT CLASS IS GYM.
Ah ha ha ha ha!
WE HAVE TO DO A LONG-DISTANCE RUN.
I DON'T LIKE THAT.
I SHOULD HURRY AND GET READY.
WHAT DO YOU THINK OF THE GIRLS IN OUR CLASS?
ISN'T THAT SADAKO SCARY?
YEAH, BUT THAT'S NOT WHAT I MEANT.
WHO DO YOU LIKE?
ARE THERE ANY CUTE GIRLS?
WELL THEN, WHO DO YOU THINK IS OKAY?
WHAT'S OKAY ABOUT?
WHY ARE YOU JUDGING GIRLS LIKE THAT, ANYWAY?
URGH
Boys are stupid !!
WHAT ABOUT ENDO?
HOW ABOUT IKEDA?
Oh, Ikeda?
Ha ha ha!
DON'T YOU THINK YANO IS DIRTY?
YEAH.
WHAT?
SHE HAS AN OLDER BOY-FRIEND.
THAT'S DIRTY!
AND SHE HAS BIG BREASTS !!
HA HA
PERVERT! Yano!
PERVERT! Yano!
SO THEY'RE HAVING FUN, HUH?

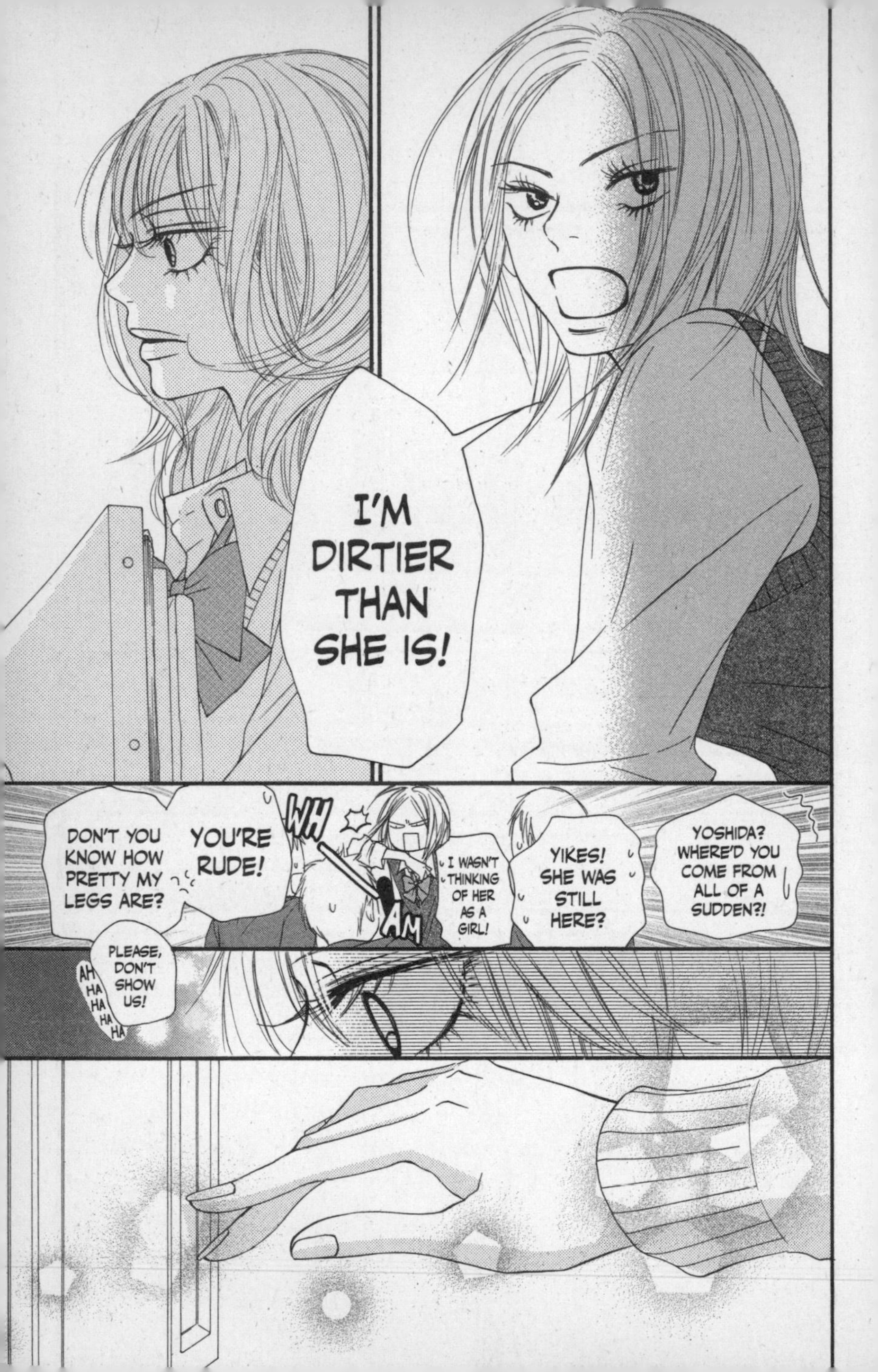
I'M DIRTIER THAN SHE IS!
YOSHIDA? WHERE'D YOU COME FROM ALL OF A SUDDEN?!
YIKES! SHE WAS STILL HERE?
I WASN'T THINKING OF HER AS A GIRL!
WH
AM
YOU'RE RUDE!
DON'T YOU KNOW HOW PRETTY MY LEGS ARE?
PLEASE, DON'T SHOW US!
AH HA HA HA HA

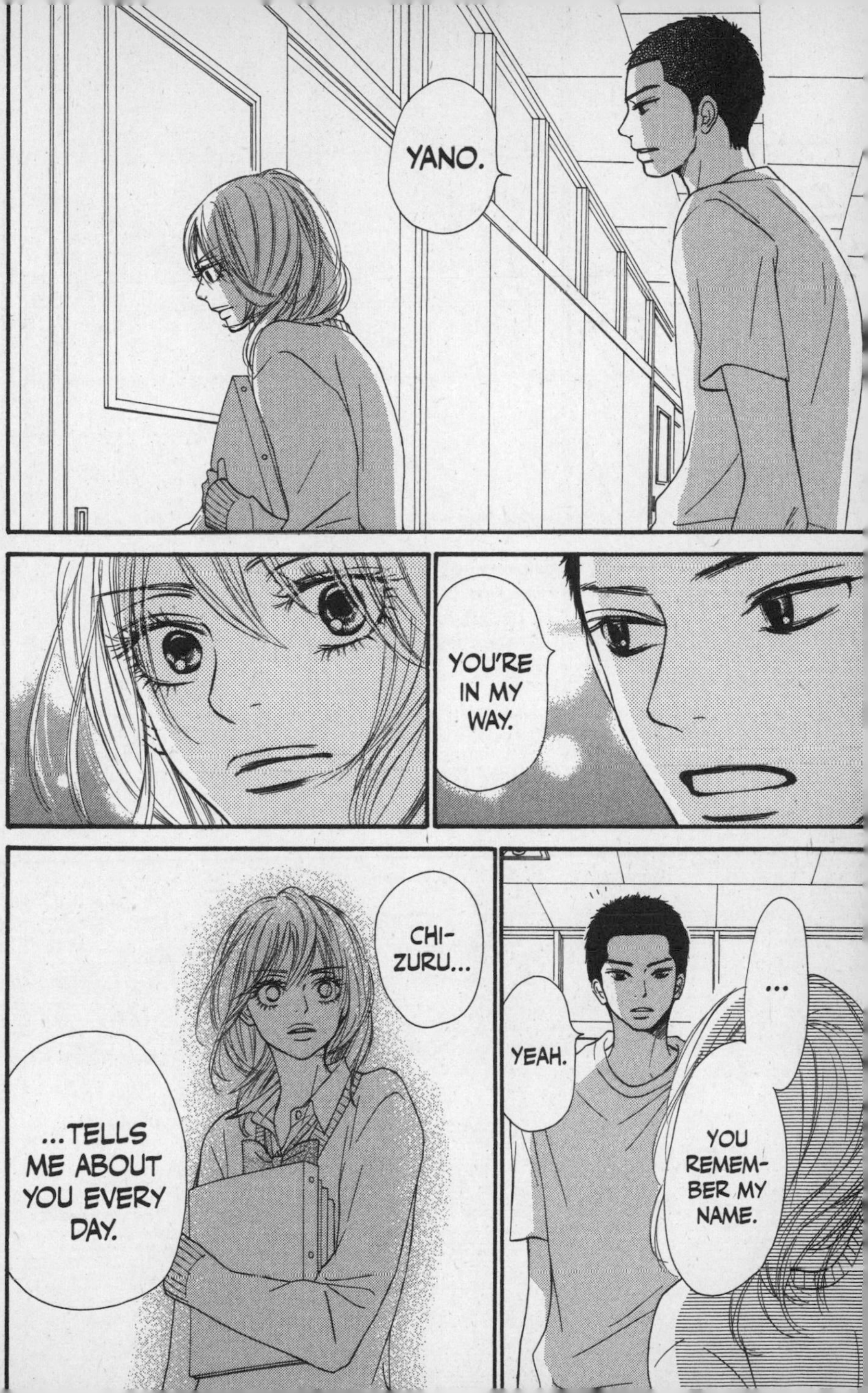
YANO.
YOU'RE IN MY WAY.
... YOU REMEMBER MY NAME.
YEAH.
CHI-ZURU...
...TELLS ME ABOUT YOU EVERY DAY.

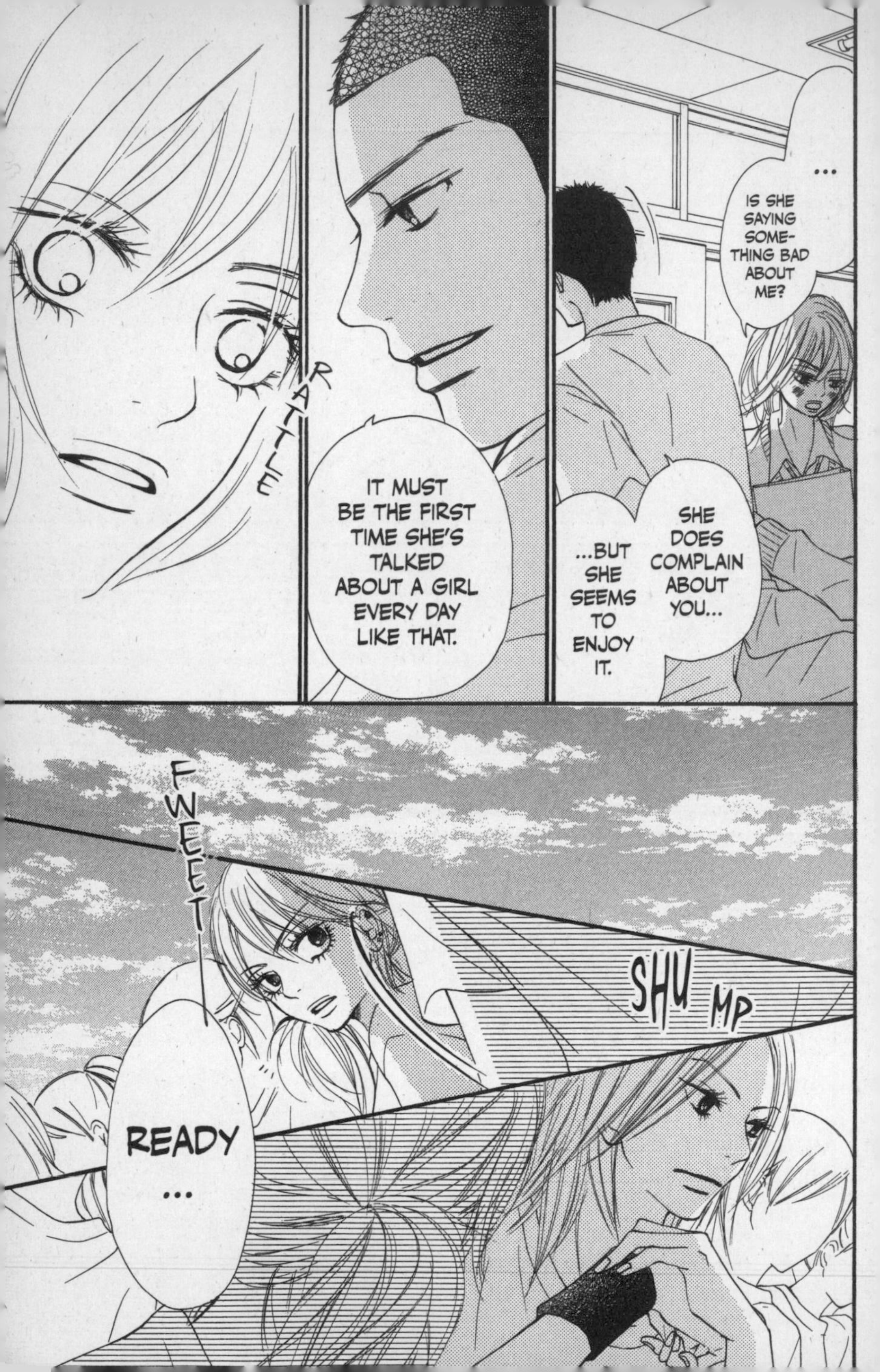
...
IS SHE SAYING SOMETHING BAD ABOUT ME?
SHE DOES COMPLAIN ABOUT YOU...
...BUT SHE SEEMS TO ENJOY IT.
IT MUST BE THE FIRST TIME SHE'S TALKED ABOUT A GIRL EVERY DAY LIKE THAT.
RATTLE
FWEEET
SHUMP
READY ...

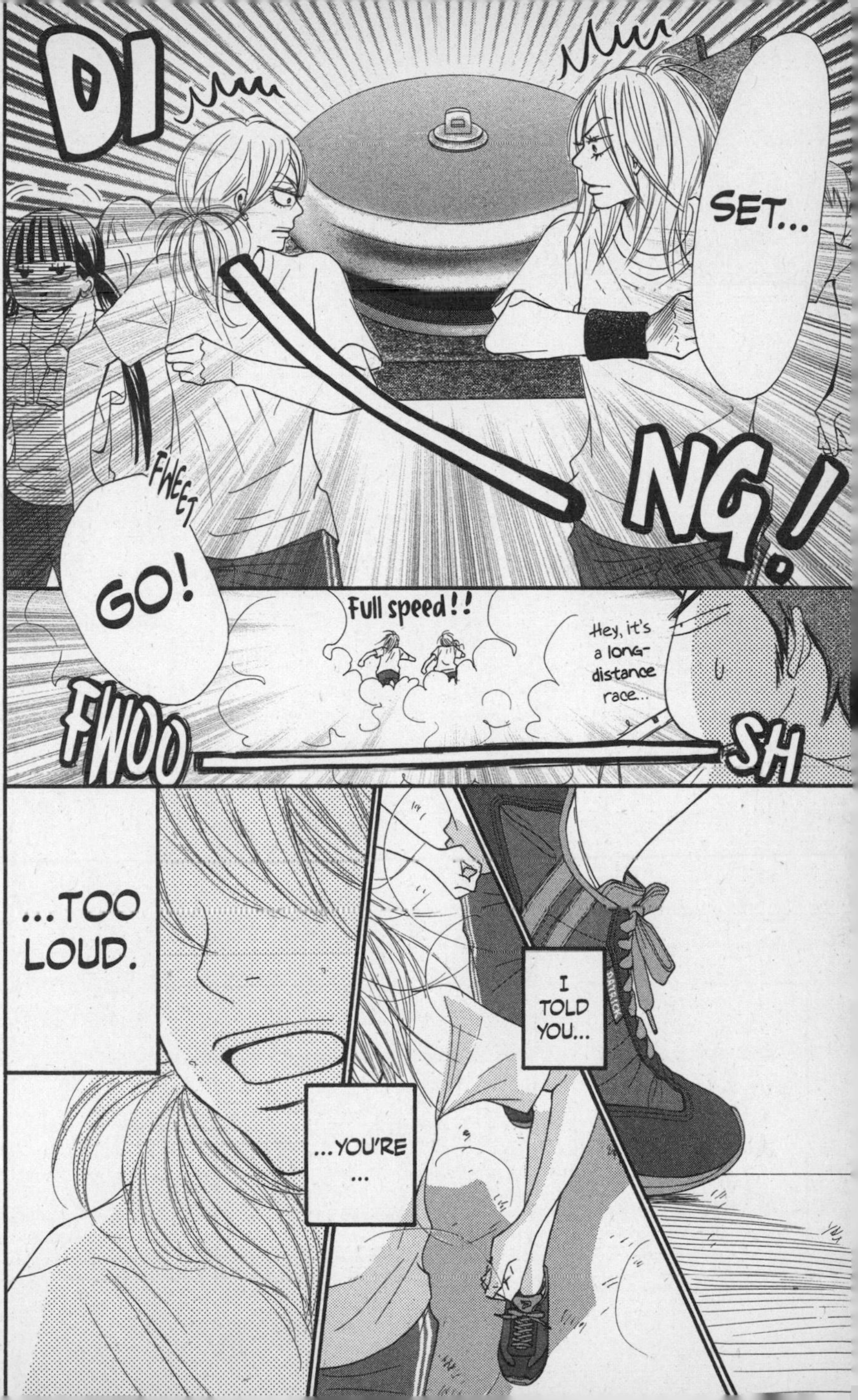
SET...
DI
NG!
FWEET
GO!
Hey, it's a long-distance race...
Full speed!!
FWOO
SH
I TOLD YOU...
...YOU'RE ...
...TOO LOUD.

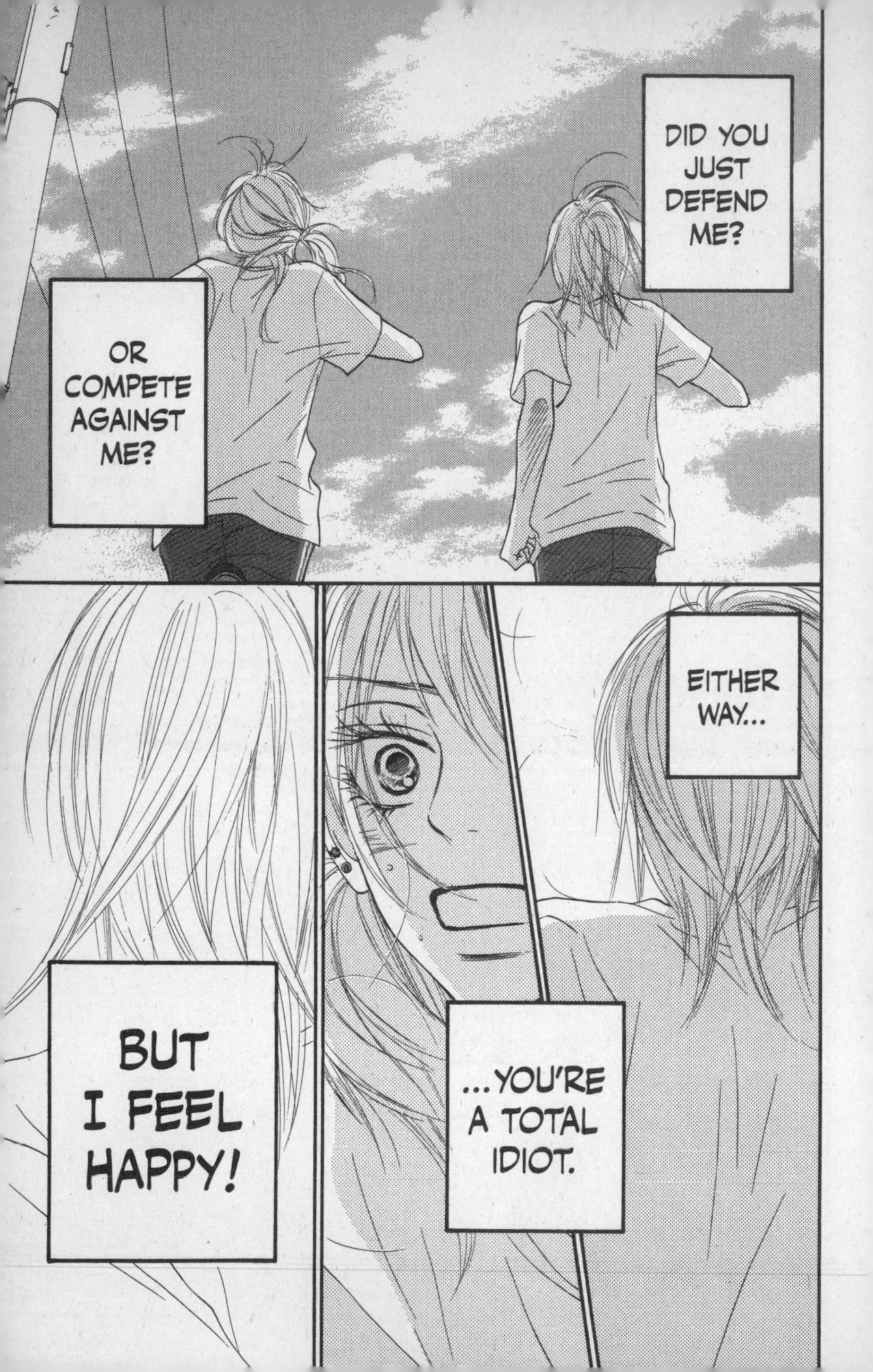
DID YOU JUST DEFEND ME?
OR COMPETE AGAINST ME?
EITHER WAY...
...YOU'RE A TOTAL IDIOT.
BUT I FEEL HAPPY!

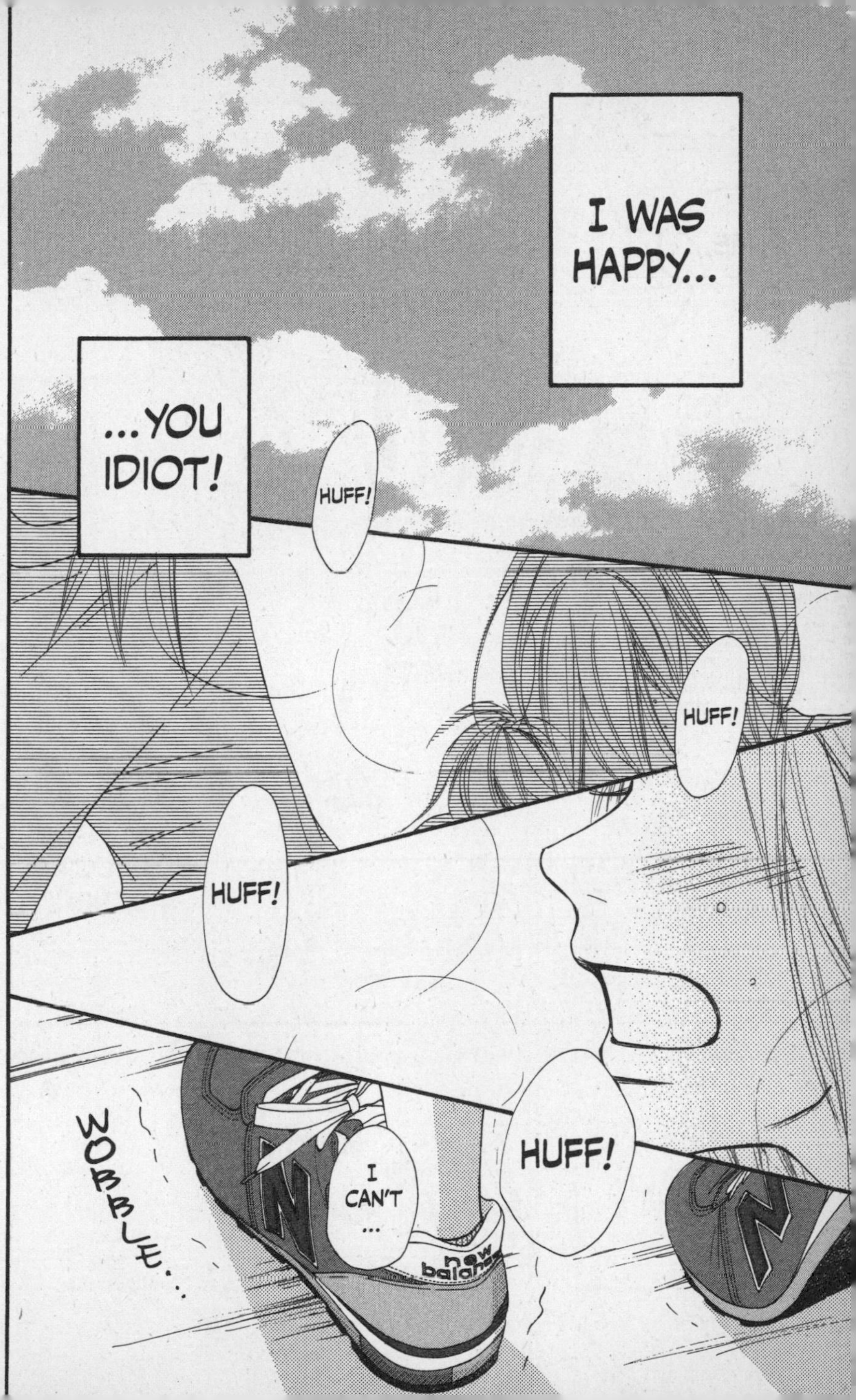
I WAS HAPPY...
...YOU IDIOT!
HUFF!
HUFF!
HUFF!
HUFF!
I CAN'T ...
WOBBLE...

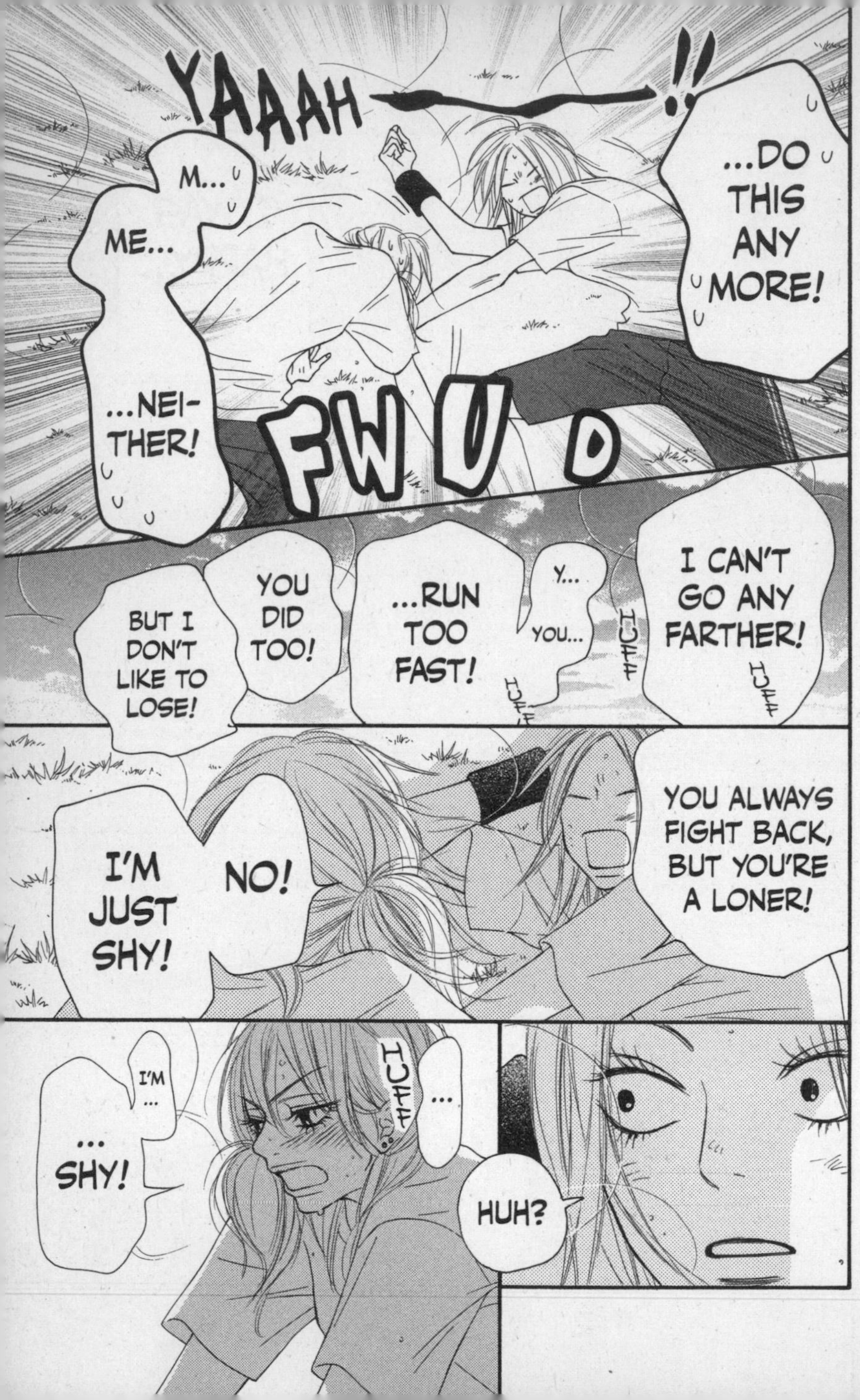
...DO THIS ANY MORE!
YAAAH!!
M... ME... ...NEI-THER!
FWUD
I CAN'T GO ANY FARTHER!
HUFF
HUFF
Y... YOU... ...RUN TOO FAST!
HUFF
YOU DID TOO!
BUT I DON'T LIKE TO LOSE!
YOU ALWAYS FIGHT BACK, BUT YOU'RE A LONER!
NO!
I'M JUST SHY!
HUH?
...
HUFF
I'M ... ... SHY!

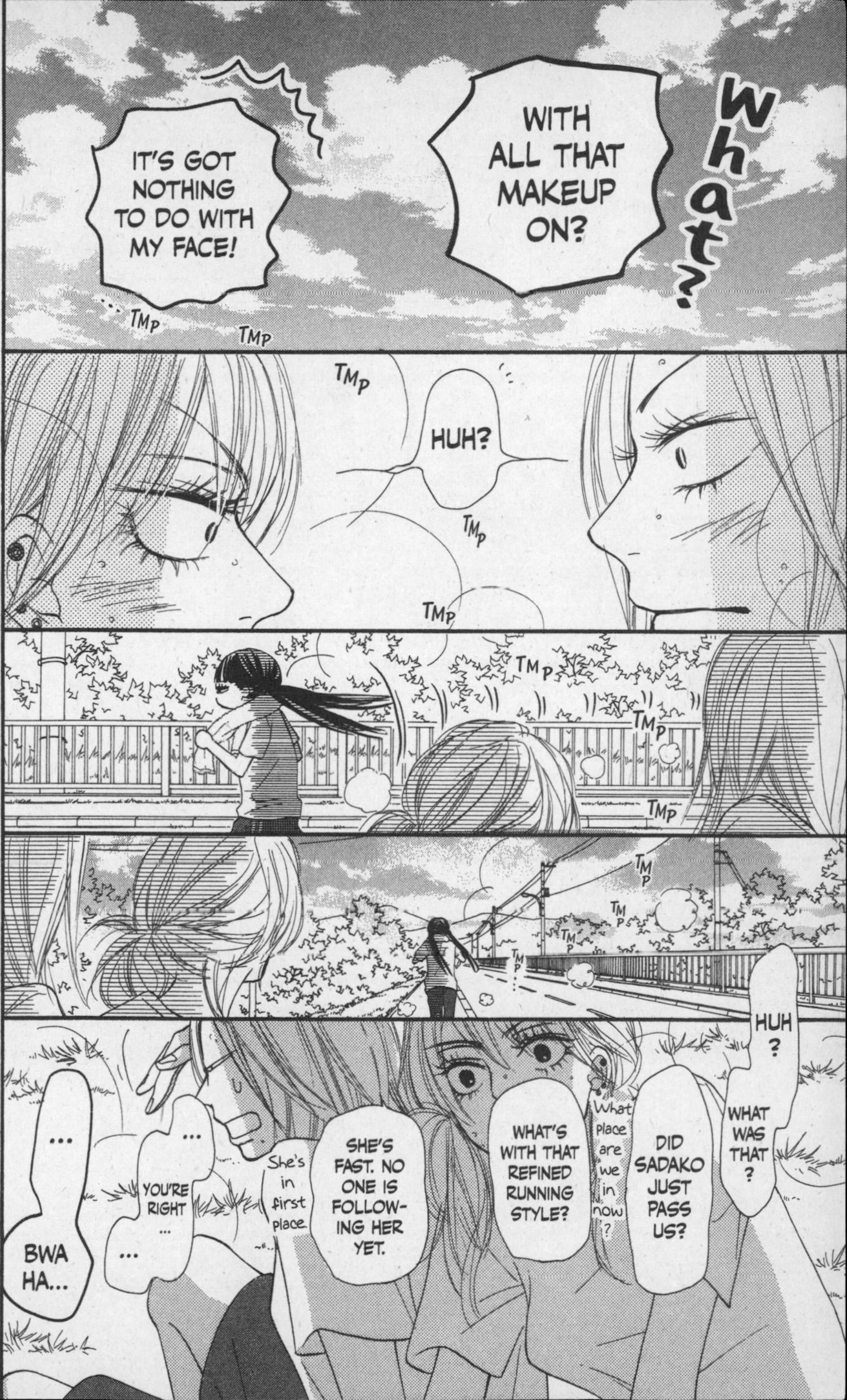
What?
WITH ALL THAT MAKEUP ON?
IT'S GOT NOTHING TO DO WITH MY FACE!
TMP
TMP
TMP
HUH?
TMP
TMP
TMP
TMP
TMP
TMP
TMP
TMP
TMP
HUH?
WHAT WAS THAT?
DID SADAKO JUST PASS US?
What place are we in now?
WHAT'S WITH THAT REFINED RUNNING STYLE?
SHE'S FAST. NO ONE IS FOLLOWING HER YET.
She's in first place.
... YOU'RE RIGHT ... ...
... BWA HA...

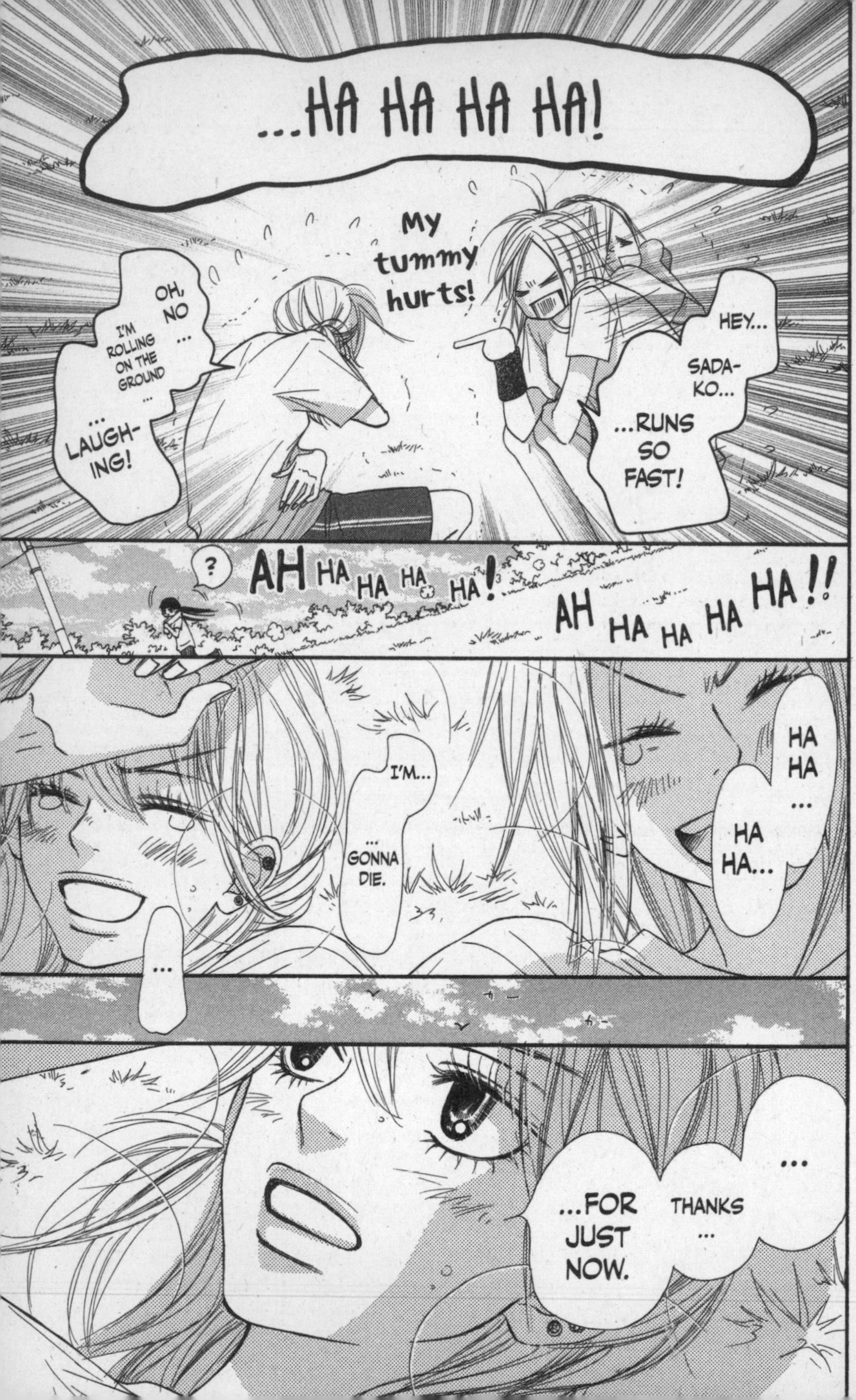
...HA HA HA HA!
HEY... SADAKO... ...RUNS SO FAST!
My tummy hurts!
OH, NO ... I'M ROLLING ON THE GROUND ... ... LAUGHING!
AH HA HA HA HA!!
AH HA HA HA HA!
?
HA HA ... HA HA...
I'M... ... GONNA DIE.
...
... THANKS ...
...FOR JUST NOW.

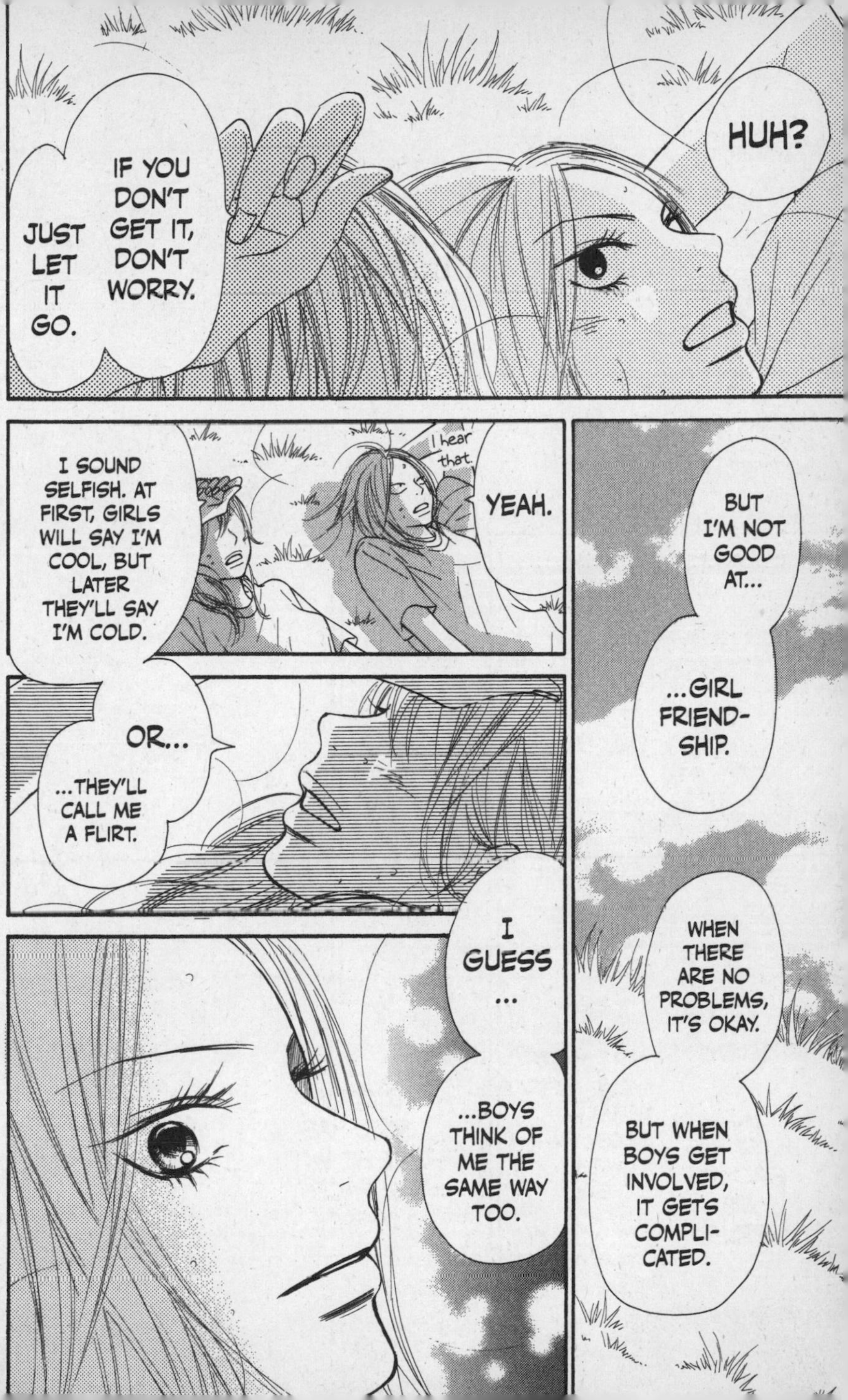
HUH?
IF YOU DON'T GET IT, DON'T WORRY.
JUST LET IT GO.
BUT I'M NOT GOOD AT...
...GIRL FRIEND-SHIP.
WHEN THERE ARE NO PROBLEMS, IT'S OKAY.
BUT WHEN BOYS GET INVOLVED, IT GETS COMPLI-CATED.
I hear that.
YEAH.
I SOUND SELFISH. AT FIRST, GIRLS WILL SAY I'M COOL, BUT LATER THEY'LL SAY I'M COLD.
OR...
...THEY'LL CALL ME A FLIRT.
I GUESS...
...BOYS THINK OF ME THE SAME WAY TOO.

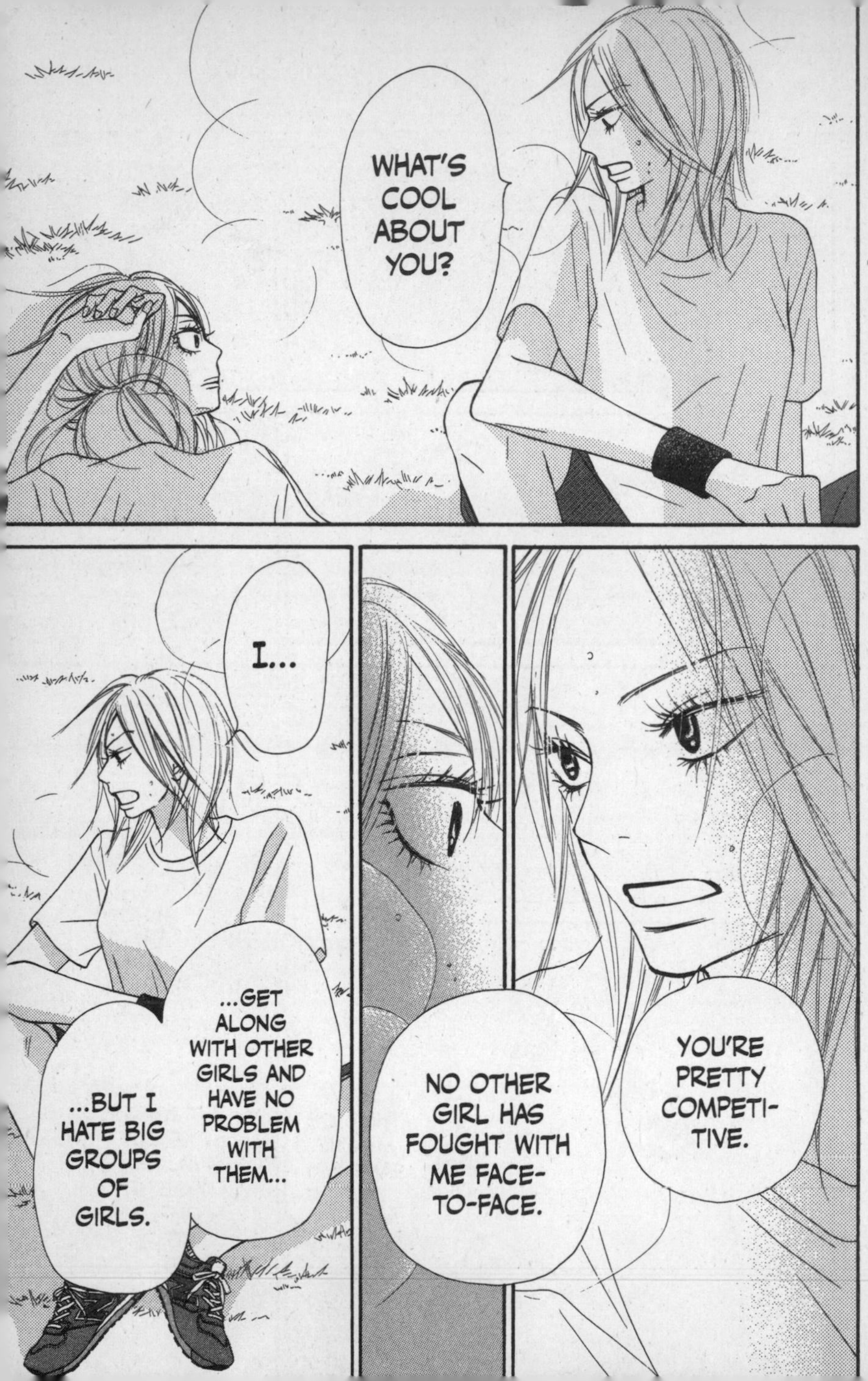
WHAT'S COOL ABOUT YOU?
YOU'RE PRETTY COMPETI-TIVE.
NO OTHER GIRL HAS FOUGHT WITH ME FACE-TO-FACE.
I...
...GET ALONG WITH OTHER GIRLS AND HAVE NO PROBLEM WITH THEM...
...BUT I HATE BIG GROUPS OF GIRLS.

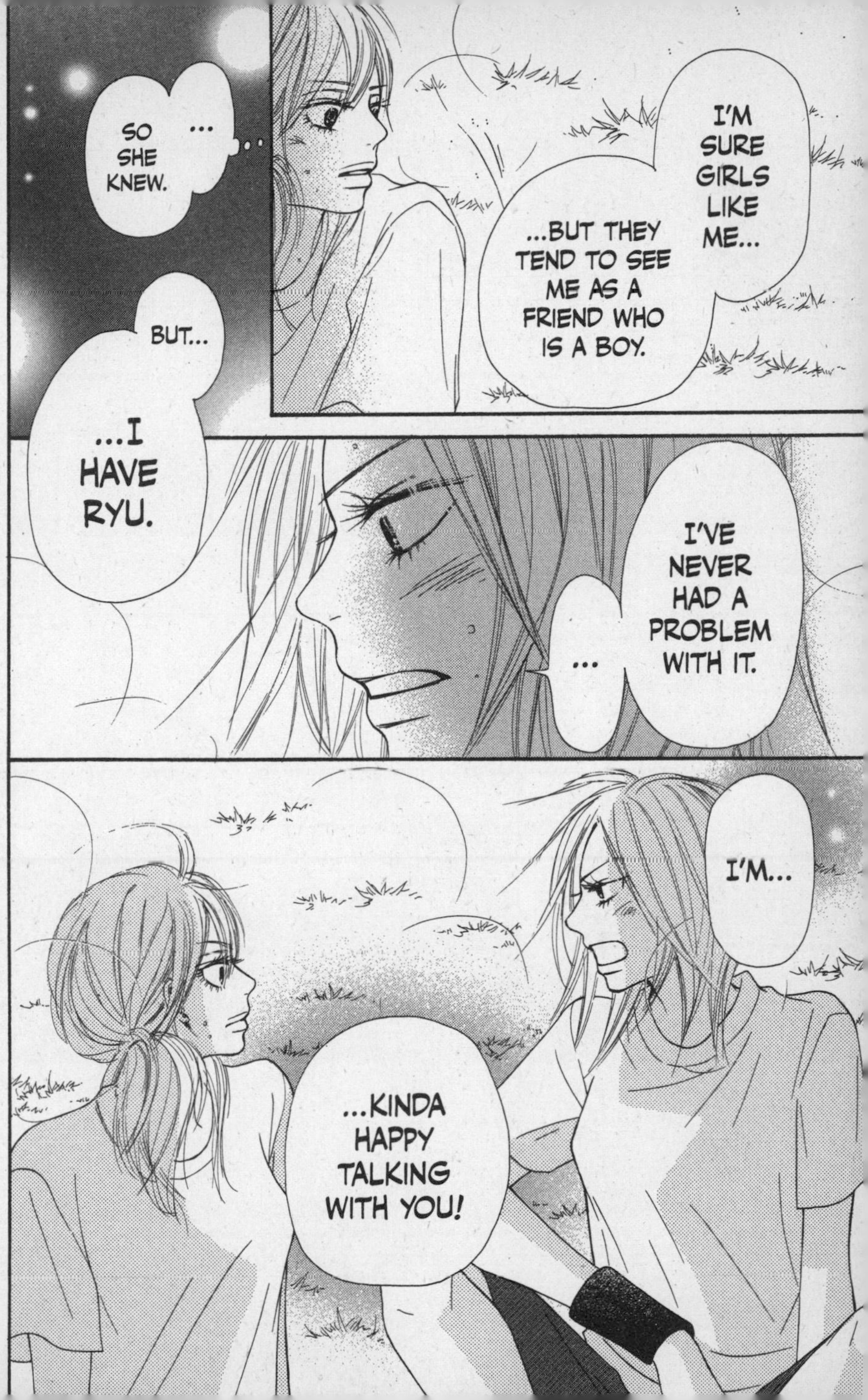
I'M SURE GIRLS LIKE ME...
...BUT THEY TEND TO SEE ME AS A FRIEND WHO IS A BOY.
SO ... SHE KNEW.
BUT...
...I HAVE RYU.
I'VE NEVER HAD A PROBLEM WITH IT.
...
I'M...
...KINDA HAPPY TALKING WITH YOU!

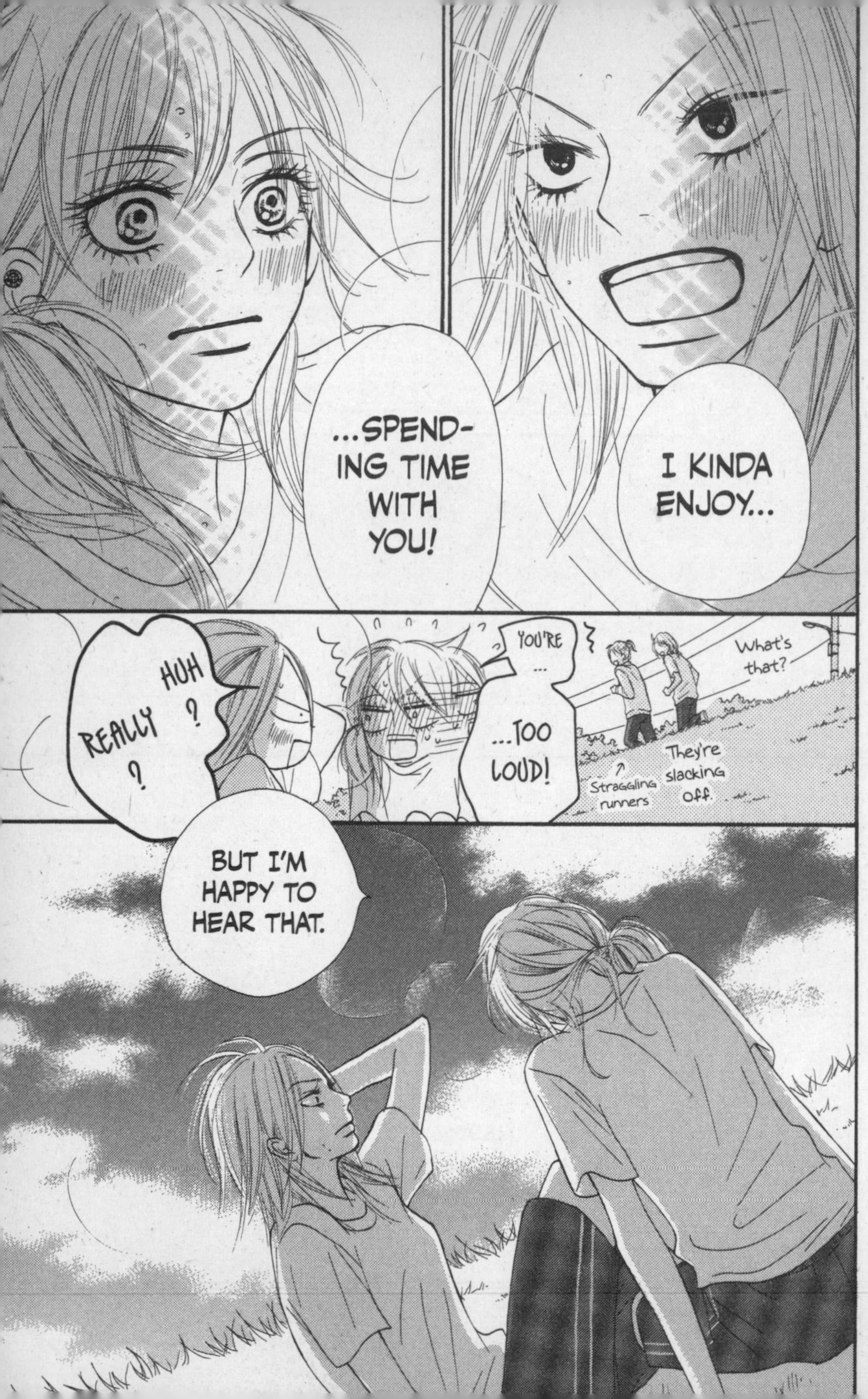
I KINDA ENJOY...
...SPENDING TIME WITH YOU!
What's that?
They're slacking off.
Straggling runners
YOU'RE ... ...TOO LOUD!
HUH? REALLY?
BUT I'M HAPPY TO HEAR THAT.

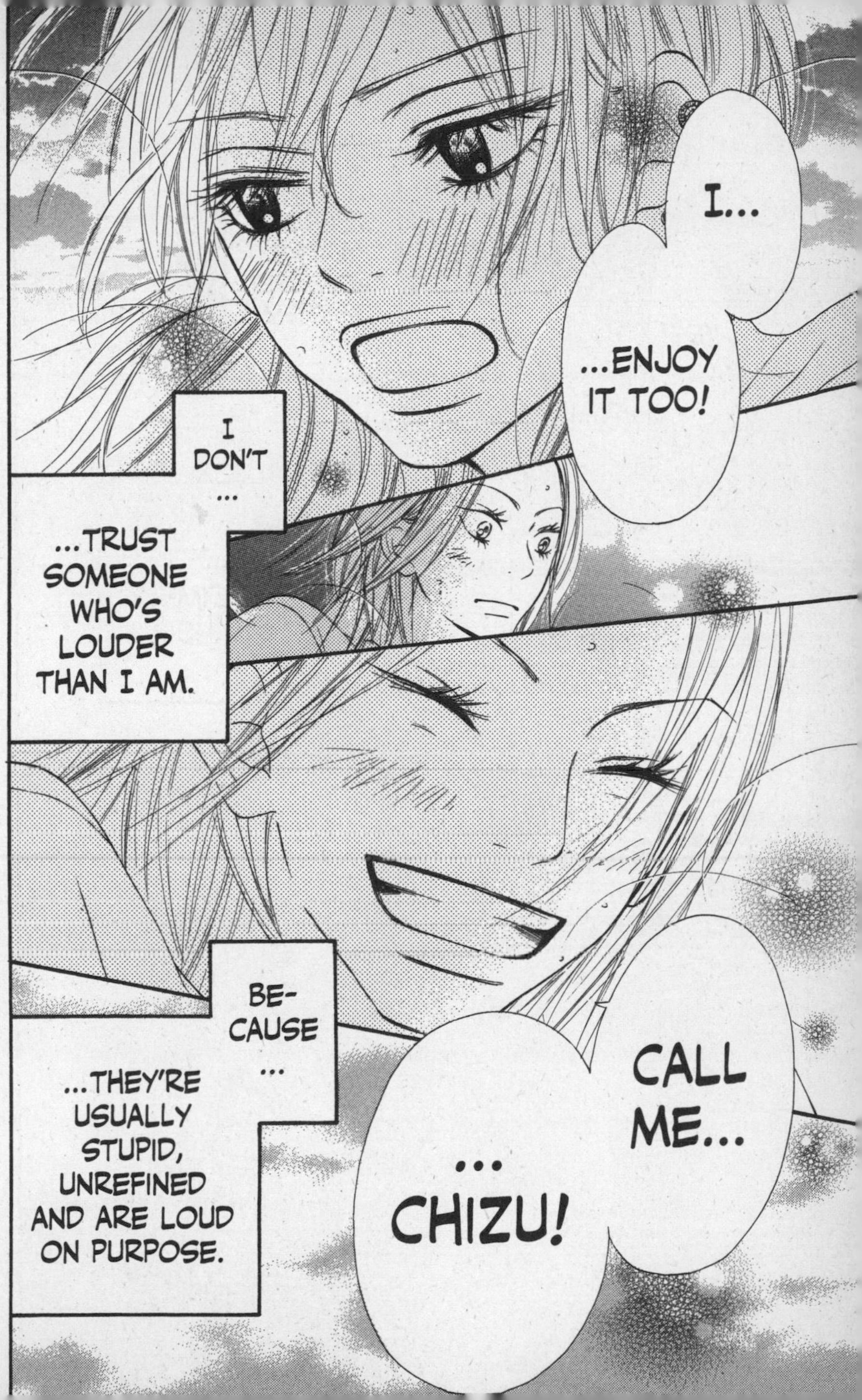
I...
...ENJOY IT TOO!
I DON'T ...
...TRUST SOMEONE WHO'S LOUDER THAN I AM.
CALL ME...
... CHIZU!
BE-CAUSE ...
...THEY'RE USUALLY STUPID, UNREFINED AND ARE LOUD ON PURPOSE.

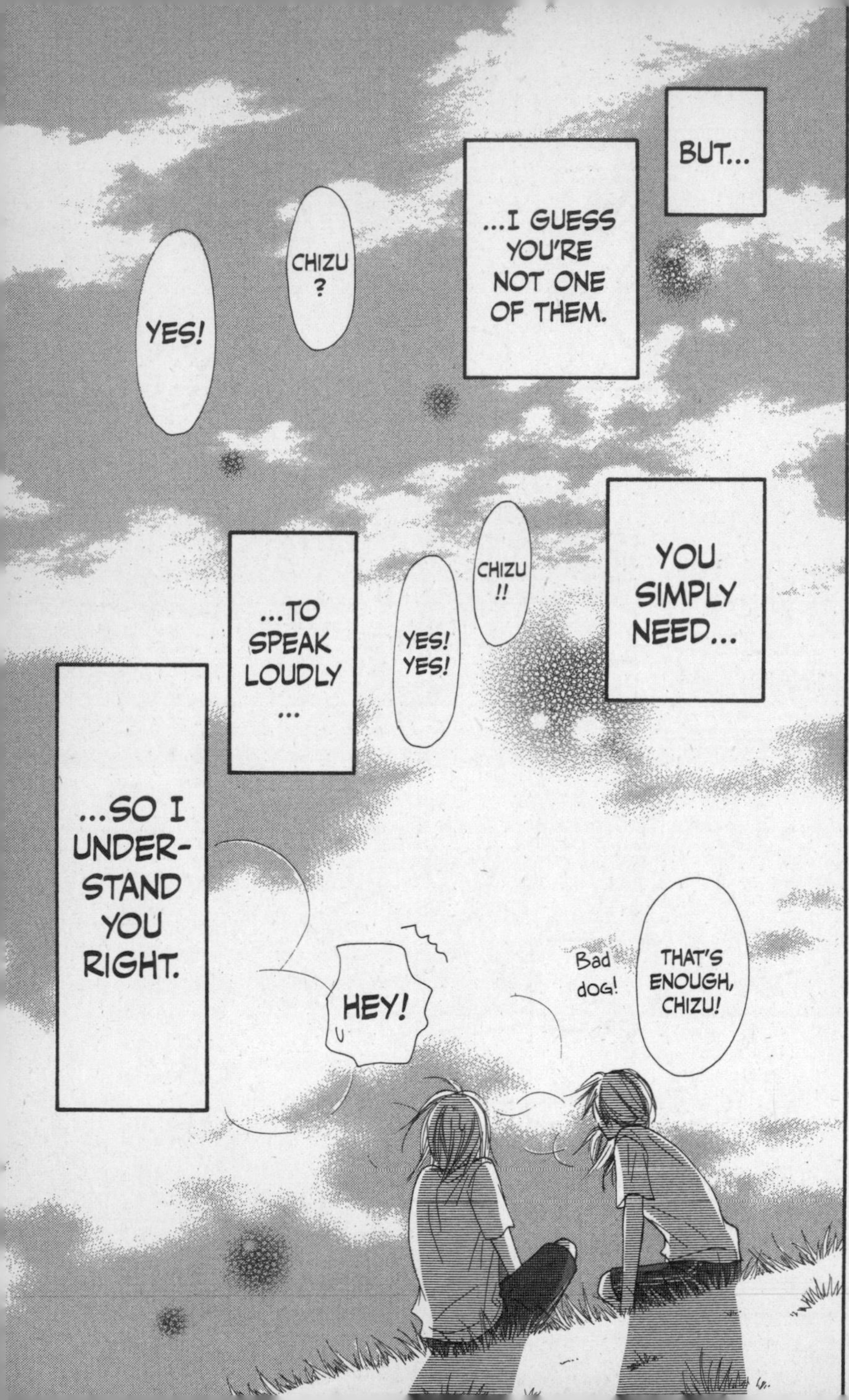
BUT...
...I GUESS YOU'RE NOT ONE OF THEM.
CHIZU?
YES!
YOU SIMPLY NEED...
CHIZU!!
YES! YES!
...TO SPEAK LOUDLY...
...SO I UNDER-STAND YOU RIGHT.
THAT'S ENOUGH, CHIZU!
Bad dog!
HEY!

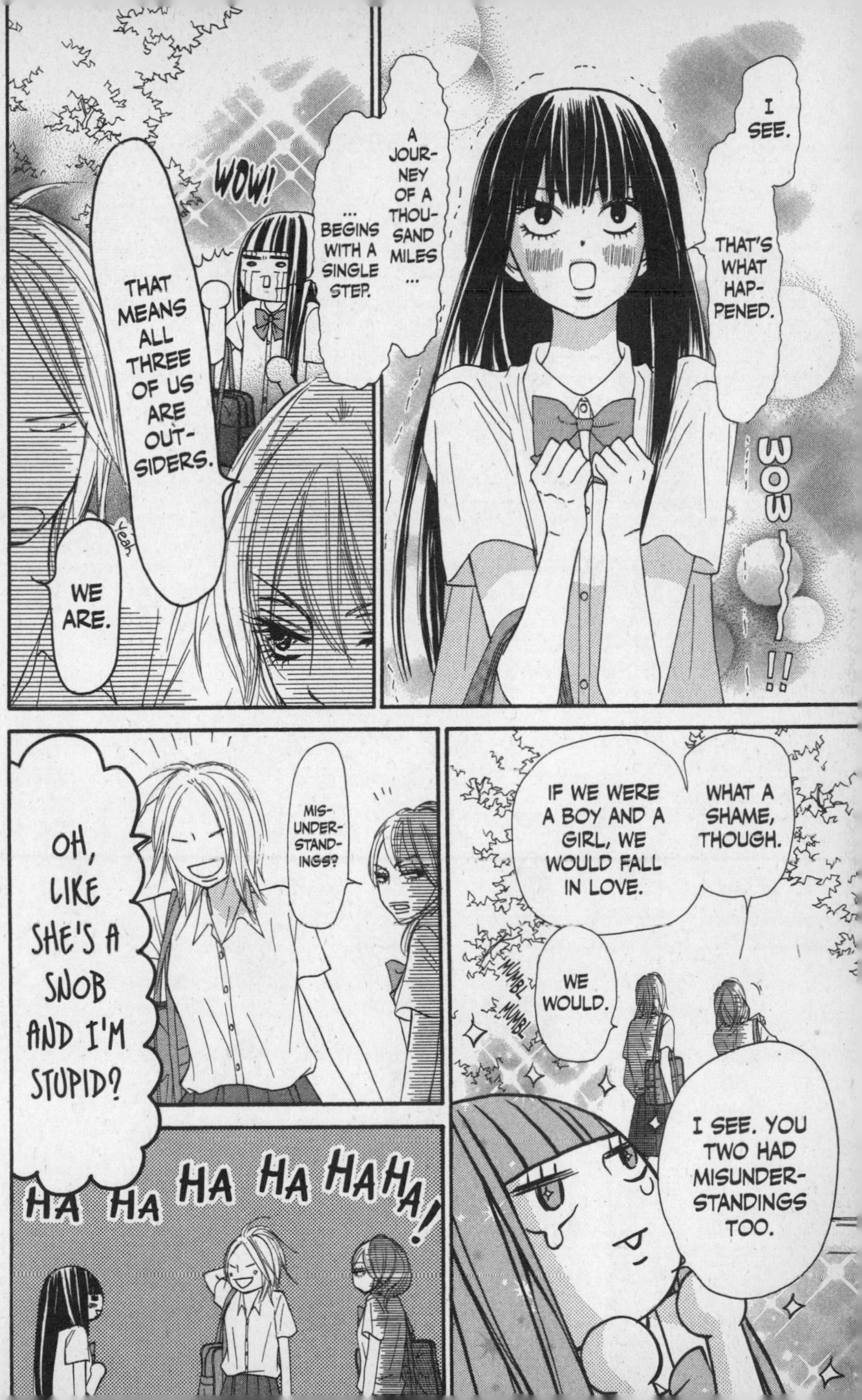

I SEE.
THAT'S WHAT HAPPENED.
WOW—!!
A JOURNEY OF A THOUSAND MILES...
...BEGINS WITH A SINGLE STEP.
WOW!
THAT MEANS ALL THREE OF US ARE OUTSIDERS.
yeah
WE ARE.
WHAT A SHAME, THOUGH.
IF WE WERE A BOY AND A GIRL, WE WOULD FALL IN LOVE.
MUMBL MUMBL
WE WOULD.
I SEE. YOU TWO HAD MISUNDERSTANDINGS TOO.
MISUNDERSTANDINGS?
OH, LIKE SHE'S A SNOB AND I'M STUPID?
HA HA HA HA HAHA!

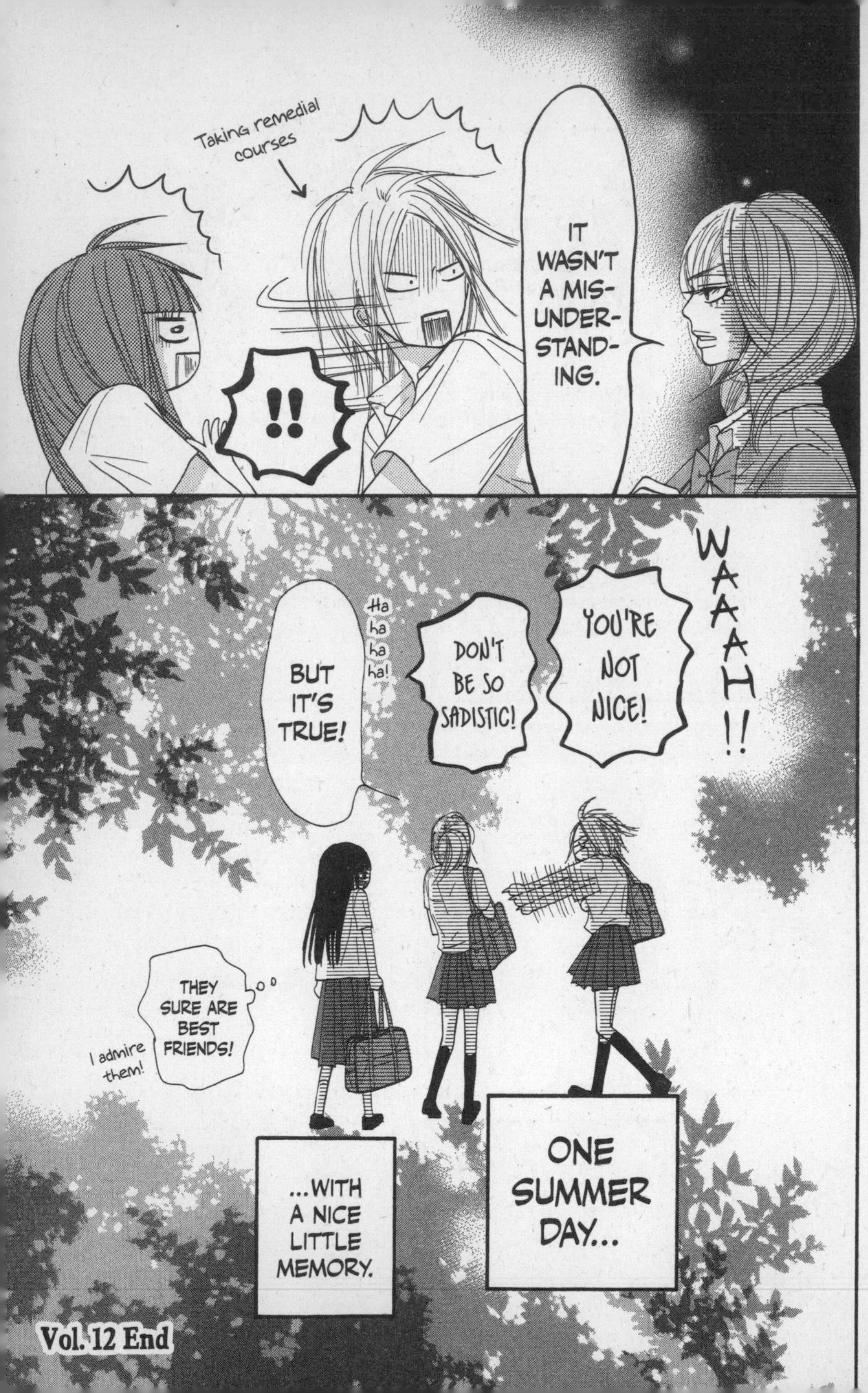
IT WASN'T A MIS-UNDER-STAND-ING.
Taking remedial courses
!!
WAAAH!!
YOU'RE NOT NICE!
DON'T BE SO SADISTIC!
Ha ha ha ha!
BUT IT'S TRUE!
THEY SURE ARE BEST FRIENDS!
I admire them!
ONE SUMMER DAY...
...WITH A NICE LITTLE MEMORY.

Vol. 12 End

From me (the editor) to you (the reader).

Here are some Japanese culture explanations that will help you better understand the references in the *Kimi ni Todoke* world.

Honorifics:

When saying someone's name in Japanese, a suffix is often attached to indicate how familiar the speaker is with the person. Some are more polite and respectful, while others are endearing. Calling someone by just their first name is the most informal.

-kun is used for young men or boys, usually someone you are familiar with.

-chan is used for young women, girls or young children and can be used as a term of endearment.

-san is used for someone you respect or are not close to, or to be polite.

Page 25, Hokkaido:

The northernmost and second largest of the Japanese islands, it is much colder than the rest of the nation.

Page 25, Bon holiday:

Bon, or *Obon*, is a summer Buddhist festival to honor one's ancestors.

Page 85, shungiku:

A zesty, edible green from the chrysanthemum family.

Page 85, shirataki:

Long, thin, translucent noodles made from the starch of the devil's tongue yam.

Page 87 and 99, Tabe-chan, Haruma-kun:

Mikako Tabe and Haruma Miura play Sawako and Kazehaya in the live-action film *Kimi ni Todoke*, which came out in Japan in 2010.

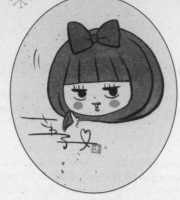

The illustration on the front cover of this volume shows the three members of the Kuronuma family. I casually asked my editor what she thought about putting the Kuronuma family on the front cover and she said she really wanted to see it, so I suddenly got serious about drawing it. I never expected to illustrate Sawako's father and mother in color. The first page of Episode 49 shows Sawako and her father when Sawako was little. When I was drawing it, I felt a little sorry for Sawako's father. Cheer up, Sawako's dad!

--Karuho Shiina

Karuho Shiina was born and raised in Hokkaido, Japan. Though *Kimi ni Todoke* is only her second series following many one-shot stories, it has already racked up accolades from various "Best Manga of the Year" lists. Winner of the 2008 Kodansha Manga Award for the shojo category, *Kimi ni Todoke* also placed fifth in the first-ever Manga Taisho (Cartoon Grand Prize) contest in 2008. In Japan, an animated TV series debuted in October 2009, and a live-action film was released in 2010.

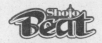

Kimi ni Todoke
VOL. 12

Shojo Beat Edition

STORY AND ART BY
KARUHO SHIINA

Translation/Ari Yasuda, HC Language Solutions, Inc.
Touch-up Art & Lettering/Vanessa Satone
Design/Nozomi Akashi
Editor/Carrie Shepherd

KIMI NI TODOKE © 2005 by Karuho Shiina
All rights reserved. First published in Japan in 2005 by SHUEISHA Inc.,
Tokyo. English translation rights arranged with SHUEISHA Inc.

Printed in Canada

Published by VIZ Media, LLC
P.O. Box 77010
San Francisco, CA 94107

10 9 8 7 6 5 4 3 2 1
First printing, January 2012

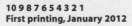

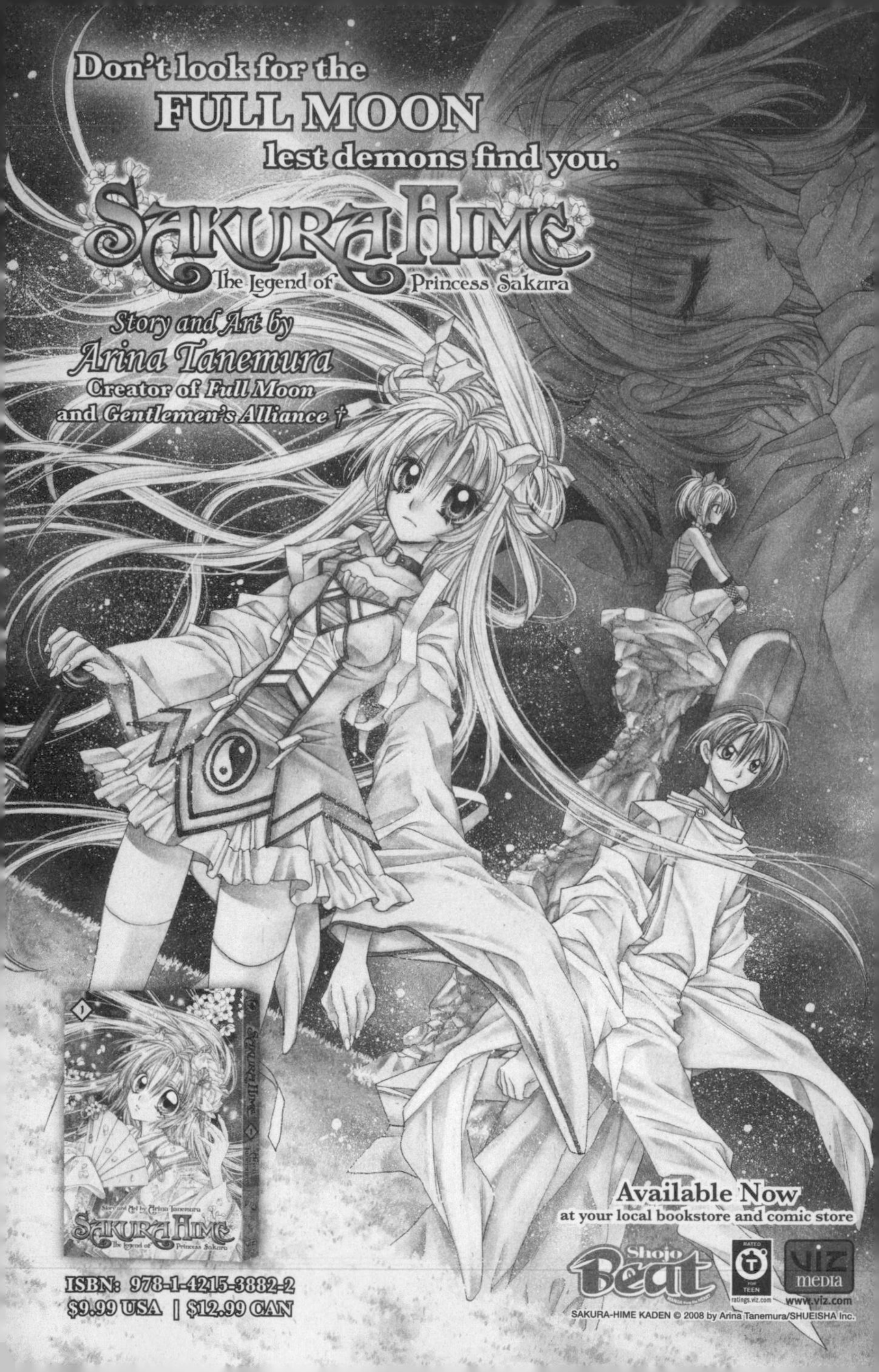
Don't look for the
FULL MOON
lest demons find you.
SAKURA HIME
The Legend of Princess Sakura
Story and Art by
Arina Tanemura
Creator of Full Moon
and Gentlemen's Alliance †
Story and Art by Arina Tanemura
SAKURA HIME
The Legend of Princess Sakura
ISBN: 978-1-4215-3882-2
$9.99 USA | $12.99 CAN
Available Now
at your local bookstore and comic store
Shojo Beat
RATED T FOR TEEN
ratings.viz.com
VIZ media
www.viz.com
SAKURA-HIME KADEN © 2008 by Arina Tanemura/SHUEISHA Inc.

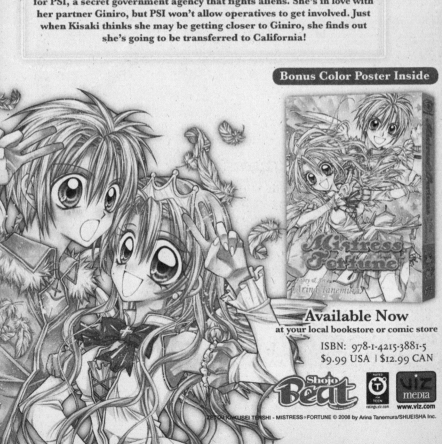

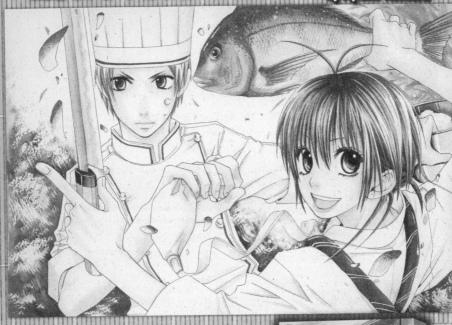
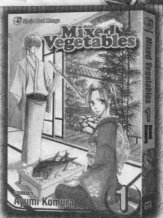
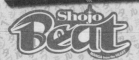

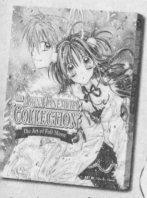